HOLLYWOOD'S WHITE HOUSE

Hollywood's
WHITE
HOUSE

The American Presidency in Film and History

*Edited by Peter C. Rollins
and John E. O'Connor*

THE UNIVERSITY PRESS OF KENTUCKY

Publication of this volume was made possible in part
by a grant from the National Endowment for the Humanities.

Scholarly publisher for the Commonwealth,
serving Bellarmine University, Berea College, Centre
College of Kentucky, Eastern Kentucky University,
The Filson Historical Society, Georgetown College,
Kentucky Historical Society, Kentucky State University,
Morehead State University, Murray State University,
Northern Kentucky University, Transylvania University,
University of Kentucky, University of Louisville,
and Western Kentucky University.
All rights reserved.

Editorial and Sales Offices: The University Press of Kentucky
663 South Limestone Street, Lexington, Kentucky 40508-4008

03 04 05 06 07   5 4 3 2 1

All photographs, unless otherwise noted, are from
the Museum of Modern Art/Film Stills Archive.

Library of Congress Cataloging-in-Publication Data

Hollywood's White House : the American presidency in film and history /
edited by Peter C. Rollins and John E. O'Connor.
    p.   cm.
Includes bibliographical references and index.
ISBN 0-8131-2270-8 (Cloth : alk. paper)
1. United States—In motion pictures. 2. Historical films—United
States—History and criticism. 3. Presidents—United States—History.
I. Rollins, Peter C. II. O'Connor, John E.
PN1995.9.U64H65 2003
791.43'658–dc21   2003005311

This book is printed on acid-free recycled paper meeting
the requirements of the American National Standard
for Permanence in Paper for Printed Library Materials.

Manufactured in the United States of America.

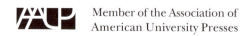

Member of the Association of
American University Presses

This book is dedicated to the American Presidents and the glorious office of the presidency.

It is our hope that the study of film and television representations will lead to a better sense of the twenty-first-century citizen's difficult duty— to sift for truth among a plethora of images.

CONTENTS

Richard Shenkman

FOREWORD

As it should be, a main theme of this book is Hollywood's failure to depict adequately the presidents of the United States. Movies almost always get the basic facts wrong. They usually present one-dimensional presidents who are either all evil or all saint; and they perpetuate hoary myths to appease the audience's expectations. As good as Henry Fonda is in *Young Mr. Lincoln*, for example, there are still vast corners of Lincoln's personality and character that the film fails to explore. Fonda portrays Carl Sandburg's Lincoln—strong, folksy, almost an innocent—an appealing Lincoln, to be sure, but one who bears little resemblance to the poorly educated child of the frontier who succeeded in becoming president. Quick: Name the president who was so hungry for power and influence that he ran for public office at age twenty-three, married a woman "above his station," and represented rich corporations. Most likely Abraham Lincoln does not come to mind.

More troubling still is Hollywood's portrayal of presidents who have little emotional depth. Watching Ralph Bellamy in *Sunrise at Campobello* the audience knows that it is only catching a fleeting glimpse of the real FDR as he strives to survive polio. Bellamy's FDR groans and appears to be in pain. He struggles to stand upright. But, for the most part, he remains a cardboard character. Does the audience realize that it took FDR a year to move his big toe?[1]

It is no wonder that Hollywood has found presidents difficult to come to grips with; they are an inscrutable bunch. Who really was George Washington? A hundred biographers have tried to pin him down and not one has yet got him quite right. Beholden to the mythology of the president who was "first in war, first in peace, first in the hearts of his countrymen," writers usually settle for the classic stuffed-shirt version of Washington. And yet, what a bewildering set of contradictions was this giant of a man. One minute he could tell a ribald joke and the next minute stare down a subordinate for daring to strike a note of informality. Such a man is not easily captured on film.[2]

The most frequent complaint about presidential movies is that they get the facts wrong. More puzzling, though character development is at the heart of the Hollywood drama, the producers, directors, and actors so seldom get the presidential character right either. Yet who could blame them? The character of a president is nearly unfathomable. Like every successful politician, a president's motives are mixed. Not one has behaved nobly at all times, and yet they all have behaved nobly on some occasions. A powerful idealistic streak runs through the presidents. An astonishingly large number—ten in all—were raised to be ministers or were the children of ministers. And yet they could be guilty of the most heinous political subterfuges and act every bit the equal of the rogues who have strolled through the histories of countries seemingly more cursed than ours.

They are a vastly heterogeneous lot. There have been insecure men such as Richard Nixon, boisterous outsized extroverts such as Teddy Roosevelt, and remote, almost shy introverts such as Woodrow Wilson. There have been tall presidents, such as the six-foot-three Washington and short ones, such as the five-foot-four Madison. No wonder Hollywood has trouble depicting them.

The first time I met a president was in 1972. I was seventeen years old, and I was in Miami to attend the Republican National Convention at which Richard Nixon was nominated for a second term as president. On the last night of the convention, after Nixon had given his acceptance speech, people in the convention hall were given the opportunity to shake the president's hand. When it was finally my turn, I told him that I was a Democrat but that I liked him anyway and wished him the best. Maybe he had not expected to meet a Democrat at that moment. Or maybe he did not believe that I liked him. For whatever reason, Nixon froze—if ever so briefly. Thirty years later, I can still see the awkward look of confusion that crossed his face. It was like nothing I have ever seen on the face of any actor playing a president in the movies.

And yet, as badly as Hollywood often presents the presidents, it has had an enduring impact on how we see them, on how they behave, and even, in a few cases, on who we elect. It is about time, therefore, for a book like this that takes seriously the American presidency in film and history.

Curiously (or maybe not), as institutions, the modern presidency and the film industry became anchored in American society at about the same time. A single event was responsible for the timely twin metamorphosis: the Spanish-American War. Before the war, few paid much attention to the presidency, which had become so vacuous by the end of the nineteenth century that Thomas Wolfe would later refer to the holders of the office as "the lost Americans . . . whose gravely vacant and bewhiskered faces mixed, melted, [and] swam together." "Which had the whiskers," he asked, "which the burnsides: which was which?" It hardly mattered. Then came the sinking of the *Maine*, the Battle of Manila, and the quick defeat of the Spanish empire. Suddenly, who was president did matter.

Hungry for news about the war, Americans turned to newspapers and movies. Any day of the week you could stroll through the downtown of an American city and see crowds streaming into theaters to catch the afternoon show, which featured newsreel footage from the war, accompanied by a live band playing the "Stars and Stripes." When the Americans on the screen battled to victory over the Spanish, loud hoots of joy could be heard as the audience broke into cheers. That much of the newsreel footage was actually shot in West Orange, New Jersey, in an open field with troops borrowed from the New Jersey National Guard did not matter. For the first time in history, thanks to Thomas Edison and other early filmmakers, Americans could see—or seem to see—what was happening on the battlefields they had been reading about in their newspapers.[3]

The great hero of the war, of course, was Teddy Roosevelt—the colonel who led the Rough Riders on their celebrated charge up San Juan Hill (actually, Kettle Hill, but what's the difference?). Much of the footage featuring TR's triumphs was faked, as the cameramen found lugging their heavy equipment on live battlefields to be difficult—and dangerous. No matter. The staged footage provided Americans with what they wanted—news of war—and the picture industry got what it wanted—a string of hits.

The two institutions were very different then. Only later would it dawn on presidents that a big part of their daily job is acting. But, beginning with Teddy Roosevelt, presidents became aware of the importance of visual images. David McCullough reminds us that when Teddy visited the Panama Canal to see what he had wrought, he "was photographed his every waking hour on the scene." The trip was, says McCullough, "the first great presidential photo opportunity in history." Even Dwight Eisenhower, salt of the Kansas earth, would find it necessary to hire an actor, Robert Montgomery, to learn how to perform on the stage that is the modern presidency. By the end of the century, Ronald

Reagan, the erstwhile actor, had been cast in the role. An actor-president was almost inevitable, was it not?[4]

Political scientists, as is pointed out in this book, say that voters do not judge presidents by image but by issues. Perhaps. But image obviously is a factor, and because it is, the presidency and Hollywood have come to seem like two very similar institutions, despite their obvious differences. Hollywood values and techniques now infuse presidential politics. Like actors, presidents are coached on what to say and how to say it. They follow scripts. They deliberately project their image and surround themselves with handlers to protect that image. The more popular a president is, the more power he has. They limit their public appearances so that the public doesn't begin to find them boring. They have to appear natural when on camera (a most unnatural circumstance), and they are judged by the quality of their performances.

Hollywood is not responsible for the preoccupation of presidents with image. Presidents have always been concerned with their images and none more so than the first; Washington understood that he was most useful as a symbol of national unity. But Hollywood showed presidents how to project their image in visual ways, and by transforming American society, has given voters a new respect for imagery. Such is the state of American culture that a president who knows how to manipulate his image is thought by many to be better suited for the office than one who is incompetent at the task. Just ask Jimmy Carter, who forfeited the brilliant image of a big-toothed smiling Man of the People for the image of an incompetent, memorialized in the stunning visual anecdote about him battling a killer rabbit from a small boat.

The images we carry in our heads of particular presidents—which surely influence the way we view the presidency as an institution and, indirectly, the way we vote—owe something to Hollywood but less than one might imagine.

Take FDR. It is not Ralph Bellamy we think of when we think of FDR, it is FDR himself, perhaps because he was a greater actor than any of the actors who have portrayed him. (FDR to Orson Welles: "There are two great actors in the country today. You are the other one.") One of the profoundly disappointing moments among many in the movie *Pearl Harbor* (2001) comes when Jon Voight reprises FDR's great speech to Congress. Who in the audience did not think that FDR played the scene far better?[5]

William Leuchtenburg noted that presidents in the postwar world lived in the "shadow of FDR." It was not his Hollywood shadow that they lived in but his real one. Reality trumped image even as the culture became more and more soaked in imagery. No movie produced by Hollywood has made a more indelible impression than Ike's smile; JFK's witty performances at press conferences; LBJ's haggard look in March 1968 as he announced his disavowal of another term; Nixon's self-serving "I am not a crook"; Ronald Reagan's "Mr. Gorbachev, tear down this wall"; or Bill Clinton's "I did not have sex with that woman." But, of course, it is the images that we remember.[6]

Ironically, Hollywood has had a profound impact on the way we think about the presidents who lived before Hollywood came into existence. In the absence of actual footage of these presidents, we have allowed Hollywood to fill in the blanks in our minds. Thus, Henry Fonda did not just play Lincoln in a movie; in a very real sense, he was Lincoln.

If Hollywood's power to shape our perception of individual presidents has been limited, its power to shape how we think about presidents in general has been great. Hollywood, more than any other force in society, has determined how people think a president should act and look. In other words, Hollywood has given us a standard by which to measure the actual people holding the office.

It is, perforce, an extraordinary standard, requiring presidents to embody the flair of Michael Douglas in *The American President,* the wisdom of Henry Fonda in *Fail Safe,* and the common touch of Ronald Reagan. Today, a president who lacks any of these qualities is at a disadvantage. To compensate, presidential candidates hire consultants to help them achieve these qualities through artifice and imagery, because no candidate for president, except perhaps FDR, has ever been blessed with all of these qualities. This effect is an unwelcome development for which Hollywood is partly to blame.

Surprisingly, given the importance that film has assumed in our national culture, only two presidents can be said to have owed their election, even in part, to film: Teddy Roosevelt and Ronald Reagan. Both men benefited from the power of film to turn largely unknown people into celebrities. Each was elected in part because of the celebrity he earned as a film star—Teddy as the star of the newsreel clips in the Spanish-American War and Reagan as an actual movie actor.

John Kennedy may be a third beneficiary of the film industry. A camera crew accompanied him on his campaign tour in 1960. The film they shot was developed on location and shipped to headquarters for use in campaign commercials and film biographies. His image was helped tremendously because he looked the part of a president: young, handsome, and charismatic. The king of Camelot. The movie star president.

One difference between Hollywood and the presidency is their relationship to facts. To the Hollywood producer, facts are little things that are easily reordered and manipulated. A drama may be "based on a true story," but it is not the true story. After the release of every movie featuring real historical characters, scholars inevitably find, as the scholars in this book do, that key facts have been distorted or omitted. To politicians, facts are more durable and cannot as easily be dispensed with. But even here the two institutions increasingly share common assumptions. Speechwriter Peggy Noonan defended Ronald Reagan— whose respect for facts was characteristically as casual as the producers for whom he long worked—by pointing out that voters, for the most part, did not particularly care whether he got the facts right or wrong. Of far more importance to them was the story line; and he nearly always got the story right. In the nineteenth century no president worried about story lines. Today no president can afford not to.[7]

You can thank Hollywood for that development, as well.

NOTES

1. About FDR: Frank Freidel, *Franklin D. Roosevelt: A Rendezvous with Destiny* (Boston: Little Brown, 1985), 45ff. About Lincoln: Richard Shenkman, *Presidential Ambition* (New York: Harper Collins, 2000), chapter 7.

2. Marcus Cunliffe, *George Washington: Man and Monument* (New York: New American Library, 1958).

3. Raymond Fielding, *The American Newsreel* (Norman: University of Oklahoma Press, 1972); Paul Smith, ed., *The Historian and Film* (Cambridge: Cambridge University Press, 1976).

4. David McCullough, "What's Essential Is Invisible," in Robert Wilson, ed., *Power and the Presidency* (New York: Public Affairs Books, 2000), 10.

5. The Welles anecdote is from David Halberstam, *The Powers that Be* (New York: Knopf, 1979), 12. The line attributed to FDR is paraphrased by Halberstam.

6. William Leuchtenburg, *In the Shadow of FDR* (Ithaca, N.Y.: Cornell University Press, 1983).

7. Peggy Noonan, "Ronald Reagan," in Robert Wilson, ed., *Character above All* (New York: Simon and Schuster, 1995).

John E. O'Connor and Peter C. Rollins

INTRODUCTION

As early as *The Candidate* in 1972, Robert Redford reminded Americans that the image was becoming more important than reality in American politics.

In the closing scene of *The Candidate* (1972), Robert Redford, playing a senatorial aspirant who has just won a heated election campaign, turns to his aides to ask quizzically: "What do we do now?" The dramatized scene is memorable partly because such revealing "behind the scenes" images are so rare, except in the few independently produced documentaries that have attempted to por-

Following the hijacking of Air Force One, Vice President Bennett (Glenn Close) briefs the press. *Air Force One* (1997).

tray political campaigns from the inside. In contrast, most of the essays in this volume discuss Hollywood's view of what a score of presidents did—or failed to do—during their terms of office. More importantly, they consider how a series of feature films came to assume the points of view that they presented and how, if at all, they may have influenced America's perception of its presidential past.

Thoughtful viewers, especially those attuned to history, may not expect "Tinsel town" to have done a very cogent job of portraying public officials or issues of state. They might be surprised. Despite a few unfortunate examples—such as Polly Bergen in office in *Kisses for My President* (1964) or comedian Bob Newhart as head of *The First Family* (1980)—a close look at films about American presidents should help Americans to understand why and how the popular views of our leaders have taken the shapes that they have over the past century. In a handful of other films, such as *The Man* (1972) and *Deep Impact* (1998), the political system has been portrayed as considerably more open than it has been in reality—in each of these cases, for example, promoting a black man to the highest office. More recently, television's *The West Wing* has expanded possibilities for American political thinking and action—although the program is not without its critics.

There has been no shortage of published studies on the office of president in recent years. Two particularly well-recognized scholars, Michael Beschloss and Doris Kearns Goodwin, have produced multiple volumes on several recent presidents, their accomplishments, and travails. But equally—if not more—interesting are the institutional studies, starting with Harold Laski's *The American Presidency: An Interpretation* (1939). Laski noted how, though the constitution had been "stingy" with power to the president and careful to balance that power with the other branches of government, over time—and especially during the then-current tenure of Franklin D. Roosevelt—the situation had changed. Rexford G. Tugwell called it *The Enlargement of the Presidency* in 1960 and developed his ideas still further in a coedited volume with Thomas E. Cronin, *The Presidency Reappraised* (1974); ironically, Tugwell had been a quintessential New Dealer who assisted in expanding federal power.

Another important scholar who traced a gradual growth of the presidents' role primarily in institutional terms is Richard M. Pious, particularly his *The American Presidency* (1979). For a more general but no less probing analysis, also see Marcus Cunliffe, *American Presidents and the Presidency* (1968) and Thomas Cronin, *The State of the Presidency* (1980). Meanwhile, others concluded that the uses presidents made of the office depended more on the personal characteristics they brought to it. See, for example, *Leadership in the Modern Presidency* (1988), edited by Fred L. Greenstein. Even more recently, Noble E. Cunningham Jr. analyzed *Popular Images of the Presidency: From Washington to Lincoln* (1991), and *The American Presidency: A Glorious Burden* (2000) was published by the Smithsonian Press to accompany a new permanent exhibit with the same name at the Smithsonian's Museum of American History in Washington, D.C. (For a fuller list of sources, especially on the more recent presidency and the evolution of the executive branch, see the bibliographical essay compiled by Myron A. Levine for this volume.)

As in the studies noted above, the issues that arise in the essays that follow touch upon every aspect of presidential responsibility. In accord with the ideas of the founding fathers, the president fulfills a "checking" and "balancing" role with the other branches of the federal government. The presidency also has a tradition of its own which affects the political system in various ways. Presidential leadership and personal style can be vastly different from one officeholder to the next. The Constitution spells out specifically the powers and limitations of the office, but some presidents have managed to stretch those limits, especially over the last seventy years when depression, war, and terrorism have called out for presidential leadership. By definition the presidency raises questions about electoral politics and political parties. One must consider the relationship of the presidency to the rest of the executive branch and to the Congress and the federal judiciary. Moreover, a president's rapport with the press and his ease before the cameras can be crucial, especially in the age of television and "sound bites."

Questions of health and personal vigor have proved central to several presidencies, and human frailties and failures of character have not been unknown. As the leader of his party, the president is involved in raising funds, campaigning for congressional and senatorial candidates around the nation, and rewarding (through patronage and other favors) those who have supported his agenda. The president is therefore, by definition, fully immersed in the political process, while constantly being urged to transcend it. Finally, the president is a symbol of the nation—its temper, its spirit, its moral values.

PART ONE: REPRESENTING AMERICAN PRESIDENTS

The first eight essays published here analyze the film depictions of six of the men who held America's highest office from the end of the eighteenth century to the middle of the twentieth century. (Lincoln earns two essays on his own, and one deals with erstwhile candidate Hubert Humphrey). Several deal with very broad historical concerns while others focus in on quite specific issues, some more personal than presidential. All the essays in Part One raise questions about the effectiveness of film for addressing the complex issues that have faced our chief executives in the past.

Stuart Leibiger credits the 1999 made-for-TV film *The Crossing* with portraying the true character and leadership of George Washington. The first on his list of Washington's "distinctive defining attributes," his "fidelity to democratic republican principles," allowed this "man who could have been king" to keep the military subordinated to civilian government. Focusing on one brilliant military foray, a decision made not alone but with a council of advisers, Leibiger shows how "admirable restraint" helped Washington earn his position as the most visible national symbol of his—or perhaps any—American generation. As important as his readiness to assume leadership at the outset of the Revolution was his willingness to step aside after two completed terms when his task was done as both military commander and as president. His character was essential not only in defining his personal role in history but in establishing our expectations for presidents to follow.

The first six episodes of *The Adams Chronicles* focus on the public and pri-

The capital city of the new nation was named in honor of its first president.

vate lives of John and Abigail Adams. Produced in 1976, in the broader cultural context of the developing women's movement as well as the Bicentennial, the series built upon the already established reputation of Abigail Adams as a strikingly intelligent, well-informed, and totally committed supporter of her well-known husband during the dramatic early days of the Revolution as well as during his crucial years abroad in diplomatic service (1778–1788). Later in the Adamses' story, Abigail's influence remains central. For example, *The Adams Chronicles* has her and John jointly planning strategy for handling the thorny XYZ Affair and other issues of his presidency. The production uses cinematic devices—such as pans, arc shots, and montages—to relate the "domestic harmony and solidity of the Adams clan" to the "newly emerging nation's principles of democracy" and uses humor to bring "historical figures into a human perspective." This episode, together with others in the very well-received series, was effective in assuring the place of the senior Adams as well as his accomplished son in the public's perception of the Bicentennial. The recent success of the 2001 best-selling biography of Adams by David McCullough has won Adams new historical attention, but *The Adams Chronicles* were effective, as well as historically faithful, in their depictions of New England's great contributions to our Revolutionary leadership.

Since motion pictures thrive on the personification of abstractions, a "presidential film" can both comment on and capitalize upon audience interest by drawing from various contemporary issues as it explores the decisions and personalities of past presidents. It was interesting that the 1995 publication of George Green Shackelford's *Thomas Jefferson's Travels in Europe, 1784–1789* coincided with the release of *Jefferson in Paris* (starring Nick Nolte) that same year, but rumors about the then-current president's affairs with the ladies may have had even more influence on how the public related to the film's portrayal of Jefferson's putative peccadillos. In "Jefferson in Love: The Framer Framed," Jim Welsh calls "astonishing" the film's framing of the story around James Earl Jones, whose character in Ohio in 1873 claims to be Jefferson's grandson. He is also disappointed by the film's presentation of our third president "more as a man of passion than of wit, judgment, and intellect." Still, according to Welsh, *Jefferson in Paris* is "tasteful by comparison" to CBS-TV's *Sally Hemings: An American Scandal* (2000), a docudrama that transformed the Clinton/Lewinsky scandal into an attack on the glorious president for whom William Jefferson Clinton was named.

The president who has been portrayed on screen more than any other is Abraham Lincoln. Two of the essays here deal with different aspects of Lincoln's presidency as seen on film. Andrew Piasecki plumbs the image of Lincoln in John Ford's silent film epic, *Iron Horse* (1925), as the "paternal and spiritual leader who brings unity and progress out of the chaos of civil war." In promoting the project of the transcontinental railroad, Lincoln foresaw the future of a great, unified nation. One of John Ford's epic Westerns of the silent era, *Iron Horse* combined its history with a melodramatic story of murder, revenge, and love, as rivals in building railroads are mirrored by rivals in courtship. The key political player in the film is Abraham Lincoln, who is shown signing the Pacific Railroad Act of 1862. Even as the Civil War raged on, Lincoln realized that, "We must not let the war blind us to the promise of peace to come or the war will have been in vain." Piasecki develops the history of several court cases related to the burgeoning railroads, the building of bridges to carry them, and "the representation of technology as a unifying force of progress." As attorney for the railroad interests in several of these cases, Lincoln lays the foundation for director Ford's later treatment of him as an apostle of progress. In the end, the transcontinental railroad becomes the fulfillment of "historical myth" for 1920s film audiences, with Lincoln providing a "guiding hand" in the story "infused with the ideology of the era."

Bryan Rommel-Ruiz examines the Lincoln portrayed in D.W. Griffith's *The Birth of a Nation* (1915). Griffith placed Lincoln in a series of "recreated historical moments," such as the signing of the document calling for "volunteers to support the rule of the coming nation over the individual states" and later as he responds to the plea of one of Griffith's southern characters that he pardon her captured son. The point is made that Lincoln intends reconstruction after the war to be a peaceful rebuilding of the nation, but his assassination opens the door to those who would protract the nation's tragedy. Reflecting the interpretations of historians contemporary to Griffith, such as John Burgess and William Dunning, the second part of the film portrays an experience of Reconstruction, which "vilifies African Americans and legitimates Jim Crow laws." White-robed members of the Ku Klux Klan become the heroes who seek to "redeem the south from Black rule." The essay ends with a discussion of how more recent films have dealt with the Reconstruction period and the influence they might have on how we think about Abraham Lincoln.

Perhaps the most personally dynamic person to have held the presidency was Theodore Roosevelt (1901–1909). J. Tillapaugh calls

Theodore Roosevelt: Charismatic leader in the White House (1901–1909).

Library of Congress.

him a "transformational leader," having brought the American people into the twentieth century and having earned "a century of national validation" as a leadership symbol. There is another transition here as well; Roosevelt is the first president we can see and hear significantly on motion picture and voice recording. The popularity of the newsreel stories on Roosevelt's "Rough Riders" and the war in Cuba tempted film producers to engage in some of the earliest examples of faked news footage. But, long after the war was over and Roosevelt had gone to his reward, filmmakers were keeping Teddy and his "Rough Riders" alive for movie audiences in a series of now vintage Westerns and, as recently as 1997, in special productions for cable television.

In personal terms, Woodrow Wilson (1913–1921) could not have been more different from the ebullient Roosevelt—an intellectual, a historian, and professor, risen to university president before being tapped by the Democratic Party for the White House. Film scholar Donald Staples credits Twentieth-Century Fox's *Wilson* (1944) with significant historical accuracy, extending beyond the treatment of Wilson himself to other historical personalities, such as William Jennings Bryan and Henry Cabot Lodge, and notes the effective use of newsreel footage, adding verisimilitude to Wilson's signing of major bills, his European trips, and his negotiation of the controversial 1919 Treaty of Versailles. The film had to end in some sadness because of the Senate's failure to endorse that treaty and because of the president's frailty after suffering his stroke, but his great accomplishments must have appeared all the greater in 1944 as yet another world war dragged on and Americans reconsidered the value of a League of Nations/United Nations body to promote world understanding and peace.

Finally, Part One concludes with Jaap Kooijman's analysis, not of a Hollywood film, but of the network television coverage of the 1968 Democratic convention and its impact on the presidential campaign of Hubert H. Humphrey. Thanks to (some would say "because of") the coverage of all the networks, "the whole world *was* watching" as the American democratic system came near to dissolution in the streets of Chicago. President Johnson, who chose not to attend the convention, watched on his television in Texas as the streets filled with protesters and Chicago police, under the command of their voluble Mayor Richard Daley, faced off against them. The impact on the electorate was inescapable. Humphrey's campaign was doomed from the outset; as Kooijman demonstrates, crucial cinematic elements of "collision montage" led to his political demise—the negative impression was not just due to overt editorializing by the media.

PART TWO: HOLLYWOOD'S "TAKE":
THE PRESIDENCY IN FICTION FILMS

It would be surprising if an institution so powerful as the presidency and a cast of characters so well known to the public had not led to a genre of entertainment films that centered on the White House. There is no shortage of recent examples, from *The American President* to a television series such as *The West Wing,* but for this volume seven authors have turned their attention to a series of films they can consider with the benefit of some distance.

Rather than focus on a specific president, the first essay in Part Two offers a more general view. Michael G. Krukones's "Motion Picture Presidents of the 1930s: Factual and Fictional Leaders for a Time of Crisis" considers the three well-known Lincoln films made between 1930 and 1940 and relates them to three fictional films about the presidency that came out of the early 1930s: *The Phantom President* (1932), *Gabriel Over the White House* (1933), and *The President Vanishes* (1934). Krukones concludes that in the same decade in which filmmakers were being "reverential" in the way they treated their past presidents— particularly Lincoln—they were devising fictional presidents who might take the more dramatic actions some saw as necessary to wrest the country from the jaws of an economic catastrophe.

Focusing in on one of these fictionalizations, Deborah Carmichael analyses *Gabriel Over the White House* in the context of the growth of protofascist movements in the United States in the early 1930s. The film, produced by Walter Wanger for William Randolph Hearst's Cosmopolitan Films, was set in a future "packed with symbols of the American past" but in a situation not unlike the plight being faced in the early years of the Depression. Fictional President Hammond (Walter Huston) is transformed by an encounter with the Angel Gabriel into a dynamic leader animated to address the nation's problems in a somewhat perverse way that "reflects and anticipates" Franklin D. Roosevelt's "New Deal." The pattern becomes more somber and troubling as the fictional president creates a federal police force and seeks to "cut the red tape" of the judicial system in the interests of "law and order." Within the context of *Gabriel Over the White House,* America is saved—in the end—by an "inspired fascist leader." The film is commonly criticized for its profascist elements but, as chilling as these may have been, for Carmichael the issue is more complex. She also sees the media mogul Hearst wanting to demonstrate how an "activist" president could respond to the nation's problems.

Ian Scott's essay demonstrates that, although they may never appear directly as characters in his films, presidential reference points are central to the historical vision of director Frank Capra. Perhaps most obvious as the "light-houses" revered so devoutly in *Mr. Smith Goes to Washington* (1939), the presidential references are more generally evident if one looks more closely at Capra's work as a spokesman for American values. According to Scott, presidential apparitions form a "constant metaphor" for Capra, "a metaphor that defines other ideas in his philosophy than those commonly listed: principles like guardianship, honor, duty, and subservience." Viewed broadly, Scott concludes, Capra "constructs a society that reflects the developing interest of *pluralism*," at the center of which was the presidency of FDR, for Capra "understood that the Roosevelt leadership was at the heart of a transformed society." But it was Capra who transformed abstract political ideals into memorable characters, such as Jefferson Smith and Longfellow Deeds, with whom the public could so readily identify. His sense of himself as a social visionary was still evident when then coeditors of *Film & History*, Martin Jackson and John O'Connor, also coeditor of this volume, met with Capra and discussed these matters over dinner in 1972.

Linda Alkana looks at three Hollywood presidents created over a span of sixty years for *Mr. Smith Goes to Washington* (1939), *The Candidate* (1972), and *Bulworth* (1998). Though still charming to watch, *Mr. Smith* seems naive in the era of "attack ads" and C-SPAN coverage of congressional committees and floor debates. Perhaps we have become too inured to candidates like Robert Redford's 1972 character, swept along by the events of the campaign until "his image is becoming more important than his words," because we have come to expect no more than is to be found in *Bulworth*, where "the institution of government is as corrupt as the process, and the victims are the people."

Robert E. Hunter opens his analysis of *Fail-Safe* (1964) and *Colossus* (1970) with a story about Jackie Kennedy disconnecting and removing an unsightly "red telephone" from the president's Oval Office and replacing it with an antique one. This humorous detail points up the "president's vulnerability, both to mechanical failures and human frailties"—in this case "his wife's whims." The first film he treats raises concerns about the reliability of technology, but is somewhat reassuring because the president is in charge. The second film raises questions about the man in charge, a president who is "weak at the outset and becomes even weaker." In *Fail-Safe*, a group of bombers fly beyond their "fail-safe" point headed toward Moscow. The president (played by Henry Fonda) must act to remedy the situation, a situation underlining the importance of presidential character in the context of the Cold War heating up (as it was in the 1960s). In *Colossus: The Forbin Project* human beings have less control.

Aliens hover over New York City in *Independence Day (1996)*.

Supercomputers have been created by both the Soviets and the Americans to automate the ultimate decision about when to use the bomb (a comparable scenario to one lightened with black humor in *Dr. Strangelove: Or How I Learned to Stop Worrying and Love the Bomb* [1964]). In *Colossus* the president, like his counterpart in *Dr. Strangelove* (Peter Sellers as President Merkin Muffley), is "befuddled" and "out of touch," raising questions about the real nature of technological "progress."

Perhaps the many portrayals of presidents in recent feature films (forty of them in the 1990s compared with only ninety of them from the beginnings of the medium to that point) can offer some hint as to why voter participation in presidential elections, especially by young people, continues to fall off. John Shelton Lawrence notes that the most successful films about presidents feature an activist chief executive, one who might even "fight foes hand-to-hand in outer space" as in *Independence Day* (1996). Perhaps the lack of a Teddy Roosevelt "take charge type" among recent presidents made it seem necessary for producers to create a fictional one. It is hard to imagine any very recent tenants of 1600 Pennsylvania Avenue taking so bold a stance, although George W. Bush, since the World Trade Center disaster on 11 September 2001, has stepped forward as a dynamic leader—to the surprise of many.

"Politics is perception"—at least that is what Martin Sheen as President Andrew Shepherd's press secretary A.J. MacInerney tells him in *The American President* (1995). But this president wants to speak, not in sound bites, but in a "noble rational controllable language—and he wants it to be his." Loren Quiring examines the presidential characters created by Aaron Sorkin—each of whom speaks in an "archetypal voice of reason." Sorkin wants his president to be a man of "his word" instead of "his image." Quiring discusses language issues in both Sorkin's *The American President* and in *The West Wing* TV series, as the author writes about "what makes an archetypal leader, especially an American one." Quiring argues that "language is perception" in the American political environment.

PART THREE: CLOSING IN ON THE PRESENT

The final seven essays in our collection bring the analysis closer to the present. Peter C. Rollins, coeditor of this volume, opens the final phase of our collection with his analysis of the "primacy of character" in the portrayal of recent Hollywood presidents. He starts with Darryl Zanuck's image of a very capable President Wilson in *Wilson* (1944) in comparison to the woefully ineffective (and thankfully fictional) President Merkin Muffley in *Dr. Strangelove* (1964). Then he notes the contrasting images of Oliver Stone's *Nixon* (1995) with the return to a "Capraesque" formula in *The American President* in that same year. Rollins demonstrates how our recent screen images of the presidency may have come "full circle," to again project strength of character in our national leaders, especially in a time of crisis.

Next, Charlene Etkind examines three films—two comedies and one contrasting drama—to understand how the myth of the presidency is often at odds with the mood of the country. *Dick* (1999) is about two schoolgirls who become incredibly entangled in the business of the Nixon White House as a result of a student tour of the building. In the other comedy, *The World of Henry Orient* (1964), two other teenage girls become infatuated with an urban pianist and "Lothario," whom they follow around New York City, stumbling into humorous situations until he seduces the mother of one of the girls, permanently trashing the girls' adoration of him. While not directly related to the presidency, Etkind sees the latter film as a "perfect morality play" for an audience that had not yet faced the political and cultural crises of the 1960s, several of which originated in the Oval Office. These experiences are recounted in Oliver Stone's *Nixon* (1995). Stone's dramatic film, in contrast to the other two, shows how an "entirely different genre can so elevate mythic properties as to incite fear and regret in the audience."

Richard Nixon is also the subject of Donald Whaley's analysis, which makes

Richard Nixon
gains a diplomatic
coup in China,
1971.

Library of Congress.

the point that—Watergate, and related bad publicity notwithstanding—by the
1990s filmmakers, like historians, had begun to reexamine the Nixon presidency. Whaley isolates three versions: the evil Nixon, first appearing in Gore
Vidal's *The Best Man* (1964) and later in *All the President's Men* (1978); the comic
Nixon of Robert Altman's *Secret Honor* (1964) and *Elvis Meets Nixon* (1997), as
well as *Dick,* noted above; and finally a tragic Nixon, as in Oliver Stone's *Nixon*
(1998). The cinematic legacy thus matches the complexity of an enigmatic
American leader.

Myron A. Levine compares the fiction film *Primary Colors* (1998) with the
documentary *The War Room* (1994), two accounts of the 1992 Clinton presidential campaign. Both films are seen as "preoccupied with exposing the machi-
nations of campaign elites" and tending to "miss the more important role played
by policy issues, substantive evaluations, and the voters themselves." *Primary
Colors,* though a fiction film, closely parallels the actual events of the 1992 Clinton
campaign, including pscudodocumentary, walk-on appearances by Geraldo
Rivera, Charlie Rose, Larry King, and Bill Maher. But the stress on events in the
contest between Clinton and Massachusetts Governor Paul Tsongas masked
the absence of issues. Filmmakers D.A. Pennebaker and Chris Hegedus's documentary, *The War Room,* treats the same campaign from the perspective of
Clinton's staff, especially James Carville and George Stephanopoulis, yet issues
again receive only fleeting reference. The operative word is "spin," as these
campaign operatives create and respond to events in ways they hope will foster
their candidate's chances. Elections, according to this *cinema verite* production,
"are about little more than image making and media control." Levine takes

Library of Congress.

Bill Clinton and the legacy of JFK.

both of these productions to task for their myopic preoccupation with media manipulation.

Luc Herman shows how the public's perception of one recent presidential campaign (and the presidency which followed) may have been influenced by selected images. In this case it was the timely release of a popular feature film that bestowed special good fortune on presidential candidate Bill Clinton. The theatrical release of Oliver Stone's *JFK* in 1991 made it possible for Clinton to "ride a new wave of Kennedy popularity in his 1992 presidential campaign." As Stone made the rounds of TV talk shows and as the new film projected Kennedy's image anew all over the newspapers and TV, the Clinton spin doctors responded. They pulled a piece of footage from the archives that presented a still vital President Kennedy in a July 1963 White House meeting seemingly passing the mantle of leadership to a teenaged Bill Clinton, who was visiting with an Arkansas school-group tour. The film clip, used first in the biographical film screened at the Democratic convention and in later commercials, was developed as an effective campaign device and was even used by the administration after Clinton took office. Herman's study is a good reminder that images can have a powerful impact when presented in manipulated contexts—all the while seeming "realistic."

The next two contributions dramatize that, in recent years, poking fun at the president has become popular entertainment. David Haven Blake, for example, concentrates on two such feature films, *Dave* (1993) and *Wag The Dog*

(1997). In discussing the impact of television, while Johnny Carson's nightly jabs were usually more friendly than caustic, more in the vein of Bob Hope's jokes about golfing with the Secret Service for caddies, John Matviko makes it clear that *Saturday Night Live* (*SNL*) was different. Partly because of its time slot, partly because of its cast of characters (not known for their respect for high offices or the people who hold them), and perhaps partly because of the program's producer—whose roots were in Canada—*SNL* could be counted on to be more biting and outrageous.

Finally, films notwithstanding, we always come back to books. Any consideration of how film and television package the American presidency must constantly touch base with basic historical and organizational studies of the White House and its supporting staff. In his bibliographical essay Myron A. Levine, who provided insight in his essay on *Primary Colors* and *The War Room*, lays out some of the more important recent references for scholars. The evolution of the presidency has been matched by the dramatically different people who have held the position over the span of more than two hundred years. It has also been shaped, in the public mind if not in actuality, by the scholars who

Former Presidents Russell Kramer (Jack Lemmon) and Matt Douglas (James Garner) confront President William Haney (Dan Aykroyd) in *My Fellow Americans* (1996).

have studied it and, at least for the past ninety years or so, by the scriptwriters, actors, and producers who have portrayed our various presidents in film and television. From the humor of *Mr. Smith Goes to Washington* to the satire of *Dr. Strangelove* to the melodrama of *Wilson*, we ignore cinematic interpretations at our own peril.

WORKS CITED

Bailey, Thomas. *Presidential Greatness.* New York: Appleton Century, 1966.

Bunch, Lonnie III, et al. *The American Presidency: A Glorious Burden.* Washington: Smithsonian Institution Press, 2000.

Cronin, Thomas E. *The State of the Presidency.* Boston: Little, Brown, 1980.

————, and Rexford Tugwell. *The Presidency Reappraised.* New York: Praeger, 1974.

Cunliffe, Marcus. *American Presidents and the Presidency.* New York: American Heritage Press, 1968.

Cunningham, Noble E., Jr. *Popular Images of the Presidency: From Washington to Lincoln.* Columbia: University of Missouri Press, 1991.

Goodwin, Doris Kearns. *Lyndon Johnson and the American Dream.* New York: St. Martins, 1991.

————. *No Ordinary Time—Franklin and Eleanor Roosevelt: The Home-Front in World War II.* New York: Touchstone, 1995.

Greenstein, Fred L., ed. *Leadership in the Modern Presidency.* Cambridge: Harvard University Press, 1988.

Laski, Harold. *The American Presidency: An Interpretation.* New York: Harper Brothers, 1939.

Neustadt, Richard E. *Presidential Power and the Modern Presidents.* New York: Free Press, 1990.

Pious, Richard M. *The American Presidency.* New York: Basic Books, 1979.

Schlesinger, Arthur M., Jr. *The Imperial Presidency.* Boston: Houghton Mifflin, 1973.

Tugwell, Rexford G. *The Enlargement of the Presidency.* Garden City, New York: Doubleday, 1960.

Part One

Representing American Presidents

Stuart Leibiger

GEORGE WASHINGTON, *THE CROSSING*, AND REVOLUTIONARY LEADERSHIP

Washington served as the first president of the United States, 1789–1797.

The Arts and Entertainment Network's 1999 film *The Crossing* recreates the harrowing but inspirational story from the American Revolutionary War of the resurrection of a general, an army, and a nation from the depths of defeat and despair. After tracing the Continental Army's desperate retreat across the Delaware River from New Jersey into Pennsylvania, the film tells how the American forces regrouped themselves, recrossed the river on the night of 25 December 1776, and captured a garrison of elite Hessian troops stationed at Trenton in a surprise attack at dawn. The protagonist is, of course, George Washington, whose fortitude and strength of character inspires his men to accomplish the seemingly impossible. But how well does *The Crossing* portray the true character and revolutionary leadership of the commander in chief of the Continental Army? As lead actor Jeff Daniels admits, our first president is one of the most misunderstood and elusive men in American history. In fact, the more one learns about him, the harder he can be to understand. Despite his complexities, Washington clearly exhibited five distinct, defining attributes as commander in chief: fidelity to republicanism, perseverance, a dignified personal demeanor, aggressive strategic thinking, and a decisive leadership style. In seeking to capture these characteristics, Daniels candidly admits not being able "to have become" Washington. Indeed, Daniels confesses coming no closer in his portrayal than to be able to "see the man" (Fast xii).

WASHINGTON'S LEADERSHIP CHARACTERISTICS

Washington's most important characteristic was his fidelity to the republican principles of the Revolution. His greatness lies less in his military genius than in his scrupulous use of power. He did not abuse the immense military authority given to him by the American people, resisting the temptation to use the army as his personal bodyguard and becoming what in his own day would have been called a "tyrant." Instead, Washington always kept the military subordinate to the civilian government—be it the Continental Congress or the state legislatures. He understood that America's Revolution was a republican revolution—a revolution for rule by the people through their elective representatives—and he remained faithful to that cause. Once the war ended, his job complete, Washington resigned his commission to Congress and retired to his Virginia plantation. He did not lust after power. The American Revolution is unusual among modern world revolutions because it produced not a dictatorship, like the French, Russian, or Chinese revolutions, but a republic. One of the main reasons for this outcome is Washington's admirable restraint (Higginbotham 69–106).

Washington's contemporaries understood better than we do today what made him great. For example, the brilliant eighteenth-century French artist Jean Antoine Houdon chose not to sculpt a glorious military victory at Trenton or Yorktown but a resignation from the army. Houdon's statue, which today stands in the Virginia State Capitol in Richmond, shows Washington in the act of retiring, returning his military cloak and sword to the state, and resuming civilian life, represented by a walking stick and plowshare. Houdon recognized that his subject exhibited greatness by returning power to the people and by voluntarily reverting to the status of an ordinary citizen (Leibiger 51–52).

Washington demonstrated unparalleled determination and persever-ance. No matter how many times he suffered defeat, no matter how little food, equipment, and men the country furnished him, no matter what disgruntled officers said behind his back, he simply would not quit, give up, or give in. Washington's perseverance was so important because he symbolized the Revolution. Americans focused their hopes on their commander in chief—who became the most visible national symbol for the infant republic (Schwartz 16–39).

Washington's demeanor commanded respect from anyone whom he encountered. James Madison thought that "what particularly distinguished . . . [him] was a modest dignity which at once commanded the highest respect, and inspired the purest attachment" (Leibiger 225). A physically imposing man, the forty-four-year-old stood six-feet, three-inches tall, weighed over two hundred pounds, and displayed impressive physical stamina. He possessed tremendous presence, carrying himself with the dignity, graciousness, and manners of a Virginia gentleman. In public, the commander in chief always remained somewhat aloof, stiff, and distant; in an age of manners, he stood out as being especially formal. Ever sensitive to popular perceptions, Washington carefully cultivated his public image, knowing that for a man in his station, every word and action received scrutiny. He possessed an inflexible sense of duty and honor, prized his personal reputation, and carefully cultivated his image (Leibiger 4–6; Abbot, "Uncommon Awareness" 7–12).

When dining in private company, he loosened up a bit, laughing as loud as anyone at a good joke but rarely told one himself. James Madison contrasted his public and private personality:

> Washington was not fluent or ready in conversation, and was inclined to be taci-turn in general society. In the company of two or three intimate friends, how-ever, he was talkative, and when a little excited was sometimes fluent and even eloquent. The story so often repeated of his never laughing . . . is wholly untrue; no man seemed more to enjoy gay conversation, though he took little part in it himself. He was particularly pleased with the jokes, good humor, and hilarity of his companions. (Leibiger 6)

Washington could also be demanding and unforgiving, and he had a temper that he usually—but not always—kept in check.

Militarily, Washington was a fighter by instinct—a very aggressive, offensive-minded general. But the weakness of his army forced him to remain on the defensive for most of the war. The solution to this incongruity was to employ an offensive-defensive strategy similar to that later used by the Confederate States of America during the Civil War. Thus he fought a defensive war of attrition most of the time, but when a favorable opportunity to go on the offensive presented itself, Washington seized the day, as he did not only at Trenton (26 December 1776) but also at Princeton (3 January 1777), Monmouth (28 June 1778), and Yorktown (October 1781) (Ferling 111–321).

Washington practiced a decisive leadership style. He held councils of war with his officers on a regular basis, gatherings where he explained the army's situation and then welcomed discussion and advice about future movements. Only after hearing everyone out, adjourning the meeting, and reflecting in private on what had been said, did he make up his mind. After reaching decisions deliberately, he executed them swiftly and resolutely. He was never a micromanager reluctant to delegate authority. Furthermore, he harbored no fear of men who disagreed with him or who did not like him or each other, provided that they were loyal and competent (Ferling 111–321).

LEADERSHIP IN ACTION: THE CROSSING

No event of the Revolutionary War better captures Washington's fidelity to republicanism, perseverance, dignified personal demeanor, aggressive strategic thinking, and decisive leadership than the three-week period culminating in the battle of Trenton covered in *The Crossing.* Not only does this episode illustrate the commander in chief's character and leadership at its best, it also marks a turning point in the war. The American victory at Trenton was incalculably important because it reversed the British "pacification" campaign in New Jersey. After chasing the Continentals out of the state at the beginning of December 1776, the British spread their garrisons across New Jersey and largely stamped out any remaining resistance. By picking off the Trenton outpost, Washington forced the British to consolidate their forces, allowing patriot militias to come out of hiding and punish those who had reaffirmed their loyalty to the Crown. This well-placed and well-timed victory, in short, shattered General William Howe's counterrevolutionary strategy and turned the war around (Gruber 154–57).

The Crossing opens with the Continental Army in headlong retreat, just barely escaping across the Delaware on 7 December 1776 with British General Charles Cornwallis in hot pursuit. Having taken all local boats across the river with them, the shattered American forces have earned a temporary reprieve in Pennsylvania. Without shipping, the British would have to wait for the Delaware to freeze to make a crossing. With his enlistments to expire at the end of the calendar year, Washington (Jeff Daniels) conceives a desperate plan: the army will recross the river into New Jersey on Christmas night, march nine miles south, and launch a surprise attack on the Hessians stationed in Trenton. The commander's first task is to sell the scheme to his officers. After waiting for former-Redcoat-officer-turned-Patriot, General Horatio Gates (Nigel Bennett), to arrive in camp, Washington unfolds his proposal at a council of war.

With obvious contempt for Washington's military knowledge and abilities, Gates arrogantly dismisses the plan as a suicide mission, insisting that the troops, their enlistments about to expire, lack incentive to fight. Gates asserts, moreover, that America's bumbling farm boys will be no match for seasoned Hessian veterans. And far from being taken by surprise, the Hessian artillery would be waiting on the Jersey shore to blast the ferryboats to bits. In the film, Washington becomes incensed at the insinuations of incompetence and hotly defends his plan. When Gates maintains his opposition, the livid commander orders him out of camp at gunpoint. Despite their disgust with Gates, Washington's officer corps knows that his predictions may well prove accurate.

Thanks largely to the heroic efforts of Colonel John Glover (Sebastian Roche) and his regiment of Marblehead, Massachusetts, fishermen, who acted as ferrymen, the Continental Army successfully crossed the ice-clogged Delaware in cargo boats from the Durham iron forge on a rainy, bitterly cold Christmas night. (Glover, a cranky, devout New Englander more devoted to duty than to his commander, has little stomach for wealthy and aristocratic Virginia planters.) After making a midnight march south and catching the Hessians at Trenton completely by surprise at daybreak, the army scores a quick and stunning victory, capturing nine hundred prisoners with minimal casualties.

The film understandably deviates from the literal truth in order to simplify events and to evoke the character of Washington. For example, the film neglects to show that Washington's success resulted in part from dumb luck when, purely by chance, a band of local militia attacked the Hessian sentries earlier that night. Assuming this skirmish to be the foray his spies had warned him to expect, Hessian Commander Johann Rall (James Kidnie) lowered his guard for the remainder of the evening, allowing Washington's men to attack without warning (Fast 139–43).

The Crossing's *Portrayal of Washington*

The film strives to portray Washington's all-important fidelity to the republican principles of the Revolution. Take the early scene where he dictates a letter to his aide, Alexander Hamilton (Steven McCarthy), pleading for more men and supplies. Although frustrated with his civilian superiors, the commander nevertheless addresses them with the utmost respect and obeisance. The film misses an opportunity to underscore Washington's fidelity to republicanism, however, in the scene where he learns that Congress has conferred dictatorial powers on him. Instead of expressing profound awe over this enormous responsibility and making a solemn vow not to abuse his authority, *The Crossing* shows Washington lying back on his bed making rather mundane comments about how oxymoronic is the term "military intelligence."

To portray determination and perseverance, the film depicts Washington as the heart and soul of the army. He is always visible to his men, always assuring them that they can accomplish seemingly impossible tasks, always motivating and inspiring them. Consider, for example, the presentation of Colonel John Glover. Washington knows exactly how to get the most out of Glover, a man with little admiration for his commander but a high sense of duty.

The Crossing takes considerable license in its portrayal of Washington's personal characteristics. The most problematic scene of the movie is the angry confrontation with General Gates during the council of war. By all accounts, Washington maintained such a dignified presence that no officer, not even one who questioned his abilities, would have insulted him to his face in the manner Gates does in the film. In reality, Gates did oppose the attack on Trenton and voiced his objections to it, but he did so respectfully. Washington, in turn, was not so insecure about disagreement that he would have answered with an impassioned defense of his own leadership. Nor did he lose control of his temper in a moment requiring unrestrained candor from his officers. No threats and counter threats were made, either in private or in front of the entire council of war. Gates did, in fact, leave the army prior to the attack on Trenton, but he did so because he was sick, not because he was expelled. In short, all of the posturing in this scene is widely off the historical mark but was "invented" for dramatic purposes to show the commander's independence and undying confidence in his men and his cause (Nelson 75–78).

The film portrays leadership style through the council-of-war scene.

Washington asks his officers for a frank and open discussion of his plan to move against Trenton. The council scene would have been historically more accurate had he not suggested the strike but had left it to one of his officers to suggest. Moreover, the real Washington would not have come to the meeting with his mind made up, and he would have adjourned the meeting and reflected on what was said before deciding to attack. It would not have been smart leadership for Washington to begin the meeting by recommending a course of action because doing so would have unduly influenced the council. Washington wanted his officers to speak their minds freely, not to be yes-men. These licenses in the film seek to emphasize decisiveness over deliberation.

The film quite accurately shows a general eager to attack. At the council of war, Washington seems more eager to fight than any of his officers, and more confident about winning. Yet his aggressiveness does not cloud his judgment. The attack on Trenton is often seen as an audacious move, a theme the film stresses. In fact, Washington did not really have much choice but to attack. His army was on the verge of going home, and he believed that General Howe was going to move against him in a matter of days once the river froze. Washington thus faced two alternatives: to attack on his own terms with an army or be attacked on his enemy's terms without an army. The decision was what we now call a "no-brainer" for such an aggressive general (Abbot, *Washington Papers* 397, 407).

The Crossing captures Washington's willingness to delegate authority and to employ men who disliked or disagreed with him. For example, in the film he makes Glover beach master (the commander in charge of the crossing) even though that officer does not like his superior and doubts that the plan can succeed. Washington nevertheless gives Glover responsibility because he knows the man is competent and will get the job done or die trying. In actuality, however, Washington's 25 December general orders name Knox, not Glover, as beach master (Abbot, *Washington Papers* 436).

Washington would not have reconnoitered the enemy alone, as the film depicts. He would have delegated that task to a trusted subordinate rather than risk capture by the enemy; in fact, he chastised his second in command, General Charles Lee, for being taken by the enemy prior to the battle of Trenton. Washington knew that he could not risk his own capture. Once again, the film opts for personalized drama over literal truth (Abbot, *Washington Papers* 371).

How good a job does the film do with Washington's other personal characteristics, such as his sense of humor? One humorous scene shows him climbing into a Durham boat and telling Colonel Henry Knox (John Henry Canavan), "Move your fat ass, Henry." Of course, his words get passed through the ranks, growing taller down the line, and soon the whole army is roaring with laughter. Whether Washington actually told Knox to move his fat ass or not, one could argue that the scene captures his skillful leadership. Of course, the commander in chief might provide comic relief to his troops at the moment they needed it most. Humor can be a valuable instrument of leadership, and Washington was smart enough to know it. But the scene is highly dubious, and Knox's biographer contends that it never happened. On the contrary, the 25 December general orders called for strict silence during the crossing. A laughing army is a loud army, something Washington could not afford during a night attack. Moreover, the real Henry Knox may have been obese, but he was also a close friend and trusted officer, not the comically pathetic person portrayed in the movie (Abbot, *Washington Papers* 436; Callahan 83).

A MODEL PRESIDENCY

Without Washington's leadership, the office of the presidency would never have become a reality. His perseverance proved critical to the long campaign to frame and ratify the United States Constitution. The inevitability that the ever-trustworthy Washington would become the first chief executive explains the willingness of the American people, wary of saddling themselves with another tyrant, to accept a powerful executive branch.

The leadership style that Washington perfected during the Revolutionary War served him well as the first president of the United States. He brought prestige to the office—unlike today, when office often confers prestige on the man who holds it. Washington, well aware that he would set precedents that would guide his successors, took pains to get things right the first time. He provided such a good role model that historians consistently rank him our third greatest chief executive after Abraham Lincoln and Franklin Roosevelt (Schwartz 44–47).

Washington surrounded himself with the best men of his day, including Thomas Jefferson as secretary of state and Alexander Hamilton as secretary of the treasury. The rivalry between these two men did not trouble him as long as both placed duty first. The first president gradually transformed his department heads into a group advisory board that we now know as the cabinet. Washington governed his cabinet meetings as he did his councils of war, hearing everyone out, reflecting on the advice, and then reaching his own decisions. Having made up his mind, he acted with swiftness and resolution. In 1794, for example, Washington resorted to overwhelming military force to stamp out the Whiskey Rebellion, setting a precedent that Abraham Lincoln would later follow in responding to secession. The first president granted his appointees considerable discretion and did not hesitate to delegate, a governing style that has often led to the incorrect accusation that he was merely a figurehead (McDonald 23–46).

President Washington ultimately returned his power to the people as he had done as general. He is widely credited with establishing one of the most sacred traditions of the American political system—the two-term tradition. So venerated has this principle become, that the nation formally added it to the Constitution with the Twenty-Second Amendment in 1951 after Franklin Roosevelt ran for a fourth term in 1944. Washington's role is widely misunderstood, however. While he recognized that his actions would guide his successors, the two-term tradition came about more by accident

Library of Congress.

Famous image of a devout Washington, later re-enacted in D.W. Griffith's *America* (1924).

than by design. He had hoped to retire after four years but was unable to because political factionalism required that he remain in office. Moreover, Washington possessed no special preference for two terms. Instead, he was more concerned with retiring from office before he died, so as not to establish a presidency-for-life. Presidents Jefferson, Madison, and Monroe, it seems, did as much to establish the two-term tradition. Upon leaving office, Washington reverted to the status of ordinary citizen, making sure full power passed to his successor (Leibiger 153–68).

CONCLUSION: THE "INDISPENSABLE MAN"

Of course, Jeff Daniels exaggerates when he opens *The Crossing* with the words, "This country was founded by one man who kept his word." Exaggeration aside, Daniels's point is well taken. Historian James Thomas Flexner said pretty much the same thing when he called Washington the American Revolution's "Indispensable Man." In other words, if one played counterfactual history by going back in time and removing him from the eighteenth-century scene, then quite possibly the American Revolution would have failed. The same probably could not be said about any other founding father with the possible exception of Benjamin Franklin, who secured the French alliance. But why was Washington such an unusual revolutionary leader? The answer is that he possessed a tremendous sense of history, of honor, and of personal reputation. James Madison remarked that his "strength of character lay in his integrity, his love of justice, his fortitude, the soundness of his judgment, and his remarkable prudence." His loyalty to his cause and his reputation outweighed any desire for power, money, women, revenge, or anything else that often corrupts leaders and makes them betray their cause. Washington's faithfulness to democratic republicanism is the key to his character and to his success as a revolutionary leader (Fast xii; Flexner xiii–xv; Leibiger 225).

Marcus Cunliffe wrote that most Americans know only Washington the cold monument, not the real man (Cunliffe 1–5). By cutting away the mythology and focusing on a representative crisis for Washington as a leader, *The Crossing* goes a long way toward replacing the monument with the man.

WORKS CITED

Abbot, W.W. "An Uncommon Awareness of Self: *The Papers of George Washington*." *Prologue* 21 (1989): 7–12.

————, et al., eds. *The Papers of George Washington*, Revolutionary War Series, Vol. 7. Charlottesville: University Press of Virginia, 1997.

Callahan, North. *Henry Knox: General Washington's General.* New York: A.S. Barnes, 1958.

Cunliffe, Marcus. *George Washington: Man and Monument.* Reprint, New York: New American Library, 1982.

Fast, Howard. *The Crossing.* Reprint, New York: Simon and Schuster, 1999.

Ferling, John E. *The First of Men: A Life of George Washington.* Knoxville: University of Tennessee Press, 1988.

Flexner, James Thomas. *Washington: The Indispensable Man.* Reprint, New York: New American Library, 1974.

Gruber, Ira D. *The Howe Brothers and the American Revolution.* New York: W.W. Norton, 1972.

Higginbotham, Don. *George Washington and the American Military Tradition.* Athens: University of Georgia Press, 1985.

Leibiger, Stuart. *Founding Friendship: George Washington, James Madison, and the Creation of the American Republic.* Charlottesville: University Press of Virginia, 1999.

McDonald, Forrest. *The Presidency of George Washington.* Reprint, New York: W.W. Norton, 1975.

Nelson, Paul David. *General Horatio Gates.* Baton Rouge: University of Louisiana Press, 1976.

Schwartz, Barry. *George Washington: The Making of an American Symbol.* New York: The Free Press, 1987.

Scott F. Stoddart

THE ADAMS CHRONICLES

Domesticating the American Presidency

John and Abigail Adams (George Grizzard and Leora Dana) move into the newly constructed White House. Adams was the second president of the United States, 1797–1801. *The Adams Chronicles* (1976), a production of WNET/ New York.

The publishing community witnessed an intriguing phenomenon in the summer of 2001 when David McCullough's biography *John Adams* debuted on the *New York Times* best-seller list at number one and remained there for fourteen weeks. The 751-page book gathered praise from throughout the critical world for its engaging style, detailing the life and career of America's second president—a president not noted for much other than being the only president to father another president (a feat only repeated after the 2000 election).[1]

However, John Adams had enjoyed popular-culture status before.[2] For the celebration of America's Bicentennial, the Exxon Corporation funded for WNET in New York a thirteen-part miniseries on John and Abigail Adams and the legacy that became *The Adams Chronicles*. Hoping to capitalize on the recent success of British television import *Upstairs/Downstairs*, the producers and writers of the Adams series desired to replicate its Emmy-winning production values. Premiering on 20 January 1976, *The Adams Chronicles* was immensely popular during the 1976 television season (the only rebroadcast was in September 1976) and paved the way for network television to begin producing programs with equally high production values—what would become the "miniseries." While the thirteen-part series helped America to celebrate its two hundredth birthday with a note of patriotic fanfare, *The Adams Chronicles* presents a prescribed portrait of John Adams, domesticating the image of the second president so as to make him seem the conscious founder of an American dynasty. The first six "chapters" of the series, following Adams from 1770 to 1801, emphasize his qualities as husband and father, rather than his career as a diplomat and politician, to create a continuing serial drama to celebrate the nation's bicentennial. In this respect, *The Adams Chronicles* becomes the precursor to the miniseries and novels-for-television that would become so popular in the late 1970s and early 1980s.[3]

SCREENING AND CRITIQUING THE ADAMS CHRONICLES

Employing six directors and nine playwrights,[4] the series based its thirteen scripts on the Adams Family Papers, letters, diaries, and journals preserved at the Massachusetts Historical Society.[5] According to the *New York Times* (11 January 1976), the series cost $5.2 million—an estimated $400,000 an episode.[6] The production values were considered so good that Coast Community College in Mesa, California, devised an early version of a distance-learning course for college credit built around studying the Adams family as an introduction to the development of political ideals and government. The course was duplicated at three hundred colleges nationwide, offering it to a total enrollment of forty-five thousand! (*New York Times*, 1 August 1976).

The series was praised by historians, including Richard B. Morris, for its intricate detail in respect to the portrayal of family life in eighteenth-century America, but some, including Morris, questioned the enlarged role of Adams in certain historical moments, feeling that the series had inflated his importance at times (*New York Times*, 11 January 1976). Claude-Anne Lopez did not agree with the portrayal of other patriots within the series, especially Benjamin Franklin, whom he thought was "vilified" in order to make Adams appear nobler (*New York Times*, 14 March 1976).[7] It is interesting to note that the producers left out of the series Adams's fifty-one-year relationship with Thomas

Jefferson. While Jefferson does figure into the fabric of the miniseries, it is clear that the real focus of the first six chapters is Adams's relationship with Abigail Smith Adams, his wife of fifty-eight years. Historians have written many volumes on Jefferson's turbulent friendship with Adams, a friendship that temporarily soured during the time both men served as president.[8] Even so, the friendship does figure slightly into the text of the series companion book, Jack Shepard's *The Adams Chronicles: Four Generations of Greatness*—a book that hit number one on the *New York Times* best-seller list and remained there for a number of weeks. These limits reveal that the structure and the content of the series maintain a certain agenda, one that ideologically coincides with television's general audience in 1976.

For one, the show's structure, like *Upstairs/Downstairs*, is a serial—a form of continuing drama. According to Nicholas Abercrombie, serials take place in the ordinary, everyday world—one that is very much a woman's world (Abercrombie 50–54). In focusing more on John Adams's family, particularly his long-distance marriage to Abigail, the producers were paying strict attention to their audience dynamics. This also makes it crucial to situate the action in the private sphere, orienting the action around the *personal* and *private* life. Therefore, using the Adams family correspondence, which deals especially in the everyday activities of John raising his sons abroad on his own and Abigail successfully maintaining the family farm, makes the series appealing to Middle-America.[9] Abigail's abilities make her an attractive heroine as well, and the period details of the Adams household surviving disease and dealing with nearby battles make the series a very attractive package for the bicentennial spectator.[10]

The evolving women's movement greatly influenced much of the television viewed in American homes in 1976. Ella Taylor believes that "the women's movement began to dig a steady, subversive path into the consciousness of both men and women, shaking up long-cherished assumptions about sex roles, marriage, and family life and demanding equality of pay and opportunity in the workplace" (Taylor 42). Taylor's perspective is correct, given that the series maintained a very strong audience in its two thirteen-week runs. She continues:

> As women entered the labor force and shouldered the multiple burdens of running domestic lives while fitting themselves into workplace cultures designed for men, the feminist critique of patriarchy in the private sphere as well as the workplace became part of the fabric of public discussion. It also became part of the fabric of television relevance. (Taylor 84–85)

What is certainly relevant here is Taylor's idea that women not only guided the television viewing in the home, but that certain shows were successful during the 1970s because they mirrored the growing acknowledgment of the place of women in American history. In that respect, the Adams family is the perfect choice for understanding how the family thrived as a unit and endured the hardships of John's very productive career—one that kept him absent for so much of the time.

ADAMS AS A SYMBOL OF AMERICAN VALUES AND IDENTITY

The Adams Chronicles can be read as a television serial in a number of ways. For instance, by calling each episode a "chapter," the method of the British-based PBS productions, and by employing techniques long associated with narrative film, the creators engage the audience in a saga of human proportions, rather than in a history lesson peopled with an aloof patriot and his family. Each of the thirteen episodes opens with a coda, recited by narrator Michael Toland, setting the tone for the lofty ambitions of the series: "Four generations of one family. Their lives and causes reveal 150 years of American history." Immediately, the writers equate the Adams family with America—the start of the Adams saga is the start of America—one narrative is the same for each. Chapter 1 of the series opens with an extended crosscut between the young, ambitious Adams (George Grizzard) and the young, privileged image of King George III (John Tillinger). Adams and George III were the same age, so it is a fitting parallel; however, the imaging of this sequence speaks volumes in respect to the ideals the series desires to impart. For instance, the first shots show a vibrant, determined Adams outdoors, hoeing a vegetable garden, pitching hay, and splitting rails for fences; these shots are crosscut with images of George III existing in opulent despair: being dressed by a coterie of valets, lounging about sumptuous divans, and feasting at large banquet tables. As the voice-over proclaims how different the men were, the images make the distinctions all the clearer, implying that Britishness is to be associated with effete dilettantes, while Americanness is imbued with the heartiness of physical work and clean, simple living.

Another cinematic technique employed by these directors involves two types of panning. Traditionally, the pan is a horizontal rotation of the camera, from left to right or right to left, to create the depth of a scene, revealing what lies before the camera on either side; however, the panning used in *The Adams Chronicles* creates a specific effect, usually humanizing the character of John Adams. The horizontal pan imbues the narrative with a sense of action in a rather static moment. For instance, the first significant use of this narrative technique is during Adams's defense of five British soldiers on criminal charges for their part in the Boston Massacre (chapters 1 and 2). To set the dramatic tension of the courtroom, the camera constantly pans the jury in much the same way that any director would use the pan in a courtroom drama. This is particularly effective during Adams's summation to the jury, a moment when he simply stands to address the jury with a long speech in which he appeals to it to "bury that beast" that he witnessed in the mobs out in front of the courthouse, crying for the soldiers' deaths only moments before. The episodes do not dwell on the details of the trial—only on Adams's summation and the court's subsequent findings. However, the unpopularity of Adams's decision to defend the soldiers necessitates a capturing of the crowd's violent desires and the young lawyer's subsequent relief that justice was served and that "the men were not found simply guilty of being British soldiers." The panning adds action as it aligns the spectator with the tension of Adams's dilemma and his words.

A second form of this technique serves to contrast the newly formed members of Congress as they meet to host the inauguration of President Washington (chapter 5) in 1789 and that of President Adams (chapter 6) in 1797. At the moment of Washington's inauguration, the president-elect (Michael O'Hare) arrives accompanied by his cabinet, and the camaraderie of the senators and representatives is evident using the panning technique as the camera frames the grinning faces jubilant with Washington's success. The panning operates in a noticeably different manner in rendering Adams's inauguration, following the political division between Adams and his longtime friend Jefferson (Albert Stratton). The panning in this sequence is noticeably slower as Adams takes the oath of office, cutting between him standing at the head of the congressional leadership and the members of the Senate and House. There are few smiles and no cheers. Instead, the camera movement shows some men standing glumly, arms folded, most scrupulously examining their new president. Polite applause ends the sequence rather than the loud bravos heard after Washington's inauguration, signaling the difficulties Adams will meet in his term as president.

Another type of panning—an arc shot—creates a sense of intrigue in the moments when Adams meets with his divided cabinet. Usually with the circular pan, the camera moves about the subject 360 degrees, conveying a bond between the characters on screen. However, this arc, whirling about the table during moments of heated discussion, replicates the dizzying effect the debate has on Adams. The method is noticeably different from the way Washington's cabinet was shot in the earlier episode—even though there is much frank discussion, particularly between Jefferson and Alexander Hamilton (Jeremiah Sullivan)—the camera never circles the table; the arguments were handled with routine cuts between the speakers. However, in discussing what will become the XYZ Affair, Adams sits at the head of the table, Hamilton's Federalist cronies to the left, and Jefferson's supporters to his right—Jefferson's seat at the foot of the table is noticeably vacant. As Adams begins speaking of building a stronger navy and increasing the might of the military, the camera circles the table, recording more of the noise than the individual responses. Again, the effect brings the spectator closer to the president as the whirling reflects his confusion and lack of control; the method empathizes with Adams, bringing his feelings of frustration to a personal level.

A significant cinematic trope employed by the series is the montage, a sequence that relies on editing to condense or expand action, space, or time. In *The Adams Chronicles* there are two significant intellectual montages that achieve very different ends. The first, occurring at the end of chapter 2, plays as John Adams, in voice-over, reads the Declaration of Independence to his family. As he reads the document, the image of the Adams clan sitting about the parlor fire dissolves into a series of lovely shots of colonial New England in the fall and of churches, their white steeples gleaming against the blue sky. There are shots of other Revolutionary War landmarks, such as Independence Hall and Mount Vernon, countered with one particular image of a forest, showing young boys climbing a set of birch trees, frolicking in the warm sun. All the while, the Liberty Bell rings in the background and finally evolves into view as Adams, still in voice-over, finishes reading the document. In all, the montage sets the tone for the rest of the series as it brings the domestic harmony and solidity of the Adams clan together with the newly emerging nation's principles of democracy, revealing that it would be impossible to have one without the other.

Another intellectual montage reveals how the technique can help in humanizing the images on-screen. At the end of chapter 4, Adams agrees to allow his only daughter, Nabby (Katharine Houghton), to marry. The sequence cuts from close-ups of the blushing bride and the happy groom, Royall Tyler (Wesley Addy), to a close-up of the proud parents standing behind. However, as the bride and groom begin to state their vows, the close-ups dissolve between the young couple, and the elder couple, John and Abigail (Kathryn Walker), look as intently into one another's eyes as do the newlyweds. The vows and the nurturing words of the bishop marrying the couple become a sort of voice-over for the overlapping images, drawing a parallel between the newlyweds and the older and wiser couple who still behave as young lovers. The imaging here is fairly obvious, making the elder Adamses into a prototype of the American family—one that stays together despite the odds, and one that stands behind all its children. Nowhere in these chapters is there any mention of Nabby's tortured relationship with Royall Tyler, nor is there any of the disparagement Adams heaped upon the man who was soon to become his son-in-law.[11] Instead, we see an image of family solidarity—a wedding celebrated to form the foundation of the continuing dynasty.

The use of humor in the series brings the image of the historical figure into a human perspective, particularly as it highlights the relationships between John and his revolutionary colleagues. As John embarks for Philadelphia in chapter 2, his wife Abigail not only admits to being a "passionate patriot," but she chastises him for not purchasing a new suit of clothes. John, much like a pouting child, claims that he could not use the allowance set aside for travel expenses to purchase a fine suit—his threadbare broadcloth suit is fine for representing the masses—particularly given how shabbily his fellow representative, cousin Samuel Adams (W.B. Brydon), dresses. However, as his carriage pulls up to his cousin Sam's home, John noticeably gasps. Samuel Adams comes out the front door dressed in a brand-new red velvet suit, a fluffy white periwig, and carrying a beautiful gold walking stick. Now dressed as a fine gentleman, Sam tells John he really should take a bit more pride in his appearance.[12]

Another sequence depicts a rather amusing anecdote concerning Benjamin Franklin (Robert Symonds), who would go on to make Adams's time in France difficult (the imaging that prompted Professor Lopez's outburst in the *New York Times*). As representatives of the Continental Congress, the men are forced to sleep in the only available room at a nearby inn—and, not only do they have to share the room, but they have to share the bed. The imagery during this sequence uncloaks the historical figures to make them more human. While discussing the need for a unanimous declaration against Britain, the shy, more puritanical Adams undresses with his back to Dr. Franklin, putting his nightshirt on over his clothes, and undressing afterward. He turns away to brush his teeth and quickly puts on his nightcap before climbing into bed. Franklin, however, takes off his shirt and parades about the room, holding forth on the day's business. He continues speaking as he brushes his teeth and spits into the bowl facing the camera. He disrobes and sits in a chair, exposed before an open window, before putting on his own threadbare nightshirt and retiring. Adams, fearful of open windows at night, believing that the night air was bad for the body and the soul, asks Franklin to close it. Franklin, espousing his idea of air-bathing to rid the body of smells and dirt, pointedly refuses. The sequence ends with the men turning their backs to one another, each sighing mightily about his uncooperative bed partner.

What the humor of these situations does is to influence the way television renders the historical figure. Obviously, the mass medium intends to reach as many spectators as possible; therefore, it is imperative that the figure of John Adams seem approachable and interesting—both in his practical outlook on life and in his reputation as an honest and stern leader. Both instances make Adams into the butt of jokes, and this contributes to a notion of him as being a very common man in the middle of rather uncommon events.

ADAMS AS DIPLOMAT AND PRESIDENT

The use of the Adams family correspondence as a basis for the series could have been deadly had the writers chosen to "record" the letters in voice-over, showing John hovered over a desk writing or Abigail sitting in a parlor reading a piece of parchment with tears in her eyes. Instead, the series writers took moments that John and Abigail recorded and dramatized them—putting them into the "active" tense to make the drama more engaging. Chapter 3 "John Adams: Diplomat," shows this method to be most particularly successful in relating the historical events of Adams's time abroad. Chapter 3 recounts the war years and relates the trials and tribulations Adams encountered in working with the British ministry and the problems Adams had with Dr. Franklin in negotiating the Treaty of Paris. Selecting engaging parts of the letters, the episode pays close attention to John Adams's gradual acculturation to the ways of the British and French. For instance, Franklin hosts a rather lavish welcome for his comrade, and French aristocrats attend, sumptuously adorned in the latest fashions of silks and satins, their huge, powdered wigs and intricate jewelry denote the special occasion. Adams, arriving with his secretary—his son John Quincy (Mark Winkworth)—appears in plain broadcloth, and, ever the pragmatic New Englander, coarsely denounces the frippery as vulgar show: "There are threes V's that plague France: Vanity, Venery, Vulgarity." The camera swirls about Adams and his son to show the chandeliers of cut crystal and the ceilings of gaudy gilt, all in an effort to replicate their displacement in this foreign land and his distain for Franklin's foolishness. Before leaving, the elder Adams chastises Franklin for this display, reminding the old man of his responsibility to keep accounts of all spending while in France.

Adams's discomfort is further heightened in a sequence that shows Adams attending the court of Louis XVI. The King (Jerome Dempsey) only speaks French, so the kindly Franklin must translate for the new minister. Adams is visibly frazzled in a close-up as Franklin and the King exchange pleasantries. However, when Franklin translates for Adams, he notes Adams's growing frustration: "I warned you not to waste your time copying our accounts; far better you spent your time learning French." When Adams and Franklin meet with the French and British emissaries, Adams's coarse frankness undoes the exquisitely polite French; the French minister asks Adams: "Have you come here to negotiate peace with Great Britain or to declare war on France?" When alone, Franklin chastises Adams for his rudeness, causing Adams to announce his intention of leaving for Holland. Franklin replies, "Mr. Adams, you can go to Holland or to hell—whichever is closer!" With these scenes, this chapter makes Adams more of an underdog, displaying his inability to negotiate with the French and British in the gallant manner they preferred. Playing off the cliché of the "innocent abroad," these sequences reveal the coarse American in juxtaposition to the refined quality of European manners, and they show Adams learning what all diplomats must: that one must become conscious of the cultural climate of a new situation in order to win favor.

Upon his return from Holland, Adams, now the member of a five-man team sent to prepare the Treaty of Paris, adopts the customs of the French in order to show up his elder rival. He dresses in smart Parisian fashions, makes small talk with the Princess of Orange (Nancy Barrett), and flirts with other ladies of the court in order to get their male counterparts interested in talking. He hosts a splendid dinner with Franklin as the guest of honor; instead of being horrified, Franklin and his entourage are splendidly surprised with the change in Adams—he now speaks French, and his reappearance at court is a qualified success. At dinner he announces, "Madame asks if I am the famous Adams. Well, I suppose I am!" With this, the scene changes as the series narrator explains that Adams, through these alterations, became the very "Washington of negotiators" and that his contributions to the discussions of peace were instrumental in maintaining French support. As the men sit down to the table, the scene gradually dissolves to Benjamin West's unfinished painting of the peace commission, revealing, once more, that the plain Adams became a great man because he could learn from constructive criticism.

Abigail's letters are also dramatized in a significant fashion, making the sequences depicting her trials on the home front much more engaging—regardless of historical accuracy. For instance, David McCullough's biography details one tribulation that Abigail encountered with a supposed friend of the family, James Lovell, one of the most active members of the Committee for Foreign Affairs at the Continental Congress. John was attending to a client in New Hampshire, and Lovell wrote to Adams appointing him to the peace commission. Abigail, suspecting that the letter was urgent, opened it, only to find that the commission was to take her husband away once more. She wrote straight away to Lovell, demanding to know how he could "contrive to rob me of my happiness. And can I, sir, consent to be separated from him whom my heart esteems above all earthly things, and for an unlimited time? My life will be one continued scene of anxiety and apprehension, and must I cheerfully comply with the demand of my country?" (McCullough 175)

As dramatized by *The Adams Chronicles* in 1976, the scene makes a bit more of a sensation. Lovell (Jack Gwillim) himself arrives to deliver the letter, and Abigail, knowing him as a dear friend and confidante to her husband, speaks of the loneliness she feels. Lovell, sitting next to Abigail on the sofa, moves closer, asking, "Why has no one ever spoken of your beauty?" As he puts his arm about her, Abigail pushes it away, rises up, and demands that he leave the house. Lovell, gathering his things, sheepishly apologizes, and leaves Mrs. Adams. As she begins to recompose herself, a servant enters, asking Abigail if Mr. Lovell will be staying to dinner. She soundly replies, "There is *nothing* on this farm that could satisfy *his* appetite!" The sequence is punctuated with humor, but it reveals an important ideological component to the story of the Adamses. Although they both suffer from the long separations, Abigail is a determined, honest woman who remains true to her husband.

THE ADAMS FAMILY VS. THE ADAMS PRESIDENCY

The problems that Adams faced as chief executive are also handled in a dramatic fashion, pitting the Adams family against the Adams presidency to show how life in the White House affected family life. This prioritizing of the family over the historical events domesticates the image of Adams all the more, witnessing Adams the husband and father contending with the forces bent on his political destruction.

This idea is exemplified in chapter 6: "John Adams: President"—an episode that could have been named "John Adams: The Man Who Didn't Want to be President." Throughout the episode, Adams finds himself at odds with his political foes in the Congress, his cabinet—led by Washington's treasury secretary Alexander Hamilton—and his ex-friend and current vice president, Thomas Jefferson. The main political event of the episode is the XYZ Affair. As historian Jack Shepard relates it, Adams sent Thomas Pinckney, Elbridge Gerry, and John Marshall to France to negotiate a trade treaty. Charles-Maurice de Tallyrand, the French foreign minister, sent three of his own ministers to the American diplomats and claimed that he would recognize them if he received a gift of $250,000 and a loan of $10 million. Shepard contends that "Adams's envoys filed their dispatches, which did not reach the president until March 4, 1798. Their reports referred to the French emissaries as X, Y, and Z, and as Adams read the dispatches, and the significance of the French rejection and bribe attempts unfolded, he knew that he faced war" (Shepard 194). Adams did not succumb to the French demands, and he made the insult public, hoping to show Jefferson and the Republican-controlled Congress that France was not such a worthy ally.

As filmed, in response to the French plot for money, Adams's cabinet advises him to call out the army and navy, asking him to declare war. The camera circles about the table as each member voices his opposition to Adams's plea for negotiation, pausing slightly when it arrives at Jefferson's empty chair. In an earlier scene, Jefferson attempts to persuade Adams to dismiss the cabinet—many members were taking direct orders from the warmongering Hamilton—and to create his own. Adams, not one to be told what to do, defies his old friend, and Jefferson then stopped attending cabinet meetings. As the president returns home for the evening, coughing and sneezing from a bad cold, the scene cuts to Hamilton reading the minutes from that day's cabinet meeting. Using Hamilton as an antagonist is crucial not only to the entertainment value of the chapter but is also crucial to the domesticated image of Adams. The characterization of Hamilton as an unmarried womanizer reveals how unscrupulous politicians can be—the John Adams we know from the previous five episodes is just too nice to be president. Even his dear friend Jefferson turns on Adams—he becomes a ruthless politician when it will benefit himself.

This is all the more underscored as John begins to bring his daily problems home to Abigail (Leora Dana);[13] his wife appears to be the only person in America he can trust for honest feedback. She stands behind him in each moment of crisis, from the small (supporting his decision not to attend a ball in George Washington's honor) to the large (supporting his break with Jefferson). When Adams decides that he must make the XYZ Affair public, she assists in his plans. After explaining the problems to her, Abby agrees that John is correct, that he must report the scandal to the newspapers: "If only you could reveal the nature of the plan without disclosing their names." Adams concurs, "I'll call them Mr. X, Mr. Y, and Mr. Z in order to pressure those men in France. Congress must find out!" In closing the scene, John and Abigail embrace on the sofa, laughing joyfully about the "intrigue" that they have created. Of course, the situation, as recorded by historians, proved to be one of the smartest moves of Adams's presidency; however, the television serial would have us believe that the Adamses plotted the details of the matter together in another moment of domestic seclusion.

Of course, the domestic scene is not all bliss for the Adams family. Later in the same episode, Adams signs the Alien and Sedition Acts into law. With the Alien Act, "the President was empowered in war or at the threat of war to seize, secure, or remove from the country all resident aliens who were citizens of the alien nation" (Smith 975). The Sedition Act "provided the penalty of a fine of not more than five thousand dollars and imprisonment for not more than five years for any persons, aliens, or citizens, who should undertake to oppose or defeat the operation of any law of the United States" (Smith 975). All the major Adams biographies concur that these acts led to his political undoing.[14]

In chapter 6, when the cabinet, the Congress, and the newspapers denounce his view on the laws, John turns to Abigail for solace. To his surprise, she joins the critics but ever so gently:

John Adams: Are you my wife or my conscience?

Abigail Adams: Both. And, your dearest friend.

The series follows the historians in identifying these acts as the major mistake of Adams's presidency; however, the show adds that he maintained peace with both Britain and France and established much of the protocol that we continue to employ today in respect to the presidency.

In 1800, six months before he left office, John Adams moved into the President's House in the newly named Washington, D.C. On 2 November 1800, he wrote to Abigail, who was nursing a persistent fever in Braintree, that, "The building is in a state to be habitable, and now we wish for your company." He then closed the letter with a prayer now carved on the mantle of the State Dining Room: "I pray heaven to bestow the best blessings on this house, and on all that shall hereafter inhabit it. May none but honest and wise men ever rule under its roof" (Shepard 209).

In *The Adams Chronicles*, John and Abigail move into the newly constructed President's House in Washington, D.C., together. As the couple wanders arm-in-arm through the drafty corridors, much as they did in the first episode, touring their bridal house by candlelight, they look over the unpainted walls and cavernous rooms. John then recites the prayer he actually wrote to Abigail. When finished, the elderly John begins to chuckle as he tells his wife, "I have yet to carry you over a threshold." Once more, the show dramatizes what was once written, and it depicts Adams as a warm, loving husband who just happened to be the second president.

In fact, it is the depiction of John and Abigail's relationship that becomes the central core of the first six episodes, and it is within these characterizations that the ideological framework of the series surfaces. Many historians attest to the fortitude between this man and wife, and the series presents Abigail as John's equal in many respects. One recurring sequence that punctuates the first four episodes shows John and Abigail preparing for bed. In chapter 1, after their stormy courtship (Abigail's mother disapproved of the young attorney), John and Abigail marry in a simple ceremony and return to John's newly appointed house, left to him by his father. The couple wanders through the rooms by lantern-light, entering the bedchamber with its warm fire and crisp, white linens. On the bed, John has left his gift to his bride—a child's primer. Abigail reads the first lesson aloud: "In Adam's fall, we sinned all" and comments, "Our sons will learn an Adams never falls, though he occasionally stumbles." As they prepare for bed, John turns to Abigail and shows her a magnet: "I felt the force of a magnet the day we met." The scene fades to black as the couple embraces, typical of series television—moving away from the scene that cannot be shown, only imagined.

The bedroom becomes a place where Adams confides in Abigail, and the trope continues through the series, revealing John and Abigail as both lovers and equals. Toward the end of chapter 1, after John has agreed to defend the British soldiers who shot at the angry mob during the Boston Massacre, he turns to Abigail before snuffing the candle and tells her that his main fear is that "law and justice" will not prevail. Abigail says nothing but listens attentively, holding her husband as he drifts to sleep. In chapter 2, after John announces he will join Samuel Adams in Philadelphia as a member of the Continental Congress, Abigail, once more in bed, speaks of her own fears in being left alone for so long, remarking, "I fear for my safety—not your success." This time, John consoles his wife, promising her that someday they will travel together. The subsequent conversation details the honesty and loving support each offered the other for a greater cause:

Abigail: I will be content with this small part of the world, if only it were free.

John: I did not know you were so passionate a patriot.

Abigail: We women are obliged to conceal our passions from the world.

The series depicts couplehood in very traditional terms, showing Abigail to be the selfless wife and mother, and John as the dedicated breadwinner and career politician.

In fact, one of the few times Abigail's frazzled nerves surface regarding John's career follows his announcement that he plans to go to France to assist Franklin in negotiating peace. While he was gone the first time, Abigail lost their second daughter to scarlet fever and caught the disease herself. Her mother came to attend her, caught the malady, and died as well. The series reflects the difficulties Abigail faced alone, nursing the sick and dying, disinfecting the house by washing the walls down with pure vinegar, as was the custom. In a letter to John, her one request is for him to bring home some pins she needed for sewing. And, on his return, he glibly informs her that he must leave much sooner than expected. Abigail's response is pricelessly sweet: "Where are the pins that I asked for? Thirteen years married, and less than half of that time have we been together. Our love, like your clothes, will go to rags without attention!" John, holding out the pins she asked for, smiles and holds his distraught wife as she quietly sobs. She resigns herself to being alone once more with the promise that she might join him in Paris once he is settled.[15]

Abigail not only joined John in Paris, but she resided in England with him after the Treaty of Paris was signed and he became Minister to Great Britain. At the Court of St. James's, Abigail accepted the duties of a minister's wife quite easily, entertaining in the manner that became a representative of the United States. However, the series depicts many of the family's trials as it adjusts to life abroad. Nabby, the eldest daughter, has had to leave her beau; John Quincy returns to America to attend Harvard College, just as his mother arrives. The sequences here are humorous as Abigail adjusts to British society. John tells her that her new dresses are "bewitching," even though she complains that they reveal too much cleavage. She writes to her sister about the necessity for maintaining appearances, yet reveals that British manners and customs are a questionable façade. Though she enjoys the naughtiness of the ballet, she does not like the frank talk of ladies having "bastard" children disposed of or of the boxes in the streets where the poor are encouraged to leave their unwanted children.

The domestic sphere takes center stage humorously as the Adamses plan a formal dinner for the British gentry to assist John's clumsy entrance into British society. Abigail enters the room with a rather sad-looking chicken; she wiggles it at her husband as she proclaims, "Thirteen shillings! Twelve to dinner! This is all that the market could offer!" Just then, a close-up reveals a large wooden crate sitting on the dining table, having been just delivered. As whatever inside begins to claw and scratch, Abigail nervously announces, "I hate surprises." John, assisted by son Charles (Thomas A. Stewart), opens the crate to discover a huge tortoise. "Good Lord, deliver us!" exclaims Abigail. "And, thank him for our dinner!" retorts husband John. The scene cuts to after dinner that evening, the guests remarking on Mrs. Adams's genius in the kitchen, not knowing whether the delicate meal was of fish or meat. Adams tells his company about the turtle and quips, "A creature when closely inspected turns out to be something completely different," referring to his own abilities as a minister, if only the British would work with him. The sequence becomes part of the family legend as the Adamses prove more capable than even they once supposed.[16]

The couple is in bed once more in chapter 5, as Adams recounts the news of his party's victory for the presidency and Adams's election as vice president. The series breaks new ground in showing the elderly John and Abigail embracing beneath the covers as they prepare to be parted once more. An American icon in bed with his wife, this time drinking warm milk, does much to redefine not only the image of the president but in reevaluating the triumphs and tragedies of the famous.

CONCLUSION

The Adams Chronicles uses the serial method to help break down the pillars of greatness to reveal that the Adamses together triumphed as a simple husband and wife and as founders of the American presidency. Writing of the formulaic television drama, Horace Newcomb underscores the necessity for historical television to adhere to generic conventions: "Television melodrama can rely confidently on one resource that is always essential to the vitality of any art form: an audience impressive not simply in its numbers but also in its genuine sophistication, its deep familiarity with the history and conventions of the genre" (quoted in Thorburn 85). Newcomb's point is valid here as it specifies *how* Americans viewed *The Adams Chronicles* as family saga. The writers of the show,

John and Abigail Adams (George Grizzard and Kathryn Walker). *The Adams Chronicles* (1976), a production of WNET/New York.

adhering to television's conventions, knew how they would catch their prospective audience—and how they wanted to make them feel as they invested thirteen weeks into the lives of the famous, yet typical, family. Newcomb's theory concerning the conflation of reality and fantasy through the medium of television is very important here, as it helps explain why this bourgeois ideology is central to the program's reception: "I would probably say now that television is more of a *mirror* than a window, that the mirror involves us with fantasies and idealizations, but that those fantasies and idealizations may be precisely what we *need* to develop values for living. That is, there's an implied distinction there between fantasy and realism" (quoted in Himmelstein 94).

This idea, both in screening the story of the Adams dynasty and in appropriating the historical for the dramatic, coincides with Abercrombie's notion of how television series affect audiences: "It is often assumed that television will have a greater effect on people the more involved they are in what is going on on the screen. If they are bound up with the action or with other characters, it seems probable that they are more likely to accept values and attitudes that appear in the programme" (Abercrombie 195–96).

In concluding his recent biography of John Adams, David McCullough reflects on what may have been Adams's last thoughts in an effort to make the former president more human: "Human nature had not changed, however, for all the improvements. Nor would it, he was sure. Nor did he love life any the less for its pain and terrible uncertainties. He remained as he had been, clear-eyed about the paradoxes of life and in his own nature" (McCullough 651). Here, the popular historian uses a technique very similar to that used by the writers of *The Adams Chronicles* in rendering the image of Adams as a man of solid, virtuous character. While never irreverent, the first six episodes that depict the career of John Adams and of his devoted wife Abigail dismantle the idea of the presidency, remaking the saga of this American dynasty as a couple of ordinary people who, after they married, worked together to do many extraordinary things.

NOTES

I want to dedicate this article to my mother, Jeanne F. Doyle Black, who not only inspired me in my love of history, literature, and film, but who watched *The Adams Chronicles* with me each week when it originally aired in 1976.

1. In fact, the book made it into an issue of *Entertainment Weekly* in a column titled "How Did They Do That?" The question regarding McCullough's book asks, "How did a 751-page, thirty-five-dollar biography of John Adams become one of the biggest best-sellers of the summer?" The article claims that the feat even took the book's publisher by surprise, though he is credited with the marketing campaign. Within two weeks of release, McCullough was interviewed on *Today, Charlie Rose,* and National Public Radio's *Fresh Air,* in addition to a two-page spread in *Newsweek* and a cover feature in the *New York Times Book Review.*

2. Peter Stone and Sherman Edwards used John Adams as the protagonist of their 1968 Broadway musical *1776,* even though his character is "obnoxious and disliked" in the play (Stone and Edwards 153). The writers claim that the events of the musical are factual, though they admit that theatrical licenses were taken; quoting a European dramatist, they observe: "'God writes lousy theater.' In other words, reality is seldom artistic, orderly, or dramatically satisfying; life rarely provides a sound second act, and its climaxes usually have not been adequately prepared for" (Stone and Edwards 153). Even so, in a brief "Historical Note" that follows the published version of the libretto, Stone and Edwards admit, "John Adams is, at times, a composite of himself and his cousin Sam Adams" (Stone and Edwards 162).

3. According to Les Brown, the miniseries was a program designed for limited runs over several nights or several weeks, as opposed to those created "in hopes of running indefinitely" (Brown 360). The miniseries came into vogue in American commercial television during the late 1970s after the success on public television of British

series, such as *The Forsythe Saga, Elizabeth R, The Six Wives of Henry VIII*, and *Civilisation*. The success of *The Adams Chronicles* is credited with the development of Irwin Shaw's *Rich Man, Poor Man* that ran on ABC in 1976 and *Roots*, which also ran on ABC in 1977.

4. The directors were Paul Bogart, James Cellan Jones, Fred Co, Barry Davis, Bill Glenn, and Anthony Page. The nine playwrights employed to compose the scripts were Anne Howard Bailey, Sam Hall, Roger O. Hirson, Ian Hunter, Corinne Jacker, Millard Lampell, Tad Mosel, Philip Reisman Jr., and Sherman Yellen.

5. The program was conceived and produced by Virginia Kassell through WNET New York. Jac Venza, director of performance programs for WNET, was the executive producer of the series.

6. The series was funded through grants from the National Endowment for the Humanities, the Andrew Mellon Foundation, and the Atlantic Richfield Company.

7. Of course, historians and critics of *1776: A Musical Play* faulted its creators for limiting and flattening the character of Thomas Jefferson, believing that the "theatrical license" underplayed his role during the Continental Congress.

8. Many of the Jefferson biographies contain much on the Adams-Jefferson connection, particularly Dumas Malone's five-volume series *Jefferson and His Times*. In particular, volume three, *Jefferson and the Ordeal of Liberty*, and volume five, *The Sage of Monticello*, attest to the trials and tribulations concerning the friendship between these two men. Also, David N. Mayer's *The Constitutional Thought of Thomas Jefferson*, Nathan Schachner's *Thomas Jefferson: A Biography*, Thomas Fleming's *The Man from Monticello: An Intimate Life of Thomas Jefferson*, and Noble Cunningham's *In Pursuit of Reason: The Life of Thomas Jefferson* have lengthy sections on the friendship—and the problems—between Adams and Jefferson. In regard to Adams biographies, Page Smith's two-volume *John Adams*, Catherine Drinker Bowen's *John Adams and the American Revolution*, and David McCullough's recent *John Adams* discuss the importance of Jefferson in Adams's life and work. For a look at their correspondence, see Paul Wilstach's edition of the *Correspondence of John Adams and Thomas Jefferson (1812-1826)*.

9. In 1975, about the same time, L.H. Butterfield, Marc Friedlaender, and Mary-Jo Kline edited a sampling of letters from the correspondence of John and Abigail Adams. Calling it *The Book of Abigail and John: Selected Letters of the Adams Family, 1762-1784*, the editors sought to "show another and more engaging human being than most of his [John's] contemporaries knew" (6) and to reveal Abigail's "total self-possession, and her artless but captivating personal style" (8).

10. Abigail herself has been the subject of major feminist biographies, including Edith B. Gelles's *Portia: The World of Abigail Adams* (1992) and Lynne Withey's *Dearest Friend: A Life of Abigail Adams* (2001).

11. Most of the Adams biographies detail Nabby's affair with the playwright Royall Tyler, who literally went mad when Abigail brought Nabby to London to be with the family. John actually found out about the engagement just before the mother and daughter arrived in Europe, having received a long-delayed letter detailing the events of Nabby's affair. Contrary to the series, Adams was in Amsterdam during most of the courting between his only daughter and his secretary, Colonel William Smith; Abigail not only made Nabby formally break with the distraught Tyler in America, but she supervised

the courtship. All Adams really did was arrive in time for the actual wedding (McCullough 362–64).

12. Because the character of John Adams was a composite of John and Samuel Adams (see endnote 2), this sequence is not played out in *1776: A Musical Play;* however, in scene 3, when John Adams enters the chamber, the libretto clearly states that he is dressed in "the somber blacks of New England" (26) in contrast to the finer silks and delicate colors of the southern contingent. In the musical, it is Benjamin Franklin who constantly ridicules John Adams's dark, shabby clothing.

13. After filming the first four chapters, Kathryn Walker left *The Adams Chronicles* to star in a new dramatic serial for CBS, *Beacon Hill.* The ambitious series, detailing the lives of a wealthy Irish-American family and its staff of servants in Boston after World War I, ran for only seventeen episodes in 1975.

14. However, Walt Brown, writing specifically on the subject of Adams and the American press, is one of the only historians who claims that he has found no evidence of Adams's support for the bills: "Despite the historiographical debate, there are no letters in any of the Adams papers collections which provide the slightest hint that Adams wanted a sedition law. Nor did Adams send any messages to Congress proposing such a law. Only in his answers to petitions did he speak of sedition" (Brown 101).

15. This is very similar to Abigail's contribution to the opening song of *1776: A Musical Play,* "Sit Down, John," where she chastises her husband for being so concerned for the well-being of the country that he cannot remember to send home a box of pins to help her to mend his clothes.

16. This anecdote seems to be an invention for the series; I have found no historical record of any similar occurrence in my reading of the published material from the Adams archives.

WORKS CITED

Abercrombie, Nicholas. *Television and Society.* Cambridge, Massachusetts: Polity, 1996.

Adams Chronicles, Episodes 1–6. PBS. WNET 13, New York. 20 January 1976–24 February 1976..

Bowen, Catherine Drinker. *John Adams and the American Revolution.* Boston: Little, Brown, 1950.

Brown, Les. *The New York Times Encyclopedia of Television.* New York: Times Books, 1977.

Brown, Walt. *John Adams and the American Press: Politics and Journalism at the Birth of the Republic.* Jefferson, North Carolina: McFarland, 1995.

Butterfield, L.H., Marc Friedlaender, and Mary-Jo Kline, eds. *The Book of Abigail and John: Selected Letters of the Adams Family, 1762-1784.* Cambridge, Massachusetts: Harvard University Press, 1975.

Cunningham, Noble E. Jr. *In Pursuit of Reason: The Life of Thomas Jefferson.* Baton Rouge: Louisiana State University Press, 1987.

Fleming, Thomas. *The Man from Monticello: An Intimate Life of Thomas Jefferson.* New York: William Morrow, 1969.

Gelles, Edith B. *Portia: The World of Abigail Adams*. Bloomington: Indiana University Press, 1992.

Himmelstein, Hal. *On the Small Screen: New Approaches in Television and Video Criticism*. New York: Praeger, 1981.

"How Did They Do That?" *Entertainment Weekly*, 3 August 2001, 25.

Lopez, Claude-Anne. "*Adams Chronicles* Vilify Franklin." *New York Times*, 14 March 1976, B25.

Malone, Dumas. *Jefferson and His Times*. 5 vols. Boston: Little, Brown, 1981.

Mayer, David N. *The Constitutional Thought of Thomas Jefferson*. Charlottesville: Virginia University Press, 1994.

McCullough, David. *John Adams*. New York: Simon and Schuster, 2001.

Morris, Richard B. "*The Adams Chronicles*." *New York Times*, 11 January 1976, A2.

O'Connor. J.J. "College Credit Course for *Adams Chronicles*." *New York Times*, 1 August 1976, B23.

Schachner, Nathan. *Thomas Jefferson: A Biography*. New York: Appleton-Century-Crofts, 1951.

Shepard, Jack. *The Adams Chronicles: Four Generations of Greatness*. Boston: Little, Brown, 1975.

Smith, Page. *John Adams*. 2 vols. Garden City, New York: Doubleday, 1962.

Stone, Peter, and Sherman Edwards. *1776: A Musical Play*. New York: Viking, 1970.

Taylor, Ella. *Prime-Time Families: Television Culture and Post–War America*. Berkeley: California University Press, 1989.

Thorburn, David. "Television Melodrama." In *Television as a Cultural Force*, edited by Richard Alder and Douglas Cater. New York: Praeger, 1976.

Wilstach, Paul. *Correspondence of John Adams and Thomas Jefferson (1812–1826)*. Indianapolis: Bobbs-Merrill, 1972.

Withey, Lynne. *Dearest Friend: A Life of Abigail Adams*. 2nd ed. New York: Macmillan, 2001.

Jim Welsh

JEFFERSON IN LOVE

The Framer Framed

Thomas Jefferson: Philosopher
and president, 1801–1809.

Library of Congress.

> All should be laid open to you without reserve, for there is not a truth
> existing which I fear, or would wish unknown to the whole world.
> —Thomas Jefferson to Henry Lee (15 May 1826)

Jefferson in Paris was the name of the picture, but *Jefferson in Love* was surely the primary agenda of the Ishmael Merchant and James Ivory film that demeaned the reputation of our third president. This was perhaps a product of the times, a decade of scandal for Mr. Jefferson's namesake in the White House when the film was made, William Jefferson Clinton. The film took an understanding and tolerant approach, as if intending to forgive the alleged attachment between

Jefferson and Sally Hemings. As portrayed in the film, their flirtation even comes close to being cute, though not so cute as the fictitious romance later concocted for *Shakespeare in Love* (1998). Should the film be forgiven for the way it attempts to humanize and explain Jefferson's alleged behavior? Or is this historical romp to be taken seriously? Was it the intent of the film to wink at Mr. Clinton's merry pranks?

Let us consider an organic metaphor, say acid reflux, commonly known as heartburn. Jefferson was certainly burned by his critics. If Jefferson was in love with his slave, Sally Hemings (as the film clearly suggests), it must have pained him to keep his heartache to himself, but it would also have embarrassed him to talk publicly about it. His dilemma is perhaps best described by the Cavalier poet Sir John Suckling (1609–1642) in the following gastrointestinal metaphor: "Love is the fart/ Of every heart/ It pains a man when 'tis kept close, / And others doth offend when 'tis let loose." Thomas Jefferson had an alleged secret that was "kept close." Ishmael Merchant and James Ivory "let loose" that secret in *Jefferson in Paris*. This is biography as scatology, then, a "fart" in the tempest of time.

Biography is not a science, not even a political science. Paul Murray Kendall wrote a book entitled *The Art of Biography*, but if it is an "art," then it can only be as good or as valid or as true as those who practice it, and it is too often practiced not by "artists" but by sensation-mongers, gossips, and frauds on the one hand and journalists and historians on the other. Such are the "artists" who practice this "art." In addition, there are the filmmakers of documentaries and feature films that one would hope would be serious, despite evidence to the contrary. Consider, for example, *Dark Prince: The True Story of Dracula*, made for and aired on Halloween 2000 on the USA cable network, allegedly "based upon" the life of the legendary fifteenth-century Romanian (actually Wallachian) Prince Vlad Tepes (the Impaler, also known as Vlad Dracul, the Dragon, the Devil). Anyone seeking the historical "truth" would do much better to look into Kurt W. Treptow's book *Vlad III Dracula: The Life and Times of the Historical Dracula*, published by the Center for Romanian Studies in 2000. The story of Vlad the Impaler gets scrambled up with the myth of Dracula, thanks to the Gothic imagination of Bram Stoker and more distortions later by communist and nationalist historiography.

Well, he was their national hero, a legend wrapped in myth. The focus here is upon Thomas Jefferson, our first secretary of state, our third president, an elegant, sophisticated intellectual who framed the Declaration of Independence; but the movie under consideration here was not intended to celebrate his intellect but rather his somewhat tarnished reputation, since, as the premier issue of *Civilization* announced, "Now some scholars detect a whiff of hypocrisy behind his republican values." The cover story by Joseph J. Ellis, entitled "American Sphinx," raised the issue of Jefferson's hypocritical attitude toward slavery and his alleged affair with Sally Hemings, Jefferson's mulatto slave, as does the Merchant-Ivory film *Jefferson in Paris*, which offers a portrait more tainted than painted. Is it shocking to think that a hypocrite could possibly reside in the White House? The intent of this work, after all, is to discuss—if not to celebrate—the traditions of the presidency as reflected by film and popular culture.

This motion picture arrived on the heels of the 250th anniversary of Jefferson's birth. Ellis noted that in 1993 alone seventeen books dealing with Jefferson were published, and that trend was to continue. Of particular interest to the viewers of this film will be George Green Shackelford's *Thomas Jefferson's Travels in Europe, 1784–1789* (1995), a scholarly but readable account of Jefferson's diplomatic mission to Paris. The frontispiece of this well-illustrated book is a map tracing Jefferson's travels north across the English Channel to Kent and Warwickshire, London and Birmingham, and also to Brussels, Antwerp, Amsterdam, Cologne, Frankfurt, Heidelberg, and Strasbourg, then south along the Bay of Biscay to Bordeaux, and east to Marseilles, Milan, and Genoa. The film totally ignores his travel agenda, with reason perhaps, but there is more to the story.

In five years Jefferson's "grand tour" covered many important cities, therefore, while he served as minister to the court of Louis XVI. Shackelford's point is that Jefferson became an internationalist well versed in French language and culture and that "to live there had become for him the only acceptable substitute for residing at home" (Shackelford 1). The film, with its romantic diversions in Paris, cannot do justice to the idea of Jefferson as an "Apostle of European Culture." Its sights are set somewhat lower, more at the heart than the head—if not below the belt.

Historian Alan Brinkley has traced the scandal back two hundred years to Jefferson's successful campaign for the presidency. Richmond (Virginia) journalist James Callender first suggested in print that Jefferson had "for many years kept, as his concubine, one of his slaves" (quoted in Brinkley 70). The story resurfaced in Fawn M. Brodie's "highly controversial" *Thomas Jefferson: An Intimate History* (1974). On 1 November 1998 the *New York Times* carried a headline announcing that, "DNA Test Finds Evidence That Thomas

Jefferson and Slave Had a Child." Now that would seem to be *real* science, not merely political science.

In fairness, it should be noted that there are still those who would deny that "evidence." *The Jefferson-Hemings Myth: An American Travesty,* was published by the Thomas Jefferson Heritage Society in 2001 to debunk that "myth." In the book, edited by Eyler Robert Coates, David Murray argues against what he considered a rush to judgment in the media, pointing out that "since few of us actually read the evidence directly in the pertinent academic journals—*Nature* and the *William and Mary Quarterly*—we actually know the facts only in their mediated form; that it, the news media so told us" (Coates 37). Later in the book the argument is made that the presumed DNA evidence might be traced to Eston Hemings, born in 1808 and judged to be legally white. The name of his father is not a matter of record but "may have been one of eight Jeffersons living in the vicinity of Monticello, including Thomas Jefferson" (Coates 180). But it should also be noted that the Thomas Jefferson Heritage Society was formed in May 2000 "to undertake an independent and objective review of all the facts and circumstances surrounding the possible paternity of Sally Hemings's children by Thomas Jefferson" (Coates 10), in other words, to clear the former president's name and reputation and to further an antirevisionist stance. If the defenders are right, the film would clearly be off base, but the intent here is to examine what the film has to suggest, not to settle an argument between revisionist and antirevisionist historians.

The film begins rather astonishingly in 1873 in Pike County, Ohio, as a reporter (Tom Choate) tracks down Madison Hemings (James Earl Jones), who claims to be the grandson of the man who framed the Declaration of Independence. According to the Coates book, Madison Hemings, born in 1805 and freed by Jefferson's will in 1827, was "believed to have been legally white" (Coates 180), and if so, James Earl Jones was surely not the best choice of actors to represent him. (The "Madison Hemings Interview," originally published in the 13 March 1873 issue of the *Pike County* [Ohio] *Republican,* is reprinted in Coates, 182–88.)

In the film, Madison Hemings tells this reporter the story handed down to him by his mother, Sally Hemings (Thandie Newton), though, since she arrived in Paris some three years after Jefferson's assignment had begun, she could not possibly have known the whole story. Thus the plot is set into motion by an unreliable narrator—not a very promising start.

At the age of forty-one, Jefferson went to Paris with his elder daughter,

Patsy (Gwyneth Paltrow), as ambassador to the Royal Court at Versailles during the last years of the reign of Louis XVI (Michael Lansdale) and Marie Antoinette (Charlotte de Turckheim). Jefferson remained in France until after the fall of the Bastille on 14 July 1789. At first Jefferson had with him only his elder daughter, Patsy, whom he enrolled in a convent school, and a servant, James Hemings (Seth Gilliam), a slave who gets a whiff of freedom in Revolutionary France, though on the issue of slavery his master, who treats him decently enough, is something of a reactionary.

Jefferson is later joined by his younger daughter, Polly (Estelle Eonnet), who arrives in the company of her nurse, Sally Hemings, who was said to be the illegitimate half-sister of Jefferson's recently departed wife. Sally was only fifteen at the time she arrived, and by that time Jefferson was deeply involved in a presumably platonic relationship with the beautiful Anglo-Italian painter and musician Maria Cosway (Greta Scacchi), who is locked into a marriage of convenience with the apparently homosexual British painter Richard Cosway (Simon Callow). The details of this ill-fated romance are central to the film, but in fact the romance would have been far advanced by the time Sally arrived.

The film shows its true colors after taking an unexpected and unexplained turn when Jefferson indulges himself carnally with this child-nurse and gets her pregnant, a common course of events, the film seems to suggest, for Virginia gentlemen slave-owners. Daughter Patsy seems to know what has occurred and is so repulsed by her randy father that she decides to become a nun and remain in France, but her father will have none of that. He has very strong opinions about granting freedom of choice to women and slaves. When questioned by the mother superior about the meaning of freedom of religion, the man seems to be a perfect hypocrite, but neither does he flinch nor falter. He also seems to be something of a fool. But of course it is nothing new these days to hear the echo of feet of clay clomping through the White House.

Jefferson argues for American slavery as a special case for which exceptions must be allowed. He manages to alienate himself from an attractive and cultivated woman of taste by his sexual dalliance with Sally, who barely speaks literate English and has little to recommend her beyond girlish high spirits. Why this Renaissance man of over forty would be so taken by an ignorant teenager is not successfully explained by either the screenplay or the acting.

When Patsy tells Maria that her father has made his slave pregnant, Maria breaks off her relationship with Jefferson and returns to England. As the French monarchy begins to collapse and the King is taken prisoner, the story ends, and viewers are transported back to that humble farmhouse in Ohio for a few final sonorous words from James Earl Jones, who is given heavy competition here from a brilliant international cast. At the very least, the screenplay has rather too many loose ends as it presents Jefferson as a sort of loose cannon struck by the blind bow-boy's butt-shaft, as Mercutio says of Romeo. Why quote Shakespeare as well as Suckling? You shall see, anon.

Of course cinema is a potential tool for the biographer, but even documentary films can distort the portrait. Commercial cinema has the added imperative to make biography entertaining, which further opens the gate for fanciful distortions, as was the case with *Shakespeare in Love*, which offered a complete, though entertaining, fabrication of Shakespeare's imagined love-life during the mid-1590s. In that film John Madden and Tom Stoppard reinvented the Bard of Avon, tweaking the unknown and undocumented biography of Shakespeare's early years in London and presenting him as a lovesick puppy. This falsification was outrageous and unsubstantiated, but the picture was packed with witty dialogue and fun to watch. The result was multiple Academy Awards and a renewed interest in the Bard of Avon and his work, from an imagined affair that never was. The Merchant-Ivory film *Jefferson in Paris* fell far short of that level of success and popularity, even though it might have more accurately been entitled *Jefferson in Love*, perhaps because it was so literal-minded in the way it adhered more closely to the historical and biographical record. That Thomas Jefferson visited Paris as ambassador is a matter of record, as is his particular affinity for French ideas and culture. That his affair with Sally Hemings developed and flourished abroad was more a matter of speculation, even though the speculation was later to be supported by the alleged DNA evidence. There are ample reasons to examine Jefferson's life and career, the film and its research, as well as the film's placement within the genre of the biographical pictures and the challenge of historical reconstruction on film.

MUTUAL EXPLOITATION: POLITICS, HISTORY, AND FILM

Just as the media constantly exploit politicians, so politicians work to exploit and manipulate the media in a process of constant cross-fertilization. The media thrive on scandal, especially when respected political figures may be involved, because scandal guarantees ratings and profits, the prime motive being to titillate readers and viewers. Tabloid journalism rules these days and has contaminated once-respected television news formats by turning smut into "news" and anchors into fishmongers. In other words, sex sells, as filmmakers have known all along, and one wonders if that was the prime motive in attempting to explore the sexual habits of the founder of the University of Virginia when the film *Jefferson in Paris* was made, a bit ahead of the curve before William Jefferson Clinton faced one of the most embarrassing scandals in the history of the presidency. The question is: how much do we need to know about the private lives of public figures? And what is to be gained, really, through such carnal knowledge?

Jefferson in Paris begins after Jefferson's death with the astonishing suggestion that Madison Hemings might have been his grandson, as that character, sitting in rural Ohio, frames the story. The framing itself is a conventional Hollywood mechanism. Perhaps this narrative device can be forgiven once the viewer is drawn into the framed story, which is, after all, based upon fact, but should it be? The film then becomes a time machine transporting viewers back in time, then abroad with Jefferson to Paris on the eve of the Revolution into a sophisticated world of aristocratic decadence and culture that looks askance on our wild colonial boy as a slave-owner. What is to be learned here of Jefferson's diplomatic mission? Very little, unfortunately. Instead, the story is dominated by rather ordinary domestic issues, his concern over his daughter's education, for example, and his courtship of a sophisticated *femme*, the musician and painter Maria Cosway, who happens to be married. But this romance fails to ignite cinematically. As Peter Travers noted, the film "catches a public figure with his pants down, and then can't bear to look" (Travers 88).

The farther back in time the film goes, the more artificial it seems. It often is reverential in its treatment of Mr. Jefferson (Nick Nolte), though presenting him more as a man of passion than of wit, judgment, and intellect. Jefferson was surely an intellectual, a man of the Enlightenment, interested in knowledge and ideas. But he was also a widower who might have been stimulated by cultured companionship, seduced by his infatuation with either Maria Cosway or by his servant Sally Hemings. The seduction might have been the selling point of the film, but that would have been a bit of a stretch for the sedate Merchant-Ivory approach of high-concept historical reconstruction. In typical Merchant-Ivory fashion the picture was stripped of passion, never daring to be vulgar. There is no real violation of taste here beyond the insinuation of a decorous and bloodless romance. Jefferson might have been in love, but Nick Nolte is not given much of a chance to show it. The film declares itself to be about "Jefferson in Paris," and that is exactly what it shows. True tabloid-style exploitation of the Sally Hemings story would come later on CBS television in February 2000 in a feature called *Sally Hemings: An American Scandal,* starring Carmen Ejogo as Hemings and Sam Neill offering what *USA Today* called a "deeply uninteresting performance" as Jefferson, playing "a founding father for a fool."

The Merchant-Ivory treatment was tasteful by comparison and certainly was marked by a stronger cast and a much more seasoned screenwriter, the novelist Ruth Prawer Jhabvala, who had worked with the Merchant-Ivory team on a total of fourteen pictures, two of which earned Academy Awards for Best Adapted Screenplay (*A Room with a View* in 1986 and *Howard's End* in 1992) in comparison to novice screenwriter Tina Andrews, once a star on *Days of Our Lives,* who scripted *Sally Hemings: An American Scandal* and who saw the story as "a star-crossed romance between lovers kept apart by social convention," treating the issue of slavery as "merely another pothole in the bumpy road to love" (Bianco E1). Maybe that is the film that should have been entitled "Jefferson in Love." Ken Ringle of the *Washington Post* stated his preference on 9 April 1995 for the PBS television documentary *Thomas Jefferson: A View from the Mountain,* produced on a budget of $400,000 in comparison to the $14 million that the Merchant-Ivory film cost. He especially ridiculed Thandie Newton's "fiddle-dee-dee" portrait of Jefferson's slave mistress, who was, he asserted, "almost certainly a woman of substance." Eve Zibart complained that "this Sally is a simple-minded and sometimes sly flirt (the word 'pickanninny' painfully comes to mind) incapable of inspiring such personally taboo passion," and she also complained that the "resonance of Sally's being half-sister to Jefferson's sainted dead wife is unexplored." Despite the magnificent arts direction, then, Zibart found the film "intellectually infuriating and thoughtlessly racist." Jefferson's repartee has been "lifted from his letters" and "sounds shaky," except when, "jerking his daughter out of a convent, he suddenly shouts sensitive-speak: 'you said you'd always be there for me'" (Zibart 45). If this film attempted to put a human face on Thomas Jefferson, at least it was not Sam Neill's, the scientist from *Jurassic Park*; but was the marine biologist from *Cannery Row* a much better alternative? Or how about the cop from *48 Hrs.*? Joe Queenan, *Movieline's* icon smasher, called the casting "capricious" and "idiotic," but Queenan hates the Merchant-Ivory style, and he considered the assignment of surveying their careers the equivalent of visiting a particularly boring level of historical hell. His most substantive criticism was that the film offered "no good sex." Queenan knows what he likes, but there must be a higher criticism.

Historians have been rather too eager to embrace filmmakers as belonging to their profession, but Oliver Stone has never referred to himself as a "cinematic historian." Rather, he sees himself as a dramatist, as his part of Robert Toplin's *Oliver Stone's USA* makes clear. Merchant and Ivory, who have specialized in films involving historical reconstruction, take certain liberties with the life of Thomas Jefferson in order to create a dramatic entertainment. But could it be otherwise? Sandra Brice, producer and writer of the Peabody Award–winning film *LBJ: The Early Years* (1986, directed by Peter Werner and starring Randy Quaid as Lyndon Baines Johnson and Patti LuPone as Lady Bird), explained at the "Images of the Presidency on Film and Television" Film and History League Conference in 2000 that although her film was extensively researched, the screenplay was organized on events that would "find" the dramatic moment. To dramatize the friction between LBJ and Bobby Kennedy, for example, Brice invented an incident

Thomas Jefferson as the author of America's Declaration of Independence, while fellow committee member, Benjamin Franklin, looks on.

Library of Congress.

extrapolated from an oral history account from one of the president's hunting buddies in which Kennedy was supplied with an overly powerful rifle and was knocked flat by the recoil. LBJ's political skills and his rise to power were, of course, central to the film, but it was more a love story than anything else and was as much about the First Lady as about the president himself. In other words, this picture might have been called "LBJ in Love." The only filmmaker who *might* qualify as a "cinematic historian" is the documentary filmmaker Ken Burns, who claims that his primary concerns are not "dramatic."

HISTORY AND BIOGRAPHY IN POSTLITERATE, MEDIA-MADE AMERICA

In his book *Screening History* (1992), Gore Vidal, perhaps more novelist than historian, claims that "half the American people never read a newspaper," and half—"the same half?" he wonders—"never vote for president" (Vidal 5). Since reading biography is rather more time consuming than reading a newspaper, the percentage of those who read biography or history must be substantially lower still. In his book *"Dumbth": The Lost Art of Thinking* (1998), the late Steve Allen quotes Al Maguire's belief that "the world is run by C-students" (Allen 6), a thought that should inspire fear and trembling in a complex world. "If stupid is as stupid does," to quote a retarded postmodern philosopher, then how are we doing as a nation? Even more depressing is the book edited by Katharine Washburn and John Thornton, *Dumbing Down: Essays on the Strip-Mining of American Culture* (1996). Are we turning into a nation of Gumps—the loveable Forrest Gump, redesigned by Robert Zemeckis and his screenwriter Eric Roth, not exactly the character originally created by novelist Winston Groom?

Where does a nation of nonreaders get its understanding of literature, history, and biography? From film and television, of course, which will most likely give simplistic or dumbed-down versions. If so, this trend invests a whole lot of authority and responsibility on such films as Oliver Stone's *Nixon,* John Ford's *Young Mr. Lincoln,* Richard Attenborough's *Gandhi,* Spike Lee's *Malcolm X,* and the Merchant-Ivory *Jefferson in Paris.* Although, in the examples just cited, the treatments may be biased, reverential, or skeptical, one doubts that any of these films intended to distort or falsify history, and all of them are probably better researched than other less worthy examples that might have been cited. Gore Vidal has suggested that written versions of history are, in fact, no more to be trusted than movie versions and are not only much less memorable but also a lot less fun. Vidal believes that, ideally, reading skills should be improved, but he adds that, "This is not going to happen for the third generation of TV-watchers" and computer addicts. "Therefore," he concludes, "let us be bold. Let us *screen history*" (Vidal 94). But to *screen* also means to *vet*, in other words, "to subject to expert appraisal or correction," and that is the responsibility of professional historians in general and of such a journal as *Film & History* in particular. Take note, Peter C. Rollins, take note. Beware of novelists and dramatists and filmmakers and cherish the cold, hard, possibly *dull* facts.

WORKS CITED

Allen, Steve. *"Dumbth": The Lost Art of Thinking.* New York: Prometheus Books, 1998.

Ansen, David. "Jefferson's Dangerous Liaisons." *Newsweek,* 3 April 1995, 69–70.

Arnold, Gary. "'Jefferson': Amorous American in Paris." *Washington Times Metropolitan Times,* 7 April 1995, C17.

Atkinson, Mark. "Jefferson in Paris." *Sight and Sound,* June 1995, 46–47.

Bianco, Robert. "Soaped-up 'Sally' plays a founding father for a fool." *USA Today,* 11 February 2000, E1.

Brinkley, Alan. "When Thomas Met Sally." *Newsweek,* 3 April 1995, 70–71.

Coates, Eyler Robert, Sr., ed. *The Jefferson-Hemings Myth: An American Travesty.* Charlottesville, Virginia: Thomas Jefferson Heritage Society, 2001.

Ellis, Joseph J. "American Sphinx." *Civilization,* November–December 1994, 34–45.

Gleiberman, Owen. "Continental Congress." *Entertainment Weekly,* 7 April 1995, 61–62.

Hinson, Hal. "In Pursuit of Happiness." *Washington Post,* 7 April 1995, D7.

Howarth, R.G., ed. *Minor Poets of the Seventeenth Century.* London: J.M. Dent, 1953.

Kendall, Paul Murray. *The Art of Biography.* London: George Allen and Unwin, Ltd., 1965.

Knorr, Katherine. "Merchant, Ivory and Jefferson in Paris." *International Herald-Tribune,* 27 May 1994, 24.

Koeppel, Frederic. "High, low notes of 'Jefferson.'" *Washington Times Metropolitan Times,* 12 May 1995, C17.

Maslin, Janet. "Jefferson's Entanglements, In History and in Love." *New York Times,* 31 March 1995, C1, C12.

McCarthy, Todd. "Jefferson in Paris." *Variety,* 27 March–2 April 1995, 74, 77.

Queenan, Joe. "The Remains of the Dazed." *Movieline,* November 1995, 65–69, 88, 94.

Ringle, Ken. "Sage of Monticello, or Fool on a Hill?" *Washington Post,* 9 April 1995, G4–G5.

Shackelford, George Green. *Thomas Jefferson's Travels in Europe, 1784–1789.* Baltimore: Johns Hopkins University Press, 1995.

Toplin, Robert Brent, ed. *Oliver Stone's USA: Film, History, and Controversy.* Lawrence: University of Kansas Press, 2000.

Travers, Peter. "Jefferson in Paris." *Rolling Stone*, 20 April 1995, 86.

Treptow, Kurt W. *Vlad III Dracula: The Life and Times of the Historical Dracula*. Iasi, Romania: Center for Romanian Studies, 2000.

Vidal, Gore. *Screening History*. Cambridge, Massachusetts: Harvard University Press, 1992.

Washburn, Katharine, and John Thornton, eds. *Dumbing Down: Essays on the Strip-Mining of American Culture*. New York: W.W. Norton, 1996.

Zibart, Eve. "'Paris': A Bad Trip." *Washington Post Weekend*, 7 April 1995, 45.

Andrew Piasecki

ABRAHAM LINCOLN IN JOHN FORD'S *THE IRON HORSE*

Both Trumpets and Silences

Abraham Lincoln, sixteenth president of
the United States, 1861–1865.

ABRAHAM LINCOLN—FOUNDER OF THE MODERN NATION

John Ford's *The Iron Horse*, released in 1924, has acquired the status of a classic
film of the Hollywood silent era. It tells the story of the building of the transcontinental railroad between 1862 and 1869, a heroic feat that exemplifies
American vision, manifest destiny, and the wisdom of Abraham Lincoln. This
momentous engineering project, undertaken by the Union Pacific and Central Pacific railroads, was completed after Lincoln's assassination in 1865; however, the president has a vital role to play in the film as the paternal and spiritual
leader who brings unity and progress out of the chaos of the Civil War. Director
John Ford depicts Lincoln as both a visionary, who sees the future of a great

nation unified by the triumph of the machine over nature, and as a crucial actor in this achievement, for it is he who ensures that the transcontinental is built by discounting all opposition and signing the Pacific Railroad Act in 1862. Thus, Ford's pictorial history shows how one of the technological wonders of the nineteenth century must be forever linked to the name of one of the greatest of all American presidents.

THE STORY OF THE IRON HORSE

The film's plot unfolds within the conventions of melodrama. Surveyor David Brandon Senior (James Gordon) is from Lincoln's hometown of Springfield, Illinois, and dreams of a mighty railroad that will cross from the east coast to the Pacific. He sets out with his son Davy (George O'Brien) to find a pass through the Rocky Mountains. One of the film's titles declares, "Brandon and his boy are impelled Westward by the strong urge of progress." In this respect their fictional life mirrors that of real pioneer surveyors like Theodore Judah and Grenville Dodge. They do find a pass, but Brandon senior is brutally attacked by Indians and bludgeoned to death by a two-fingered white man in disguise; the attack was witnessed by a terrified Davy, hiding in nearby bushes.

The film then jumps forward in time to the moment when Lincoln (Charles Edward Bull) signs the Pacific Railroad Act of 1862. Davy is now working to build the railroad west. By chance he meets up again with his childhood sweetheart, Miriam Marsh (Madge Bellamy), whose father has become a railroad contractor. Unfortunately for Davy, she is now engaged to the villainous and cowardly Mr. Jesson (Cyril Chadwick). While out scouting with Davy for a shortcut pass, Jesson seizes the opportunity to kill Davy by cutting the rope while he descends into a ravine. Jesson has been put up to this act of treachery by the corrupt land baron Deroux (Fred Kohler), who wants the rewards that will come from the railroad taking a longer route that will cross his land. Davy miraculously survives the fall and returns to deal with Jesson. Miriam intervenes and makes Davy promise that he will not fight her betrothed, but Jesson attempts to shoot Davy in the back. A fight ensues, and Jesson is killed, further straining Davy's relationship with Miriam. Later, while out laying ties, Davy and his crew are attacked by Indians. Davy goes after a sniper who turns out to be the two-fingered Deroux and kills him in hand-to-hand combat, thereby avenging his father's death. Still estranged from Miriam, he leaves to join the rival Central Pacific, which is building the railroad from the west. Finally, they meet up at Promontory Point, Utah, and are reunited just as the two railroads, the Union Pacific and the Central Pacific, are conjoined.

Ford makes full use of the new cinematic possibilities of the era by interweaving this melodramatic drama of murder, revenge, and love with a historical documentation that enables him to make a film on a truly epic scale. The story of the romantic lovers and their emotional struggle is played out against the vast panorama of the American continent and the struggle to overcome the geographical and human forces that stand in the way of progress.

The Iron Horse was Fox Studio's response to the success of *The Covered Wagon*, an epic Western produced by Paramount in 1923. The cast of 5,000 extras gives a sense of the scale of *The Iron Horse*. It included: "a complete regiment of U.S. cavalry, 3,000 railway workers, 1,000 Chinese laborers and 800 Pawnee, Sioux, and Cheyenne Indians. Among the livestock were numbered 2,800 horses, 1,300 buffalo and 10,000 head of cattle" (Tuska 99). Ford's film depicted many scenes that are now established classics of the Western genre, such as an Indian attack, a cattle drive, a saloon brawl, and the appearance of mythical figures, such as Buffalo Bill and Wild Bill Hickock. There is even a recreation of Hell on Wheels, the wild frontier town that moved on as the railroad advanced westward. Shots of the wide-open landscape are used to create a sense of space against which human beings can seem insignificant. Ultimately, though, it is the courage and sacrifice of ordinary people that is able to tame this wilderness and conquer the West.

A WORK OF GIANTS

The Iron Horse exemplifies, then, the American ideal of man's triumph over nature. The building of the transcontinental across such a vast and inhospitable landscape was a remarkable achievement and paved the way for the industrial and economic development of the latter part of the nineteenth century. In short, it "made modern America" (Ambrose 22). Ford's film has helped to establish this feat as a significant moment in the story of American progress, a story that illustrates the virtues of human endeavor, vision, and courage. The race of the two railroad companies to lay more track is used by Ford to create a sense of suspense and excitement. The race itself reinforces the capitalist virtues of competition and enterprise. More recently, Stephen Ambrose has provided a detailed historical account of the project, and his book, *Nothing Like It In The World* (2000), portrays it in a heroic light similar to that found in Ford's film. Ambrose explores how the movers and shakers behind this enterprise overcame the many geographical, political, and financial obstacles that stood in their way. In paying tribute to the thousands of laborers, mainly Chinese and Irish, who carried out the manual work, Ambrose cites the words of one of their contemporaries, William T. Sherman, who described their achievement in Herculean and patriotic terms as "a work of giants. And Uncle Sam is the only giant I know who can grapple the subject" (Ambrose 63).

The heroic achievement of ordinary men is a central theme of Ford's film. He avoids becoming embroiled in the managerial and business aspects of the transcontinental project, preferring instead to focus on the gargantuan labors of the construction workers and engineers who, in his film, are spiritually guided by the vision of Abraham Lincoln. This presidential influence is established early in the film by a subtitle in the form of a dedication "to the ever-living memory of Abraham Lincoln, the Builder—and of those countless engineers and toilers who fulfilled his dream of a greater Nation."

The Iron Horse encapsulates a sense of awe through its use of wide panoramic shots and scenes focusing on the toiling workers, dwarfed by the landscape but laying down the tracks industriously and interminably. There is, then, in this film an overwhelming sense of the marvelous achievements of an earlier age, which is still shared today. As railroad historian Oliver Jensen puts it, looking back from the twenty-first century "is to wonder whether we are today the equals of men who with their bare hands laid those long ribbons of metal over a century ago" (Ambrose 64).

LINCOLN—A VISIONARY WITH A COMMON TOUCH

Lincoln's role in the film is crucial inasmuch as it reinforces his identity as the father and spiritual guide of the modern America. His portrait frames the action in the form of an ethereal floating bust, which appears at the beginning and the end of the film. In this silent film, Lincoln has a ubiquitous silent presence as an offstage guiding force that brings unity and harmony out of chaos and struggle. His supreme status as a unifying force is reinforced from the start by a title affirming confidently that, "More than to any other man, the nation owes gratitude to Abraham Lincoln whose vision and resolution held (together) the North and the South, while moulding with blood and with iron the East and the West." The technology of the railroad is the physical unifier of landscape and people, and the railroad is a paean to Lincoln. Ford's film provides a fusion of technological determinism and "great man history."

Yet, despite being elevated almost to the status of a deity, Lincoln is also portrayed in the "Honest Abe" tradition as a friendly, down-to-earth American with a common touch. Ford would develop further these qualities of presidential leadership in *Young Mr. Lincoln*. In the early scenes of *The Iron Horse*, Ford focuses on the domestic world of Lincoln's native town of Springfield, Illinois. The future president is seen standing behind a split-rail fence, watching over the young Miriam and Davy with paternal affection, while they play in the snow at railroad surveying. Their childhood games imitate the preoccupations of the adult world. Shortly after this scene, there is a neighborly discussion in which Miriam's father expresses his doubts about Brandon senior's dream of a transcontinental railroad. Lincoln intervenes and a subtitle reveals his prophetic words: "Someday you'll be laying rails along that rainbow." His physical presence shows him as both a part of the scene and, at the same time, strangely detached from it. In a final glimpse of him in Springfield, Ford places him again in the position of the onlooker. This time he is held in shot, looking off-screen at the scene of Davy departing with his father on a railroad-surveying adventure. A subtitle reinforces the significance of the moment: "He [Lincoln] feels the momentum of a great nation pushing Westward—he sees the inevitable." In the film's narrative, the transcontinental railroad has its genesis in Springfield, Illinois.

LINCOLN IN CONGRESS

When Lincoln next appears in the film, he has been elected president, and the year is 1862. While the Civil War rages, Lincoln remains calm and authoritative. His qualities of leadership in a time of crisis are reaffirmed by the terse subtitle ("I have decided") that accompanies the shot of him putting his signature to the Pacific Railroad Act. Although flawed and requiring revision two years later (Ambrose 94), the act provided generous public subsidies to the railroad companies, without which the project could not have been undertaken. Ford's film does not dwell on the political complexities of this moment, though it does give some sense of the lobbying activities by the factions for and against the act. By interweaving the main plot into this scene (Miriam and her father arrive to make the railroad-builders' case), Ford makes Lincoln responsive to the aspirations of good American citizens. The arguments are reduced to one simple point: you are either for or against progress. Lincoln warns those in Congress who are opposed to the act that, "We must not let war blind us to the promise of peace to come or war will have been in vain." Lincoln recognizes that risks must be taken, and he has a long-term vision that cannot be compromised. His presidential virtues are distilled into a single subtitle: "The far seeing wisdom of the great rail-splitter President is the beginning of the Empire of the West." Having shaped the course of events to come in terms of America's wider destiny, Lincoln takes no further part in the action of the film.

THE WILY MR. LINCOLN AND THE EFFIE AFTON CASE

Ford's depiction of Lincoln both draws on and develops his legendary status as railroad president. The "real" Mr. Lincoln certainly did have an interest in railroads, but prior to becoming president, he was more than a rail-splitter. As a self-made man who prospered as a lawyer, railroad suits provided a lucrative source of income; indeed, the Illinois Central Railroad became one of Lincoln's major clients. According to one biographer, Lincoln had no "consistent legal philosophy that he sought to push" in relation to his work (Donald 157). His position was pragmatic rather than ideological, and he was, says Herndon, his law partner, "purely and entirely a case lawyer" (Donald 157). Disputes often arose when rail bridges interfered with river traffic. While Lincoln saw the economic benefits (presumably to himself as well as the nation) of developing the railroads and representing their interests, he was equally willing to represent steamboat interests if asked to do so.

One railroad-steamboat dispute that he worked on is revealing to look at as a microcosm that offers a very different kind of history to that presented in *The Iron Horse*. It reveals much about the character of Lincoln and also about the complex way in which history unfolds and technologies develop. This episode does not appear in the film. It would have disrupted the plot, reduced Lincoln's heroic stature, and undermined the film's representation of technology as a unifying force of progress. In 1856, the Chicago and Rock Island Railroad (hereafter C.R.I.) constructed a bridge across the Mississippi River at Rock Island, Illinois. The bridge was the first across the great river and threatened to undermine the economic power of the South by diverting goods away from a river route to St Louis, Memphis, and New Orleans to a new west-east railroad system, which would increase the power of Chicago and the eastern seaports. Such a fundamental threat to those whose livelihoods depended on water transportation was not to go unchallenged, and the Rock Island Bridge project became a crucial site of struggle between people whose local interests were interwoven in a broader struggle between North and South (Agnew, "Jefferson Davis" 14; Beveridge 598; Zobrist 172).

The C.R.I. chose the crossing point because the island in the middle of the river (Rock Island) made the task of building a bridge across to Davenport on the west bank significantly easier and cheaper. However, a problem for the C.R.I. was how to justify such an ambitious project if it appeared merely to link up two towns whose commercial interests were so closely tied to river transportation. The answer was to locate the project within a grander scenario, which could be shown to override parochial interests and serve the "national interest." The town of Council Bluffs, further west on the Missouri River, was rapidly developed so that the bridge-building project could be presented as a way of linking up with this new and "vital" town (Brown 7). Significantly, it was the town of Council Bluffs that Lincoln was to designate as the starting point for the Union Pacific in 1863, and it was also where he acquired his own land interests.

The bridge-building project became a test case in a power struggle between North and South. The struggle itself was fought out partly through a series of court cases, thus locating political and economic rivalries within a legal framework in which the conflict would be expressed in terms of justice and democratic rights. Steamboat owners from St Louis objected that the bridge, while it was still in its planning stage, was "unconstitutional, an obstruction to navigation, dangerous, and it was the duty of every western state, river city, and town to take immediate action to prevent the erection of such a structure" (Brown 7). Such objections from southern interests firmed up as soon as actual building started in 1854. At this time the secretary of war was Jefferson Davis, a powerful spokesman for southern interests, who was to become president of the seceding Confederate States of America in 1861. He ruled that Rock Island could not be a legitimate crossing point because of its former use as a military reservation. This move was rapidly followed by a federal injunction, taken out by the steamboat interests, which charged the bridge-builders with trespass, destruction of government property, and obstruction of steamboat navigation (Zobrist 164).

In July 1855, however, the judge ruled in favor of the Railroad Bridge Company (a subsidiary of the C.R.I.). An important precedent was established because it was now officially adjudged and recorded that "railroads had become highways in something the same sense as rivers; neither could be suffered to become a permanent obstruction to the other, but each must yield something to the other according to the demands of the public convenience and necessities of commerce" (Zobrist 164). In legal terms, then, railroads were put on an equal legal footing with steamboats, and a giant step had been taken toward the development of a transcontinental rail link.

However, the east-west axis was not going to be developed uncontested. On 6 May 1856, just a few days after the bridge had been opened, a packet boat named the *Effie Afton,* which was steaming mysteriously well away from its usual route between New Orleans and Louisville, collided with the bridge and set it on fire. This calamity was much appreciated by local river transporters, some of whom coincidentally had already prepared a banner for just such an eventuality, which read: "Mississippi bridge destroyed. Let all rejoice" (Brown 9). The owner of the *Effie Afton* promptly sued the bridge company for damages, claiming that the bridge structure was an impediment to safe river transport, and he was strongly supported by the St Louis Chamber of Commerce. For its defense, the Railroad Bridge Company hired Abraham Lincoln as its lawyer. So the legal battle intensified and embroiled on opposite sides two men, Abraham Lincoln and Jefferson Davis, who would play out the national struggle on a devastating scale five years later in the Civil War. In Ford's film, Lincoln remains sublimely above the fray; in reality, he was very much a part of it.

While the battle was being fought in the Chicago courts, the conflict was extended to the public domain by the newspapers of Chicago and St Louis. The *Chicago Tribune* accused St Louis of being the real plaintiff in the case, while making its own allegiances clear: "facts . . . do not warrant the incessant clamour kept up by those who insist that the magnificent structure shall be torn down. . . . We trust that . . . the outcries of the St Louis and river press may be silenced" (Beveridge 599). Meanwhile the St Louis papers made their own case:

> The Railroad Bridge at Rock Island is an intolerable nuisance. . . . It is utterly impossible for any man not an idiot to note the disasters at Rock Island and honestly ascribe them to any other cause than the huge obstruction to navigation which the Bridge Company have built there and insist shall remain, even though lives by the score and property by the million are destroyed every year. . . . We have rarely seen such illustration of supercilious insolence, as have been presented by the bridge. (Beveridge 600)

Lincoln's defense was constructed cannily around two arguments. First, he attempted to persuade the jury that the expansion of railroads, and their crossing of rivers, was bound up with inevitable progress: "There is a travel from east to west whose demands are not less than that of those of the river. It is growing larger and larger, building up new countries with rapidity never before seen in the history of the world. This current of travel has its rights as well as that of north and south" (Starr 108). Here the real Lincoln has much in common with Ford's motion picture Lincoln. Both invoke manifest destiny and adopt the Whig view of history as progress. Secondly, he scrutinized the internal "facts of the case" with a rigorous attention to detail (reminiscent perhaps of the famous use of the almanac in the trial scene in *Young Mr. Lincoln*). He produced empirical evidence, based on careful observations and measurements of the river currents, to prove that the *Effie Afton's* starboard wheel was not operating at the time of the accident. Thus, the jury was asked to reach a verdict on the basis of detailed evidence, but at the same time, the concept of rights in terms of geographical movement was introduced as a foundation for the whole case.

The jury failed to reach a verdict so that Lincoln, effectively, won the case, though there were a few more skirmishes to come. Now in retreat, the Southerners attempted to rally in 1858 by pressing for a congressional law forbidding bridges over navigable rivers. Although this measure failed, they won a Pyrrhic victory later that year when an Iowa judge declared the bridge to be "a common and public nuisance" (Zobrist 170) and ordered the part of the bridge that lay within the state of Iowa to be dismantled. The dispute was played out, then, at state and federal levels. The C.R.I. duly appealed, and the matter was finally settled in 1862 when the Supreme Court of the United States ruled in favor of the C.R.I. A report on the final verdict describes the case as being:

> valuable as marking the evolution of the Lincoln doctrine that a man has as good a right to go across a river as another has to go up or down the river, that the two rights are mutual, that the existence of a bridge which does not prevent or unreasonably obstruct navigation is not inconsistent with the navigable character of the stream. (Starr 115)

Thus, the economic interests of a coalition of railroad owners, financial backers, and politicians are expressed in terms of mutual rights, which are then enshrined in law. Lincoln's role in this affair was later elevated to that of prime mover in the course of progress by conferring on him the title of "author of the American doctrine of bridges" (Starr 116).

The geographical constraint of water implied one kind of logic for human settlement and economic activity, while bridges implied another. Railroad bridges became a powerful iconographic representation of a technology that could simply override the apparent constraints of the "natural" landscape. Acts of sabotage against them were not uncommon. The events that took place in the aftermath of the *Rock Island* case reveal much about the skullduggery of railroad magnates in manipulating so-called "market forces" and maneuvering to establish strategic advantage in the race to complete the first transcontinen-

Jefferson Smith (James Stewart) seeks inspiration at the Lincoln Memorial in *Mr. Smith Goes to Washington* (1939).

tal link (see Agnew, "Iowa's First Railroad" and "Mississippi and Missouri"; Brown; Donovan). In its muddled way this case was a critical incident in railroad expansion and the development of a transcontinental "system." It brought together a wide array of forces operating in the pre–Civil War decade and illustrates how railroads used the courts to legitimize technological development. Of course, the bridge case was just one small incident in the development of a technology, but it suggests that the development was complex and by no means predetermined (though whether such a view of history can easily be translated into cinema is another matter). It is clear also that Lincoln had an important role to play in the case, but it is only in mythology and film that he can be presented as the Promethean figure who forged the American nation.

THE PROGRESSIVE ERA

However, Ford's film offers a heroic version of events that inevitably simplifies history and reflects the optimism of the era in which it was made. In 1924, the mass production of Henry Ford's motorcar had already superseded the iron horse. In just over half a century since the transcontinental had been completed, America had established itself as a world power with a consumer market that was rapidly developing a taste for luxury goods. Looking back from this period of economic prosperity and growing consumerism, it was only to be expected that history would be presented as a simple narrative about the march of progress. *The Iron Horse* concludes with the two railroad barons, Leland Stanford and Thomas Durant, of the Central Pacific and Union Pacific respectively, facing each other like two heroic pioneers, surrounded by their laborers and guests of honor at the railroads' meeting point. The carefully composed mirror image of the two parties symbolizes the national unity predicted by Lincoln earlier in the film. The two railroads that competed against each other are only rivals in the progressive sense that they are spurred on by the race to get the job done and help build the nation. The story of the transcontinental project becomes a historical myth "to support the 1920s version of the doctrine of Progress" (Kirby 201).

There is no place in the film for any mention of the many disputes over the exact route that the transcontinental should take. This issue of routes was a crucial matter in the power struggle between north and south (Ambrose 31). Even when the route became relatively fixed (the exact route was always somewhat fluid), the disputes continued. When the two companies actually began to run their tracks past each other in parallel, instead of meeting up, President Grant had to force an agreement for a final meeting point at Promontory Point. The film is silent about the chaos and corruption in the railroad industry as a whole, the briberies and the bankruptcies and the skullduggery of magnates like Jay Cooke, upon whom the government relied to prop up the economy during the Civil War (Brown 203–17). Nothing is said of the ruthless way in which the "native problem" was dealt with or of the vast public-relations operation needed to induce a population of idealistic homesteaders across the Atlantic in order to dump them onto hostile—and often infertile—plains, where many were held in near-feudal servitude by their debts to the railroad companies. Idealism would turn to resentment and opposition, which came to a head in the 1870s with the birth of the Granger movement (Piasecki, "Railroad Trumpet," 63). Certainly in Ford's depiction, there are local difficulties to be overcome, striking workers, barbaric Indians, and villainous landowners, but there is no muckraking agenda here (as there might have been in less confident times at the turn of the century). In this schematic version of history, forces of opposition are all obstacles to a process that is inevitable. The confidence of the 1920s is underwritten by a teleological view of the past, assigning credit to the guiding hand of Abraham Lincoln.

Judging by the film's box office success, such a view was clearly in keeping with contemporary demand for tales of the frontier and the developing genre of the Western, a demand that was being met by popular fiction and magazines, such as the *Saturday Evening Post*, as well as by Hollywood in films like *The Covered Wagon* (1923). There is no single source for *The Iron Horse*. The fictional plot is based firmly in the tradition of melodrama. According to the *Silents Are Golden* online review of the film, "in its historical details it closely follows the railroads' own records" (*Silents Are Golden* 1). Clearly there was some direct involvement from the railroads themselves; the Central Pacific and the Union Pacific loaned original locomotives to Ford for the making of the film (Tuska 99). Such collaboration does suggest that the railroads may even have had an interest in using this film to promote their own declining business. American railroads had been very adept at exploiting the power of popular media for promotional purposes throughout their history (Kirby 21; Piasecki, "Railroad Trumpet," 55).

The Iron Horse is inevitably infused with the ideology of the era. Its depiction of the past is eulogistic, and history is presented as a grand narrative in which progress is assured because Americans are, for the most part, made of "the right stuff." Ford was clearly fascinated by human endeavor on an epic scale, and the film certainly succeeds in portraying the building of the transcontinental railroad as an awesome achievement, crucial for the future development of the American nation. That said, it is also a partial view of history with convenient silences and omissions. The transcontinental project could equally well have been an appropriate subject for investigation in the muckraking tradition, though no Hollywood film studio would have backed such an approach. The film also illustrates many of Ford's own preoccupations as a film director. There is a sentimental longing in many of his films for a mythical frontier world where men can express themselves, free from the trappings of civilized life. The frontier spirit, guided by Lincoln, provides the creative force that engenders progress. There is a certain irony here, though, in that the building of a great nation, through technological progress, leads to the destruction of the frontier itself. Ultimately, this is the price that must be paid for the triumph of the machine over nature. In later life, Ford looked back on *The Iron Horse* as one of his best films, perhaps partly with nostalgia for the actual making of it, which was a kind of epic western adventure in itself (Sinclair 34–35). He had directed close to forty Westerns before embarking on this film, and the Western was the genre for which he became best known. Abraham Lincoln, a midwesterner with a legendary renown for plain speaking, was an ideal president for Ford to assimilate into the Western genre. At a mythical level he becomes a symbol for America itself (Kirby 204). Yet, just as in Ford's later film *Young Mr. Lincoln*, his greatness also lies in his ability to relate to the common man.

WORKS CITED

Agnew, Dwight L. "Iowa's First Railroad." *Iowa Journal of History* 48 (1950): 1–26.

———. "Jefferson Davis and The Rock Island Bridge." *Iowa Journal of History* 47 (1949): 3–14.

———. "The Mississippi and Missouri Railroad, 1856–1860." *Iowa Journal of History* 51 (1953): 211–32.

Ambrose, Stephen E. *Nothing Like It In The World: The Men Who Built the Transcontinental Railroad, 1863–1869.* New York: Simon and Schuster, 2000.

Beveridge, Albert J. *Abraham Lincoln, 1809–1850.* Vol. 1. London: Victor Gollancz, 1928.

Bijker, Wiebe E., and J. Law, eds. *Shaping Technology/Building Society.* Cambridge, Massachusetts: MIT Press, 1992.

Bogdanovich, Peter. *John Ford.* Berkeley: University of California Press, 1978.

Brown, Dee. *Hear that Lonesome Whistle Blow.* London: Chatto and Windus, 1977.

Cahiers du Cinema. "John Ford's Young Mr Lincoln." In *Movies and Methods,* edited by Bill Nichols, 493–529. Berkeley: University of California Press, 1976.

Charnwood, Lord. *Abraham Lincoln.* Garden City, New York, 1917.

Donald, David H. *Lincoln.* London: Jonathon Cape, 1995.

Donovan, Frank. "The Race to Council Bluffs." *The Palimpsest* 43 (1962): 545–56.

Kirby, Lynne. *Parallel Tracks, The Railroad and Silent Cinema.* Exeter: University of Exeter Press, 1977.

Mackenzie, Donald. *Knowing Machines, Essays on Technical Change.* Cambridge, Massachusetts: MIT Press, 1996.

Meinig, D.W. *The Shaping of America: A Geographical Perspective on 500 Years of History.* Vol. 2 of *Continental America, 1800–1860.* New Haven: Yale University Press, 1993.

Piasecki, Andy. "Blowing the Railroad Trumpet." *Public Relations Review* 26 (2000): 53–65.

———. "The Rock Island Line is a Mighty Good Road." *Komunikacie* 1 (2000): 93–97.

Pitt, H.G. *Abraham Lincoln.* Gloucestershire: Sutton Publishing, 1998.

Silents Are Golden. 20 October 2001 <http://www.silentsaregolden.com/ironhorsereview.html>.

Sinclair, Andrew. *John Ford.* London: George Allen and Unwin, 1979.

Slotkin, Richard. *The Fatal Environment: The Myth of the Frontier in the Age of Industrialisation.* New York: Atheneum, 1985.

Smith Merritt R., and L. Marx, eds. *Does Technology Drive History?* Cambridge, Massachu-
    setts: MIT Press, 1994.
Starr, John W. *Lincoln and the Railroads.* New York: Mead, 1927.
Tuska, Jon. *The Filming of the West.* London: Robert Hale, 1978.
Zobrist, Benedict K. "Steamboat Men Versus Railroad Men: The First Bridging of the
    Mississippi River." *Missouri Historical Review* 59 (1965): 159–72.

Bryan Rommel-Ruiz

REDEEMING LINCOLN, REDEEMING THE SOUTH

Representations of Abraham Lincoln in D.W. Griffith's *The Birth of a Nation* (1915) and Historical Scholarship

Library of Congress.

In America's memoirs: President Lincoln, the Great Emancipator or the determined defender of the Union?

In 1922, President Warren Harding, Chief Justice William Taft, Civil War veterans, and Dr. Robert Moton of Tuskegee College led the ceremony commemorating the Lincoln Memorial on the National Mall in Washington, D.C. The presence and speeches of these distinguished men illuminated the division over the nation's historical memory of President Lincoln: Was he the man who saved the Union? Or was he the man who freed the slaves? While we may think that he did both, the answer was not so simple for a nation which seven years prior to the dedication of the memorial was commemorating the fiftieth anniversary of the end of the Civil War. For the majority of white Americans, the dedication of the Lincoln Memorial was another in a series of events to salute national reconciliation. For African Americans, of course, the commemoration ceremony was about the ambivalent (not to say bloody) legacy of emancipation and Reconstruction, and Tuskegee President Moton said as much: "The claim of greatness for Abraham Lincoln lies in this, that amid doubt and distrust . . . he put his trust in God and spoke the word that gave freedom to a race" (Schwartz, "Collective Memory" 1). Lest anyone be confused about the reasons for the gathering and for the Lincoln Memorial, President Harding stressed, "the supreme chapter in American history is [union,] not emancipation" (Schwartz, "Collective Memory 1).

Images of President Lincoln embody our nation's mixed historical memory about the meaning of the Civil War (Schwartz, *Lincoln* 2-12), and nowhere is this ambivalence more evident than in Civil War films and historical interpretations of Reconstruction. In both cases, President Lincoln's life and death symbolize the controversial history provoked by the trauma and bloodshed of Reconstruction. Specifically, filmmakers and historians have raised the issue of what form Reconstruction would have taken had Lincoln survived his presidency. The myth and memory of Lincoln were invoked by political partisans immediately after the Civil War ended, each contending that his program of Reconstruction championed Lincoln's vision. By the early twentieth century, historians and filmmakers continued this retrospection with strikingly similar perspectives.

In 1915, D.W. Griffith released *The Birth of a Nation* as part of the fiftieth anniversary of the end of the Civil War. Despite the film's controversial narrative, Griffith could expect an audience who shared his opinion that Reconstruction was a failure. Not everyone would have agreed with Griffith's view that the Ku Klux Klan saved the South from corrupt northern officials and ignorant black politicians; but historians and white Americans would not have contested his portrayal of vindictive Radical Republicans, carpetbaggers, and unqualified black legislators. In fact, historians such as John Burgess and William Dunning rose to prominence for championing this version of history.[1]

This essay compares the works of the historians Burgess and Dunning with contemporary Civil War films like *The Birth of a Nation* to understand the ways their portrayals of Lincoln meshed with larger cultural questions about the meaning of the Civil War and Reconstruction. Much like the controversies surrounding the Lincoln Memorial, cinematic and historical representations of President Lincoln addressed issues about America's identity and mission. Involved were competing narratives about national reunification, freedom, and democracy. Visions of sectional reconciliation and racial equality were fundamentally at odds, given the success of southern Redeemers who were intent upon consolidating their power by reinstating a racial caste system, unofficially known as "Jim Crow." Despite the important writings of black scholars such as W.E.B. Dubois,[2] early historians denigrated the role of blacks and Radical Republicans as they wrote their national histories. Like Griffith's *The Birth of a Nation*, their works would shape American perspectives of Lincoln, Reconstruction, and white supremacy for generations.

THE CIVIL WAR, ABRAHAM LINCOLN, AND THE MEANING OF NATION IN EARLY CIVIL WAR FILMS

The Civil War had been the subject of numerous plays, nickelodeons, and short films well before the release of Griffith's *The Birth of a Nation* (hereafter *BON*). In fact, Griffith himself had starred in a play and directed eleven one-reelers about the war. While *BON* is a landmark film in cinematic history for its innovative camera and editing techniques while it presents Griffith's particular vision of the Civil War (Rogan 250), most of the film's historiography reflects established conventions and tropes. These conventions often described the war as a tragedy that divided families, friends, and lovers, showing battles that emphasized the miseries and sufferings of war. Since the 1880s, northern and southern publishers fed a voracious literary market for autobiographies, biographies, and fictions about the conflict. Invariably, these stories portrayed a lost world of loyal slaves, idyllic social relations, and pastoral bliss in the antebellum period. As David Blight notes in *Race and Reunion*, literary works of reconciliation and reunion recaptured this "lost world," particularly popular in an age of rapid industrialization and tense race relations (Blight 227–31). As historian Paul Buck observed over fifty years ago, white Americans wanted sectional healing so desperately that they were willing to sacrifice racial equality (Buck 297).

The images of union and family were not new to movie audiences in the early 1900s. Abraham Lincoln, of course, invoked the family—and the Bible—as metaphor when he stated that, "A house divided against itself cannot stand." For filmmakers, the family tragedy/melodrama was among the more popular themes in their productions concerning the Civil War. Closely tied to it was the lover's quarrel (and inevitable reconciliation). These narratives of families and lovers divided and then reunited paralleled the national struggle, enabling filmmakers to personalize complex issues that revolved around questions of regional politics, economy, culture, and society. Two early films to mobilize these formulas were *The Battle of Shiloh* (1913) and *The Crisis* (1916). In *The Battle of Shiloh*, two young women, Ellen Winston and Ethel Carey, have tried to discourage their brothers, Tom and Frank respectively, from joining the Union and Confederate armies, only to save them from execution and imprisonment after their capture. During the war, Frank and Ellen become lovers while Ellen becomes a spy for the Confederacy. After the brothers leave the prison camps, Ethel and Tom likewise become romantically involved. By the end, the film's themes are quite clear: first, family and love define the film's characters, establishing inviolable ties which even war cannot break; second, the "marriage" of the two regions is essential to national happiness.[3]

Instead of employing the divided-family theme, *The Crisis* focused upon lovers from the different regions quarreling and then reconciling. The plot connects the Civil War to historical figures like Abraham Lincoln and the issue of emancipation, which was not done in *The Battle of Shiloh*. In *The Crisis*, Stephen Bryce, a lawyer from Boston—and recently arrived in the South—seeks the love of Virginia Carvel. Although attracted to Bryce, Virginia rejects him because of his abolitionism, and chooses Clarence Colfax, a southern gentleman. While fighting for the Union, Bryce is wounded and then becomes an aide to President Lincoln. In the meantime, Virginia loses interest in Colfax and calls off their engagement. However, when he is captured by Union forces and is condemned to death, she seeks out President Lincoln and pleads for his life. Lincoln, wanting to show his forgiveness of a defeated South, commutes Colfax's death sentence. Seeing Bryce as the president's aide, she remembers her feelings for him. The two lovers embrace, and the film ends with their anticipation of a united future.[4]

The Crisis reveals what *BON* demonstrates more forcefully: cinematic representations of the past can shape the perception of historical issues. In this case, abolitionism drives a wedge in an otherwise harmonious relationship between the North and South. Lincoln himself is not seen as an abolitionist (let alone the Great Emancipator), but a leader distraught over the fate of his divided country. The Civil War is fought over the folly of abolitionism, and it is incumbent upon the president to reconcile the true principle of the nation—unionism. In this context, his pardon of Colfax is emblematic of his true feelings for the South: the prodigal son needs to be shown mercy so that the family can be reunited. The marriage of Virginia and Stephen is the foundation of

Director D.W. Griffith with famous cameraman Billy (G.W.) Bitzer.

the new family (which Lincoln helped reunite), whose children will people a peaceful nation.

REPRESENTATIONS OF ABRAHAM LINCOLN IN THE BIRTH OF A NATION

The relationship of blood, race, nation, and the role Lincoln plays in their definition in post–Civil War America is most provocatively shown in Griffith's *BON*. Based closely upon Thomas Dixon's novel *The Clansman* (1905), *BON* traces the origins of the Civil War, southern defeat and humiliation under Radical and Black Reconstruction, and the "Redemption" of white southern power by the Ku Klux Klan. Griffith believed that, "The bringing of the African to America planted the first seed of disunion" (*BON* 7),[5] a point demonstrably made from the film's beginning. While this film weaves two major themes of the Civil War genre—the divided family and quarreling lovers—Griffith adds a critical dimension to his interpretation: for him, the central question of the Civil War and Reconstruction was the history and future of blacks in America. Ironically, scholars at the opposite end of the political spectrum, such as W.E.B. Dubois, would argue the same point. However, where Dubois contended that blacks needed to be extended civil rights and integrated into political society, Griffith argued that they must be disenfranchised and expelled.[6] Again, Griffith could claim connection to President Lincoln, as the president himself had advocated African colonization and racial separation (Foner 6; Schwartz, *Lincoln* 2). While it is unclear what Lincoln believed about the history of slavery in America, for Griffith the importation of African slaves set the stage for a family divided and fratricidal conflict.

The image and portrayal of Lincoln pivot on his relationship with the two families of the film: the Stonemans and the Camerons. Austin Stoneman (Ralph Lewis) was a northern congressman whose staunch support of abolitionism and lust for his mulatto servant has clouded his concern for his family—and, by extension, the nation.[7] His sons are Phil (Elmer Clifton) and Tod (Robert Harron) who serve in the war, and his daughter Elsie (Lillian Gish) is the love interest of the film's hero, the Southerner Ben Cameron (Henry B. Walthall). Elsie is also the love interest of the film's antagonist, Silas Lynch (George Siegmann), Stoneman's mulatto henchman who intends to destroy southern white society and establish black rule. Ben Cameron is the eldest son of the Cameron family, whose idyllic plantation—shown in lavish detail during the first half of the film—embodies the hierarchical order of an idealized, antebellum South Carolina.

The narrative begins with Ben inviting his former schoolmate Phil and his brother to the Cameron plantation, where Phil meets and falls in love with Ben's sister, Margaret (Miriam Cooper). In this scene, Griffith also introduces the other members of the Cameron family. In the film, the elder Cameron (Spottiswoode Aitken), the honorable patriarch of the family, will represent the political and social humiliation of the South during Reconstruction but whose masculinity and dignity will be restored by Ben through the triumph of the Ku Klux Klan. Mrs. Cameron (Josephine Crowell) is the sacrificing, virtuous matron who, after losing a son in the Civil War, will beg President Lincoln (Joseph Henabery) to save her sole-surviving son. Finally, there is Flora (Mae Marsh), the "pet sister," an innocent, virginal southern girl who will be preyed upon by the family's former slave, Gus (Walter Long, in blackface).[8]

During the Stonemans' visit, Tod quickly befriends one of the Cameron brothers. The initial squabbles and friendly jostling suggest that these boys have become friends, perhaps closer to one another than to their own brothers (*BON* 65–70). By highlighting the friendship between the two boys, Griffith draws the audience into an emotional relationship that will be wounded by war. At the end of the visit, the boys promise to see one another again (*BON* 137); tragically, Griffith fulfills this promise by having them meet on the battlefield (*BON* 296–307). After the Cameron brother is shot, Tod rushes to stab him with his bayonet, only to recognize his friend. As he attempts to help his friend, Tod is shot, and they die in each other's arms. It is this confrontation that *BON*'s Lincoln feared.

PRESIDENT LINCOLN AND RECONCILIATION IN THE BIRTH OF A NATION

The president is introduced as he signs a proclamation raising seventy-five thousand volunteers. Griffith begins this scene with the notation, "An historical facsimile of the President's Executive office on that occasion (the raising of troops after Ft. Sumter), after Nicolay and Hay in *Lincoln, a History*" (*BON* 144). This title is the first of numerous efforts Griffith makes to connect his film to real events and figures by replicating historical moments, using them as rhetorical devices to authenticate his historical interpretation. In this sequence, Lincoln is reluctant to call upon Americans to fight one another, and it is advisers who present him with the proclamation. Lincoln paces and ponders before he decides to sign the historic document. After this scene, Griffith inserted a title stating, "Abraham Lincoln uses the Presidential office for the first time in history to call for volunteers to enforce the rule of the coming nation over the individual states" (*BON* 146). The following shot shows Lincoln signing the proclamation; after his advisers leave, he sits alone, takes a handkerchief from his hat, wipes tears from his eyes, and clasps his hands in prayer (*BON* 147).

For Griffith, Lincoln was not the rabid abolitionist Southerners feared and reviled on the eve of the Civil War but a distraught father of a divided family and a noble leader who kept radicals in his party at bay. Lincoln is next seen hearing Ben Cameron's mother plead for her son (*BON* 480). Mrs. Cameron came to Washington to tend to her captured and convalescent son. At the hospital Ben finally meets his love, Elsie Stoneman. Hearing that Ben has been condemned to be hanged, Elsie tells Mrs. Cameron, "We will ask mercy from the Great Heart" (*BON* 478). Meeting the president, Mrs. Cameron implores him to pardon her son. The president initially declines her appeal but then concedes. With her kneeling next to him in supplication, Lincoln sits at his desk and writes Ben Cameron's pardon (*BON* 493). After Mrs. Cameron and Elsie exit, Lincoln remains at his desk. The president removes his glasses in a gesture parallel to the earlier scene when he raised the volunteers (*BON* 495). With this juxtaposition, Griffith demonstrated how Lincoln's pardon of Ben Cameron forgave the president for raising an army against the South. To reinforce this point, he has Mrs. Cameron say to her son, "Mr. Lincoln has given your life back to me" (*BON* 497). By accepting Mrs. Cameron's plea (a mother who has sacrificed a son for the war) and saving Ben's life, Lincoln has honored the dignity of those who fought and supported the Confederacy. In this dramatic sequence, Lincoln has begun to restore the South to the national family, a point Griffith will further during a confrontation between President Lincoln and Austin Stoneman.

In the same room where Lincoln signed the proclamation and Ben Cameron's pardon, the president welcomes Stoneman, who has come to "protest against Lincoln's policy of clemency for the South" (*BON* 529). The comparisons are quite clear. Lincoln will treat all Southerners as he treated Ben Cameron. Just as Ben was condemned to be hanged, Stoneman came to Lincoln declaring that the South's "[L]eaders must be hanged and their states treated as conquered provinces" (*BON* 531). As Stoneman wildly protests Lincoln's ideas, the president calmly replies, "I shall deal with them as though they had never been away" (*BON* 533). Stoneman leaves in anger while Lincoln stands reflectively. According to Griffith, Lincoln would have allowed the South to direct its own reconstruction. The next scene directly presents this interpretation, as it begins with the title, "The South under Lincoln's fostering hand goes to work to rebuild itself" (*BON* 535). Ben Cameron is then shown rolling up his sleeves and, with other members of his family, setting about putting the family's life back together.

This optimism is abruptly punctured with the following segment—the assassination of President Lincoln. As Griffith states, "And then, when the terrible days were over and the healing time of peace was at hand . . . came the fated night of April 14, 1865" (*BON* 537). Among the longer scenes in the film, Griffith dramatically restages the tragic night of the president's assassination to dramatize how this bloody act changed the course of Reconstruction. Instead of a benevolent rebuilding of southern society, the former Confederacy will be treated as Stoneman's conquered provinces. The following two scenes reinforce this point as Griffith shows Stoneman and his mulatto servant Lydia plotting their scheme of Black Reconstruction (*BON* 607–12), followed by the mournful Cameron family reading a newspaper describing the assassination (a facsimile of the *New South*, 22 April 1865). Upon reading the news story, Ben Cameron says, "Our best friend is gone. What is to become of us now?" (*BON* 617). In the next shot, Ben looks grimly at his father, who, in a gesture similar to Lincoln's after he had signed the volunteer proclamation, puts his hands over his eyes and bows his head (*BON* 618).

It is significant that part one of the film ends here. The Camerons' mourning of Lincoln suggested a peaceful and reconciliatory rebuilding of the nation. From this perspective, the South was willing to accept defeat and restore its society under "Lincoln's guiding hand." Accordingly, Griffith's Lincoln was not an interventionist; he would not have undermined southern institutions—of course, how emancipation would have factored into his interpretation is unclear. This brilliant juxtaposition does more than provoke sympathy for the Confederacy. It demonstrates emotional attachment to the president (he forgives them for seceding, and the South forgives him for calling the volunteers) and legitimates the actions the South will take under the Ku Klux Klan. From this perspective, terrorizing blacks and undermining Radical Reconstruction not only redeems the South, but it does so in consonance with Lincoln's plan for the region.

Griffith's representation of Lincoln as one sympathetic to a defeated South may appear exaggerated and perhaps odd to the modern viewer, but this perspective was not too far from the views of white Americans in 1915. After Lincoln's assassination, white Americans had constructed myths about him. With most Americans disappointed in Reconstruction by its end in 1877, Civil War pageants and holidays (such as Memorial Day) became occasions of reconciliation and mythology (Blight 2, 64–93). It was at these moments when the mythological Lincoln helped Americans define the meaning of the conflict. A Lincoln emerged who bore little resemblance to the president who led the nation in the Civil War. While he had promoted unionism, in historical memory he became an advocate of reunion and reconciliation, not emancipation. Significantly, this is the portrait of Lincoln postwar historians would enshrine in their scholarship.

PRESIDENT LINCOLN, NATIONAL RECONCILIATION, AND THE HISTORICAL PROFESSION

Although journalists disputed Griffith's portrayal of Reconstruction as a visceral, bloody race war (Hackett 161–63), contemporary historical scholarship described how "fanatical" abolitionism and black suffrage produced racial antagonism. Griffith even drew upon this scholarship to support his ideas. Using Woodrow Wilson's *History of the American People*, Griffith quoted passages such as "The policy of congressional leaders wrought . . . a veritable overthrow of civilization in the South . . . in their determination to 'put the white South under the heel of the black South.'"[9] Another excerpt stated that, "The men were roused by a mere instinct of self-preservation . . . until at last there had sprung into existence a great Ku Klux Klan, a veritable empire of the South, to protect the Southern country" (*BON* 621–25; Wilson 19–20, 49–50, 60). More than quoting the prominent historian and president, Griffith used these passages to frame the narrative of part two, divided into the rise of the black South, the disenfranchisement of the white South, and, in closing, the restoration of white supremacy. Wilson's scholarly template was visually extended to support Griffith's historical interpretation that vilifies African Americans and legitimates lynching and Jim Crow laws. It is precisely because the film works as history— not merely as epic spectacle—that President Wilson noted that *BON* was "History written in Lightning" (Rogan 251).

While Griffith quoted the historian Woodrow Wilson in his epic, much of the film's historical background was consistent with the leading scholarship about Lincoln's role in the Civil War and Reconstruction held by John Burgess (1844–1931), William Dunning (1857–1922), and Claude Bowers (1879–1958). Burgess argued in *Reconstruction and the Constitution* (1902) that Reconstruction under Lincoln had already been instituted in states like Louisiana, Arkansas, and Tennessee, where the "Great Heart" intended to let the states manage their own return to the Union. In these states, men who swore allegiance to the Union and accepted emancipation were appointed to manage the return. According to Burgess, the states that joined the Confederacy were still part of the Union, and thus did not need to be reconstituted. They needed only to be controlled by men who had supported the Union in the 1860 election or had pledged allegiance to the Constitution (Burgess 10–11). Lincoln recognized that federal intervention was necessary at times during these early years of Reconstruction, but Burgess thought this position and the requirement that state governments would be established only when one-tenth of the number of people voting in the election of 1860 swore a loyalty oath were "erroneous" and "destined to result in mischievousness" (Burgess 9). Even though such federal mandates violated the concept of a state according to Burgess, Lincoln's intention to allow states to rule themselves was contrary to what many members of Congress had in mind in the aftermath of a bloody war (Burgess 11,13).

Griffith's cinematic encounter between Lincoln and Stoneman followed the historical portrayal of Lincoln and the radicals in Congress offered by Burgess. Griffith quoted Lincoln stating, "I will treat them [the secessionists] as if they never left," because historians such as Burgess argued the very same point. Burgess concluded his chapter on this topic by showing the peaceful reentry of states in the Union (like Tennessee) and then poignantly stated, "Such was the condition of things when the assassin's bullet ended the life of the great and good President and brought the Vice-President, Mr. Johnson, into the office" (Burgess 13). In *The Tragic Era*, Claude Bowers went even further than Burgess, stating, "Nowhere did the murder [of Lincoln] fall so like a pall as in the South." Quoting a Georgian, Bowers wrote, "Then God Help us! If [Lincoln's death] is true, it is the worst blow that has yet been struck the South" (4). This statement could have worked nicely as the final title for part one of the film. In fact, it closely parallels Ben Cameron's final statement, "Our best friend is gone. What is to become of us now?" (*BON* 617).

William Dunning's *Essays on the Civil War and Reconstruction* described Lincoln's approach to Reconstruction as a matter of state determination, much as Burgess had done. According to Dunning, "Lincoln stated his conviction that the Union could not be broken by any pretended ordinance of secession . . . [and] that the inhabitants of states [which had seceded] were to be in insurrection against the United States" (Dunning 65). To understand Lincoln's vision of reconstruction, Americans need to examine his attitudes about federalism and secession. According to Dunning, Lincoln "issued a proclamation . . . which recited the subversion of the state governments by persons in rebellion and hence guilty of treason, and the desire of certain of these persons to reinaugurate loyal governments 'within their respective states'" (Dunning 66). Discussing the 10 percent rule, Dunning noted that Lincoln would pledge to recognize state governments composed of men who swore to a loyalty oath (Dunning 65–66). Dunning concluded, "Mr. Lincoln was thus true to the position assumed at the outbreak of the war. The executive department, in short, was fully committed to the doctrine that the corporate existence of the seceding states was not interrupted by the war" (Dunning 66). Dunning's conclusion thus suggested that Lincoln's Reconstruction plan would have treated the South as if it had "never left."

However, where Dunning and Burgess conceded that Lincoln would allow more state control over rebuilding, they were circumspect over the issue of southern social institutions like slavery. On this matter, Dunning noted that Lincoln required states to accept federal laws, even those made during the war.

Dunning was unsure about the degree to which this included the issue of slavery, noting that "[T]he [Emancipation Proclamation] was merely presented as a rallying point, which might bring people to act sooner than they otherwise would, and was not intended as a final solution of all the delicate questions involved" (77). That is, it was a wartime measure that loyal Southerners would be allowed to coordinate in their respective states. To underscore the problem of slavery during the war, Dunning pointed to the issue of runaway slaves to Northern armies. Even before the Emancipation Proclamation, slaves had run away from border and Confederate slave states. While more recent historians see slave flight as black agency and freedom, scholars such as Dunning argued that, "Commanders were seriously embarrassed by the great crowds of improvident blacks that attached themselves to the armies in their campaigns" and by caring and providing for these runaways, "[T]he status of the negroes thus seems to have been practically that of wards of the national government, with rights totally undetermined" (Dunning 73, 75). Dunning's perspective on freedmen and slavery during the conflict was important because it affected his view of Radical Reconstruction, which described blacks as unqualified and ignorant freedmen. Dunning's argument (like others concerning black empowerment, white disenfranchisement, and Radicals like Thaddeus Stevens) were major themes to guide Griffth's vision of Reconstruction in part two of *BON*.

John Burgess and William Dunning were among the more influential early writers of Reconstruction. Their histories stood among the many written in the early twentieth century whose objective was to reconcile the southern narrative with the larger national drama of the Civil War and Reconstruction. Historian Peter Novick notes that these historians emerged in a social climate that had seen Reconstruction as a failure and accepted black inferiority. Burgess wrote that, "A black skin means membership in a race of men which has never of itself succeeded in subjecting passion to reason" (Novick 75). Dunning would write that blacks "had no pride of race and aspiration or ideals save to be like the whites" (Novick 75). In *That Noble Dream*, a famous history of the historical profession, Novick states, "The near unanimous racism of northern historians . . . made possible a negotiated settlement of sectional differences in the interpretation of the Civil War and Reconstruction" (77). Consequently, they "became harshly critical of the abolitionists as they were 'irresponsible agitators'" (Novick 77). They agreed with southern historians in denouncing the "criminal outrages" of Reconstruction. Although they would agree that slavery was wrong and secession was unconstitutional, Burgess said that Reconstruction was a "punishment so far in excess of the crime that it extinguished every phase of culpability upon the part of those whom it was sought to convict and convert" (Novick 77).

Dunning viewed Reconstruction as such an "unmistakable disaster, leading among other atrocities, to 'the hideous crime against white womanhood which now assumed new meaning in the annals of outrage'"(Novick 77). Dunning's observation is the fundamental premise of Griffith's history of Reconstruction. In Griffith's version, interracial marriage and miscegenation were the ultimate goals of black politicians, and those motivations lay behind white disenfranchisement. Black pursuit of white women fundamentally legitimated the organization of the Ku Klux Klan and its effort to redeem the South from black rule.

LINCOLN IN RECENT RECONSTRUCTION HISTORIOGRAPHY AND FILMS

Our understanding of Lincoln and Reconstruction has changed significantly in the last fifty years. The Civil Rights movement radically transformed American visions of justice and democracy; accordingly, historical scholarship on the Civil War and Reconstruction has changed. Today, historians praise the role of African American soldiers in the war and take note of the civil rights legislation that the Radicals in Congress promoted (Foner xxii–xxiv; McPherson, *Battle Cry*). Indeed, the Radicals, who were too extreme for the earlier generation of historians, are now seen as progressive—men ahead of their time. Furthermore, the social and cultural revolution engendered by the Civil Rights movement has redefined much of the controversy over Lincoln and emancipation. In fact, debating Lincoln's sincerity about emancipation encourages outrage among students who have grown up with the firm belief that Lincoln freed the slaves.[10] Despite the transformation in the scholarship on Reconstruction, however, filmmakers and American society are reluctant to alter their vision of the Civil War. While films like Edward Zwick's *Glory* (1989) have substantively altered American understanding of the role of blacks in the struggle, television dramas, such as *The Blue and the Gray* (1982) or John Jakes's *North and South* (1985, 1986) continue to replay traditional formulae about families and lovers divided by the conflict. Slavery may be broached, but it remains tertiary to the melodrama.

In *The Blue and the Gray* (1982), for example, the film's hero, John Geyser (John Hammond) leaves his family's Virginia farm after the state secedes and a black friend has been hanged for sheltering runaway blacks. Reversing the theme of the film *The Crisis*, he rejects his family because it tolerates slavery. In the end, though, he fights on his family farm after serving as a war correspondent because his family ultimately defines his identity. The film concludes with his marriage to a northern girl.[11] As in *BON*, the nation's unity is reconciled in a marriage between Northerner and Southerner. The film ends with promise of reunion rather than a detailed exploration of the impact of Reconstruction on the nation in a way similar to the conclusion of *The Crisis*. In *The Blue and The Gray*, Reconstruction is mentioned but never examined.

As in *The Crisis* and *The Birth of a Nation*, Lincoln plays a significant role in *The Blue and the Gray*. As in the earlier films, he is portrayed as a paternalistic figure that regrets the impact of the war on families. In one scene, he advises John Geyser to become an illustrator for a national magazine so he does not have to "raise a gun against his family." It is John's dilemma that becomes the national problem; in the film he is an impartial observer of the war's horror and tragedy. Lincoln is intimately tied to the film's main characters; this personable Lincoln, however, is a depoliticized president. He signs the Emancipation Proclamation, but his positions on Reconstruction and the future of African Americans, democracy, and freedom are not clearly defined. *The Blue and The Gray* clearly overlooks recent historical scholarship which proclaims that the concept of freedom defined the Civil War. In fact, even traditional questions about states' rights and the Constitution are largely ignored. By marginalizing the issue of slavery and federalism, the film effectively depoliticizes the war itself. In this context, Lincoln's death is a moral and personal tragedy. The nation perseveres after his death. It reunites and reconciles in his absence, symbolized in the film by the marriage of the Virginian John Geyser and his lover from Massachusetts (with his aunt, uncle, and cousins from Pennsylvania attending).

Since Reconstruction remains a source of controversy for Americans, current filmmakers are probably hesitant to examine this period. By concentrating solely on the Civil War in dramas such as *The Blue and the Gray*, though, they sustain a genre that perpetuates the national reconciliation narrative. Amputating the Civil War from Reconstruction enables them to sentimentalize and memorialize the dead without exploring the vital issues for which America's soldiers fought. Whereas historians and filmmakers once agreed upon the narrative of the Civil War and Reconstruction, they now disagree. Historians such as Eric Foner, August Meier, and Sidney Mintz link the Civil War and Reconstruction, arguing that the constitutional controversy that led to the war be-

Library of Congress.

The type of historical moment reenacted in *The Birth of a Nation* (1915).

came by 1863 a larger struggle about black freedom (Foner xxiv–xxvii). Film-makers with their continued efforts to separate the Civil War from Reconstruc-tion, in contrast, seek to avoid these interpretive debates and arguably obfuscate the meaning of the conflict. Was the war about union or freedom? Among histo-rians like Foner, Lincoln continues to play an important role in the emancipa-tion debate (Foner 6–13; Berlin; McPherson, "Who Freed The Slaves?"). Among filmmakers, Foner's views about slavery are marginalized because they interfere with their melodrama about division and reconciliation. Not surprisingly, cur-rent films about the Civil War rarely include the president because of the contro-versies associated with the competing historical memories he signifies.

As this essay has examined the relationship between the historical profes-sion and filmmakers, it has also raised the issue about the relationship between history and historical memory. Representations of President Lincoln in histori-cal scholarship and popular culture have long been areas where these two visions of history converged. In the past their perspectives have been similar, and, more recently, they have diverged. In both cases they raise larger ques-tions about how Americans identify themselves and the ideals to which they aspire. Michael Kammen has written that Americans are a people of paradox—a people of celestial ideals who struggle to live up to them. Efforts to understand Lincoln and the Civil War are exercises in this perpetual struggle. In historical memory, the American story is a biblical epic, with our Principled Puritans failing to live up to their religious vision of America as the Eden of Freedom. Like the Hebrew people of the ancient world, Americans desire to renew the Puritan covenant. The Civil War, however, represents a virtual self-immolation that almost destroyed the American epic. Like Noah who led his children through the Flood, Abraham Lincoln guided America through the carnage and destruction of the Civil War, reestablishing the covenant of freedom. Indeed, Lincoln's Gettysburg Address redeemed the carnage of the Civil War by connecting the war to the meaning of the American Revolution and the American ideals embodied in the Declaration of Independence (Wills). D.W. Griffith understood this portrayal of Lincoln and his relationship to Reconstruction. Today's historians have been able to reconcile this traditional vision of Lincoln with a revised social history that includes African Americans. It remains to be seen if today's filmmakers have the boldness that Griffith once showed to rewrite a cinematic biblical narrative of Reconstruction in this modern vein—to attempt, in a contemporary context of racial awareness—to write history with lightning.

NOTES

1. For the roles John Burgess and William Dunning played in shaping Reconstruction historiography, see Eric Foner, *Reconstruction*, xix-xxi, and Peter Novick, *That Noble Dream*, chapter 2. The work of Dunning and Burgess on Reconstruction was also influenced by contemporary ideas about race, emancipation, and slavery. As they wrote their works, U.B. Phillips was writing *American Negro Slavery*, which in effect argued that slavery was a benign institution and a "school" for civilizing blacks. Kenneth Stampp's *Peculiar Institution* (1953) was the first major monograph to challenge Phillips's interpretation. Not until Stanley Elkins wrote *Slavery: A Problem in American and Institutional Life* in 1959 did a sea change begin in the scholarship regarding slavery and its consequences for African Americans and American race relations. While African American scholars, such as Carter G. Woodson, Rayford Logan, and John Hope Franklin, had long combated Phillips's interpretation, Elkins's *Slavery* reached a broader scholarly and popular audience, including Daniel Patrick Moynihan, who drew upon Elkins's work to suggest public-policy initiatives in the 1960s in what became known as the *Moynihan Report*. For an excellent discussion on the role of Elkins's *Slavery* upon the historical profession and the ways it encouraged the field of African American history in the 1960s and 1970s, see August Meier and Elliot Rudwick, *Black History and the Historical Profession*.

2. W.E.B. Dubois, *Black Reconstruction: an essay toward a history of the part which black folk played in the attempt to reconstruct democracy in America, 1860-1880.* A landmark study of Reconstruction, it was initially dismissed by the historians because of its Marxist analysis. See Peter Novick, *That Noble Dream*, 232; August Meier and Elliot Rudwick, *Black History and the Historical Profession*; and Eric Foner, *Reconstruction*, xxi. For how Dubois's work has led revisionist scholarship on Reconstruction, see Foner, *Reconstruction*, xxiv-xxv.

3. The following is a more complete plot summary of the film, providing the reader with a better understanding of the strong personal connections between the regions: As the war ensues, Ellen has become a spy for the South, and her brother, Tom, sees her pass a message to her lover, Frank Carey, Ethel's brother and Confederate soldier. Tom seizes the note but allows Frank to leave. The note is later discovered in Tom's hands, and Union army officers declare him a traitor and sentence him to death, despite his heroic efforts at the battle of Shiloh. The execution is commuted when Frank admits that the letter was intended for him. Before he is executed, Frank escapes, then is recaptured. Meanwhile, Tom has been captured by Southern troops while visiting his sister. Ethel and Ellen promote the exchange of their imprisoned brothers, and the film ends with the lovers Frank and Ellen heading South and Tom and Ethel going North. The confusing narrative parallels the internecine and discombobulated nature of the Civil War. Family and love are the only rational and loyal relationships established in the conflict. Politics and war are not only disconnected but artificial in comparison to blood relationships. Whether the modern viewer believes this interpretation, it must be taken into account that contemporaries saw the Civil War as a human tragedy (and, in some cases, the apocalypse), and reaching for human understanding was central to rationalizing what occurred. As much as we see political instruction from the conflict, contemporaries sought to distance themselves from such claims because of the immediate emotional dimension of their experiences with the war. *The Battle of Shiloh*, dir. Joseph Smiley, Lubin Manufacturing Company Distributing Company, General Films Company, release, 15 December 1913.

4. *The Crisis,* dir. Colin Campbell, Selig Polyscope, 1916.

5. *The Birth of a Nation*, or alternate title, *The Clansman*, dir. D.W. Griffith, David W. Griffith Corp., Griffith Feature Films Distribution Co., Epoch Producing Corp., release 2 August 1915 (© Epoch Producing Corp. and Thomas Dixon David W. Griffith Corp. 2 August 1915, 2 December 1915. See also Lang, *The Birth of a Nation, D.W. Griffith, Director*, 44. Throughout this essay I have drawn upon Lang's excellent text, which breaks down each shot of *The Birth of a Nation*. For reference and bibliographic purposes, discussions of the film will draw upon this text and cite the shot numbers for readers as (*BON*, shot #).

6. In fact, in an earlier version of *BON*, Griffith advocated the expulsion of African Americans from the United States, which included a deleted scene where blacks were herded upon a ship. Arguably, the scene included in the most recent version of *BON* suggests a crueler fate: Black male assault upon both white women and society deserves nothing less than extermination. For a discussion of the deleted scene, see Michael Rogan, "'The Sword Became a Flashing Vision': D. W. Griffith's *The Birth of a Nation*," 254.

7. Other than President Lincoln, Austin Stoneman is the closest representation of

a historical figure in the film, in this case Thaddeus Stevens, a staunch abolitionist Republican from Pennsylvania. Thaddeus Stevens embodied much of the "radical" sentiments of the Republican Party, including emancipation, black suffrage, and racial equality. Stoneman's likeness to Stevens is quite clear, including the pursed lips and clubfoot. One can only speculate that giving Stevens a pseudonym in the film enabled Griffith to develop the fictionalized narrative of the northern family. Arguably, the similarity to Stevens allows Griffith to further connect history and fiction, confusing the two even further, but, given that Griffith believed his representation of Reconstruction was "history," he probably thought he was giving an accurate portrayal of Stevens's plans for Reconstruction.

8. The character of Gus is as critical as the other two major "black" (played by white actors in black-face) characters, Mammy and Silas Lynch. Mammy, of course, represents the loyal slave who will stay with the family through Reconstruction and criticize Northern freedmen and soldiers. This characterization of Mammy as the loyal slave has a long history in plantation literature. Joel Chandler Harris and Thomas Nelson Page popularized this perspective in their stories about Uncle Remus and Marsc' Chan. In *BON*, Gus was "corrupted" by emancipation and the desires of free black men to prey upon white women. Although Gus will chase Flora until she jumps from a cliff to retain her virtue, it is unclear whether Ben and the Ku Klux Klan will kill him for his pursuit of Flora or for his betrayal of the Cameron family. In any case, Gus symbolizes how blacks were "unsuited" for freedom, according to Griffith. For more about the representations of the family and loyal slave in the plantation-literature genre, see David Blight, *Race and Reunion*, 222–31. For a discussion on the Plantation Illusion in *BON*, see Everett Carter, "Cultural History Written in Lightning: The Significance of *The Birth of a Nation* (1915)."

9. Underline Griffith.

10. This debate has arisen in the context of recent research on the role slaves played in the emancipation process. For an overview of these arguments, see Ira Berlin, et al., *Slaves No More: Three Essays in Emancipation*. For a response to these perspectives, see James McPherson, "Who Freed the Slaves?"

11. Much of *The Blue and the Gray* is derivative of *The Birth of a Nation* and other early, romantic Civil War films (and perhaps therein lies its continued popularity—at least among Civil War film viewers who write film reviews at Internet sites such as Amazon.com). John's romantic relationship, however, closely resembles Elsie and Ben Cameron's, as John's lover, the daughter of an Austin Stoneman-like character, works as a nurse during the war.

WORKS CITED

Battle of Shiloh . Dir. Joseph Smiley. Lubin Manufacturing Company, 1913.

Birth of a Nation, or alternate title *The Clansman*. Dir. David W. Griffith. David W. Griffith Corporation, 1915.

Blue and the Gray. Dir. Andrew, McLaglen, 1982, 1985.

Crisis. Dir. Colin Campbell. Selig Polyscope, 1916.

Berlin, Ira, et. al. *Slaves No More: Three Essays in Emancipation.* New York: Cambridge University Press, 1989.

Blight, David. *Race and Reunion: The Civil War in American Memory.* Cambridge, Massachusetts: Harvard University Press, 2001.

Bowers, Claude. *The Tragic Era: The Revolution after Lincoln.* Cambridge, Massachusetts: Houghton Mifflin, 1929.

Buck, Paul. *The Road to Reunion, 1865–1900.* New York: Little, Brown, 1938.

Burgess, John. *Reconstruction and the Constitution: 1866–1876.* New York: Charles Scribner's Sons, 1902.

Carter, Everett. "Cultural History Written in Lightning: The Significance of *The Birth of a Nation* (1915)." In *Hollywood As Historian,* edited by Peter C. Rollins, 9–19. Lexington: University Press of Kentucky, 1983.

Dubois, W.E.B. *Black Reconstruction: an essay toward a history of the part which black folk played in the attempt to reconstruct democracy in America 1860–1880.* Edited by Cedric Robinson. South Bend, Indiana: University of Notre Dame Press, 2001.

Dunning, William A. *Essays on the Civil War and Reconstruction, and Related Topics.* New York: Macmillan, 1904.

Elkins, Stanley. *Slavery: A Problem in American and Institutional Life.* Chicago: University Press of Chicago, 1959.

Foner, Eric. *Reconstruction: America's Unfinished Revolution, 1863–1877.* New York: Harper Collins, 1988.

Hackett, Francis. "Brotherly Love." In *The Birth of A Nation, D.W. Griffith, Director,* edited by Robert Lang. 161–63. New Brunswick, New Jersey: Rutgers University Press, 1994.

Kammen, Michael. *A People of Paradox: An Inquiry into the Origins of American Civilization.* New York: Oxford University Press, 1980.

———. "The Birth of a Nation: History, Ideology, and Form." In *The Birth of a Nation, D.W. Griffith, Director,* edited by Robert Lang, 3–24. New Brunswick, New Jersey: Rutgers University Press, 1994.

Lang, Robert, ed. *The Birth of a Nation, D.W. Griffith, Director.* New Brunswick, New Jersey: Rutgers University Press, 1994.

Lincoln, Abraham. "Speech Given at the Illinois Republican State Convention." 16 June 1858. <http://home.att.net/~rjnorton/Lincoln78.html>.

McPherson, James. *Battle Cry of Freedom: The Civil War Era.* New York: Oxford University Press, 1988.

———. "Who Freed the Slaves?" *Proceedings of the American Philosophical Society* 139 (1995): 1–10.

Making of Birth of a Nation. David Shepard. Film Preservation Associates, 1992.

Meier, August, and Elliot Rudwick. *Black History and the Historical Profession.* Urbana: University Press of Illinois, 1986.

Novick, Peter. *That Noble Dream: The Objectivity Question and the American Historical Profession.* New York: Cambridge University Press, 1988.

Rogan, Michael. "'The Sword Became a Flashing Vision': D.W. Griffith's *The Birth of a*

* Nation." In *The Birth of A Nation, D.W. Griffith, Director,* edited by Robert Lang, 250–93. New Brunswick, New Jersey: Rutgers University Press, 1994.

Schwartz, Barry. *Abraham Lincoln and the Forge of National Memory.* Chicago: University Press of Chicago, 2000.

———."Collective Memory and History: How Abraham Lincoln Became a Symbol of Racial Equality." *Sociological Quarterly* 38 (1997): 469. AN: 9708301680.

Wills, Garry. *Lincoln at Gettysburg: The Words That Remade America.* New York: Simon and Schuster, 1992.

Wilson, Woodrow. *Reunion and Nationalization.* Vol. 5 of *The History of the American People.* New York: Harper, 1901.

J. Tillapaugh

THEODORE ROOSEVELT AND THE ROUGH RIDERS

A Century of Leadership in Film

Theodore Roosevelt, the twenty-sixth president of the United States, 1901–1909.

Library of Congress.

Theodore Roosevelt was a transformational leader who brought the people of the United States, sometimes kicking and screaming, into the twentieth century. His image was carved on a mountain in South Dakota, along with Washington, Jefferson, and Lincoln. These presidents transformed their nation through commitments to change, as opposed to those caretakers who only transacted presidential business. Despite the occasional critic, the quality of TR's leadership has passed all the tests for a century of American history.[1]

Roosevelt's rise to national leadership coincided with the inventions that permitted the development of the motion picture industry. He embraced the new technology and allowed his image to be conveyed to a broad audience. He proved to be an energetic study for the rest of his life. Movies of Roosevelt and the Rough Riders show that they came to heroic attention at the very start of moving film. The original footage gives instruction about the importance of these warriors to TR's career and times. After his death, a series of patriotic representations kept the historic Roosevelt before the public. By the mid twentieth century, the Rough Riders had become a Western genre in their own right, as the cowboys continued to ride for good over evil. Finally, a centennial celebration, the cinema's best efforts commemorated TR and his men to an audience of Americans whose heroes were few.

THE FIRST PRESIDENT IN MOTION PICTURES

Theodore Roosevelt was the first president recorded significantly on film that moved. "Significantly" is the key word. Our understanding of TR cannot, and should not, be separated from his cinematic image. That we can see him now in motion and hear his voice is a triumph for American accomplishments, and for historians. For the third of his life that he held positions of leadership, he left his people and their descendants with a new type of record by which to assess him.

In 1897, *Hon. Theo. Roosevelt, Ass't Sec'y, U.S. Navy, Leaving White House* provided a motion-media event. He walked briskly down a sidewalk, turning before the camera for a good profile, with the White House in the background. Historians argue for the year 1896 as the best date for the start of this medium, largely based on the patents of the Edison interests and their competitors (Hampton 21). TR was savvy enough, and well founded as a Roosevelt, to be assertive in these experiments. He did so within a year, for better or worse. Born 27 October 1858, he was not yet forty years old. At this age previous presidents had been visually recorded, if at all, only by artists and still photographers. He was ambitious and qualified as an emerging leader.

TR served in a new Republican administration that would preside over the coming of the twentieth century. President William McKinley was the last of the Union's generation of soldiers who saved the nation in the Civil War and governed it thereafter. McKinley campaigned from his front porch in Ohio, and he became the first president ever to be recorded by motion media while in office. An assassin's bullet in 1901 denied more of his filmed image. McKinley remains a visually murky nineteenth-century figure, characterized by blending with his predecessors of the decades that closed the old era. They appear in interchangeable photographs as fat, old, ugly, bearded white men. Historians value the filming of McKinley's state funeral as well as the visual archives of the new century's young new president.[2]

THE ROUGH RIDERS

Films related to the Spanish-American War won widespread attention at the beginning of the new medium. Such current-event newsreels were "a revelation, and in 1898–1899 these were the first animated pictures to be seen by many people." The Edison Wargraph Company advertised "War views. All the best views of the Spanish-American War. Wonderfully realistic, thrilling and appalling" (Hampton 37).[3]

The American Mutoscope and Biograph Company provided two fine examples of TR and his volunteer cavalry. They featured what the public wanted to see—action and speed—as the riders thundered toward the viewers and then turned their horses. *Roosevelt's Rough Riders at Drill* was most likely filmed at the Rough Riders' camp in Texas before they departed for Florida and Cuba. For more emphasis on the colonel, TR led the riders to the camera, dismounted, and exited to his tent in *Col. Theodore Roosevelt and Officers of his Staff.* This movie was made after the successful campaign, in Camp Wikoff on Long Island, circa September 1898.

Some of the war movies were early newsreels that kept the public informed visually about breaking events. The Edison Company, with William Paley on camera, made many such films that documented the army's progress in war. *Military Camp at Tampa, Taken from Train,* circa 10 May 1898, gave a panoramic view of the large camp and its activities. A camera on a rapidly moving train shot the interesting film. *Roosevelt's Rough Riders Embarking for Santiago* showed the troopers busy on the docks on 8 June 1898. Similarly, *U.S. Troops Landing at Daiquiri, Cuba* recorded the first arrivals of General William Shafter's expeditionary force on 22 June 1898. The motion picture camera had gone to war. Or did it, really?

The people's patriotic enthusiasm for the victorious campaigns lasted much longer than did the war. The need to keep the arcades and nickelodeons supplied with fresh portrayals led to staged productions of events where the motion camera had never been. News and entertainment became confused at a time when the emerging industry's business was not yet much subject to ethics. The Edison Company accommodated its needs with the New Jersey National

Guard in the Orange Mountains of New Jersey in May 1899. *U.S. Infantry Supported by Rough Riders at El Caney* gave action entertainment—docudrama—devoid of historical veracity. The infantry fired, advanced, and fired again, followed by mounted Rough Riders "riding like demons, yelling and firing revolvers" (Library of Congress: *Spanish-American War in Motion Pictures*). Horses and guns also characterized *Skirmish of Rough Riders,* where no battle was even cited. For another example, Edison copyrighted and distributed a Vitagraph production *Raising Old Glory Over Morro Castle.* Promotions heralded the action: "Down falls the symbol of tyranny and oppression . . . and up goes the Banner of Freedom. In the distance are the turrets and battlements of Morro, the last foothold of Spain in America." Vitagraph used its studio rooftop in New York City, in front of a painted backdrop (*Spanish-American War in Motion Pictures*).[4]

THE CAVALRY'S LEADER

The cinema art, whether real or imagined, certainly elevated Colonel Roosevelt as a genuine war hero. He was immediately elected to be governor of New York, and then vice president in 1900. The American Mutoscope and Biograph Company caught his ceremonial prominence on 30 September 1899, in *Governor Roosevelt and Staff.* The occasion was New York City's homecoming parade for Admiral George Dewey, the hero of the recent war in the Pacific theater. The cameramen always sought their focus on TR.

Military units on horseback would escort Theodore Roosevelt wherever he attended important events for the rest of his life. Mounted honor guards of aging Rough Riders showed up whenever they could manage to be with him. Twelve of them did so for the former president in *TR's Reception in Albuquerque, N.M., 1916,* joined by another of their colleagues whom Roosevelt had appointed territorial governor of New Mexico. In *TR with Rough Rider Friends,* perhaps from the same western tour, their leader gently positioned their discussion for the motion camera's advantage. After all, the First Volunteer Cavalry as cowboys, governors, or president had become a national symbol held in the highest respect for its transformational leadership for a quarter of a century.

PATRIOTIC REPRESENTATIONS

The Rough Riders stimulated the author's interests in history and film. While researching the First Cavalry Regiment's decade of duty (1923–1933) at Fort D.A. Russell in Marfa, Texas, the military records offered a great story: the

Theodore Roosevelt, scholar and
soldier.

Library of Congress.

troopers of the historic regiment played the Rough Riders in a major movie.
The records presented the cavalry's experiences in the filming from August to
October 1926. The whole notion seemed terribly appropriate. Who better could
recreate the First Volunteer Cavalry than the First Cavalry Regiment? Hollywood used various units of the military services, so this was an early—if not
unique—cooperation.

In 1926, the nation was at peace, and the film industry paid. The army
could not afford to conduct innovative maneuvers at the Mexican border that
year. Officers were willing to make available their considerable resources in
men and animals. The mission of the project intended a heroic portrayal worthy of the subject. Its managers showed respect by paying for the train to transport its military actors, who were accustomed to marching across Texas, to the
actual sites in the San Antonio area where Roosevelt had gathered his troops.
On 16 August 1926, the First Cavalry Regiment entrained from Marfa on a
great adventure (*Cavalry Journal* 166).

Paramount and the Famous Players-Lasky recruited a real army for the commemoration. The twenty-sixth president's funeral in January 1919, which was filmed, had not been forgotten. The thirtieth anniversary was at hand of the public's discovery of Theodore Roosevelt—and of war and great power. Others of the regiment at Fort Clark, Brackettville, Texas, increased the size of the contingent.[5] The numbers involved in this project actually paralleled those of the real Rough Riders. Cecil B. DeMille was temporarily not with Paramount, but the publicity touting a "cast of thousands" approached accuracy.

At Roosevelt Field, San Antonio's old fairgrounds, the troopers and their mounts began making a movie. They were cast in scenes enlisting recruits, drilling recruits, and riding wild horses. In one shoot, the actor portraying Lieutenant Colonel Roosevelt formally reviewed the First Cavalry/Rough Riders. The men enjoyed the "de luxe" camp provided by the movie company as well as the amenities of the city.

The filming resumed at Camp Stanley, Texas, in order to recreate the battles of Kettle Hill and San Juan Hill. The troopers charged and recharged up hills, "until even the Director said we had this battle business down pat." Unfortunately, the novelty of the change from routine work and training began to wear off. At Camp Stanley, "practically marooned on a Texas hillside, with long hours of waiting in the sun for the movie director to receive an inspiration, the regiment decided that the movie game is a very poor occupation for the Regular Army" (*Cavalry Journal* 167, 171).[6]

THE MONUMENTAL SILENT FILM

Adolph Zukor for Paramount and Jesse Lasky for his Famous Players presented a large production in *The Rough Riders*. There were some problems. Theodore Roosevelt's portrayal presented one of them. The popular president remained well fixed in the public mind during the mid-1920s. No known actor was awarded the role. Hundreds of applicants were tested to play TR. The part went to an unknown citizen named Frank Hopper, simply because of his physical resemblance to Roosevelt. (Hopper got to be the "star," but it became his one and only movie credit.) The story ending also caused trouble. The filmmakers vacillated over how happy or sad the ending should be. They reshot the scene several times from different perspectives, and they used previews to help determine the final choice (*The Rough Riders* 1927).[7]

Eventually, in October 1927, the monumental film debuted about TR and his Rough Riders during the Spanish-American War. The thirteen reels ran for 105 minutes. It was an expensive extravaganza, following Metro-Goldwyn-Mayer's *Ben Hur* and Cecil B. DeMille's *The King of Kings* as the estimated fifth-most-costly movie. Providing for a real army certainly contributed toward the $1.6 million of expenses. Unfortunately, the Paramount Famous Players-Lasky production came at a time of major transition for the industry. It ended the era of the silent screen and missed the arrival of the honors of the Academy Awards (Hampton 342).

SIDNEY BLACKMER AND ANOTHER WAR

Unlike the unknown Frank Hopper, who got fifteen minutes of fame from Paramount, the actor Sidney Blackmer repeatedly portrayed Theodore Roosevelt during his career. Renewed interest in TR accompanied the presidency of his cousin and nephew, Franklin, especially as the world of the late 1930s exploded into another world war. Sidney Blackmer played President Theodore Roosevelt in six movies during the decade of conflict and trial from 1937 to 1948. Of course, the Rough Riders received attention from the film industry and the nation at war.[8]

Blackmer as Roosevelt began and ended with Hollywood fluff.[9] In between, Blackmer appeared in two of the Rough Rider Western genre (discussed later) and two dramatic historical productions. Warner Bros. in its films echoed the antifascist warnings to the nation of Time-Life, Henry Luce's print empire. *The Monroe Doctrine* (1939) developed educational parallels among the several presidents' efforts to block foreign intervention in the Americas. The legacy of John Quincy Adams and Henry Clay continued through Blackmer's TR and invited a second Roosevelt's role.[10]

Warner Bros. and Vitaphone hammered on the historical lesson in 1940 with *Teddy the Rough Rider*. Blackmer headed the cast in the documentary short that presented TR's political career from 1895 to the presidency in 1901. Foreign threats required the nation to fight, and the charge up San Juan Hill in Cuba was recreated. Rousing, patriotic music helped to rally the people, with "A Hot Time in the Old Town Tonight," "America," "Auld Lang Syne," and "There's a Long, Long Trail." This Rough Rider movie, at another time of great national danger, won the Academy Award for best short subject. The attack on Pearl Harbor followed later in 1941.

Warner Bros. went to war with *March on America!* (1942). The documentary short showed the heritage that Americans were fighting for, reviewing the struggle for freedom from the Pilgrims to Pearl Harbor. In Technicolor, it used excerpts from the studio's *Historical Featurettes*, interestingly combined with some original film as well as newsreels. Footage was incorporated from both *The Monroe Doctrine* and *Teddy the Rough Rider*.[11] The transformational leadership of Theodore in war, as portrayed by Sidney Blackmer, was importantly invoked as Franklin led the people in another conflict. The story of the Rough Riders again inspired and validated the American experience.

THE WESTERN GENRE

The winning of the American West actually continued when the motion camera arrived in the decade of the 1890s. The struggles with the Native Americans had ended, as had the open range with its near-continental cattle drives. The railroad had crossed the vast lands and then opened and integrated them into the national system. Still, an increasingly urban America, which had lost its demographic frontier, found in the man on horseback tending to his stock— the cowboy—links in both reality and imagination to the epic western settlement. The movie industry developed the story of the cowboy from its start. Western films became a staple, filled with action, danger, and romance. They featured early stars, such as Tom Mix, and many others followed over time. Not surprisingly, the Rough Riders became a focal point within the genre.

Theodore Roosevelt won his own credentials as a cowboy. A scion of advantage, he had traveled often through the old European world before he first visited the American West in 1883. After the death of his young bride, Alice Lee, he sought solace in 1884 on the Badlands frontier. He bought ranchlands and established herds at the western border of the Dakota-Montana territories. There he learned firsthand about working with rough men against beasts, nature, and each other. TR experienced the customs and plight of Native Americans, as well as law and order at the end of a revolver. The rugged majesty of western natural sites and resources engaged the New York Knickerbocker, who became more rounded as an American. Others managed his ranch for many years after he returned east, and he pursued the interests of conservation for the rest of his life of transformational leadership.[12]

It was in 1886, during border tensions with Mexico, that Theodore Roosevelt first proposed the raising of a volunteer cavalry of cowboys. Still in his twenties during his Dakota period, he could see himself leading his western comrades into foreign war. Congress provided the occasion in April 1898 by authorizing the muster from the remaining continental territories of Arizona, New Mexico, Oklahoma, and the Indian Territory. He and Leonard Wood, his friend from the regular army, secured their commissions and headed to Texas. The choice of San Antonio for the gathering and training of the westerners brought many Texans into the ranks. About fifty men from backgrounds of old families and Ivy League halls came from Roosevelt's own privileged class. Most of the states added some representatives in the force of one thousand men. TR often spent his own money to help his men meet the national emergency of war with Spain.[13]

The cowboy cavalry caught the people's attention and became the popular heroes of the campaign in Cuba. TR accepted the name "Rough Riders" and used it thereafter for the First Volunteer Cavalry. Before departing from Florida, the officers were forced to reduce the numbers to less than six hundred men for their part in the invasion of Cuba. The lack of transport ships also required all but the officers to leave their horses and mules behind. "Little Texas" was the name of TR's own pony. His men fought as dismounted cavalry. A quarter of them, both distinguished and common, were wounded and killed in battle. Within six months, Roosevelt wrote his account, *The Rough Riders*. Finley Peter Dunne's character "Mr. Dooley" quipped that the title should have been "Alone in Cubia." TR was "delighted." His Rough Riders had made the facts of war, and the national legends would follow (Roosevelt).

HOLLYWOOD AND THE COWBOY ROUGH RIDERS

Hollywood soon found in the Rough Riders all the necessary elements for its Western movies. Roosevelt's men from Texas and the territories had included cowboys and Indians, sheriffs and outlaws, rangers and gamblers. They had come together to fight for the virtues of truth, justice, and the American way. After the era of President Roosevelt and silent films had faded, the memory of his common cowboys could still inspire the imagination about the winning of the west. The creation of cinema stories about fictional, individual Rough Riders added credentials to the otherwise formula Westerns. They rode horses and fired guns, and they chased bad guys and saved women. Hollywood was less interested in the historical events than in the heroic legacy of the Rough Riders.

The opening scenes feature newspapers with sensational headlines about war with Spain and victories in Cuba. Then the railroad delivers the veteran to his cow town's welcome. Soon he discovers that bad men were after the gold from the mine and the deed to the ranch. With a toast of campfire coffee to the Colonel, the hero summons old colleagues like "Arizona Jack" to the new cause. A location in Texas near the border allowed for Spanish complications and stereotypes. Eventually, the Rough Riders outsmart and vanquish the slackers, and the hero wins the beautiful daughter. Such entertainment was the contribution of Republic Pictures to the genre in *Rough Riders Round-up.* Roy Rogers got to sing. The lessons in this portrayal in 1939 invoked another round-up for the nation in foreign peril.[14]

The plots and places changed as the Rough Riders ranged across the Old West in these movies. The cowboy veterans often served as lawmen—marshal, sheriff, border patrol—in these films about the winning of the West.[15] The character of Theodore Roosevelt was not necessary, but Sidney Blackmer was available. He played TR in two Westerns worthy of mention: *Buffalo Bill* (1944) and *In Old Oklahoma* (1943). All sense of actual historic times and events became blurred and lost.[16]

Eventually, the story, or at least the title, made the transition from the silver screen to television. *The Rough Riders* became a TV series during the 1958–1959 season from ZIV Television Programs. General Eisenhower was president, and he enjoyed Westerns, especially the works of Zane Grey. By then, the name of TR's cavalry was used generically pretty much for anybody who rode across the West doing good over evil. This time three veterans of the Civil War banded together, a rebel and two Yankees, to provide continuity for these thirty-nine programs that won the West.[17]

Over a century the cowboy gave inspiration to movie and television portrayals of the settlement of the frontier. The same has been true for art, history, and literature. Even the story of Roosevelt's cowboy cavalry in the Spanish-American War has become a part of the larger Western genre. The cowboy as a veteran hero, divorced from the historic details of time and place, and sometimes even singing, still displayed the virtues that made legends. With or without their colonel and president as leader, TR's men have captured and held the nation's attention. The Rough Riders became both legend and symbol.

A CENTENNIAL CELEBRATION BY TURNER NETWORK TELEVISION

The Spanish-American War closed the nineteenth century, but it also opened the new twentieth century as the United States assumed global great power. Thereafter the nation's people and treasure would often be tested outside its continental borders. These military conflicts over the decades were usually understood and supported, but there were those who called the American mission into question. As the twentieth century passed, reflections on the Span-

Library of Congress.

The Cowboy Rough Riders in victory, 1898.

ish war can be made in this larger context from a perspective of one hundred years. Turner Network Television (TNT) undertook the cinematic task with a centennial celebration of a much-remembered part, *Theodore Roosevelt and the Rough Riders*. Turner's four-hour epic production represented the best efforts of film art. The commemoration invites examination of historical portrayal by way of the movies.

The conflict of 1898 goes down on the collective record as one of the good wars. Its purpose to end the chaos in Cuba and evict the Spanish imperialists was broadly backed at home. The policy of the Monroe Doctrine—hands off the western hemisphere—appeared to be justification, and the Teller Amendment, which asserted that Cuba would not be claimed by the United States, elevated the mission. The people mobilized to offer their sons, who fought with valor and honor. Victory was achieved rapidly in the "Splendid Little War." William Jennings Bryan, the leader of the opposition party, tried to participate, although he ended up in a hospital tent in Florida with dysentery, and he failed to rally the doubters in 1900. President McKinley won reelection on his record by a landslide with a genuine war hero standing by his side.[18]

CRITICAL VIEWS

This patriotic interpretation remains popular and valid, even though specialists know much about the bad side of the war. Historians debate the origins of the war as a manifestation of imperialism, but they accept the results as a fact of empire. The motivations based on economics and power usually pass scrutiny, although not without serious challenge to the exploitive ways of the newly industrializing United States. The emotional motivation, however, compromised patriotism with the racism of the day. The Teller Amendment was qualified by the Platt Amendment, which attached strings to Cuba's sovereignty and fostered dependency. Castro's revolution followed fifty years later. The Philippines was another story. Naval warfare took Americans there, but there was no need to stay. Empire later required a nasty war of imposition. How could a democracy subjugate others against their will? It could not in the long run. The annexation of Hawaii brought vulnerability to attack but eventually turned out well through war and statehood. The status of Puerto Rico, however, remains unresolved after a century.

CAN THESE OPPOSING VIEWS BE RECONCILED?

Leadership helps to cut the knots. The Spanish war began righteously by the old century's terms, but its results demanded transformation of the nation in the world by the new century's leaders. Theodore Roosevelt's leadership demonstrated both of these truths. He wanted it, fought it, and managed matters afterward. The nation accepted the responsibilities and did well by them over time. This war provided military and political heroes as did both world wars. Korea confused military and political objectives, and it left difficult results that still need to be addressed. Nevertheless, both Truman and MacArthur were heroes as leaders despite their partisans and critics. The lesson indicates that quality leadership is important in both war and peace and that sometimes it comes from the same person: Washington, Jackson, Grant, both Roosevelts, and Eisenhower. What is wrong with having a real hero? What is wrong with recognizing leaders who never had to say "I am not a crook," "Trust me," and "I never had sexual relations with that woman"?

The motion media has much to say in answer. The industry often muddles the message in delivery while affirming the result in the popular culture. Take the last half of the twentieth century and its battle with Soviet communism. The Cold War and its Vietnam chapter dominated the times. Nothing about the misery of Vietnam involved U.S. leader heroes. American leadership failed under Kennedy and Johnson. Film art has given many outstanding creations to help heal the nation's wounds. They all deal with victims, especially badly used soldiers. Was Richard Nixon the only unsung victim because he ended the Vietnam War? The Cold War was the larger global context. It has many real leader heroes, portrayed in Hollywood as part of the historical perversion and consensus. Should the historical record credit Truman more for starting it than Reagan for ending it? The motion media leaves records of popular culture to help find the answers.

The decades of the 1890s and the 1990s parallel each other. Each faced economic difficulties and offered enormous technical opportunities without a strong ethic of the public welfare. McKinley and the first President Bush led the nation through successful wars of ambition and interest. Both handled the military victories well, and both left behind political challenges. There the history differs: McKinley left Roosevelt in power; Bush was defeated. Bill Clinton had many merits, but he fumbled with the military abroad without defining his world of the post–Vietnam and Cold War eras. He even ordered "wag the dog" bombings across the continents at suspicious times of personal setbacks. (Zippergate replaced the honor gates at the White House.) Now President Bush faces war with historical models provided by TR and others, including his father.

HISTORY AND FILM OVER A CENTURY

Turner Network Television's *Rough Riders* came at a time of presidential disgrace rather than heroic leadership. It was made with a notion of history that fitted the popular culture of television. The production looked to patriotic interpretations for its centennial view, and most of the contentious issues about empire remained unargued. It kept to the specifics of its focus on TR and his brave volunteers.[19]

A positive popular response to a series of recent war films placed the TNT work with distinguished contemporaries. To mention just a few, Turner Picture's *Gettysburg* (1993) dealt with the Civil War, Steven Spielberg's *Saving Private Ryan* (1998) with World War II, and Oliver Stone's *Platoon* (1986) with the Vietnam War. Several of TNT's major actors appeared in such war movies. Tom Berenger was in *Platoon*, *Gettysburg*, and others before his masterful portrayal of TR. Also in *Gettysburg* were Sam Elliott, as the Arizona lawman, Bucky O'Neil, and Gary Busey, whose old Confederate General "Fighting Joe" Wheeler injected comic relief. In *Rough Riders*, at a turn of a battle in Cuba, he shouted "We've got the Yankees on the run!" The military heritage expressed in these movies gave reassurance in the 1990s as the nation searched for its new mission and role in the world.

Roosevelt's own version of *The Rough Riders* provided a basic textbook. He was far from "Alone in Cubia," as Mr. Dooley had quipped, and his characterizations of his men became the basis for many of the screen personalities. These portrayals, whether of real or composite figures, ranged from Colonel Leonard Wood (Dale Dye) through Indian Bob (Bob Primeaux). They included other such important roles as Craig Wadsworth (Christopher Noth), Henry Nash (Brad Johnson II), and Rafael Castillo (Francesco Quinn). While TR himself was introduced as more of a novice—a four-eyed eastern dude—than his earlier military experiences warranted, his maturation soon followed with the realities of war. Roosevelt's colorful prose gave inspiration for much of the TNT commemoration. Motion-film archives also allowed the study of past portrayals, so in a sense previous productions became additional historical footnotes.

Writer and director John Milius followed a theme that TR had developed: the uniting of the north and south with the west as a new generation beyond the Civil War fought for a common national cause. His film gave witness to TR's words:

> Everywhere we saw the Stars and Stripes, and everywhere we were told, half-laughingly, by grizzled ex-Confederates that they had never dreamed in the bygone days of bitterness to greet the old flag as they now were greeting it, and to send their sons, as now they were sending them, to fight and die under it. (Roosevelt)

On the one hand, Milius significantly included the Native-American and Mexican-American volunteers along with the African American troops of the regular army, as had Roosevelt in his writing. Development of the current politically correct emphases, fortunately, brought enhancement to the historical record. "Black Jack" Pershing importantly led "Smoked Yankees" in Cuba. While TR did not refer to the future general of World War I, whose reputation was also enhanced by action in the Philippines, TNT emphasized the convergence in the Cuban campaign of their heroic statures.

On the other hand, license beyond history occurred in the thematic handling of yellow journalism. TR never dealt with the topic of the jingo press as such, but he covered exploits of newsmen Edward Marshall and Richard Harding Davis. They became compressed as one while Frederic Remington and Stephen Crane, never mentioned by TR, received creative credits. Tying in the author of *The Red Badge of Courage* as more of a drunk than a coward, Crane got to take the photograph of the victors at TR's request: "Will you be so kind, Mr. Crane, with your camera, to take a picture of this regiment on this glorious hill, for we will always live in its shadow" (*Rough Riders* 1997).

Roosevelt ignored the occasion in his account, and William Dinwiddie lost his fifteen minutes of fame as the real photographer. Vastly more regrettable, George Hamilton, as William Randolph Hearst, pranced on horseback in fantasies around battlefields in Cuba. TNT would have served the record better by turning the camera around. There was yellow cinema as well as yellow press. The presence in Cuba of the very pioneers of motion movies never got into the show. Historians sometimes do battle for the last word in popular culture.

The quality of TNT's *Rough Riders* as an action drama about war rests with the battle scenes over the San Juan heights. The filmmakers went to considerable lengths to elevate their art, perhaps as much through changing technology as had Paramount with the First Cavalry Regiment in 1926. The actors trained together arduously during the filming in Texas, and careful technical measures sought authenticity. For example, the use of firearms and artillery can pass critical scrutiny. TR wrote enough on the subject as to leave virtually a technical manual. The overall results were strikingly effective and downright impressive. Here, as elsewhere, the lapses and distortions from the historical record detracted little from the film's achievements. The fact that TR rode into battle on "Little Texas" would surely not concern the viewers. For them, Tom Berenger successfully captured the warrior's spirited leadership in the test under fire. The war scenes accomplished the thematic goals. This production was a fine, entertaining movie.

HISTORY, FILM, AND POPULAR CULTURE

Filmmakers may seek the objective of "reality," but their cinematic arts serve other, subjective purposes as well. Entertainment is an end in itself, and docudrama is the "reality" of the results. The popular culture can be perverted by awful products whose makers assert that they can "intuit" history. Oliver Stone has made this claim without apology. Even historical studies can be abused by such arrogance. Consider the irresponsible techniques of Edmund Morris and his publisher for their fantasy that poses as a biography of Ronald Reagan. On the other hand, fortunately, the popular culture may benefit from well-made productions that reach a much broader audience than the usual dissertations of history. Turner Network Television's *Rough Riders* took the high ground. The historical credentials can be recognized and the portrayals at least can be defended while the message of a centennial TR film renewed America in a time of need.

The story of Theodore Roosevelt and the Rough Riders continues to manifest long-held truths and traditions. Film portrayals for the public began at the time when motion media was an experimental exploration through technology. As the industry returned to the Rough Rider story often during both peace and war, it is interesting that caricature on occasion resulted while revisionism never did. History and popular culture made common cause. TR and his volunteer cavalry won the endearment of the nation and have held it for the hundred years since. They became both American legend and symbol of the rare transformational leadership still sought as George W. Bush leads in a new kind of war at the start of the twenty-first century.

NOTES

1. For a recent analysis of presidential leadership, see James MacGregor Burns and Georgia J. Sorenson, *Dead Center: Clinton-Gore Leadership and the Perils of Moderation.*

2. Historical preservation has provided film images of Roosevelt. The credit goes first to the Theodore Roosevelt Association (TRA). The decades of work to gather a large quantity of motion picture negative and positive stock earns the TRA listing with preservationists such as Ann Pamela Cunningham, who did Washington's Mount Vernon. The TRA turned over its historical treasure in 1962, when the Roosevelt House became the Theodore Roosevelt Birthplace National Historic Site. The Library of Congress received grants from the National Endowment for the Humanities, beginning during Gerald Ford's presidency in 1975, for providing cataloging and computer access to its entire Roosevelt collection. The Roosevelt records are among the most prominent at the Library of Congress, partly because of the creation of separate presidential libraries that begin with the Herbert Hoover administration (1929–1933). The Motion Picture, Broadcasting, and Recorded Sound Division (MP/B/RS) opened its motion-film archives of TR and his times to the World Wide Web in September 1999, another centennial celebration.

The collection reveals that no president was more cooperative and photogenic during the era of the silent newsreel. The TRA passed on 381 titles of nitrate-base films, now preserved on safety-base stock. During the 1920s and 1930s, about fifteen subject documentaries combined newsreels and other films with photographs, and eight of these are still distributed by the TRA. The Library of Congress chose 104 motion pictures and four sound recordings for Internet access in *Theodore Roosevelt: His Life and Times on Film*. Based on the quality of footage and events, eighty-seven came from the TRA, supplemented by seventeen films from the Paper Print Film Collection at MP/B/RS. Other Paper Print films are also available on line, especially from MP/B/RS's *The Spanish-American War in Motion Pictures*. The Edison Company made sound recordings during the presidential campaign of 1912. All together, the preservationists of the Library of Congress have given ready access to a remarkable, comprehensive collection about TR and his America (Library of Congress: Gillespie).

3. These early films appeared in peep-show parlors and penny arcades, as well as on life-size screens at the "Nickel-Odeon" theaters. Footage varied, from fifty feet for peep-cabinet showings to one thousand feet (one reel) for the screen productions lasting fifteen to twenty minutes. Edison battled with early competitors, such as Biograph, Vitagraph, and Mutoscope. The films circulated widely, and copyrights received little respect before 1912 (Hampton chapter 1).

4. Regardless of how such films were represented to the public then, the Library of Congress collections have been carefully annotated for the benefit of historical understanding.

5. The border fort site would later become home to the "Waynamo," the imaginative version of the site of Texas independence created by John Wayne and others.

6. After two months, the cavalry's role in the film finally ended; the troopers and their horses departed on 20 October 1926. The First Cavalry began a four-day march of some 150 miles to Fort Clark. From a military standpoint, acting as extras for the movies may have been "the poorest training possible" (*Cavalry Journal* 171). The cavalry had demonstrated, however, the professional prowess of men and mounts that the movie company had sought for the public. The First Cavalry Regiment again enjoyed the Pullman route for the return to Fort D.A. Russell and the command of the Big Bend border with Mexico. Its site at Marfa in Presidio County would be revisited often by moviemakers, to mention only *Giant* (1956), the national film of Texas.

7. The patriotic representation has also been entitled *The Trumpet Calls*. A distinguished historian and Roosevelt scholar, Dr. Hermann Hagedorn, received credit for the story. Victor Fleming directed the movie, and James Wong Howe did the cinematography. The Famous Players cast included Noah Beery, Mary Astor, George Bancroft, Charles Farrell, Charles Emmett Mack, and Fred Kohler. Fred Lindsay played Colonel Leonard Wood, the First Volunteer Cavalry's commander from the regular army.

8. Sidney Blackmer (1895–1973) grew up during the TR era. He gained his first movie credit as a teenager in the film classic *The Perils of Pauline* (1914). Fifty movies later, he had reached the age of forty, the same age as TR when he became a national leader. TR had been well documented on film, and Blackmer became Hollywood's Roosevelt. His minicareer as TR, however, did not end in typecasting. He appeared in fifty other movies during the same years. Additional films after his last TR role and his transition to television helped him to accomplish a remarkable achievement of 119 movie and 18 notable TV acting credits. He last performed on TV in 1970 at age seventy-five.

9. In 1937 Darryl F. Zanuck and Twentieth Century Fox offered *This Is My Affair*, with an impressive contract studio cast headed by Robert Taylor, Barbara Stanwyck,

Victor McLaglen, Brian Donlevy, and John Carradine. The plot was impossible. Sydney Blackmer as President Roosevelt sent a navy lieutenant to infiltrate a gang of well-placed bank robbers in the midwest. Taylor wooed Stanwyck. A critic observed: "If the representation of Teddy Roosevelt in this movie is accurate, how did anyone stand being around him?" (*Internet Movie Database*). A tear-jerk Warner Bros. drama, *My Girl Tisa* (1948), gave Lilli Palmer inspiration as a devoted immigrant girl trying to bring her father to the United States. San Wanamaker and Akim Tamiroff were involved in the parlor piece from the play *Ever the Beginning*. Blackmer took his final exit as TR.

10. Nanette Fabray, as the Spanish female love interest, and George "Superman" Reeves also performed.

11. The historical montage also included editing from *Give Me Liberty* (1936), *The Declaration of Independence* (1938), *The Bill of Rights* (1939), and *Lincoln in the White House* (1939).

12. For Roosevelt bibliographies, see Theodore Roosevelt Association, <http://www.theodoreroosevelt.org/index.html>; *American Presidents: Life Portraits*, <http://wwwamericanpresidents.org/bibliography/25.asp>; *TR on Film*, <http://memory.loc.gov/ammem/trfhome.html>.

13. For Rough Rider bibliographies see *U.S. History Interactive Site Contents: Theodore Roosevelt—Rough Riders*, <http://www.geocities.com/heartland/pointe/3048/bio/tr/trchap6.html>.

14. Duncan Reynaldo, born in Romania, played a Mexican, before the Cisco Kid found a sidekick named Poncho.

15. Buck Jones was *Arizona Bound* (1941) in a rather dark and brooding Monogram Picture, also known as *Rough Riders*. Buck was called upon to save a stage line from a gang of robbers. He gets framed and must prove his innocence while springing a trap on the desperados. A series of *Rough Rider Adventures* was made. Republic Pictures returned to the thematic genre without Roy Rogers as its singing cowboy but rather with Tom London as the star in *Rough Riders of Cheyenne* (1945) and *Rough Riders of Durango* (1951).

16. *Buffalo Bill* (1944) traced the legendary life of William F. Cody from scout to showman. Joel McCrea, Maureen O'Hara, and Linda Darnell headed the cast for Twentieth Century Fox. Anthony Quinn played an Indian and Edgar Buchanan a sergeant. The dime novelist Ned Buntline was acknowledged with a role, as were presidents Hayes and Roosevelt—and even Queen Victoria. Perhaps as mythic, *In Old Oklahoma* (1943), also known as *War of the Wildcats*, in which a cowboy and an oilman competed for leases on Indian lands and for the schoolmarm. This John Wayne movie from Republic included Dale Evans, "Gabby" Hayes, and Blackmer as TR. The action Western, "Glorifying the Romantic Pioneer Spirit of America," was nominated for Oscars for best music and best sound in 1944.

17. The Union's "Captain Flagg" and his Rough Riders, one of whom wore his six-shooters backward, appeared with an impressive cast of guest stars in each episode. Recognition here goes only to actors known by the author: John Carradine, Lon Chaney Jr., James Coburn, Mike Connors, William Conrad, Russ Conway, Broderick Crawford, DeForest Kelly, Joyce Meadows, Leonard Nimoy, Jeanette Nolan, Warren Oates, and Dan Sheridan. Ronald Reagan was not on the list.

18. For war bibliographies see *The World of 1898: Spanish-American War,* <http://lcweb.loc.gov/rr/hispanic/1898/> and *The Spanish-American War in Motion Pictures,* <http://memory.loc.gov/ammem/sawhtml/sawhome.html>.

19. Producers Tom Berenger, Moctesuma Esparza, Robert Katz, Larry Levinson, and William MacDonald, *Rough Riders,* 1997, <http://tnt.turner.com/movies/tntoriginals/roughriders/prod.home.html>.

WORKS CITED

American Presidents: Life Portraits. <http://www.americanpresidents.org/bibliography/25.asp>.

Burns, James MacGregor, and Georgia J. Sorenson. *Dead Center: Clinton-Gore Leadership and the Perils of Moderation.* New York: Scribner, 1999.

Cavalry Journal. 36 (January 1927).

Hampton, Benjamin B. *History of the American Film Industry: From its Beginnings to 1931.* 1931. Reprint, New York: Dover Publications, 1970.

Internet Movie Database. <http://www.imdb.com>. All motion pictures cited in the text and notes.

Library of Congress. Gillespie, Veronica M. *T.R. on Film: The Theodore Roosevelt Association Collection at the Library of Congress.*

_____. *Last Days of a President: Films of McKinley and the Pan American Exposition. 1901.* <http://memory.loc.gov/ammem/paper/mckhome.html>.

_____. *Spanish-American War in Motion Pictures.* <http://memory.loc.gov/ammem/sawhtml/sawhome.html>.

_____. *Theodore Roosevelt: His Life and Times on Film.* <http://memory.loc.gov./ammem/trfhtml/trfhome.html>. Includes *About the Collection, The Paper Print Film Collection at the Library of Congress,* and *Sound Recordings of Theodore Roosevelt's Voice.*

Morris, Edmund. *Dutch: A Memoir of Ronald Reagan.* New York: Random House, 1999.

Roosevelt, Theodore. *The Rough Riders.* 1902. Reprint, New York: Da Capo Press, 1990.

Rough Riders. 1997. <http://tnt.turner.com/movies/tntoriginals/roughriders/prod.home.html>.

Smythe, Donald. *Guerrilla Warrior: The Early Life of John J. Pershing.* New York: Charles Scribner's Sons, 1973.

Stone, Oliver. "In Filming History: Question, Disbelieve, Defy." *The Chronicle of Higher Education.* 14 July 2000.

Theodore Roosevelt Association. <http://www.theodoreroosevelt.org/index.html>.

U.S. History Interactive Site Contents: Theodore Roosevelt-Rough Riders. <http://www.geocities.com/heartland/pointe/3048/bio/tr/trchap6.html>.

World of 1898: Spanish-American War. <http://1cweb.loc.gov/rr/hispanic/1898/>.

Donald E. Staples

WILSON IN TECHNICOLOR

An Appreciation

Woodrow Wilson, twenty-eighth president
of the United States, 1913–1921.

WOODROW WILSON AND THE CINEMA

In 1915, D.W. Griffith released his masterpiece film, *The Birth of a Nation*, to the
public; he also held a private screening in the White House for President
Woodrow Wilson. This was the first recorded showing of a feature film in the
White House, and President Wilson reacted by stating that, "It is like writing
history with lightning" (Cook 77). As a historian who wrote extensively, Wilson
was obviously impressed. It was to be expected, however, Griffith played on
Wilson's academic ego by quoting from Wilson's writings on the screen. Since
this was a silent film with all of the description and dialogue printed on the
screen, audiences were used to reading complicated title cards. Griffith gave
them historical quotations complete with attribution; he even referenced cer-

tain photographs and cartoons that he recreated on motion picture film. Below are frame quotes from Wilson's *History of the American People:*

> Adventurers swarmed out of the North, as much the enemies of one race as of the other, to cozen, beguile, and use the Negroes . . . In the villages the negroes were office holders, men who knew none of the uses of authority, except intolerances.

Next frame:

> The policy of the congressional leaders wrought . . . a veritable overthrow of civilization in the South . . . in their determination to "*put the white South under the heel of the black South.*"
>
> Woodrow Wilson

Next frame:

> The white men were roused by a mere instinct of self-preservation . . . until at last there had sprung into existence a great Ku Klux Klan, a veritable empire of the South to protect the Southern country.
>
> Woodrow Wilson (Griffith 4-14)

Even though Wilson was nineteen years older than Griffith—and had therefore personally experienced the War Between the States as a young boy—both men had similar backgrounds and shared similar views of the Civil War and Reconstruction. Both men grew up in the South and had fathers who had been officers of the Confederate Army. The stories they heard were much the same from the veterans, and these facts and folklore informed both Wilson's writing and Griffith's filmmaking, especially for *The Birth of a Nation.*

Many historians, journalists, and other citizens condemned the film as racist, and protests were organized in several cities in response to the film. At least eight states banned the film, and President Wilson "was forced to retract his praise publicly and to suggest that the film had used its brilliant technique in the service of specious ends" (Cook 78). The NAACP vilified both Wilson and Griffith for their images of Reconstruction in volume five of *The History of the American People* and in *The Birth of a Nation* and also because neither Wilson nor Griffith capitalized the word "Negro," a word for which the NAACP had been crusading for at least four years. Even Griffith soon realized that bits of the film were inflammatory, and he removed about ten minutes of film, 169 shots (Cook 77).

Historian John Hope Franklin commented on the power of movies to influence public opinion and refashion history:

> As an eloquent statement of the position of most white Southerners using a new and increasingly influential medium of communication and as an instrument that deliberately and successfully undertook to use propaganda as history, the influence of *The Birth of a Nation* on the current view of reconstruction has been greater than any other single force. (Griffith 443)

As a matter of fact, the Klan did use the film for decades as a recruiting tool.

WOODROW WILSON AS CINEMA

Woodrow Wilson could hardly have imagined that, thirty years later, his life would be the subject of another propaganda film, Darryl F. Zanuck's *Wilson* (1944). Like *The Birth of a Nation*, *Wilson* was a long (154-minute) statement on the need for peace in the world, for a type of "reconstruction" if you will. The general public, however, met the film with apathy like it did the League of Nations, and it has been pronounced a "flop." But it was not a flop to this writer, who, at the age of ten, thought that *Wilson* was a wonderful and inspiring motion picture experience. At least in the eyes of one youth, the images were beautiful, the sets gorgeous, the costumes brilliant, and the acting was at a very high, believable level. The story was consuming for its entire 154 minutes, and Alexander Knox, as Wilson, was on the screen most of the time with his commanding stature and imperious look. Knox's mellifluous voice was hypnotic, and the use of newsreel footage was fascinating. The professionals of the film industry understood the value of what they had seen on the screen; the members of the Academy of Motion Picture Arts and Sciences nominated the film for ten Academy Awards, and *Wilson* won five of them. Color cinematography and color art direction were two of the awards given at a time when these categories had both color and black-and-white sections. *Wilson* was photographed in full three-strip Technicolor using Technicolor film, Technicolor cameras, Technicolor processing, and Technicolor consultants. It was beautiful and memorable on the big screen at the Belle Meade Theatre in Nashville, Tennessee.

Other significant nominations were for best picture, best director (Henry King), and best actor (Alexander Knox). Darryl F. Zanuck received the special

Irving Thalberg Award often given to outstanding producers and in this case
for a labor of love.

THE VISION OF DARRYL F. ZANUCK

Zanuck was a very patriotic American and good Methodist, born and raised in
Nebraska, who had planned to make a significant film after he returned from
World War II as a colonel. (He never bothered to correct persons who wrongly
presumed that he was one of the cabal of film moguls whose roots were Jewish
and middle–European.) He felt that the American public was ready for a serious film that involved politics and the future of the world. He had become a
good acquaintance of the Roosevelts while at the same time becoming a very
close friend of Wendell Willkie. Of Willkie he said, "He's such a nice decent
man. He's the only pol I know who doesn't fill the basin with muck every time
he washes his hands" (Mosley 212). Willkie and Zanuck were both fans of
Woodrow Wilson, admiring his politics, his ethics, and his old-fashioned
Presbyterianism, so Zanuck abandoned his prewar plans for a film on the life
of labor leader Samuel Gompers and turned to the story of a professor who
became a politician—Woodrow Wilson. Zanuck had worked for Wilson once
when he was an army private and Wilson was his commander in chief during
World War I.

The production of *Wilson* was to Darryl F. Zanuck what *Gone With the Wind*
was to David O. Selznick. These were films from the heart, and every ounce of
energy, money, and time was utilized to create their epics. Zanuck was convinced that the American public was ready for films that mattered. In an interview he stated:

> You might ask why I am doing *Wilson*. First off, I am doing it because I think it is
> the right thing to do at this time. I think that it will serve a tremendous purpose
> for our company, for our industry, and for our country, and furthermore, I will
> not start shooting it until I am completely satisfied that I have the opportunity of
> making it a popular entertainment. I will at least be compensated by making an
> important contribution that has the advantage of being significant and impor-
> tant. (Gussow 109–10)

WILSON: THE FILM

Wilson opens with the seal of the President of the United States of America with
the words "Twentieth Century-Fox presents Darryl F. Zanuck's production of"

(and then a full frame in caps) "*WILSON*" superimposed on top of it; then two paragraphs in two different frames are superimposed.

The first reads:

> Sometimes the life
> of a man mirrors the life of
> a nation. The destiny of
> our country was crystallized
> in the life and times of
> Washington and Lincoln . . .
> and perhaps too in the life
> of another president . . .

The second:

> . . . this is the story of
> America and the story of
> a man . . . Woodrow Wilson.
> 28th president
> of the United States.

Zanuck insists that the audience in the theater should know that this is an important, serious film and that they should sit up and look and listen with gravity. This is reinforced with the orchestral music on the soundtrack—"Hail To the Chief" and "God Bless America."

"Princeton University 1909" is then superimposed over pictures of the campus moving from right to left. This is not the way we read, and it is somewhat distasteful aesthetically and often physically uncomfortable. Nevertheless, the images of Princeton in the fall are lovely, and ivy-covered walls are featured. After a couple of still shots of buildings, the scene quickly dissolves into the marching band at the Princeton–Yale football game of that year. The teams run out onto the field; the scoreboard is shown; and the Wilson family is on the front row. The camera dollies in to heroic low-angle shots of Wilson cheering the team on and the doctor waiting with his bag and a couple of sets of crutches. The shots of the various types of 1909 football headgear start a series of comic sidebars that continue throughout the film. At the end of this sequence, Wilson consoles the Princeton quarterback with a line that foreshadows the ending of the film: "You played a great game, but, anyone is allowed to stumble once in his life."

Mr. and Mrs. Wilson's southern heritage is reinforced one evening when they and their three daughters sing "My Old Kentucky Home" around the piano. This is one of several musical interludes, the most formal being a stage performance by Eddie Foy Jr. portraying his famous father, a vaudeville performer.

When Senator "Big Ed" Jones approaches Wilson to run for governor of New Jersey, Mr. Wilson's academic publications are shown on his library bookshelf early on with a comic bit: one of Senator Jones's political cronies implies that he has read *History of the American People, Constitutional Government in the United States,* and *Mere Literature.* Wilson's college textbook, *The State,* was not shown (Smith 27).

Henry King directed *Wilson;* however, we usually refer to it as a "Zanuck film." For an *auteurist* critic, this is a wide departure but a necessary one. King was Zanuck's favorite director in the 1930s and 1940s. This meant that King did exactly what Zanuck wanted him to do, with style and flourish. On this production Zanuck was even more demanding: appearing on the set, writing memos, rewriting the script, and micromanaging the project. One sequence was copied from *Citizen Kane,* which had been released three years prior to *Wilson.*

Wilson's first major speech in the New Jersey gubernatorial race is delivered in a huge auditorium, a scene quite reminiscent of Kane's speech in Madison Square Garden. The gigantic portrait of the candidate is mounted on the back of the stage, dwarfing the real-life person. The low angle from the orchestra floor makes the candidate grow into the large stature of a political personality. An extremely long, high-angle shot from the back of the balcony looks like the matte shot in *Citizen Kane* where Boss Jim Gettys views the proceedings from a technical booth in the back. Both have a line in their speeches that gets a laugh. In *Wilson* it is, "Good heavens, no political experience? I wonder if any of these gentlemen have ever attended a faculty meeting or seen the wives of the trustees in action." In both films, the candidates make headlines by swearing to get rid of the "bosses." Visually there are many similarities, and the cuts to close-ups of the family and the use of arms and other body language by the speakers are identical. The advantage in *Wilson* is Technicolor. The colors are saturated, and the red, white, and blue of the conventions and rallies stand out in patriotic assurance. The presidential conventions of 1912 and 1916 are beautifully recreated with all of the pre-TV manic show and commotion. The use of hand fans continually gives action and motion to every scene of the crowds, with the loud speeches and bands playing adding an audio frenzy.

Critics writing about *Citizen Kane* often mention the use of ceilings, both low and high, because they had not been dominant in past films. William Wyler had shown them in 1939 and John Huston in 1941; however, this practice was not popular because of the expense and technical difficulty imposed by blocking off an area normally used for motion picture lighting units and microphones. In *Wilson* ceilings are used extensively and to very good effect. This is particularly evident in the shots of the interior of the White House and specifically in the Lincoln Bedroom with accompanying dialogue about the bed itself. The use of dark shadows and area lighting provides a dramatic feel to even the most routine scenes. The chiaroscuro lighting conveys the loneliness at the top and foreshadows the tragedy of the end.

In one scene Wilson is shown doing his own typing. This must have been a surprising note for 1944, but he had been a teacher and writer in an era when the typewriter was a refreshing innovation. The schoolteacher label is mentioned several times, and one campaign sign reads, "Elect the Princeton School Master." Senator "Big Ed" Jones often dismisses Wilson's actions and words by saying, "You have got to remember that he's a school teacher and sometimes he treats us like one of his students." Wilson does a brilliant job of dressing down the German ambassador and sending him back to Germany. This and other speeches show his eloquence; he had a larger vocabulary than most of our presidents, with the imperious look and patrician attitude that Alexander Knox brings to the role.

One of the cinematic triumphs of *Wilson* is the use of montage sequences and newsreel footage. The campaigning montages combine newspaper headlines, smoking locomotives, speeding trains, speeches from the rear platforms of Pullman cars, boxing rings, and farms. Together with rousing music, they convey the frenzied activities of the campaign's public presentations. The effort to stay out of the war and then the energy to win the war are well conveyed in dramatic scenes; however, it is the black-and-white documentary newsreel footage of the war that shines forth on the silver screen, showing the military preparation and the hell of trench warfare. This sequence lasts four minutes, and it condenses the American experience in World War I into a concise view of the activities and personalities as presented by Fox News. Reaction back home and a scene with the president and first lady dispensing doughnuts and coffee in the Washington, D.C., railroad station complete the war section.

Throughout *Wilson* the historical personalities are accurately portrayed, whether they are servants or senators. The two Mrs. Wilsons, Senator Henry Cabot Lodge, Colonel House, Dr. Grayson, William Jennings Bryan (from Nebraska), cabinet members, and the vice president are all limned to perfection with distinct character and distinctive clothing. Many of President Wilson's major speeches are presented word for word, albeit edited for length. Scenes of Wilson signing major bills are shown in close-up, and his European trips are presented through original newsreels or detailed recreations. The signing of the Versailles Treaty is a beautiful example of the latter. The White House and the chambers of Congress were gorgeously reproduced. Historical accuracy lengthened the film and gave it a veracity that most other biopics lack. Darryl F. Zanuck was especially impressed that President Wilson, like President Theodore Roosevelt before him, had received the Nobel Peace Prize.

When Zanuck returned on 10 October 1944, to his hometown of Wahoo, Nebraska, before the premiere of *Wilson* in Omaha, he ended a civic luncheon speech by saying, "If any of my movies have reflected the spirit of America, the inspiration came from my boyhood days in Nebraska. I am proud to be a Nebraskan." This may have been his last visit to Wahoo, but his statement about roots was sincere (Mosley 214).

THE RESPONSE TO WILSON

The critics raved about the film, and it received universally good reviews. The industry agreed with its ten Academy Award nominations; however, the public stayed away. With World War II drawing to a close, there were few audiences for patriotic speeches and exhortation. The word-of-mouth evaluation of *Wilson's* entertainment value was negative. A family doctor from Wahoo was quoted as asking, "Why should they pay seventy-five cents to see Wilson on the screen when they wouldn't pay ten cents to see him alive?" (Gussow 111). It was a sad time for Darryl F. Zanuck who only returned to Lincoln, Nebraska, once more— to receive an honorary Doctor of Humanities from the University of Nebraska in 1975.

This author has an additional take on the failure of *Wilson*. When it was released and distributed in 1944, Americans were still dying overseas. It was premature. No one wanted to learn about this new "reconstruction." This was a patriotic nation that wanted to kill the Germans and the Japanese. Americans were still making war and had little interest in peace. They were involved in their own world war and did not want to see a film about one whose ultimate objectives were not achieved. The 1944 Academy Award for best picture went to *Going My Way*, and Bing Crosby received the best-actor award. If *Wilson* had been released at the time of the founding of the United Nations, the box office figures might have been quite different, and the Academy Award winners might have been different. Sometime later, the American Nobel Committee asked Darryl F. Zanuck to address them because of his "vital contribution to the cause of world peace."

Historians usually quibble about the ending of the film. President Wilson was very ill during the last two years of his presidency. He had suffered a "thrombosis in his brain" sometime during April 1919 (Smith 106) that had been misdiagnosed as influenza, and he was often bedridden or in a wheelchair. His thought processes were erratic and his speech was affected. He could only walk a few steps even with help.

On the real inauguration day in 1921, President Wilson had to be lifted into an open automobile for the drive to the Capitol and lifted out upon his arrival. Just before the inauguration Wilson determined that he was too weak to continue and spoke his famous line, "The Senate has thrown me down, but I don't want to fall down" (Smith 185). He was taken from the Capitol to his new home on S Street and did not participate in the ceremonies. As a dramatist and filmmaker, Zanuck determined that this was no way to end a patriotic

The Democratic National Convention of 1912 as recreated by cinematographer Leon Shamroy. *Wilson* (1944).

film; however, this line was used verbatim in the scene of his departure from the White House.

Darryl F. Zanuck ended *Wilson* with the staff and congressional leadership saying their good-byes. Earlier, the leave-taking was set up with President Wilson saying, "I'm very sorry I won't be able to stay for the inauguration, but Mr. Harding and Mr. Coolidge have been kind enough to excuse me." Wilson leaves on his wife's arm, with a cane supporting his right side, striding down the foyer steps as a chorus sings the ending of "America the Beautiful":

> Long may our land be bright,
> With freedom's holy light.
> Protect us by thy might.
> Great God our King.

It was a very patriotic film. We all stood and clapped our hands at the end, which was a very unusual reaction for my family. Kids often cheered and yelled at the Westerns; however, this was a serious movie.

Wilson, then and now, is the kind of film that ends and you say, "Yes!" out loud. Perhaps Darryl F. Zanuck might have silenced us, because his most often-quoted remark is, "For God's sake, don't say yes until I finish talking!" (Katz 1261).

WORKS CITED

Birth of a Nation, The. Dir. David Wark Griffith. Blackhawk Films, 1915.

Cook, David A. *A History of Narrative Film.* New York: W.W. Norton, 1996.

Gussow, Mel. *Don't Say Yes Until I Finish Talking.* New York: Pocket Books, 1972.

Katz, Ephraim. *The Film Encyclopedia.* New York: Putnam, 1979.

Mosley, Leonard. *Zanuck, The Rise and Fall of a Hollywood Tycoon.* New York: McGraw-Hill, 1985.

Smith, Gene. *When the Cheering Stopped.* New York: William Morrow, 1964.

Wilson. Dir. Darryl F. Zanuck. Twentieth Century-Fox, 1944.

Jaap Kooijman

A Juxtaposition of Conflicting Images

Hubert H. Humphrey and the Television Coverage of Chicago, 1968

Vice President Hubert Humphrey,
1965–1969.

"The whole world is watching! The whole world is watching!" demonstrators in the streets of Chicago shouted while the television cameras were rolling (Barnouw 419; White 299). And the world was watching. Held in Chicago on 26-29 August, the 1968 Democratic National Convention was extensively covered by the television networks of the day: ABC, CBS, and NBC. In the words of *Newsweek* columnist Kenneth Crawford, the networks presented the convention "in glorious living color, big as life and twice as natural" (Crawford 36). For many Americans, Chicago 1968—both the violence in the streets as well as the disorder on the convention floor—was a major television event. As a viewer from Cincinnati, Ohio, stated, "I watched the entire Democratic Convention coverage, on a Zenith television set with remote control, which allowed me to switch from station to station from the armchair, where I sat" (Humphrey Papers, Stone to Daley, 4 September 1968).

When four months earlier, Vice President Hubert H. Humphrey announced his candidacy for the Democratic presidential nomination, he exclaimed that he wanted to return to "the way politics ought to be in America," namely "the politics of happiness, the politics of purpose, and the politics of joy" (Eisele 330). To many, Humphrey's statement appeared naïvely unrealistic in such controversial and violent times. The Tet Offensive in Vietnam, riots in American inner cities, and the assassination of Dr. Martin Luther King were clear signs of the grim and violent character of American politics in 1968. The assassination of his competitor Robert Kennedy in June and the dominance of violence at the Democratic National Convention in August proved that Humphrey's call for "joy" was wishful thinking—at least in 1968 (Matusow 395–439).

The televised disorder and violence of the convention evoked two questions that were extensively discussed in the media. First, "Had Democratic hopes—already dim—died in the bloody streets of Chicago?" (*Newsweek*, 9 September 1969). In other words, did Hubert Humphrey and the Democratic Party still stand a chance to win the presidential election after such negative exposure? Second, had the television networks presented a biased view by predominantly focusing on police brutality and neglecting to cover provocations by demonstrators? (*Broadcasting*, 19 August 1968; *Newsweek*, 16 September 1968; Witcover 5–9). Particularly the second question led to heated public and political discussions, eventually resulting in a congressional investigation by the Special Committee on Investigations of the House Committee on Interstate and Foreign Commerce (Special Committee 1969). This study will try to go beyond the issue of bias by focusing on the juxtaposition of the images of a smiling Hubert Humphrey and his politics of joy on the one hand and the images of violent protests and police brutality on the other. As I argue, the television coverage of the 1968 Democratic National Convention was not so much an example of manipulation by the media, as a demonstration of how the juxtaposition of images (or "intellectual montage" in cinematic terms) can provoke strong reactions from television viewers at home and generate unintended meanings, revealing the power of television as a volatile—and sometimes inflammatory—medium of visual communication. Moreover, the television coverage of Chicago 1968 established the conflicting visual connection between the image of an allegedly carefree vice president and the harsh images of chaos, disorder, and violence resulting from presidential politics—a connection that still can be found in television coverage today.

CHICAGO *1968*

In more than one sense, the 1968 Democratic National Convention was a rather extraordinary political event. Chicago had been chosen by President Lyndon B. Johnson in close consultation with Chicago Mayor Richard J. Daley. Johnson, however, decided not to go to Chicago, and instead watched the convention on television in Texas, where he celebrated his sixtieth birthday (Dallek 571–75; White 260). The Democratic Party was strongly divided on the issue of the war in Vietnam, a division that was emphasized by the candidacy of Eugene McCarthy. McCarthy supporters, many of them belonging to the student antiwar movement, went to Chicago to raise a voice of protest against the war policies of the Johnson administration, both inside the convention hall as well as outside in the streets (Herzog 193–239; Matusow 410–11). In addition, more radical groups of antiwar protesters, such as Yippie! (Young International Party) and the National Mobilization Front, were planning to demonstrate in Chicago. As the Humphrey campaign staff believed, it was the intention of the radical protest movement to "be met by the massive force promised by Mayor Daley and Governor Shapiro and to gain wide audience through the media showing a peaceful demonstration being broken by force and blood" (Humphrey Papers, Neigher to McCandless, 21 August 1968).

The extraordinary character of the convention was enhanced by outside circumstances. The Soviet Union had invaded Czechoslovakia a week before the convention started, thereby increasing the tension between the supporters and the opponents of the war in Vietnam over the theme of Communist aggression. Back in Chicago, preparations for the convention were hindered by striking taxi drivers and telephone workers. As a result of the telephone strike, the television networks were able to broadcast live coverage only from the convention hall. Coverage of any events outside the convention hall had to be collected on videotape, leaving at least half an hour between the shooting of the events and the eventual broadcast (*Newsweek*, 26 August 1968). Suspicion arose among the journalists that the limitation of live coverage to the convention floor was a deliberate move by Mayor Richard Daley to curtail the power of the press. A week before the convention, the head of CBS News, Richard Salant, expressed his concern that "the power structure here" in Chicago clearly believed that the television coverage could be controlled. "They obviously don't want us to cover any of the demonstrations live" (Whiteside 46). Regardless of whether the limitation of live coverage was a deliberate attempt of censorship by Mayor Daley, the resulting intercutting of previously collected footage of events outside in the streets into the live events going on in the convention hall had a major montage-style impact on the overall television coverage.

Vice President Hubert Humphrey found himself in a difficult position, as he could empathize with the nonradical antiwar protesters, but he still remained closely tied to the war policy of the Johnson administration (Dallek 469–97; Van den Berg 59–72). He detested the radical antiwar movement and distrusted the media, particularly television. As Humphrey later stated, "TV has its own built-in activator, and when the hot coals of protest and dissent are already present and mobilized, bringing in a TV camera is like adding gasoline" (Humphrey, *Education* 290). Humphrey's campaign staff was not sure how to counter the threat of protests. One suggestion was to have "several busloads of attractive, clean-cut young ladies in H-line[1] dresses available as 'flying squads' to be sent wherever some demonstrating by the other side seemed likely" as "they could win the place quite easily from the opposition" (Humphrey Papers, Spivak to Hayes, 8 July 1968). Even though the staff did realize that the "young ladies" might be exposed to "the danger of violence or of unpleasantness," this unintended example of the "politics of joy" reinforced the notion of naïvetè that seemed to define the Humphrey campaign.

In retrospect, the Humphrey campaign staff was also rather naïve in its view of the convention's television coverage. Less than two weeks before the convention, the staff started a word-of-mouth campaign to point out to the convention delegates that "the television cameras are ever alert to pick up a delegate who is reading a newspaper during a speech, sleeping, or acting in some undignified manner." As the memo continued:

> The delegates should be constantly impressed with the fact that the whole Convention is on television and that while the Convention can be good fun, it also should be portrayed to the great American public as a serious exercise entered into for serious purposes, and certainly politeness, courtesy and attentiveness are the least that can be accorded to the speakers. (Humphrey Papers, O'Brien to McCandless, 15 August 1968)

Little did the Humphrey campaign staff know that the power of television they so rightfully recognized would work in an unexpected manner. Instead of revealing the dreaded lack of interest by delegates, the television cameras ended up showing—in detail—the conflict and eventual disorder within the Democratic Party, which was further intensified by the coverage of violence in Chicago's streets. Similar to the way in which television had brought the violent "reality" of the war in Vietnam into American living rooms, the television coverage of Chicago captured the ideological conflict that dominated American domestic politics in 1968.

CHAOS, DISORDER, AND VIOLENCE ON THE TELEVISION SCREEN

In historical accounts of the Chicago convention, the television coverage of the demonstrations and police brutality in the streets of Chicago has overshadowed the chaos and disorder that also occurred inside the convention hall. As one television viewer stated, "With all the barbed wire and the over-abundance of police and security agents *on the floor* of the convention, my impression was that a supposedly democratic process was taking place in a highly un-democratic atmosphere" (Humphrey Papers, Morey to HHH, 29 August 1968, emphasis in original). From the opening live performance of "The Star-Spangled Banner" by soul-singer Aretha Franklin—which, in the words of Theodore White, "sounded more like a yodel than the national anthem" (White 276)—to the closing acceptance speech by the then-nominated Democratic candidate, Hubert Humphrey, the convention proved to be a chaotic four days of political controversy. Television viewers witnessed delegates being removed from the floor while reporters were hindered and hassled by the convention's security guards. When during one of these incidents CBS journalist Dan Rather was punched in the stomach, his colleague Walter Cronkite erupted on national television, "I think we've got a bunch of thugs down there" (*Newsweek*, 9 September 1968; Rather 307–10). The chaos reached its climax during the discussion on the Vietnam plank, ending in an almost surrealistic cacophony. After the majority plank, supporting the war policy of the Johnson administration, had been accepted, the supporters of the minority peace plank started singing "We Shall Overcome," led by folksinger and New York delegate Theodore Bikel (Chester, et al. 581). At the order of Mayor Daley, the Democratic house band tried to drown these voices of protest by playing "Happy Days Are Here Again," a classic Democratic campaign theme but within this context a misplaced leitmotiv of Humphrey's politics of joy.

The inability of the networks to present a live broadcast of the events outside the convention hall forced them to make difficult editing decisions about when to interrupt the live coverage of the events on the convention floor with previously collected footage of the demonstrations. The resulting television coverage turned out to be a montage of conflicting images, specifically the juxtaposition of political procedures on the convention floor on the one hand, and the protests and police brutality on the other. Such a juxtaposition resembled the "intellectual montage" of the early-twentieth-century Soviet cinema, most often associated with Sergei Eisenstein. As Eisenstein argued, the juxtaposition of conflicting shots creates a new meaning, through dialectical montage instead of traditional narration (Eisenstein 72–83). In other words, the resulting collision of the images of the actions on the convention floor with the images of the violence in the streets of Chicago was more than merely an accumulating coverage of news events, but it created (whether or not intended by the editors) a juxtaposition of images that challenged the authority of the political establishment in general and of Hubert Humphrey in particular.

The intellectual montage became most apparent during the live coverage of the nomination speeches, on Wednesday evening (28 August). While the delegates on the convention floor continued to present their nomination speeches, the television networks interrupted the live coverage with images that, as Walter Cronkite told the television viewers, spoke for themselves (Whiteside 48). Cronkite was referring to the excessive force used by the Chicago police to break up the groups of protesting young Americans, collected on video forty-five minutes earlier. Even though demonstrations and rioting had occurred during the days before, the images of the Chicago police severely beating up young men and women at eight o'clock Wednesday evening, near the Hilton hotel where Hubert Humphrey was staying, became emblematic of Chicago 1968.[2] One viewer wrote Humphrey that she had "watched with horror the events occurring in the streets of Chicago—the cops who swung with vicious and savage glee their clubs on the heads of little more than children, *backed up with national guard troops*" (Humphrey Papers, Fioriglio to HHH, 29 August 1968, emphasis in original). The images of the police aiming loaded grenade launchers at young Americans presented a striking contrast with the images of the political procedures on the convention floor. Yet, the shocking images did not only have a strong impact on the television viewers at home but also on the delegates in the convention hall. In the middle of his speech nominating George McGovern, Senator Abraham Ribicoff (D-Connecticut) made his now-notorious statement referring to the "Gestapo tactics on the streets of Chicago." The television cameras immediately zoomed in on Mayor Richard Daley, who, though unintelligible to the viewers, appeared to use an expression that lip readers later translated as "Fuck you. You Jew son of a bitch!" (Chester, et al. 584–85; Matusow 421; Viorst 459).

Even though Hubert Humphrey was not present on the convention floor, he followed the nomination speeches on television in his Hilton hotel room. After the rioting in the streets had ended, but while the nomination speeches were still going on, Humphrey told the press: "We knew this was going to happen. It was all programmed" (Chester, et al. 584). Almost simultaneously, both CBS and NBC switched from live coverage of the convention floor to footage of the rioting earlier in the evening. As a result, the nomination speech by Carl Stokes, the African American mayor of Cleveland, was replaced by images of police brutality. The intercutting infuriated Humphrey and his staff because the nomination by Stokes was intended as a reminder of Humphrey's decades-long commitment to the Civil Rights movement. Instead, as Theodore White wrote, only "Stokes' dark face is being wiped from the nation's view to show blood—Hubert Humphrey being nominated in a sea of blood" (White 302). That same evening, the juxtaposition of the images of a victorious Humphrey and the images of young people being beaten by the police became transfixed. When, close to midnight, the nomination of Humphrey was secured, television cameras captured Humphrey leaping from his chair, clapping his hands, and kissing the television screen, which showed a close-up of his wife Muriel sitting in the convention hall (Chester, et al. 585–86; White 303). Shortly after, the networks reran sequences of the demonstrations in the streets.

As Humphrey had not been present on the convention floor during the live coverage of the nomination speeches, the intercutting of previously collected footage into the live events never juxtaposed the images of a smiling Hubert Humphrey with the images of the violence in the streets, as had happened with images of Mayor Richard Daley. Nevertheless, as the images were again and again repeated on television and in other media, the contrast between a happy Humphrey of the Democratic establishment and a victimized younger generation suggested that Humphrey not only endorsed the violence but also was responsible for it. Humphrey was aware that he needed to address the situation in his acceptance speech the following evening to distance himself from the image that had been constructed in the media. As he remembered in his autobiography:

> Finally it was time. I moved to the podium, my moment of triumph. Faces looking up, the hall filled, the color, the lights, the thirteen thousand people, mostly cheering, some possibly ready to embarrass me. (Where are they? I thought. New York back there. California.) Signs waving. The noise level building. And the TV cameras going to carry what I have to say to 20 million Americans. (Humphrey, *Education* 295–96)[3]

Starting out by quoting a prayer of St. Francis of Assisi (which included the line "where there is hatred, let me sow love") Humphrey did address the "troubles and violence" that had dominated the convention but failed to make his own position clear. "We do not want a police state, but we need a state of law and order," Humphrey exclaimed, continuing, "and neither mob violence nor police brutality have any place in America" (Humphrey, "New Day"). Instead of distancing himself from the violent images, Humphrey's equivocal response heightened the negative juxtaposition between his moment of victory and the casualties in the streets. A television viewer revealed the impact of this collision of images by asking Hubert Humphrey the rhetorical question: "How can you smile while people in the street are being beaten?" (Humphrey Papers, Harris to HHH, 31 August 1968).

VIEWER RESPONSES

The television coverage of the Democratic National Convention, particularly the Wednesday evening broadcast, prompted several hundreds of viewers to write letters of protest to Hubert Humphrey in which they expressed their "shock" and "disbelief" about what they had "witnessed."[4] Many of these viewers reacted immediately after watching the violent images on their television screens. They refer to the act of watching, often expressed as "witnessing," and explain how the violent images had a direct physical effect on them, ranging from feeling sick or angry to having an urge to cry or scream:

As I sit viewing the television screen this evening at 10:00 P.M., I cannot believe my eyes—and my eyes are filled with tears. I cannot believe that while the "Democratic" National Convention is going on inside—the rioting, the club swinging—the horrors to which our citizens have been subjected—is going on outside. I thought I was viewing a scene from Nazi Germany—instead it was my beloved United States. (Humphrey Papers, Rudolph to HHH, 28 August 1968)

My living room was filled with police brutality, the like of which my family has never witnessed. My living room was filled with the sight of bleeding heads and blood-drenched streets. My God! My God! Was this America! Was this Germany 1939! (Humphrey Papers, Luongo to HHH, 30 August 1968)

We saw girls given an extra club after they were in the paddy wagon. We saw six police run after one boy. We saw people on the ground beaten after they were down. And we heard on TV that Hubert Humphrey was so close he could smell the gas. It was so bad I screamed right in my own living room, and I'm not given to that. (Humphrey Papers, Tressman to HHH, 30 August 1968)

One "amazed and horrified" television viewer had expected Hubert Humphrey to condemn the police brutality in his acceptance speech; she could not believe that he could condone "this unnecessary blood-shed." However, Humphrey failed to do so, neither in his acceptance speech nor later in the campaign. "Imagine my horror the next morning when you said on the *Today Show* that we do not need demonstrations in America and that we cannot have anarchy in America. I agree—we cannot have anarchy, but neither can we tolerate police brutality" (Humphrey Papers, Morey to HHH, 29 August 1968).

Even though the majority of letters sent to Hubert Humphrey during the week after the convention broadcast were protests against the police brutality and Humphrey's alleged indifference, Humphrey also received letters from viewers who supported the actions of the Chicago police. Moreover, many of these viewers believed that the television networks had been biased in their coverage and that, in fact, the networks were responsible for the violence, as they had encouraged the demonstrators and "showed up the worst of the situation instead of playing down the violence" (Humphrey Papers, Allen to HHH, 4 September 1968).

A good club on the head to the hippies and yippies was readily understood by the unwashed scum. (Humphrey Papers, Surinak to HHH, 31 August 1968)

I also sincerely believe that the American People are all fed up with the news media and their Nazi tactics; thank goodness they again are in the minority. All the TV networks last night blasted the police and condoned these demonstrators who had hoisted the Viet Cong Flag. (Humphrey Papers, Burns to HHH, 29 August 1968)

We hope you can persuade the national television networks to desist from their inflammatory broadcasts that incite our more susceptible citizens to violence. (Humphrey Papers, Kelly to HHH, 31 August 1968)

Dear Walter Cronkite brought the Yippies to our screens. Ridiculous, I thought. Facetious. Wasting time on this nonsense? . . . But it turned out to be not nonsense, not kid stuff, but Revolution. Revolution turned on for the TV cameras as that . . . Revolution turned on to sway delegates at a political convention, so that force would outweigh majority sentiment. (Humphrey Papers, Chandler to HHH, 1 September 1968)

Even though neither the letters of protest nor those of support can be considered representative of the general American public, they do tell something about the impact of television. In particular the difference between the response of the protesters and the response of the supporters is significant.

The letters of protest tend to present a direct (physical) reaction, often including detailed descriptions, to the violent images on the screen, resulting in a strong exclamation of disbelief and disgust. The letters of support, on the contrary, tend to question and even rationalize the violent images by assuming that the broadcast had been biased. Those viewers who were shocked by the images tend to refer to the demonstrators as "children" and "girls and boys" while those viewers condemning the television coverage refer to them as "hippies" and "Yippies." Moreover, the large number of protests, written immediately or shortly after the broadcast, clearly showed a significant increase while the relatively small amount of support did not significantly outnumber the regular expressions of support, suggesting that the television coverage evoked such a strong reaction among "disgusted" viewers that they—even those who normally were not prone to do so—felt compelled to send in their protest.

QUESTIONING THE BIAS

Initially, many Americans, including the press, were outraged by the violence that had dominated the television screens during the coverage of the Democratic National Convention. Within two weeks, however, the indignation seemed to dwindle. Polls showed that a majority of Americans believed that Mayor Richard Daley and the Chicago police had handled the situation correctly. Newspapers, such as the *Washington Post*, which earlier strongly had condemned the police brutality, now reversed their positions (Chester, et al. 592–94). However, the discussion about whether the television coverage had been biased continued. All three major networks, ABC, CBS, and NBC, strongly denied the claim, stating that the coverage had been fair, particularly considering the difficult circumstances (*Broadcasting*, 7, 21, 28 October 1968). Moreover, the networks believed that the criticism was partially based on a misunderstanding of how television works. "Like no other medium in history, television catches the flavor, the immediacy, the excitement, the tension and the confusion, too, of the moment," as CBS president Frank Stanton explained both the strength and the weakness of television:

> The proof of this impact was borne out by the fact that newspapers from all over the world covered the same story, and in many cases said much harsher things about Chicago than did our pictures. Yet it was television that drew the bulk of the criticism." (*Broadcasting*, 30 September 1968)

The complaints that the television coverage by the networks had been biased eventually resulted in an investigation by the Federal Communications Commission and a report by the Committee on Interstate and Foreign Commerce of the House of Representatives. The committee's report, simply entitled *Television Coverage of the Democratic National Convention, Chicago, Illinois, 1968*, was presented in July 1969, and it was based on the premise that "serious charges of misconduct and unfairness on the part of the national news media—especially television—were made during and after the convention" (Special Committee 1). Of the eight issues examined, ranging from the bias and animosity among the press and the staging of events, to the alleged cooperation with demonstrators, only three proved to be relevant to this study, namely the "prejudicial selection of film," the "prejudicial editing," and the "unfair juxtaposition and intercutting of live and taped material." After examining the outtakes of the footage collected in the streets of Chicago, the committee concluded that the networks had not, at least deliberately, been biased in the selection and editing of the footage. The committee was more critical, however, about the alleged unfair juxtaposition and intercutting, specifically referring to the CBS broadcast in which previously shot footage of the demonstrations was alternated with a live interview with Mayor Richard Daley on the convention floor. "This intercutting technique may be used to keep the viewer in continuous contact with two or more simultaneously occurring events," but, as the report concluded, "It may also be used, as it was in Chicago, in attempt to add irony or drama to a news situation" (Special Committee 24–29). In other words, even though the committee concluded that the television coverage in general had not been biased, the *intended* use of intellectual montage was perceived as a biased distortion of reality.

THE JUXTAPOSITION OF VIOLENCE AND HUMPHREY'S POLITICS OF JOY

The question of whether the networks had been biased in the coverage of the 1968 Democratic National Convention—suggesting that they made a deliberate attempt to connect the violent images to the leadership of the Democratic Party—becomes less relevant when addressing the juxtaposition of the violent images and the images of Hubert Humphrey and his politics of joy. In fact, one can wonder if a deliberately constructed juxtaposition would have had the same strong impact. Two months after the convention, the campaign of Humphrey's Republican opponent, Richard Nixon, capitalized on this montage technique with a controversial television ad, broadcast only once during an episode of

Rowan and Martin's Laugh In (giving some television viewers the impression that the ad was part of the program). Using the song "Hot Time in the Old Town Tonight" as soundtrack, the ad started out with images of the Democratic National Convention in Chicago alternated with stills of a victorious Hubert Humphrey and the rioting in the streets. The intercutting continued with images of the war in Vietnam and a poor family in Appalachia. As Katherine Hall Jamieson has concluded in her analysis of the ad, the juxtaposition of the smiling Humphrey and the images of war, disorder, and poverty tried to give the impression that either Humphrey was to blame, or that he simply did not care about, or even enjoyed the misery (Jamieson 245–47).

Even though both the television coverage of the Chicago convention and the Nixon campaign ad presented a constructed image of conflict through the use of intellectual montage, their impact was quite different. As the controversy caused by the Republican ad suggests, the obviously deliberate attempt to construct conflict turned out to be far less convincing—and thus far less powerful—than a similar juxtaposition presented by television through the "live" coverage of the events in Chicago. Viewers could easily recognize the political ad as a deliberate attempt to hurt Humphrey by connecting him to the images of violence. In the television coverage of Chicago 1968, on the contrary, this intent was more difficult to discern. Ironically, the montage of the television coverage had the effect on the audience that the Nixon campaign had tried to achieve. Many of the television viewers who wrote to Hubert Humphrey connected the images of a smiling Humphrey to the violent images of the police brutality. The joy of winning the nomination was translated into an approval of, and even a delight in, the violence in the streets. As one viewer wrote:

> I do not understand how I can support a man who is capable of pulling the drapes of his [hotel] room and joyously dancing in celebration of a personal victory—while the streets below are wet with human blood and injured men and women who lie unattended in his very hotel. (Humphrey Papers, Stewart to HHH, 31 August 1968)

Hubert Humphrey's self-acclaimed politics of joy enhanced the conflict made visible by his victory amidst a violent political climate. Different than Mayor Richard Daley (who "merely" had become the embodiment of the police brutality in Chicago), Humphrey symbolized the political establishment that refused to recognize and to validate the growing concern among the American population, particularly the younger generation. As historian Dan Cohen has pointed out, his "exuberance, seen against a background of tragedy, had a devastating impact," suggesting that Humphrey was "indifferent to the suffering going on about him, so self-involved with his personal triumph that nothing could penetrate his bubble of happiness, his politics of joy" (Cohen 336–37). Humphrey's image of naïvetè and reluctance to face the reality of the situation was strongly reflected in the letters of the television viewers. "I'm sorry, but this is your image. And you projected it yourself," one former supporter wrote Humphrey. "No, I'm not a hippie. I'm 66 and I'm a librarian" (Humphrey Papers, Tressman to HHH, 30 August 1968).

Campaign button from 1968: the politics of joy.

Library of Congress.

CONCLUSION

In a *Newsweek* column written less than three weeks after the 1968 Democratic National Convention, Kenneth Crawford claimed that the television coverage had been "oversimplified and overdramatized to the point of gross distortion, if not of falsification" (Crawford 36). Even though the juxtaposition of the images of a victorious Hubert Humphrey and the images of the violence in the streets of Chicago may have been a simplification of the complex political circumstances of 1968, the dilemma it brought forward was everything but false: how could the American political system—and specifically the Democratic leadership—continue to function in its traditional ways without taking account of the grim and violent character that had come to define American politics in 1968? The conflict as presented by television, whether it was a simplification or not, was readily understood by the viewers, who often responded in disbelief and disgust. These viewers were no "hippies and Yippies" but "average" American citizens who were genuinely shocked by the violence they witnessed, particularly in comparison to "regular" American political practice. The juxtaposition presented a collision between tradition and reality, between convention and actual experience. Humphrey's "politics of joy" appeared naïve and outdated when contrasted to the violence in the streets of Chicago.

The fear expressed by the Humphrey campaign staff of a violent confrontation between the Chicago police and the antiwar protesters, broadcast "live" on television, had become true. The questions of whether the violence was the result of provocation by radical demonstrators, whether the presence of television cameras incited a more violent confrontation, or whether the television networks were biased in their coverage become less relevant when discussing the actual effect the coverage had on the viewers in the American living rooms. The power of television as a medium of visual communication has to be found in its ability to present a montage of images that obtain a new meaning through conflict rather than through narrative. As the responses of television viewers show, the constructed conflict in the "live" television coverage of the 1968 Chicago convention proved to be convincing, even when (or perhaps because) the editors of the television networks never intended to present such dialectic images. Through the montage of conflicting images—the political procedures on the convention floor and the violence in the streets of Chicago—the contrast between a smiling Hubert Humphrey, representing the Democratic establishment, and young Americans being beaten by the Chicago police provided a telling message of how American politics had become estranged from the realities of American popular sentiments.

Even though the extraordinary circumstances of Chicago 1968 (both the practical obstacles encountered by the television networks and the historical context) undoubtedly contributed to the way the television coverage presented conflicting images, the resulting juxtaposition is not uniquely connected to one specific moment in American political history. In 1991, for example, the television network CNN presented a smiling President George Bush Sr. in the White House Rose Garden in juxtaposition to footage of Gulf War bombing in Iraq. One could argue that postmodern television viewers have acquired such a level of visual media literacy that they easily recognize the intellectual montage, and thus reactions, such as those experienced by "disgusted" viewers of Chicago 1968, will no longer occur. However, one could also argue that, in spite of the acquired literacy of contemporary television viewers, the act of the intellectual montage in television coverage continues to prove its power by exposing political conflict in dialectic terms, not only in 1968 but also in contemporary times. Up to this day, the mediation of the politician's image depends on how the image is presented on television, making the politician dependent on the television editor—similar to the way the image of the film actor is ultimately controlled by the director and editors. "Why? Why? Why, didn't you speak up and stop the mess?" one television viewer asked Humphrey, continuing, "It was in your power to do so" (Humphrey Papers, Luongo to HHH, 30 August 1968). However, even if Hubert Humphrey had spoken up, he could not have been able to overcome the powerful juxtaposition of conflicting images presented by television.

NOTES

1. "H-line" refers to Humphrey's campaign symbol, based on his initials HHH.

2. Most of the television coverage referred to in this article is included in the 1995 American Experience documentary *Chicago 1968*, produced by Chana Gazit.

3. Humphrey's estimation of a television audience of twenty million is obviously an underestimation and may be a misprint. *Newsweek* columnist Kenneth Crawford, for example, estimated that the television audience amounted to one hundred and forty million viewers (Crawford 36).

4. The number of letters of protest written during the week after the television coverage (around five hundred) is roughly five times the amount of regular protest and support mail. In fact, there was no significant increase in the number of support letters sent, an observation based on an examination of the 1968 Campaign Files of the Hubert H. Humphrey Papers, which are located at the Minnesota Historical Society, St. Paul, Minnesota.

LETTERS CITED

All letters can be found in the Hubert H. Humphrey (HHH) Papers: 1968 Campaign Files, available at the Minnesota Historical Society, St. Paul, Minnesota.

Allen, Geo E. to HHH, 4 September 1968, 150.F.18.4F.

Burns, Burley to HHH, 29 August 1968, 150.F.18.4F, box 23.C.8.7B.

Chandler, Otis to HHH, 1 September 1968, 150.F.18.4F.

Fioriglio, Louise to HHH, 29 August 1968, 150.F.17.6F, box 4-15.

Harris, Mrs. F.A. to HHH, 31 August 1968, 150.F.17.6F, box 4-15.

Kelly, Thomas A. and Elizabeth L. to HHH, 31 August 1968, 150.F.18.4F.

Luongo, Anthony A. to HHH, 30 August 1968, 150.F.17.6F, box 4-15.

Morey, Sharon L. to HHH, 29 August 1968, 150.F.17.6F, box 4-15.

Neigher, Alan to Bob McCandless, 21 August 1968, 150.G.5.5B, box 7-1.

O'Brien, Larry to Bob McCandless, 15 August 1968, 150.G.5.5B, box 7-1.

Rudolph, Helen to HHH, 28 August 1968, 150.F.17.6F, box 4-15.

Spivak, Al to Larry Hayes, 8 July 1968, 150.G.5.5.B, box 7-1.

Stewart, Edwin S. to HHH, 31 August 1968, 150.F.17.6F, box 4-15.

Stone, W. Allen to Richard J. Daley, 4 September 1968, 150.F.18.4F.

Surinak, J.J. to HHH, 31 August 1968, 150.F.18.4F.

Tressman, Ruth to HHH, 30 August 1968, 150.F.17.6F, box 4-15.

WORKS CITED

"ABC Defends Chicago Coverage." *Broadcasting*, 21 October 1968, 63–64.

Barnouw, Eric. *Tube of Plenty: The Evolution of American Television*. New York: Oxford University Press, 1975.

"Battle in Chicago"/"The Winner: How—And What—He Won." *Newsweek*, 9 September 1968, 24–34.

Chester, Lewis, Godfrey Hodgson, and Bruce Page. *An American Melodrama: The Presidential Campaign of 1968.* New York: Viking Press, 1969.

"Cliffhanger in Chicago." *Broadcasting,* 19 August 1968, 28–30.

Cohen, Dan. *Undefeated: The Life of Hubert H. Humphrey.* Minneapolis: Lerner, 1978.

Crawford, Kenneth. "In Living Color." *Newsweek,* 16 September 1968, 36.

"Cronkite Defends TV's Objectivity." *Broadcasting,* 7 October 1968, 47–48.

Dallek, Robert. *Flawed Giant: Lyndon Johnson and His Times, 1961–1973.* New York: Oxford University Press, 1998.

"Dementia in the Second City." *Time,* 6 September 1968, 21–24.

"Down to the Barbed Wire." *Newsweek,* 26 August 1968, 17–19.

Eisele, Albert. *Almost to the Presidency: A Biography of Two American Politicians.* Blue Earth, Minnesota: The Piper Company, 1972.

Eisenstein, Sergei. "Methods of Montage." In *Film Form: Essays in Film Theory.* 1929. Edited by Jay Leyda, 72–83. Reprint, New York: Harcourt, Brace, Jovanovich, 1949.

Herzog, Arthur. *McCarthy For President.* New York: Viking Press, 1969.

Humphrey, Hubert H. "A New Day For America." 29 August 1968, Humphrey H. Humphrey Papers: 1968 Campaign Files, 150.F.18.4F, box 23.C.8.7B. Minnesota Historical Society, St. Paul.

———. *The Education of a Public Man: My Life and Politics.* 1976. Reprint, Minneapolis: University of Minnesota Press, 1991.

"Is the Press Biased?" *Newsweek,* 16 September 1968, 66–67.

Jamieson, Katherine Hall. *Packaging the Presidency: A History and Criticism of Presidential Campaign Advertising.* New York: Oxford University Press, 1996.

Matusow, Allen J. *The Unraveling of America: A History of Liberalism in the 1960s.* New York: Harper & Row, 1984.

"Mule Teams At Work." *Newsweek,* 9 September 1968, 68–69.

"NBC Defends News Objectivity." *Broadcasting,* 28 October 1968, 67.

Rather, Dan, with Mickey Herkowitz. *The Camera Never Blinks: Adventures of a TV Journalist.* New York: William Morrow and Company, 1977.

Special Committee on Investigations of the Committee on Interstate and Foreign Commerce, House of Representatives. *Television Coverage of the Democratic National Convention, Chicago, Illinois, 1968.* Washington, D.C.: Government Printing Office, 1969.

"Stanton Rebuts Chicago Critics." *Broadcasting,* 30 September 1968, 46–47.

Van den Berg, Erik E.W. "Supersalesman for the Great Society: Vice President Hubert H. Humphrey." *American Studies International* (October 1998): 59–72.

Viorst, Milton. *Fire in the Streets: America in the 1960s.* New York: Simon and Schuster, 1979.

White, Theodore H. *The Making of the President–1968.* New York: Atheneum, 1968.

Whiteside, Thomas. "Corridor of Mirrors: The Television Editorial Process, Chicago." *Columbia Journalism Review* (Winter 1968/1969): 35–54.

Witcover, Jules. "The Press and Chicago: The Truth Hurt." *Columbia Journalism Review* (Fall 1968): 5–9.

Part Two

Hollywood's "Take"

The Presidency in Fiction Films

Michael G. Krukones

MOTION PICTURE PRESIDENTS OF THE 1930S

Factual and Fictional Leaders for a Time of Crisis

In 1933, President Franklin D. Roosevelt promised a "New Deal."

Library of Congress.

Motion pictures tell us something about ourselves, who we are as a people; express our aspirations; and reveal much about our national character. Review the movies produced in the United States during any era and you will discover a cinematic canvas of the nation's history on which is presented the attitudes and beliefs of the people toward its leaders and political institutions. This study examines presidents in film in one of the earliest periods of movies, the decade of the 1930s, an era of great unrest in the nation. The Great Depression, the election of Franklin Roosevelt and the creation of the New Deal programs, the rise of fascist groups, and the rumbling of a world war produced an unsettled time in the country. The presidency experienced significant changes during the same time period, primarily in the shift from the laissez-faire Hoover administration to the activist Roosevelt presidency. The movies both advocated and reflected this sea change in presidential power. The decade of the 1930s is

President Lincoln (Joseph Henabery) is shot by John Wilkes Booth (Raoul Walsh, future director) in Ford's Theatre on Good Friday, 1865. *The Birth of a Nation* (1915).

also important for the film industry with the development of the studio system and advances in motion picture technology, such as color and sound. The political system and the film industry interacted more with one another during this time through state censorship boards, the Hays Office, and the development of the Production Code in 1930 (Christensen 41).

Six films on the American presidency from the 1930s are examined, three of which deal with a real president and three in which a fictionalized president or candidate running for the presidency is the subject of the movie. Comparisons of the two types of film presidents and the motion pictures themselves allow valuable insight into the period.

THE REAL PRESIDENT

Abraham Lincoln (1930)

Three major American films of the 1930s dealing with a real president were centered around Abraham Lincoln. In cinematic terms, although some sixty-five years after his demise, the era could rightfully be called the decade of Lincoln (Cameron 58). The decade opened with D.W. Griffith's melodrama, *Abraham Lincoln* (1930), the first biographical talkie about an American president and Griffith's first sound film. It was also the only one of the three Lincoln films of the 1930s to cover his entire life.

Griffith's version begins and ends with storms that bracket Lincoln's life and create the image of a man who was in constant turmoil. His love for Ann Rutledge (Una Merkel) is portrayed along with his depression over her death, and he is shown to be fearful of Mary Todd (Kay Hammond) before their marriage. After losing the 1858 senatorial election to Stephen Douglas (E. Allyn Warren), Lincoln (Walter Huston) considers himself to be a failure, but he is later asked by the Republican Party leaders to be their candidate for president, and the movie spends most of its time relating Lincoln's years in the White House.

Griffith made the preservation of the Union an overriding theme of the movie. At many points, Lincoln states that saving the nation is his only goal and that he is more concerned about the nation than his place in history. He is also shown to be a president who wants to bring both sides together after the Civil War, and he demonstrates this belief by regarding the people of the South not as traitors but as rebels who should be taken back "as if they were never away." His compassion is further shown in a scene where he pardons a soldier during a court-martial. Even at Ford's Theatre on the night of his assassination, Lincoln makes the statement that there should be "malice toward none and charity toward all" (from his Second Inaugural Address). At the end of the film, the Lincoln Memorial, built as a tribute in 1922, is photographed with a halo effect around Lincoln's head and a voice-over narrator declaring that, "Now he belongs to the ages."

Abraham Lincoln is episodic in nature and presents Lincoln's life as a series of historical vignettes. Because of Griffith's southern background, the region is portrayed in a positive light, and, in one scene, General Lee (Hobart Bosworth) countermands an order to have a spy shot. The acting is stilted—which may be because of Griffith's inexperience with the new sound medium—but the overall effect of the film shows Lincoln as a worried yet humane president whose thoughts were forever on a peaceful reconciliation of the North and the South.

Young Mr. Lincoln (1939)

Young Mr. Lincoln considers Abraham Lincoln in his early years before public office. The story is a collection of Lincoln anecdotes, including an incident from an 1857 trial in which Lincoln proved his client's innocence by consulting an almanac (McBride 305). In the film, two brothers are accused of murder after neither wishes to implicate the other in the crime. The idea of two

A tall and awkward young lawyer (Henry Fonda) rides into town in *Young Mr. Lincoln* (1939).

defendants came from a trial covered by the film's screenwriter, Lamar Trotti, as a young reporter in Georgia (Gallagher 162). Lincoln (Henry Fonda) is the attorney for the brothers, and he uses homespun logic and wit in their defense during a series of courtroom scenes. The situation appears to be an open-and-shut case against the brothers; Lincoln is even told by the judge to consult Stephen Douglas (Milburn Stone), a more experienced attorney, for advice. But, Lincoln does not take up the judge's offer, and he is able to gain acquittal for the brothers by proving through a *Farmer's Almanac* that a witness to the murder, which took place at night, could not have seen the crime because it was a moonless night. He is even able to elicit a Perry Mason–style confession of the crime from the witness (Ward Bond) who testified against the brothers.

The film juxtaposes the idea of legality and the lynch mob ("A Collective Text" 704). Lincoln trades some dry goods from a pioneer family for a copy of *Blackstone's Commentaries*. The same family will later be the one whose brothers he defends. He is shown to be fascinated by the law and indicates that he knows "what's right and what's wrong." He also takes on a lynch mob that is after the two brothers and is able to talk the mob out of the act by telling them "they can't take the law into their own hands."

As was the case in the Griffith film, Lincoln is seen as an unassuming man who is not concerned with glory. At the beginning of the film, he is shown running for the Illinois state legislature, and he admits that he does not care whether he wins or loses. Also, Ann Rutledge (Pauline Moore) has an impact on his life, not through her death, as in the previous film, but as a guiding spirit of his career who urges him to have confidence in himself and follow the noble career path of law (Neely 126).

Lincoln is shown to be a man of compassion and unification in a number of instances in the film: he settles a dispute between two men; he later has trouble deciding which pie is the best at a fair; and finally, he attempts to save the lives of both brothers when the prosecuting attorney offers the freedom of one in exchange for the death of the other. At the end of the film, Abraham Lincoln climbs a hill while a symbolic storm gathers in the distance. He walks out of the frame of the picture toward his destiny and into American history.

Abe Lincoln in Illinois (1940)

Abe Lincoln in Illinois closed the "Lincoln decade" of the 1930s. The film was based on a Pulitzer Prize–winning play by Robert E. Sherwood and starred Raymond Massey, who had created the role on stage. The play and film cover the life of Lincoln from his adolescence to the brink of the presidency. Of the three films on Lincoln in this era, it is the most romantic and contains only snippets of Lincoln's speeches and pronouncements on liberty, slavery, and union (Cameron 60). Lincoln is viewed as a potential great leader, not so much by what is learned of him from the film but because of what Lincoln will do as president (Cameron 60).

The film confuses the chronology of Lincoln's early years in a similar fashion to *Young Mr. Lincoln* (Neely 127). What is most evident and most embarrassing to some is the presentation of Lincoln as a man who has little ambition himself and who is pushed into the White House by others (Christensen 49). Ann Rutledge (Mary Howard) again acts as a catalyst on Lincoln's life, but it is Mary Todd (Ruth Gordon) who states that she will push him toward his destiny. Lincoln is portrayed as a man who does not want to be a politician, is uneasy around people, and believes that he is a failure. On top of these negatives, Lincoln is told by a group of women that he is the homeliest person they have ever seen. Overall, he is viewed as a person who would be easily controlled by others once in the White House.

Raymond Massey in his greatest role as a flawed—but dedicated—leader in *Abe Lincoln in Illinois* (1940).

When Lincoln gains the presidency, he is despondent because he realizes that his victory will lead to the secession of the southern states. The final scene of the film shows Lincoln standing at the rear of the train with Mary as he heads for Washington. The figure of Lincoln becomes more distant as he fades into history while smoke from the engine both signifies the fires of discord he will face in the years to come as well as his forthcoming glory.

A number of conclusions can be drawn from these films on Lincoln. In each of these presentations, he is viewed as an unpretentious man who is not personally ambitious for a political career or fame, even to the point of having others push him toward his life in politics. He exhibits homespun thinking and humor and, thus, shows his connections with the people. He is a man of the law who will not allow the mob to have its way. He is also a person who believes in compromise and unification, and who tries to see a disagreement from multiple perspectives.

Liberties have naturally been taken with some of the ideas and events presented in these movies on Lincoln. One of the most glaring inaccuracies is the portrayal of Lincoln as a man without political ambition. In fact, Lincoln had vast electioneering skills and great drive, which one would need to arrive at the presidency, and his law partner, William Herndon, referred to Lincoln as "a little engine of ambition that knew no rest" (Donald 81). Nevertheless, the image of Lincoln in films from the 1930s, both as president and in his early years, is one that shows great reverence for a saintly man.

On the one hand, most movies about real politicians that were made before Vietnam and Watergate presented the chief executive in a favorable light (Edelman 323). On the other hand, Hollywood has not been as kind in portraying fictional politicians (Genovese 15). This difference will become evident in the examination of the next three films on presidents from the 1930s.

THE FICTIONAL PRESIDENTS

The period of the early 1930s in the United States was a desperate time. With the onset of the Great Depression, the unemployment rate stood at 24.9 percent in 1933, up from only 3.2 percent at the time of the 1929 stock market crash. Insecurity about the banking system caused people to withdraw their money, which prompted more bank failures. Crime, especially of the gangland style, continued to increase primarily because of rivalries over the liquor market within the context of federal Prohibition, which began in 1919. In 1932, thousands of World War I veterans marched on Washington to demand immediate payment of a promised bonus by the federal government. They settled in squatter camps not far from the National Mall, and, at least on one occasion, they trapped congressmen and staff members in the Capitol Building itself. Their requests, though, were ignored by President Hoover, who believed that communists and criminals had infiltrated their group; he ordered General Douglas MacArthur to disperse the gathering and destroy its shanties (Pitney 47).

The nation was in a true "depression." There was a distrust of authority, a disbelief in the fairness of the law, and a feeling that government was not interested in the problems of the people (Combs 23). Political leadership was perceived as being ineffective, and there were even cries for some type of dictatorship for the nation. *Vanity Fair* in June 1932 proclaimed: "Appoint a Dictator," and *Liberty* magazine suggested that the president be given dictatorial power (Pitney 48). Because of his perceived ability to run his government efficiently, Benito Mussolini was seen as a model for politicians to emulate, and fascism—seen from a safe distance—became an answer in some circles.

Political movies of the early 1930s reflected this mood of the nation. Politicians were portrayed as shysters and crooks, politics was viewed as a sham, and corruption was shown to dominate the entire political system (Klein 15). Part of the reason for the appeal of the gangster film in this era was that the gangster was seen as accomplishing things even if it meant going outside the law. In two of the three films in this section, the presidents engage in deceitful activity that would be considered beyond the scope of the law in order to accomplish their ends. Audiences, though, seemed to enjoy watching these reel activists rather than having to live under the weak leadership of their real political leaders.

The Phantom President (1932)

The Phantom President is the most lighthearted of the three films on fictional presidents in this era. The central character is not the president but a man who is running for the presidency. A group of senators believe that Theodore Blair (George M. Cohan) is the best man to get the nation out of the depression, but he lacks a strong personality to run for the office. When Blair's exact double Peter Varney (also played by George M. Cohan), who is a traveling medicine man, appears in town, the senators decide to use him in the campaign because of his pleasing personality and then place Blair in the White House after the election. Both men agree to the plan, and to confuse matters, Blair's girlfriend, Felicia (Claudette Colbert), falls in love with Varney, thinking that he is Blair who is undergoing a personality change. Blair becomes resentful of the plan and plots to have Varney kidnapped, but Felicia discovers the plot and has Blair kidnapped instead and sent to the Arctic. Varney wants to reveal this scam over the radio to the nation, but he is stopped from doing so; with Felicia's help, Varney decides to run for president using his own name. He wins the election and marries Felicia.

The movie, although a musical comedy and not a serious drama, has much to say about the political atmosphere of the day. The film satirizes political campaigns and makes it appear that voters are more interested in a person with a smiling face than in someone with ideas (Roffman and Purdy 38). The fact that the man who is eventually elected president is a medicine man—in effect a con man—trivializes political campaigns. The movie thus becomes an early representation of "the selling of the candidate" theme that would become more widely used in the 1960s and beyond in such films as *The Candidate,* *Bob Roberts,* and *Primary Colors.*

The film cries out for a strong leader. The opening musical number has Washington, Jefferson, Lincoln, and Teddy Roosevelt indicating that the "country needs a man," presenting in comic fashion what the country wanted in reality. Peter Roffman and Jim Purdy have concluded that the 1932 presidential campaign mirrored the movie in that Hoover was similar to the Blair character who failed to project strong leadership while FDR was similar to Varney in his ability to exude charm and inspire confidence (Roffman and Purdy 40). The film speaks to issues of the Depression. Hollywood, for the most part, dealt with the Depression in its early years by ignoring it and downplaying the situation (Platt 61). *The Phantom President* makes light of the Depression through Jimmy Durante, who plays Varney's partner, Curly. In the film, Curly asks the rhetorical question, "What's a depression?" He answers that, "A depression is a hole." He then asks, "What's a hole?" and he responds by stating that, "A hole is nuttin'." Thus, on the one hand advocating the need for a strong leader, on the other hand the film seeks to minimize the importance of the Depression because it appears as if, for the time being, there is nothing to do but live through it without much assistance from government.

Gabriel Over the White House (1933)

Gabriel Over the White House is a much darker movie than *The Phantom President* and touches on the problems of the era in a more serious manner. The film tells the story of a recently elected president, Judson Hammond (Walter Huston), who enters the presidency, following the advice of a fellow politician that he should not worry about keeping his campaign promises. The president mouths platitudes to reporters concerning questions of unemployment, racketeering, and foreign debt. At the same time, he ignores the growing number of unemployed who are being led by a man named John Bronson (David Landau).

After being involved in a car accident that puts the president in a coma, the angel Gabriel appears before him; as a result, he turns into a completely different person. He becomes a more determined and serious executive. He meets with his cabinet and tells it that he has power to do what he wants and fires, on the spot, one of his cabinet members. The president indicates that he will not send troops against the unemployed, but instead he will create an "army of construction" which will build new roads and buildings. He goes before Congress and asks for a declaration of national emergency which will give him dictatorial power, and he states that his dictatorship is based on Thomas Jefferson's definition of democracy—"A government for the greatest good of the greatest number." He declares martial law and dismisses Congress, thereby overturning the Constitution.

The president proposes a number of aid programs along with a repeal of Prohibition. He informs the racketeers that the government will muscle in on the liquor business. Later, when some gangsters bomb a government liquor store, they, along with their leader, are arrested, convicted by a court-martial, and executed near the Statue of Liberty. In an observation that can be taken as an understatement, an associate of the president remarks that the president has cut the red tape of legal procedures.

In foreign affairs, the president declares that the United States will no longer be outmaneuvered by crafty European politicians and that these nations must be economically responsible. He holds a conference with European representatives and tells them to stop building up armaments so that they can instead repay what they owe other nations. To prove his commitment to disarmament, he has two American battleships blown up in front of the conference members. In the final scene of the movie, the foreign representatives agree to a peace covenant and to repay what their nations owe; as the president signs the covenant, he dies.

The film was a call for strong leadership, and its story of a president who assumes dictatorial power to run the country must be seen in the context of the fascist dictatorships of Europe during this period. William Randolph Hearst's production company, Cosmopolitan Productions, financed the movie, and while Hearst never advocated a fascist takeover of the United States, he did have an interest in fascist ideology and spoke in admiration of Mussolini (Pitney 49); he viewed fascism as a movement to oppose any left-wing uprisings in the nation. Hearst was a proponent of a strong president, but he had found his candidate in FDR, whom he supported in 1932. Many of the programs of FDR's New Deal and Judson Hammond's New Order in the movie are similar, including the repeal of Prohibition, the creation of a federal police force, and government sponsorship of building projects staffed by the unemployed (Roffman and Purdy 72). The closeness of their ideas about government could be attributed in part to the belief that Hearst had written some of the speeches for the character of President Hammond while at the same time writing some of FDR's speeches (Shindler 112). Ironically, Hearst later became disenchanted with

FDR after the president accomplished many of the things Hearst advocated—but in ways that Hearst opposed (McConnell 25).

Aside from promoting a strong president, *Gabriel Over the White House* is noteworthy for the care with which the president assumes dictatorial power (McConnell 25). The movie achieves a certain credibility through the style the president uses to gain control of the nation's problems, and audiences reacted favorably to the actions of the president in the film, especially his promise of jobs for the unemployed (Levine 175). While some critics, such as the reviewer for the *Nation*, denounced the film for trying to convert American movie audiences to "a policy of fascist dictatorship," the journal also conceded that the movie was a welcome first attempt by the Hollywood establishment to focus attention on current social and economic ideas; finally, the dream factory was beginning to accept the Depression as fact (McConnell 24).

Although the movie is a fictional portrayal of a president, there are connections to FDR and other real presidents, especially Abraham Lincoln. For example, President Hammond uses Lincoln's quill pen to sign the disarmament covenant; there is a bust of Lincoln in the Oval Office; and jobless veterans sing the "Battle Hymn of the Republic" before the gates of the White House. These examples of patriotic symbolism were used in the movies of the 1930s to present situations of extraordinary figures who had suffered through their own difficult times, therefore, giving the public some confidence in its own future (Levine 181).

The movie produced a variety of reactions. Louis B. Mayer, head of Metro-Goldwyn-Mayer, which released the picture, and Will Hays of the Motion Picture Producers and Distributors of America were appalled by the production, not for its fascist overtones, but because it seemed pro-FDR, and they were staunch Republicans. Mayer, after a preview, reshot some scenes and modified others (Christensen 34). Members of Congress complained about how Congress was treated in the film by the president, and the State Department was also dissatisfied with Hammond's iron-fisted foreign policy. Not surprisingly, President Roosevelt enjoyed the film and saw it several times (Christensen 34).

Gabriel Over the White House was a movie that clearly revealed the yearning of the nation for a strong president during difficult times. Its popularity with audiences in 1933 indicated that it touched a nerve by putting on film what many in the nation fantasized the president and government should do (Christensen 34). The extreme solutions in the film required the divine intervention of an angel to get the president to move the country out of the

Depression; on a more secular plane, the people now placed their faith in FDR to do the same thing.

The President Vanishes (1935)

The President Vanishes, another film dealing with the president in critical circumstances, was released two years after Gabriel Over the White House. The President Vanishes, like Gabriel, placed the president in a proactive position to cope with America's crisis.

In the film, war has broken out in Europe and President Craig (Arthur Byron) has taken a position of nonintervention, even though Congress wishes him to intervene. A number of powerful men, including a banker, a steel magnate, a newspaper owner, a judge, and an oil tycoon, meet in a lobbyist's house in Washington to discuss how they can get the U.S. involved in the war for their economic benefit. They settle on the slogan "Save America's Honor," hoping to sway public opinion. They ally themselves with a fascist group called the Gray Shirts who also want America involved in the war.

The president is fearful that he will be impeached if he does not accede to the wishes of Congress for intervention, but he disappears on the day he is supposed to appear before Congress to ask for a declaration of war. The secretary of war leads an investigation to find the president, and the public directs its attention to the missing president and away from thoughts of war. It is later discovered that the president has hidden himself in a garage that is used by the Gray Shirts for their meetings to make it appear as if he had been kidnapped. The head of the Gray Shirts, Lincoln Lee (Edward Ellis), comes to the garage to kill the president, but one of his associates saves him by killing Lee. The president reveals that he plotted his own kidnapping to bring the people back to their senses, and he then speaks to the nation about his opposition to war and his faith in the American people.

The President Vanishes presents another cinematic example of a strong president who takes action, in this case to combat right wing and big-moneyed interests who wish to profit from war industries. Both The President Vanishes and Gabriel clearly have antiwar and isolationist themes in keeping with the public mood of the times, and fascism plays a part in both films. In the case of The President Vanishes, though, the president is seen combating fascist ideology rather than embracing a fascist mentality as he did in Gabriel. At the same time, the president uses tactics of a deceptive nature to fight fascism. Instead of using appropriate methods of constitutional debate, he takes matters into his own hands through a scheme that challenges the democratic process. Furthermore, the president comes across as a paternalistic leader who says he has faith in his public; yet he speaks critically of it when he states that he needs to bring the American public back to its senses (Levine 179). Such actions give the president elitist overtones.

The movie was not as concerned with the Depression as was *Gabriel*, possibly because FDR had already taken steps to alleviate some of the more egregious problems of the economic crisis. War in Europe now became a new concern of the American public. Also, phrases that the president and others used in the movie, such as "my friends" in addressing the public and "new deal," alluded to the rhetoric of FDR (Roffman and Purdy 73-74). In *Gabriel Over the White House*, in contrast, the movie was suggesting that FDR emulate the fictional president.

The President Vanishes was one of the first movies to depict the highest levels of American government or industry so directly and critically outside the genres of musical comedy or social satire (Bernstein 97). The Production Code Administration was critical of *The President Vanishes* for the way it portrayed industrialists as conspirators, and it suggested a number of revisions in the film before a production code certificate could be given, including changing one of the conspirators from a senator to a judge and making the vice president a stronger character, not a weakling or a fool.

In times of war and struggle, Americans turn to the legacy of Abraham Lincoln.

Library of Congress.

The President Vanishes, like *Gabriel Over the White House,* depicted a nation in disarray and in need of strong leadership. In both films the president used tactics that would certainly be questionable and would be challenged today—especially as a result of our increased concern about constitutional rights for individuals in conflict with the state. The public of the 1930s, though, was not as concerned about tactics as it was about its own economic and political emergency, and movies such as these gave it fantasy leaders and cinematic panaceas.

CONCLUSION

Two styles were used in depicting presidents in films of the 1930s. In three historical dramas concerning Abraham Lincoln, the president in office or in his earlier years was viewed in reverent tones. He was seen as a modest man with few aspirations for the presidency, and he was influenced by others, including his sweetheart, Ann Rutledge, and his wife, who pushed him in his career toward the White House. Lincoln was also viewed as a man who had concern for the law and what is right. These characteristics were in many ways the opposite of how the citizenry viewed contemporary politicians. In the minds of the public, most politicians were ambitious and interested in their own careers over the interests of the people. Corruption was also considered a prime trait of politicians. Furthermore, people had lost faith in their political leaders and institutions because of the Depression; this accounts for the popularity of gangster films where individuals could gain advantages in society and make a success of themselves even if it was outside of the law. The public, though, saw Lincoln in film as a man who, even with his own failings, could still become president and carry the country through an extremely difficult struggle. Lincoln, thus, gave the public hope that the nation could produce great presidents in times of trial—both in the past and, more importantly, in the future.

In the case of the films on fictional presidents from the 1930s, the characters were people whose actions worked toward ends that the public supported. Americans had mixed feelings regarding presidential power and leadership, which could be denounced one year, such as during the Hoover administration, and supported the next under FDR (Schlesinger 285). The citizenry wanted a strong president to bring them out of the Depression, even if the president took some liberties with laws and rights. Depression breeds disorder in society, and the public responded favorably to film presidents who could restore order by having lawbreakers rapidly tried and executed. When industrialists favored entry into war for their profit in *The President Vanishes,* the president outsmarted them through his own "kidnapping," and since the public placed much of the blame for the Depression on wealthy capitalists, the film gave the public the chance to imagine that the average person might occasionally come out ahead of the privileged. The public seemed to approve of the authoritarian measures of these film presidents in order to gain the needed ends. If it took a benevolent dictator and shortcuts in the democratic system to bring the nation back on track, the public did not seem to object to some bending of constitutional principles—at least in the nation's movie houses.

Some movie politicians were also viewed as con men whose winning personalities seemed more important to the public than the positions they took. At the same time, film politicians saw the citizenry as the foundation of the nation in whom they had faith while also referring to the public as stupid and lazy and needing to bring it back to its senses (Levine 178–79). In essence, both the public and the film politicians of the 1930s viewed each other with ambivalent feelings.

Movies of the 1930s, thus, revered real presidents, as movies would continue to do for the next three decades, while creating images of bold fictional presidents who could move the nation forward and solve its problems. In fact and fiction, films depicted presidents to the public who were strong leaders, and the people hoped for and accepted this type of president in order to restore economic stability and political normality. The screen personas of the presidents became the public's model for a real president of the era.

WORKS CITED

Bernstein, Matthew. *Walter Wanger: Hollywood Independent.* Berkeley: University of California Press, 1994.

Cameron, Kenneth. *America on Film: Hollywood and American History.* New York: Continuum Press, 1997.

Christensen, Terry. *Reel Politics: American Political Movies from* Birth of a Nation *to* Platoon. Oxford: Basil Blackwell, 1987.

"A Collective Text by the Editors of *Cahiers du Cinema:* John Ford's *Young Mr. Lincoln.*" In *Film Theory and Criticism,* edited by Gerald Mast and Marshall Cohen. New York: Oxford University Press, 1985.

Combs, James E. *American Political Movies: An Annotated Filmography of Feature Films.* New York: Garland Publishing, 1990.

Donald, David Herbert. *Lincoln.* New York: Touchstone, 1996.

Edelman, Rob. "Politicians in the American Cinema." In *The Political Companion to American Film,* edited by Gary Crowdus, 322–30. Chicago: Lake View Press, 1994.

Gallagher, Tag. *John Ford: The Man and His Films*. Berkeley: University of California Press, 1986.

Genovese, Michael. "Art and Politics: The Political Film as a Pedagogical Tool." Paper presented at the annual meeting of the American Political Science Association, 1995.

Klein, Maury. "Laughing Through Tears." *American History Illustrated*, March 1983, 10–21.

Levine, Lawrence. "Hollywood's Washington: Film Images of National Politics During the Great Depression." *Prospects* (1995): 169–95.

McBride, Joseph. *Searching for John Ford*. New York: St. Martin's, 2001

McConnell, Robert L. "The Genesis and Ideology of *Gabriel Over the White House*." *Cinema Journal* 16 (1976): 7–26.

Neely, Mark E. "The Young Lincoln." In *Past Imperfect: History According to the Movies*, edited by Mark C. Carnes. New York: Henry Holt, 1995.

Pitney, John J. "Fascism in *Gabriel Over the White House*." In *Reelpolitic: Political Ideologies in '30s and '40s Films*, edited by Beverly Kelly, 45–60. Westport: Praeger, 1998.

Platt, David. *Celluloid Power: Social Film Criticism from* Birth of a Nation *to* Judgment at Nuremberg. Metuchen: Scarecrow Press, 1992.

Roffman, Peter, and Jim Purdy. *The Hollywood Social Problem Film: Madness, Despair and Politics from the Depression to the Fifties*. Bloomington: Indiana University Press, 1982.

Schlesinger, Arthur M., Jr. *The Cycles of American History*. Boston: Houghton Mifflin, 1986.

Shindler, Colin. *Hollywood in Crisis: Cinema and American Society: 1929–1939*. London: Routledge, 1996.

Deborah Carmichael

GABRIEL OVER THE WHITE HOUSE (1933)

William Randolph Hearst's Fascist Solution for the Great Depression

President Judson
Hammond (Walter Huston)
lays down the law in a
nationwide address in
Gabriel Over the White House
(1933).

In today's vocabulary, "fascism" carries ominous implications from historical hindsight, but during the Great Depression many Americans believed that a fascist government was needed to relieve the nation's distress. Emotionally overwhelmed by the problems facing the country, citizens were willing to surrender individual rights to an executive given centralized control economically, politically, and socially. *Gabriel Over the White House* brought William Randolph Hearst's version of this fascist solution to the screen shortly after the 4 March 1933 inauguration of Franklin Delano Roosevelt.[1] The players behind the scenes are as fascinating as the characters on the screen. This 1933 MGM release, produced by Walter Wanger, written by Carey Wilson, and directed by Gregory LaCava for William Randolph Hearst's Cosmopolitan Films, reflects the political beliefs not only of Hearst but also of many concerned Americans. Even Charles Lindbergh, America's hero, advocated a monocratic government. These were the days when Father Charles E. Coughlin preached fascism from his radio pulpit while Huey Long practiced what he preached. An angry Francis E. Townsend proposed an Old Age Revolving Pension Plan, and William Dudley Pelley organized the Silver Shirts. Economist Lawrence Dennis penned *Is Capitalism Doomed?* in 1932 and went on to write an approving book entitled *The Coming American Fascism* in 1936. Mothers' movements led by women such as Elizabeth Dilling and Agnes Waters called for radical reforms. The left, particularly the Communist Party of the United States (CPUSA) with allies in labor movements including the Farmer-Labor Federation, fought equally hard for drastic change. The CPUSA, the importance of which is now often downplayed in a historical backlash to McCarthyism (1950–1954), was led by men answering directly to the Soviet Comintern (as the availability of records in 1991 reveals).[2] Both leftist and right-wing political activists responded to the crisis facing America in the 1930s—the stock market crash, rampant unemployment, reduced prices and markets for both farm and industrial production, bank foreclosures, and bank failures—and looked to Washington for leadership. The mood of the nation was one of desperation: "Even if they did not lose their jobs or go hungry themselves, even if the terror of want passed over them without touching them, most Americans felt its passage like a cold, unforgettable wind" (Watkins 12).

Although the fascist premise of *Gabriel Over the White House* may seem startling or even preposterous now, audiences in the 1930s were well aware of these multivocal appeals for a strong leader during what Arthur Schlesinger Jr. called a "crisis of the old order." These radical solutions tapped public fears and a growing frustration with government. At the time that the movie was produced, William Randolph Hearst was a strong supporter of Franklin Roosevelt, as were Father Coughlin and Huey Long. *Gabriel Over the White House* projects hypothetical solutions beyond constitutional boundaries into the realm of a fascist state, a totalitarian rhetoric very freely proposed in the media of the day.

The despair and frustration of the American public during the Great Depression spawned numerous political prophets. Father Coughlin preached a doctrine of currency reform and a restructuring of financial institutions, targeting bankers and wealthy capitalists as the source of America's problems. Coughlin provided radio support for FDR with slogans such as "Roosevelt or Ruin" and "The New Deal is Christ's Deal" (Brinkley 108–9). Huey Long proposed the "Share Our Wealth Society" and drafted the eloquent Gerald L.K.

Smith as its national organizer. Long's plan offered middle-class status to every American family by confiscating income from those citizens making more than one million dollars a year. Instead of a chicken in every pot, Huey Long promised that every family would have a home, an automobile, a radio, and a guaranteed annual income of two to three thousand dollars a year (Jeansonne, *Gerald* 35). Again, wealthy bankers and financiers were the villains. Townsend came up with a solution for both unemployment and for the security of the elderly. Anyone over sixty would receive $150 a month from the federal government, which the pensioners would be required to spend by the end of the month, putting money into the economy and creating new jobs. This plan would be supported by a sales tax on both retail and wholesale transactions (Brinkley 223). The Mothers' movements grew out of antiwar sentiment and into anticommunist crusades advocating a fascist form of government over a socialist one (Jeansonne, *Women* 1–15). Many, including William Randolph Hearst, had suggestions to offer an American public disillusioned with the laissez-faire approach of Presidents Coolidge (1923–1929) and Hoover (1929–1933).

THE POWER OF MEDIA

William Randolph Hearst understood the power of both the printed word and the visual arts to promote a message, just as Father Coughlin recognized the effectiveness of radio. Producer Walter Wanger gained firsthand experience of the power of media, serving in World War I with the Committee on Public Information (CPI). He later met documentary film pioneer John Grierson, who shared his belief that movies "had the very special duty to interpret the contemporary scene." Wanger once wrote a friend, "The talking motion picture is the greatest step in civilization. . . . It even exceeds the printing press in importance [for it can] bring to the poorest person in the street the greatest academic advantages of the day" (Bernstein 31, 72, 73). Hearst used both film and newsprint to advance his political views. Infamous for his manipulative methods, Hearst used his film company to do more than advance Marion Davies's screen career. He also promoted his political views in *Gabriel Over the White House*, which reflected both Hearst's personal desire to be politically influential and his belief that fascism was a viable national ideology.

As Andrew Robertson demonstrates in *The Language of Democracy*, "hortatory rhetoric" entered the American political arena after the French Revolution, linking "the audience in an immediate, emotional way to events, principles, or policies, mostly real, often exaggerated, sometimes illusory" (Robertson 11).[3]

By the beginning of the twentieth century, print technology had advanced to the point at which visual images were no longer difficult to reproduce. The written word often took a subordinate role to pictorial representations, especially cartoons. "The yellow press's celebration of 'unity' required *ad odium* negative references. The word that came to denote such references was originally a printing term: stereotypes" (Robertson 208–9). The Hearst-Pulitzer battle for the "Yellow Kid" cartoonist R.F. Outcault in 1895 illustrates the importance of visual journalism. "Negative references" were used to attack political rivals, and they also pandered to prejudices regarding "foreigners." Robertson notes that, "The first stage of rhetorical transformation is the use of familiar themes set in a new context" (Robertson 216).[4] William Randolph Hearst was well aware of the political impact of visual editorial comment, especially for a mass audience: "The policy of his *Evening Journal* was 'to engage brains as well as to get the news, for the public is even more fond of entertainment than it is of information'" (Robertson 208). George Seldes indicates that, although "surveys have shown that thousands of Hearst readers hate[d] his views," they continued to buy his newspapers because they liked Hearst comics (Seldes 100).

Hearst entered the motion picture business in 1913, beginning with newsreels produced for Hearst-Selig News Pictorial. Hearst productions quickly became "omnipresent" in movie theaters, offering weekly newsreels, serials, and cartoons based on his Sunday comics with Gregory LaCava managing his animation studio in 1915 (Nasaw 237). "By 1919, Fox, Pathe, Hearst and Universal were each producing two newsreel issues a week, reaching an average audience of 40 million people" (Muscio 18). As Andrew Bergman notes, "During the most abysmal days of the early thirties, . . . movie attendance still averaged an astonishing sixty to seventy-five million persons each week," although unemployment was nearing fifteen million and the number of under-employed also grew (Bergman xi). Hearst used both the power of the press and the cinema to impose his political message on that audience of millions.[5]

Although Hearst never formally endorsed fascism, he was often criticized by his opponents as being pro-Hitler and pro-Mussolini. After visiting Mussolini in 1931, Hearst wrote of Il Duce, "'He is a marvelous man. . . . It is astonishing how he takes care of every detail of his job'" (Swanberg 430). Many Hearst critics felt the publisher ran his newspapers as a tyrant, who, like Mussolini, left few details to the care of others.[6] Hearst met Adolph Hitler in 1934. In 1936 Ferdinand Lundberg published *Imperial Hearst*, which was representative of the criticism Hearst received from contemporaries. Lundberg wrote, "Today Hearst is the keystone of American fascism, the integrating point in a structure around which political reaction is attempting to develop a movement which, if it succeeds, will tragically dupe America." Lundberg goes on to reveal that Hearst had been quoted in the German press as saying, "If Hitler succeeds in pointing the way of peace and order and an ethical development which has been destroyed throughout the world by war, he will have accomplished a measure of good not only for his own people but for all humanity. . . .This battle, in fact, can only be viewed as a struggle which all liberty-loving peoples are bound to follow with understanding and sympathy" (Lundberg 343–44). Hearst may not have been a "self-proclaimed" fascist, but he certainly respected the authoritarian regimes of both Mussolini and Hitler.

The inflammatory radio commentary of Father Coughlin received favorable publicity from Hearst newspapers in the 1930s. Lundberg even charged that Father Coughlin "is obviously a Hearst puppet" (Lundberg 277). As Swanberg notes, two of the three Hearst biographies appearing in 1936 were "written by liberals who regarded Hearst as a fascist" (Swanberg 477). Lundberg's book is dedicated "To Heywood Broun and the American Newspaper Guild," a group Hearst strongly opposed. In 1935, Alfred Bingham called for a Commonwealth Party made up of labor and farm-union members. Because of Hearst's strong antilabor and anticommunist stance, it is not surprising that Bingham would indict Hearst as "the obvious type of backer for a Fascist movement and whose power could be used to make a Long-Coughlin movement definitely anti-red, anti-labor and militantly jingoistic" (Bingham 188). Also in 1935, Raymond Gram Swing published his book, *Forerunners of American Fascism;* it proved so popular that a second edition appeared in April of that year. Swing wrote, "Mr. Hearst did not arrive at this fascist faith by sudden conversion, or perhaps even conscious of the full implications of what he was advocating. He did not plump for fascism as such, and so far he never has. Even if he were a conscious fascist, it would be poor business to admit it" (Swing 145). During the 1932 presidential campaign, Herbert Hoover included Hearst in his "roll of revolutionists," labeling them "'exponents of a social philosophy different from the traditional American one'" (quoted in Schlesinger 434–44). Describing the attacks on Hearst as a fascist proselytizer, Swanberg writes, "The charge was echoed, re-echoed and widely believed during the peculiar ideological frenzy of the Thirties. Those who looked for a bogeyman found it in Hearst." This biographer continues by noting that some echoed Swing, saying they "thought it possible that Hearst entertained fascist ideas without even knowing it" (Swanberg 444–46). It seems impossible to state unequivocally that William Randolph Hearst considered himself a fascist. His political loyalties were too mercurial; he shifted his allegiance from a Democratic to a Republican and back to a Democratic presidential candidate. At the time that Hearst was approached by Walter Wanger about producing *Gabriel Over the White House*, he was a staunch supporter of Franklin Roosevelt.

PRODUCTION HISTORY

Walter Wanger, after working at Paramount and Columbia, joined MGM in 1933. He had already produced *Washington Merry-Go-Round* (1932), a prototype for Frank Capra's *Mr. Smith Goes to Washington* (1939). Within days of arriving at the newest studio, Wanger "asked MGM's story editor Samuel Marx to purchase" the screen rights for *Gabriel Over the White House*. The producer acted quickly to get the film underway on a "program picture" budget, perhaps to avoid the scrutiny of Louis B. Mayer, a dedicated Republican. Carey Wilson, a protégé of Irving Thalberg, was assigned to write the screenplay. "After two weeks of script preparation and the assignment of comedy expert Gregory LaCava to direct the film," Wanger had gained the financial backing of William Randolph Hearst. After being fired by Paramount in 1931, Wanger hoped to start an independent film company and considered leasing Cosmopolitan's Harlem studio, but he was unable to find investment capital for his plan (Bernstein 79–84). Much earlier, Wanger had negotiated Irene Castle's contract to star in Hearst's 1917 serial, *Patria* (Bernstein 30). Wanger's acquaintance with Hearst and his political leaning indicated that Cosmopolitan Films would be the ideal production company for this project. Cosmopolitan had been on the MGM lot since 1923, and it had been a mutually beneficial arrangement. Marion Davies's films were distributed by MGM, and MGM received favorable reviews in the Hearst press (Bernstein 84). Early in February, Hearst began to provide his input on the script for *Gabriel*.

The film was based upon an eponymous book published anonymously by Thomas W. Tweed, an aide to former British Prime Minister David Lloyd George. The dystopian novel dramatized a time of high unemployment, governments in jeopardy, war debts unpaid, rampant crime, and angry veterans. Wanger chose to set the film in the present, using inaugural newsreel footage to add to the realism. William Randolph Hearst immediately put his personal political stamp on the screenplay, often dictating changes or writing them himself. Hearst chose to soften the "social ills" of the narrative, while emphasizing solutions to the country's problems as initiated by an "activist" president. The summit-conference speech, delivered by *Gabriel's* President Hammond (Walter Huston), was written by Hearst himself, echoing the editorial pages of his newspaper empire. Hearst had found another avenue for promoting his current political philosophy, emphasizing public works and the financing of federal programs with money collected on Europe's World War I debts to America (Bernstein 84).

With the Hearst-Wilson script complete, production moved quickly on *Gabriel*, taking only ten days to shoot (from 16–26 February). To keep costs down, only two well-known Hollywood actors were signed to the film: Walter Huston (D.W. Griffith's *Abe Lincoln* [1930]) and Karen Morley (*Washington Masquerade* [1932]). Production costs came in at $180,000, and the film ultimately showed a profit of over $200,000 (Bernstein 84–86). Wanger previewed his movie in March 1933 in Glendale, California, at which time Louis B. Mayer discovered the nature of his producer's latest effort. Mayer, angered that *Gabriel* was openly anti-Hoover and pro-Roosevelt, sought to suppress the film. As David Nasaw writes, President Hammond had "been transformed from a Warren Harding–like hack who speaks in Herbert Hoover–like platitudes to a man of Lincolnesque stature who sounds like a Hearst editorial" (Nasaw 464). The Production Code Administration (PCA), the self-policing administrative organization instituted by the Hollywood studios to avoid government censorship, took exception to some of the film's content. As early as January 1933, James Wingate of the Hays Office had expressed concerns about the script, and only a week after Franklin Roosevelt's inauguration, the film had become a concern at the real White House.

Roosevelt's press secretary, Stephen Early, contacted PCA head, Will Hays, with objections to *Gabriel's* plot. Irving Thalberg, Nicholas Schenk, and Louis B. Mayer offered assurances that script changes would be made (Nasaw 464–65). Wingate, Mayer, and the new administration had three main concerns: first, the depiction of a mob marching on Washington might lead to real mob violence reminiscent of the 1932 Bonus March (the *Gabriel* march was moved to Baltimore); second, the unflattering portrayal of Washington politicians might alienate Congress, resulting in a negative scrutiny of Hollywood studios (President Hammond's speech to Congress was revised); and third, in March 1933, the State Department was holding negotiations with Germany on arms limitations. Hammond's ultimatum to world leaders was moved from a naval vessel to a private yacht (Bernstein 84–85). Although White House aides had read the screenplay, Hays feared repercussions from Congress in the form of "punitive tax or censorship legislation" (Musico 92). Two script revisions were provided to the Hays office, and although the second revision was accepted, additional changes were made (Nasaw 465). By 29 March, *Gabriel Over the White*

House had received the production code seal. Although Hearst, Wanger, LaCava, and Wilson were disappointed with the final result, the film, suffering only minor cuts at the state level, became a box office success—one of the top six movies of April 1933 (Bergman 118). Although Hearst's rhetoric reached theaters in a softened version, the film certainly connected with an audience lacking confidence in government policy and hoping for some economic miracle.

FASCIST RHETORIC

Fascist rhetoric and ideology in America in the 1930s played more to emotions than to reason and often offered vague solutions and shadowy causes and culprits. *Gabriel Over the White House* worked upon audience emotions with an extensive use of patriotic music and symbolism while demonstrating the need for change in government. Lawrence Dennis introduced *The Coming American Fascism* by noting that, "Terms like communism and fascism, just as terms like Christianity, Americanism, or due process of law, must mean many different and often mutually exclusive things to different people" (Dennis vii). Fluid definitions of fascism, or any "ism" being promoted, grew from personal circumstance and popular media representations as in *Gabriel*. Mostafa Rejai offered three main components of a totalitarian ideology, outlining them as: first, a total rejection of "existing order as corrupt, immoral, unjust, beyond hope, and beyond repair"; second, an offer of "a utopian vision of grand myth"; and third, a "statement of plans and programs intended to realize the alternative order" (Rejai 70). This description suggests that certain conditions must be present for a totalitarian voice to be accepted: dissatisfaction with current conditions, a nostalgia for the past or hope for a better future, and a demand for corrective action. "Demagogy makes its appearance whenever a democratic society is threatened with internal destruction" (Lowenthal xi). An "activist" leader can argue convincingly for suspension of both individual freedoms and democratic government while promising solutions to present social and economic conditions. Leo Lowenthal and Norbert Guterman discuss what they label as "Themes of Agitation."[7] To convince citizens that radical change is necessary, these authors believe that "Social Malaise" is a prerequisite for acceptance of such change by the general public or, more specifically, those with the most to lose, the middle-class.

Victor Ferkiss, in his article "Populist Influences on American Fascism," rejects the idea that fascism grew from Progressive or Populist movements but concedes that fascism in this country appealed to the same people, "a middle class composed largely of farmers and small merchants which feels itself being crushed between big business—and especially big finance—on the one hand, and an industrial working class which tends to question the necessity of the wage system and even of private property itself on the other (Ferkiss 91). Playing upon these fears of left-wing ideologies, a demagogue denouncing economic, political, and moral injustices could trigger emotional responses and feelings, such as distrust, helplessness, anxiety over the future, and disillusionment with the current political system (Lowenthal 12–14). Outspoken proponents of fascism, whether speaking in the press or the cinema as Hearst did, or from Father Coughlin's Detroit pulpit, or from Huey Long's Louisiana statehouse, played upon the fears and misgivings of a depression audience using common themes of suspicion.

Lowenthal and Guterman outline twenty-one "themes of agitation." They first describe the "hostile world" in which Americans may be convinced they inhabit. Propaganda to support this claim includes emphasis on a conspiracy of dishonest politicians and financiers "duping" the general public, fueling resentment of both plutocrats and government—the "haves" versus the "have nots" (Lowenthal 20–37).[8] Another common strategy to promote a radical ideology calls upon fears of a "ruthless enemy" in the guise of corrupt leaders in league with racketeers here at home or foreign enemies seeking to destroy America through political infiltration and economic upheaval (Lowenthal 38–51). Lowenthal and Guterman point out that the rhetoric of insurrection is purposefully vague, calling upon common values and shared traditions in the name of ill-defined goals (Lowenthal 6–7). The voice of totalitarianism seeks to appeal to the submerged fears of each person with a call for collective action. Arthur Schlesinger Jr. considered the winter of 1932–1933 as a time when, "A cult of direct action was beginning to grow." Al Smith, comparing the Depression to war, reminded Americans that, "In the World War we took our Constitution, wrapped it up and laid it on the shelf and left it there until it was over." Walter Lippmann advocated a presidency given "the widest and fullest powers, [with] limit[ed] congressional rights of debate and amendment" (Lowenthal 460–61). Hoover's policy of seeking solutions for the Depression in local governments was proving unsuccessful. Farmers, union members, the growing numbers of unemployed, as well as economists and public leaders began to look for centralized relief provided by a federal government, even if this meant relinquishing constitutional rights. "'There was serious talk of revolution as early as 1931' . . . thus were opportunities provided for a . . . horde of ambitious leaders in the preparatory stages of fascism'" (Schonbach 228–29).

Fascist rhetoric relied upon many elements of frustration and discontent, especially within a hard-working middle class of farmers and small merchants who saw themselves as abandoned by their government. Charismatic leaders, such as Coughlin and Long, were happy to voice their quasi-fascist plans. And *Gabriel Over the White House* was released at a time that was ripe for the message Hearst, Wanger, LaCava, and Wilson brought to the screen. That message of the benefits of a benign dictator heavily relied upon an American iconography of nostalgia for a patriotic and better past.

BIBLICAL CONNECTIONS

With Hearst, Wanger, and LaCava's understanding of the power of visual representations, it is not surprising that *Gabriel Over the White House* is packed with traditional symbols of America's political legacy. The title's archangel, whose presence is signaled by soft music and a fluttering lace curtain, links President Hammond (Walter Huston) to the Puritan mission to build a new Jerusalem. In the biblical Book of Daniel, Gabriel reveals,

> I am now come forth to give thee skill and understanding . . . for thou *art* greatly beloved: therefore understand the matter, and consider the vision. Seventy weeks are determined upon thy people and upon thy holy city, to finish the transgression, and to make an end of sins, and to make reconciliation for iniquity, and to bring an everlasting righteousness. . . . Know therefore and understand, that from the going forth of the commandment to build Jerusalem . . . the street shall be built again, and the wall, even in troublous times. (Daniel 9: 23–25, King James Version)

President Hammond, transformed after a car accident and subsequent coma, embarks upon a "holy" mission to reform government, vanquish iniquitous gangsters, and preserve America's future through war-debt repayment. Like Gabriel, he will be a messenger of both mercy and vengeance, bringing truth and hope to the nation. Hammond, the shyster politician from the opening scenes, reminded by cigar-smoking political cronies that he owes them the election, stuns his cabinet with his sudden recovery, announcing that he is no longer concerned with party politics. Hammond will answer only to "the people."

This cinematic conversion mirrors William Dudley Pelley's encounter with the spirit world. Pelley, a successful writer, including time in Hollywood as a screenwriter, claimed that he died in May 1928, received instructions while in heaven, and returned from the dead, continuing to communicate with God (Jeansonne, *Women* 37–38). "He always referred to the date of his founding the Silver Shirt Legion as January 31, 1933, simultaneous with Hitler's gaining the chancellorship," and he sometimes described himself as the "American Hitler" (Schonbach 305). For those in the theater audience familiar with Pelley's story, the reforms President Hammond enacted would come as no surprise. However, Hammond is not only changed in spirit but also in appearance, providing visual confirmation of his metamorphosis. When his disgruntled personal secretary demands to see the president, she is met with a ghostly figure seated in a pose calling up visions of the statue of Lincoln by Daniel Chester French in the Lincoln Memorial. The archangel Gabriel has transformed Hammond from a party hack into a gaunt figure resembling a wartime Abraham Lincoln, with the implication that he now believes in a government "of the people, by the people, and for the people."[9]

After the president's embrace of the people and his rejection of party politics, his private secretary argues that although he might sound crazy, "a simple, honest man can solve anything" (evoking for the audience the humble beginnings of Honest Abe); she speaks of "divine madness." When the president fails to recognize his speech for Congress until a mysterious luminescence fills the Oval Office, his secretary becomes convinced of a third presence within Hammond. His past political self has been cast off and replaced, after his accident, by a benevolent defender of the "little guy," who is now infused with a godlike spirit. Pendy (Karen Morley), Hammond's personal secretary, reveals to Beek (Franchot Tone), the press secretary, that God has sent Gabriel as an "angel of revelation." Beek muses on the idea of "Gabriel over the White House." The film cuts back to the president in the Oval Office as he hears the strains of "The Battle Hymn of the Republic." As he turns to the window, a choir of "common men" appears on the lawn and then abruptly vanishes. Hammond moves past a bust of Lincoln, which now has facial features that are pale and indistinct, although the clothing remains crisply detailed. The spirit of Lincoln has "entered" President Hammond while the archangel Gabriel keeps watch over him, the White House, and the country. Both God and the Great Emancipator inspire the actions the president will take.

HISTORY AND PATRIOTISM

The use of "The Battle Hymn of the Republic" also connects President Hammond with an earlier sequence in the film set in Central Park. Activist

John Bronson prepares a "Million Man March" on Washington with his Army of the Unemployed.[10] Early in the film, Hammond had played hide-and-seek with his nephew in the Oval Office, with a bust of Lincoln prominently displayed, while ignoring Bronson's radio plea to relieve the plight of the unemployed. Bronson (David Landau) is summoned by two thugs to the posh art deco apartment of gangster Nick Diamond (C. Henry Gordon), seen bribing a police officer. Diamond hopes to bribe Bronson to remain in Central Park, distracting the police from enforcing Prohibition laws. Bronson refuses to cooperate and is soon gunned down. With his dying words, he urges the Army of the Unemployed to advance without him, as the sound of "The Battle Hymn of the Republic" swells in the background.[11] The recurring use of this Civil War anthem connects Hammond with both Lincoln and "a people" committed to a redress of grievances. In the next scene, President Hammond dismisses the secretary of war who has suggested mobilizing the army against the marchers.

The first of the film's fascist motifs appears here as the president orders food for these men, vowing to "feed our own," not foreigners. The foreign "other" has been introduced into the story line. Hammond travels to Baltimore to speak before the Army of the Unemployed. Promising "the last full measure" of protection and help for these men, the president declares them to be the first recruits as soldiers in the Army of Construction, with military pay and military rules; they will remain in service until industry can hire them. This state-of-emergency decision will remain in effect until the president declares the crisis over. (Hammond has begun to expand his executive powers.) An upbeat rendition of "The Battle Hymn of the Republic" closes this scene. President Hammond has established a new military branch, staffed by grateful citizens loyal to his policies. With food and rhetoric, the president has won their hearts and minds. The film's Army of Construction prefigures FDR's Civilian Conservation Corps (CCC), a paramilitary service corps, which provided work for many unemployed youths.

This resolution of the march on Baltimore directly calls into question Herbert Hoover's response to veteran requests for a lump-sum payment of the bonus approved by Congress in 1924. Schlesinger recounts the march on Washington in 1932 by thousands of angry and frustrated veterans—the Bonus Expeditionary Force. In July 1932, a nervous police officer fired into a crowd of veterans; the use of federal troops was immediately approved by Hoover. Such later notables as Douglas MacArthur, Dwight David Eisenhower, and George Patton Jr. supervised the infamous charge made upon the veterans' camps, killing one and wounding several others (Schlesinger 257–65). "Newsreels showed tanks rumbling through the streets. . . . From coast to coast, theater audiences booed and hissed as they viewed the shocking scene" (Freidel 75). A second Bonus Army traveled to Washington in May 1933. Instead of being met by tanks and tear gas, this group was greeted by a sympathetic Eleanor Roosevelt, creating a positive media event, reminding newsreel audiences of Roosevelt's inaugural promise to lead the "great army of the people."

With executive measures in place and the entire cabinet dismissed, the ensuing scene, set in the Senate chamber, opens with a call for impeachment of the president. President Hammond strides into the room past the American flag and a portrait of Washington. Declaring himself a representative of the people, "the roots" of the country, he demands that Congress declare an official state of emergency and immediately adjourn, giving him full power to guide the nation. In response to charges of "dictatorship," he calls upon the principles of America's iconic leaders—Washington, Jefferson, and Lincoln—"in the name of the people." Aligning his goals and those of the nation's founders with the words of the Communist Manifesto, for the "greatest good for the greatest number," he declares martial law, justified by his power as commander in chief of the armed forces. President Hammond reinterprets Jeffersonian democracy as Ezra Pound had done. Rather than a decentralized government, this president centers total power solely on his own decisions.[12] Hammond takes decisive action as demanded by the seriousness of the national crisis; he becomes the "activist" president Hearst envisioned.

President Hammond moves quickly to explain his plans to the country through a radio broadcast reminiscent of FDR's "Fireside Chats."[13] Announcing new banking laws, including no foreclosures, promising fifty-five million dollars in aid to farmers, Hammond goes on to repeal the Eighteenth Amendment and establish state-owned liquor stores. Early in 1933, Roosevelt informed a Hearst representative that "he considered farm relief the first priority; then unemployment relief and public works, though he described Hearst's five-billion-dollar program as 'too large at present'" (Schlesinger 453). Roosevelt acted as quickly and decisively as the fictional President Hammond. "The night of his inauguration he [Roosevelt] ordered Secretary of the Treasury Woodin to prepare emergency banking legislation. The next day he forbade further transactions in gold, proclaimed a bank holiday, and called Congress into a special session beginning March 9." On the first day of that special session both the House and Senate passed Roosevelt's requested banking legislation (McJimsey 35–36). The Agricultural Adjustment Administration (AAA), the

Federal Emergency Relief Administration (FERA), the Civilian Conservation Corps (CCC), and the Tennessee Valley Authority (TVA) quickly found acceptance from Congress. And on 5 December 1933, Prohibition was repealed. *Gabriel's* fictional events reflected and anticipated Roosevelt's swift action during his first one hundred days as well as the later programs of his administration.

ETHNIC GANGSTERISM

President Hammond's encounter with the mob creates a fictionalized scapegoat for the country's woes. The film cuts to the mocking, gin-running mobster Nick Diamond (C. Henry Gordon), as he enters the White House. Meeting with President Hammond in the Oval Office, Diamond, dwarfed by a painting of Washington, is offered the opportunity to "return to his own country." Diamond is not only the "gangster" enemy; as an immigrant exploiting nontraditional avenues to success, he has become a "foreign" enemy threatening America. After his refusal to comply, two government "heavies" escort Diamond from the Oval Office. Nick Diamond and his henchmen quickly retaliate by bombing a government liquor store and by spraying bullets through the front doors of the White House in a drive-by shooting—during which Pendy, the president's personal secretary, is seriously wounded. The attack on the "people's home" signifies an attack on the nation, the presidency, and innocent citizens. Such a threat requires drastic executive action.

President Hammond responds by creating a mobile Federal Police and assigns Beek to head up this extralegal force, ordered to be "ruthless and merciless against gangsters." With cannon-equipped armored cars attacking Diamond's warehouse, the mob is captured in short order. In the most chilling scenes of *Gabriel*, a military tribunal court-martials the gangsters in a set reminiscent of a Kafka narrative.[14] Condemning his prisoners to death for their gangland killings, Beek, presiding over the trial in military uniform, praises the president for "cutting the red tape" of the civil judicial system by getting "to first principles," that is, "an eye for an eye." The mobsters are bound, blindfolded, and summarily shot by a firing squad as Lady Liberty looks on from New York Harbor. President Hammond's Federal Police have assumed the role of gangsters, publicly executing government enemies without due process of the law. Fascist "law and order" replaces the right to a trial before a duly appointed judge and jury. Hammond has become both of these, with the American public benefiting from this execution of the "last of the racketeers." With the approval of Lady Liberty, the president has eliminated one group of "foreign enemies," subverting the humanitarianism of her message, "Give me your tired, your poor, your huddled masses yearning to breathe free."

Next the president moves to render external "foreign" enemies defenseless. Calling world leaders to meet on the presidential yacht, they are angered to learn, once at sea, that their negotiations will be broadcast to the public by radio. With American battleships gliding past, Hammond demands that all war debts be repaid. Americans have been pickpocketed by foreign nations. He informs these captive diplomats that if they fail to agree to his demands, the Naval Limitations Agreement will be broken. Hammond holds the world hostage. America will begin to build a new navy to "defend" the country. In a show of power, the president commands the Naval Air Corps to sink two American battleships.[15] As these ships slip beneath the waves, Hammond predicts that future conflicts will rely upon air power, which will destroy cities as well as armies, resulting in the depopulation of the earth from the use of poison gases and "death rays." He calls for a mutual arms-destruction agreement, with the United States to comply last, as the means for bringing "peace on earth; good will to men." America will gain the power to function as the totalitarian "peacekeeper" of the world.

Agreeing to Hammond's "Washington Covenant," the world's leaders meet for the signing ceremony with radio microphones at hand as each "foreign" representative adds his signature to the document. After all have participated, a weary president slowly enters the East Room, accompanied by the sound of "The Battle Hymn of the Republic." Taking up the pen Abraham Lincoln had used for the signing of the Emancipation Proclamation, Hammond adds his signature, finalizing the disarmament treaty, and then collapses. His limp body is carried to his bedroom, recalling the journey of the wounded body of Lincoln carried from Ford's Theatre. President Hammond has performed his last act on an international stage. Placed on a leather chaise with the bust of Washington just beyond his shoulder, he remarks that it is "his heart" that has given out and caused his collapse. As the curtains flutter, the Gabriel leitmotif sounds once again. Refusing medication from his doctor, saying, "there is nothing you can do for me," his tired, sunken face, closely resembling that of Lincoln, slowly transforms into the heavy-jowled politician first seen in the film. As Hammond expires in Pendy's arms, Gabriel's musical theme is played a final time as the curtains stir at the window. Gabriel may be standing vigilant above the White House, but the spirits of Lincoln and Hammond appear to have departed the room. Pendy names him the "greatest man who ever lived," as the sound of "The Battle Hymn of the Republic" swells louder. Pendy and Beek announce to the anxious diplomats that the president wishes "peace on earth" for a millennium, and then announces, "The President is dead."

An inspired totalitarian leader has saved America because the death scene comes after President Hammond has "emancipated" the country from both internal and external "enemies." This suggests that his role as "benign" dictator has been successful in leading America to a brighter future. The closing shot reveals the American flag being lowered to half-mast, as average Americans look on. One does not know if Gabriel still watches over the White House, but the grand old flag endures to the end, and martial law remains in place as the screen fades to black.

CRITICAL RESPONSE

Variety described the film as, "A cleverly executed commercial release, it waves the flag frantically, preaches political claptrap with ponderous solemnity, but it won't inspire a single intelligent reaction in a carload of admission tickets" (Balio 288). Although the *Nation* criticized *Gabriel* as profascist, the reviewer pointed out that, "Now for the first time Hollywood openly accepts the depression as fact," addressing "the current popular interest in social and economic ideas" (Mitchell 219). Andrew Bergman notes that a Michigan theater manager found it to be "one of the best pictures ever played," while a theater patron in Mississippi stated, "Well if I was President of this fool old U.S.A., I would okay this great picture . . . it will give them a brighter hope for tomorrow." The *New Republic* bitterly noted that the film "represents pretty well its public" (Bergman 118). President Roosevelt wrote to Hearst:

> I want to send you this line to tell you how pleased I am with the changes you made in *Gabriel Over the White House*. I think it is an intensely interesting picture and should do much to help. Several people have seen it with us at the White House and to every one of them it was tremendously interesting. Some of these people said they never went to movies or cared for them but they think this a most unusual picture. (Nasaw 466)

Roosevelt's comments are a study in ambiguity—interesting, unusual, useful—words designed to neither condemn nor offer high praise for the film. Choosing these words carefully, Roosevelt would maintain favorable coverage in the Hearst papers until early in 1935, when the publisher took exception to the proposed American membership in the World Court and later to higher income taxes (Nasaw 511–13). In typical Hearst fashion, the publisher would later back Roosevelt once again.

THE "ACTIVIST" PRESIDENCY

Although political ideologies in the 1930s were as quixotic as Hearst's political allegiances, *Gabriel Over the White House* dramatizes common elements of totalitarian rhetoric. Bronson's Army of the Unemployed (visually all men) underscores the frustration of a depression audience longing for a return to traditional order and the virtue of the common man as honest laborer. This army of discontented men implies a fracture of the American family and the values the family represents. President Hammond embodies the spirit of the American myth, becoming a charismatic leader of Lincolnesque physical appearance, creating practical programs offering food and work. His ideology embraces "the people"—"a simple, honest man can solve anything." Reminding the public of America's glorious past, Hammond borrows from Washington, Jefferson, and Lincoln with the blessing of the archangel Gabriel connecting his policies to the Puritan mission for the country. No interior shot of either the White House or the Capitol building lacks a bust or portrait of one of America's founding fathers.

To establish an equitable distribution of wealth, prosperous scapegoats must be identified and punished. *Gabriel Over the White House* avoids labeling bankers and financiers as the villains of the Depression, although Hammond bans foreclosures. Instead, wealth is located in the hands of mobsters profiting by ignoring the laws of the land and foreign governments ignoring responsibility for war debts while allocating funds for rearmament. Martial law guided by a benign dictator offered solutions to the Great Depression. The visual message of *Gabriel Over the White House* reached a wider audience than Hearst publications could engage, providing William Randolph Hearst with a unique opportunity to advance his political agenda. As Andrew Bergman points out, "Every movie is a cultural artifact." The box office success of *Gabriel Over the White House* indicates that the film "depicted things lost or things desired" (Bergman xii). Hearst hoped to demonstrate that an "activist" president offered solutions. Moviegoers of 1933 hoped to regain prosperity with a new administration and a New Deal. Roosevelt acted quickly to respond to depression conditions and the mood of desperation gripping the nation. The success of the fictional President Hammond in *Gabriel Over the White House* foreshadowed the decisive, wide-ranging programs of Franklin Delano Roosevelt's first year as president of a country fearful of the future but hopeful that strong leadership would end the Great Depression. The "first hundred days" of the Roosevelt administration produced more sweeping changes than Hearst's cinematic president could have ever imagined. Roosevelt "sent fifteen messages up to the hill, . . . [he saw] fifteen historic laws through to final passage," including legislation on "agricultural and industrial recovery experiments, mortgage relief, welfare and public works, and reform ranging from securities regulation to the establishment of the TVA" (Leuchtenburg 125; Freidel 105). Hearst's vision of a benevolent, totalitarian, Lincolnesque president taking determined control in *Gabriel Over the White House* pales in comparison with FDR's pragmatic opportunism, yet parallels persist. Both Hearst's President Hammond and President Roosevelt understood the power of the media to reach "the people." And both presidents experienced a transformation once in office. It was written of Roosevelt that, "The oath of office seems suddenly to have transfigured him from a man of mere charm and buoyancy to one of dynamic aggressiveness" (Leuchtenburg 125). President Hammond's transformation delighted audiences; FDR's policies transformed America.

NOTES

1. The exact release date remains unclear. The MGM web page (http://www.mgm.com/cgi-bin/c2k/search_result_alpha.html&from=g&to=h) lists a 1 January release date, but if Matthew Bernstein's research is correct, the film was shot 16–26 February. David Nasaw notes a March preview and production code approval in late March.

The *New York Times* included a review of *Gabriel* in the 1 April edition, and *Variety* ran a review on 4 April 1933.

2. For an analysis of the CPUSA as a minimal threat to American government see Ellen Schrecker's *The Age of McCarthyism: A Brief History with Documents* or her longer work, *No Ivory Tower: McCarthyism and the Universities.* For an examination of communications between the Comintern and the CPUSA, see Harvey Klehr, John Earl Haynes, and Kyrill M. Anderson's *The Soviet World of American Communism.*

3. This hortatory rhetoric was more inflammatory than the laudatory form preceding it. Robertson calls hortatory rhetoric a "cry of 'Fire' in the theater" (11). Political rhetoric shifted from a positive, laudatory focus to an alarmist, emotional (rather than intellectual) form. Addressing the fears or dissatisfactions of the audience created a more direct response.

4. Robertson writes that Abraham Lincoln "had the moral vision to frame issues and set them in a context that would be clear to an audience" while using "mythic imagery" (216–17).

5. Walter Lippmann described *Gabriel* as "a dramatization of Mr. Hearst's editorials" (Bergman 115).

6. Charles Foster Kane, a thinly disguised portrayal of William Randolph Hearst in Orson Welles's *Citizen Kane* (1941), displays these characteristics.

7. It should be noted that Lowenthal and Guterman's *Prophets of Deceit* is part of a series called Studies in Prejudice published by the Department of Scientific Research of the American Jewish Committee.

8. *Gabriel Over the White House* touches only briefly on the supposed evildoings of the banking community.

9. Lincoln took command of the Union troops, relieving General George McClellan of command.

10. Only one black American is included in the crowd of unemployed.

11. Julia Ward Howe wrote "The Battle Hymn of the Republic" in November 1861 after watching Union troops march into battle. She wrote and lectured on women's suffrage and black emancipation (*Columbia Encyclopedia*). Frank Capra effectively used both patriotic anthems and national monuments to rally Americans behind the war effort in *Prelude to War* (1942), the first film of his *Why We Fight* series.

12. As early as 1909, Herbert Croly in *The Promise of American Life* wrote, "The time may come when the fulfillment of a justifiable democratic purpose may demand the limitation of certain rights" (36).

13. In 1936, Elliott Roosevelt, FDR's son, was named vice president of Hearst's radio businesses (Swanberg 477).

14. After the terrorist attacks on America of 11 September 2001, President George W. Bush advocated the formation of military tribunals to bring foreign terrorists to justice in a manner that would bypass the court system of the United States.

15. Early in the 1920s, Billy Mitchell demonstrated the effectiveness of air attacks on ships at sea. His persistent campaign to promote air power resulted in his court-martial for insubordination in 1925 (Schlesinger 74). During World War II, Mitchell's predictions about air power were vindicated. Lindbergh admired the highly advanced aircraft industry of Nazi Germany and received the German Medal of Honor from Hermann Goering in 1938, leading to accusations that he was a Nazi sympathizer. A staunch isolationist, Lindbergh resigned from the Army Air Corps after Roosevelt publicly attacked him. After Pearl Harbor, Lindbergh's request to reenlist was refused. In 1944, Lindbergh served as a civilian advisor in the Pacific theater and flew some fifty combat missions.

WORKS CITED

Balio, Tino. *The Grand Design: Hollywood as a Modern Business Enterprise, 1930–1939.* New York: Scribner's Sons, 1993.

Bergman, Andrew. *We're in the Money: Depression America and Its Films.* New York: New York University Press, 1971.

Bernstein, Matthew. *Walter Wanger, Hollywood Independent.* Berkeley: University of California Press, 1994.

Bingham, Alfred M. *Insurgent America: Revolt of the Middle-Classes.* New York: Harper & Brothers, 1935.

Brinkley, Alan. *Voices of Protest: Huey Long, Father Coughlin, and the Great Depression.* New York: Alfred A. Knopf, 1982.

Columbia Encyclopedia. 6th ed. <http://www.bartleby.com/65/ho/Howe-Jul.html>.

Croly, Herbert. *The Promise of American Life.* 1909. Reprint, Cambridge: Belknap Press of Harvard University Press, 1965.

Dennis, Lawrence. *The Coming American Fascism.* New York: Harper & Brothers, 1936.

Ferkiss, Victor C. "Populist Influences on American Fascism." In *Populism: The Critical Issues,* edited by Sheldon Hackney. Boston: Little, Brown and Company, 1971.

Freidel, Frank. *Franklin D. Roosevelt: A Rendezvous with Destiny.* Boston: Little, Brown & Company, 1990.

Jeansonne, Glen. *Gerald L.K. Smith: Minister of Hate.* New Haven: Yale University Press, 1988.

———. *Women of the Far Right: The Mother's Movement and World War II.* Chicago: University of Chicago Press, 1996.

Klehr, Harvey, John Earl Haynes, and Kyrill M. Anderson. *The Soviet World of American Communism.* New Haven: Yale University Press, 1998.

Leuchtenburg, William E. "The Historic 'Hundred Days.'" In *The Great Depression,* edited by Don Nardo. San Diego: Greenhaven Press, 2000.

Lowenthal, Leo, and Norbert Guterman. *Prophets of Deceit: A Study of the Techniques of the American Agitator.* New York: Harper & Brothers, 1949.

Lundberg, Ferdinand. *Imperial Hearst: A Social Biography.* 1936. Reprint, Westport, Connecticut: Greenwood Press, 1970.

McJimsey, George. *The Presidency of Franklin Delano Roosevelt.* Lawrence: University Press of Kansas, 2000.

Mitchell, Greg. *The Campaign of the Century: Upton Sinclair's Race for Governor of California and the Birth of Media Politics.* New York: Random House, 1992.

Musico, Giuliana. *Hollywood's New Deal.* Philadelphia: Temple University Press, 1997.

Nasaw, David. *The Chief: The Life of William Randolph Hearst.* Boston: Houghton Mifflin, 2000.

Rejai, Mostafa. *Political Ideologies: A Comparative Approach.* Armonk, New York: M.E. Sharpe, 1991.

Robertson, Andrew W. *The Language of Democracy: Political Rhetoric in the United States and Britain, 1790–1900.* Ithaca: Cornell University Press, 1995.

Schlesinger, Arthur M., Jr. *The Crisis of the Old Order, 1919-1933.* Vol. 1 of *The Age of Roosevelt.* Boston: Houghton Mifflin, 1957.

Schonbach, Morris. *Native American Fascism During the 1930s and 1940s: A Study of Its Roots, Its Growth and Its Decline.* New York: Garland, 1985.

Schrecker, Ellen. *The Age of McCarthyism: A Brief History with Documents.* Boston: Bedford, 1994.

———. *No Ivory Tower: McCarthyism and the Universities.* New York: Oxford University Press, 1986.

Seldes, George. *You Can't Do That: A Survey of the Forces Attempting, in the Name of Patriotism, to Make a Desert of the Bill of Rights.* New York: Modern Age Books, 1938.

Swanberg, E.A. *Citizen Hearst: A Biography of William Randolph Hearst.* New York: Charles Scribner's Sons, 1961.

Swing, Raymond Gram. *Forerunners of American Fascism.* New York: Julian Messner, 1935.

Watkins, T.H. *The Great Depression: America in the 1930s.* Boston: Little, Brown, 1993.

Ian Scott

Populism, Pragmatism, and Political Reinvention

The Presidential Motif in the Films of Frank Capra

Director Frank Capra (1897–1991).

Photo by Bill Hamilton.

When the hero of Frank Capra's 1936 film, *Mr. Deeds Goes to Town*, makes a pilgrimage to the tomb of America's eighteenth president, Ulysses S. Grant, it was a warning that all was not as it seemed in Capra's movie world.

Longfellow Deeds, who has recently arrived in New York to claim a $20 million inheritance, takes a bus trip with newspaper reporter Babe Bennett (Jean Arthur) to the site of Grant's Tomb. On a murky, foggy evening, Babe introduces the monument. "Well, there it is, Grant's tomb. Hope you're not too disappointed," she sighs. Longfellow clearly feels it is anything but disappointing and comments that he thinks the monument is wonderful. Babe replies that most people are "awfully let down" by it. Longfellow responds by reciting Grant's poor-farmboy-from-Ohio story, encapsulating it within the framework of nineteenth-century progress and the promise of the American dream. Babe's indifference might suggest an apolitical contemplation of the Civil War general on her part, but it also presents an alternative presentation of the man and his times, indicating that Grant's later political failings, and the tarnished image of the "gilded age" as a whole, remain problematical considerations for the film.

For Patrick Gerster, the one minute and fifteen seconds of this scene "does much to invest the film with its overall meaning." Grant's tomb, he asserts, "exploits the ideological dynamics of symbolic displacement" (Gerster 42). In other words, the scene is critical because its selective engagement with history maintains the luster of Grant's military record—and thus his heroic intent—while remaining disassociated from his presidential record. History gets edited into a mythological treatment by filmmakers, suggests Gerster, and that viewpoint is elaborated upon in this essay. *Mr. Deeds Goes to Town* is thus an important watershed for any examination of Frank Capra's films precisely because it provides a distinctive set of clues about the director's ideals and political beliefs in relation to the American presidency.

Capra achieved this historical contemplation because his social and ideological comment was complemented by a subtle amount of time referencing American presidents. Through textual and visual symbolism, Ulysses Grant, Thomas Jefferson, Woodrow Wilson, Harry Truman—and most especially, Abraham Lincoln—cast long shadows over Capra's protagonists and spread their iconic values throughout his films. He conditioned his audiences to accept the humanist, Christian traditions outlined by these leaders, as they reoccurred throughout his work; but implicit in this reiteration of leading chief executives was an assessment by Capra of the contemporary occupant of the White House, Franklin Delano Roosevelt (1933–1945).

An estimation of Roosevelt helps to reposition the concepts of populism, individualism, liberty, and democracy in Capra's films, but it also offers a previously unaccredited appraisal of presidential power, performance, and pragmatics in the 1930s and 1940s. FDR came to balance practical political service with the more indeterminate notions of historical symbolism, the spirit of leadership, and, critically, of the changing democratic pretensions of the state. These were the issues that meant presidential apparitions formed a constant metaphor for Capra, a metaphor that defined other ideals in his philosophy than those commonly listed: principles like guardianship, honor, and duty. But these ideals were condensed into a cinematic motif that increasingly acted, in Capra's films from the mid-1930s onward, as both a warning from history and prophecy about the future.

THE GHOSTS OF PRESIDENTS PAST

The faces and features of past presidents crop up in many of Frank Capra's films, usually at the critical junctures. In *Mr. Smith Goes to Washington* (1939) the famous trolleybus tour around Washington, D.C., concludes at the Lincoln Memorial. Grandpa Vanderhoff's (Lionel Barrymore) "ismology" speech in *You Can't Take It With You* (1938) mentions Jefferson and Washington, while Long John Willoughby (Gary Cooper) in *Meet John Doe* (1941) and Grant Matthews (Spencer Tracy) in *State of the Union* (1948) both have moments that refer to, or lyrically symbolize, the strength of America's past leaders.

The presidential personification of history is not solely confined to Capra's principal characters. Jefferson Smith's home-state supporters adorn his send-off rally with pictures of Washington and Jefferson, and in *It's a Wonderful Life* (1946) George Bailey's father, Peter, has an office decorated with the portrait of Woodrow Wilson, solemnly invoking a life of commitment and public service. Almost inevitably, though, George's rebuilt family home includes a portrait of Lincoln, hanging in one corner of the living room over his architectural plans.

More than mere apparel for the narrative conduct of his characters, there is a linear connection between presidential references in Capra's films as the war years loom and then pass by. The scenes are less a symbol of political intent than an invocation of presidents acting as guardians of an essential American spirit. Joyce Nelson has remarked of *Mr. Smith Goes to Washington* that here is a film that draws upon iconic names and where mythological characters are eulogized in a distinctly American world of heroes and villains.[1]

Other Capra scholars have elaborated upon similar ideas. Raymond Carney argued: "Grant, Lincoln and Jefferson are referred to in the later films in their capacities as pragmatic individual performers, as fathers of their country, in the entirely practical sense of the word. It is their individuality that Capra's heroes admire and emulate, not their institutional abstractness". (Carney 52). Charles Maland believes that the visit to Grant's tomb and the poor-farmboy-from-Ohio story is a homologous tale for Longfellow Deeds and a call to his own personal succession in this American tradition. But, while the focus of individualism in the film lies with Deeds, Grant's historical legacy is being put into context by Babe Bennett. The sequence in *Mr. Deeds* invokes the memory of the Civil War and Grant's contribution to the reuniting of the union rather more than his record in presidential politics—hence Bennett's remark about people being "let down" by the tomb. Grant is thus a classic link for Capra, a connecting figure bolting back together the fissure of Civil War strife and also upholding constitutional federalism. The point is critical because, if Grant never easily fitted into the Capra mythology of "great political leader," his place in history—and particularly his place as a war leader—is determined by the powerful traditions of the founding fathers.

But why and how did a more overt political vision, such as that presented in *Mr. Deeds*, begin to infuse Capra's films from this moment on? One of the most significant factors is the collection of favorite collaborative writers whom the director enlisted for his films. Robert Riskin, Jo Swirling, and Sidney Buchman were all much more politically active than Capra, and it was actually these writers who first courted and then adapted the director's moderate ideological views. Riskin in particular encouraged a greater diversion into political topics as his and Capra's relationship deepened into a "symbiotic one, on every level, including that of politics" (McGilligan xxviii).

There is plenty of evidence to support the view that Capra cultivated a growing interest in political stories, especially presidential biography. Twice during the 1930s, for instance, he attempted to adapt a stage play about George Washington—*Valley Forge*—the second time, in 1938, with a plan to have Gary Cooper starring in the lead role.[2] *Valley Forge* was by Maxwell Anderson, a writer whom Capra greatly admired. His plans for translating the work to the screen were thwarted by Columbia boss Harry Cohn, who felt that the subject matter would be inappropriate, especially for British audiences then under the threat of war with Nazi Germany. Such enthusiasm from Capra for the subject matter should, though, come as no surprise. Patriotic adherence to all things star-spangled came easily to the Italian immigrant. In a time of crisis his natural instinct was to recall not simply an era of similar turmoil but to focus on a leader who arose to save the nation.

Most of Capra's films from the mid-1930s onward, therefore, directed their attention, by means of presidential figures as well as through their narratives, to questions of leadership and the inheritance of constitutional principles invoked by the office of the presidency. Nostalgia and tradition were the order of the day, and they additionally spoke to the social milieu as well as to the malaise that emerged from the mid-1930s setting for *Mr. Deeds*. "Formulas had to be restructured, not discarded," argues Patrick Gerster.[3] But what were these formulas beyond the humanist, mythological, Christian tradition in Capra's work? Where did debates over the New Deal and the future of American life fit into the set of unavoidable legacies in Capra's career that made for an increasingly assertive mindset within him?[4]

Even more fervently, Capra explored the changing conditions in America. If *Mr. Deeds* was Capra's gentle reminder about constitutional principles, then its entreaty was later transformed into a polemical diatribe by the time of *Meet John Doe* (1941). Long John Willoughby (Gary Cooper) is the hero who accepts the part of a "John Doe" stooge in a newspaper stunt concocted by columnist Ann Mitchell (Barbara Stanwyck). One by one, however, Willoughby, Mitchell, and newspaper editor Connell (James Gleason) come to realize that they are pawns in a far larger plot built around tycoon D.B Norton's (Edward Arnold) White House aspirations. At the film's moral climax, Willoughby meets Connell in a bar; in a scene high on rhetorical emotion and political pleading, writer Robert Riskin demonstrates how much darker his and Capra's vision had grown. Connell has belatedly discovered the truth about Norton's political ambition; he professes that, "I get boiling mad, and right now John I'm sizzling. I get mad for a lot of other guys besides myself. I get mad for a guy named Washington. And a guy named Jefferson. And Lincoln. Lighthouses, John, lighthouses in a foggy world."[5] (The "lighthouses" reference was so striking to Capra that he later included it in the first of his World War II propaganda films for the military, *Prelude to War* [from the *Why We Fight* series]).

Meet John Doe emphasized that the presidency was no longer an institutional symbol of longing and traditional reorientation. It had now become a bulwark against domestic fascism. And that fascism, Capra realized, was not cultivated solely in ambitious men with evil intent but is translated through propaganda, through the new voices of the media, and within urban environments where the pace of life and society's demands condition acceptance and passivity. Capra returns to such a symbolic model of order in his most underrated, and most important, presidential film, *State of the Union* (1948). Lead character and aspiring presidential candidate Grant Matthews (Spencer Tracy) is an embodiment of an American society undergoing radical change in the wake of World War II and unsure of the competing interests rising through the ranks of a revitalized, postwar nation.[6]

Even more than in *Meet John Doe*, Capra references political deceit and misleading semantics, all promoted in the name of democracy. *State of the Union* went beyond any of Capra's other political statements by naming parties and defiantly having Matthews as a candidate for the Republicans in 1948. Ironically enough, Capra's partnership with Riskin had been effectively dissolved, and while the writing of Anthony Veiller and Myles Connolly was less subtle, it did create various characters in the film, notably newspaper hack Spike (Van Johnson), who made pointed criticisms of the incumbent Truman administration. Through Spike's eyes, politics is paraded as no more than fodder for hungry paparazzi loitering around the characters. Capra's disillusionment with political and media relations in these immediate postwar years was compounded by his desire for Truman to take the satire to heart. Capra never voted for Truman just as he never voted for Roosevelt. But he saw this respectable, decent person overtaken by a transformation of the office and of society going on around him that he seemed to have little control over. Did Truman really want loyalty oaths, the National Security Act, the seizure of the steel mills, and the investigation of the House Committee on Un-American Activities (HUAC) of Hollywood? Capra thought not, but used the symbolism at the heart of *State of the Union* to reveal the new pressures and demands on leaders in the postwar era. The conclusion was that the legacy of those presidents evoked in his past films had been changed by the era of Franklin Roosevelt. Politics and the presidency, Capra correctly adjudged, would never be the same again.

Franklin D. Roosevelt utilizes the force of rhetoric on the stump during his presidency.

POPULISM AND *FDR*

What was it about the New Deal, Roosevelt, and the shift from the depression of the 1930s to the postwar development of the 1940s, in general, that sparked a more critical tone in Capra's films? According to Michael Parrish, "most of the New Deal bore the stamp of many authors, arose from no master plan, and did not fit neatly into a single ideological box" (Parrish 83). Others—such as Peter Fearon—deduced that the New Deal bore no coherent economic strategy but was rather a calculated exercise in political power (Fearon 69, 98). Conclusions such as these are essential for any investigation of Capra as a public spokesman in the 1930s and 1940s.

The New Deal had no easy ideological home and, for a while, neither did Capra. But it is not simply this convenient assertion that needs reinforcing. The Depression, populism, Roosevelt, and the New Deal have often been linked in writings about Frank Capra as a magical compound of elements that added up to the social vision. Capra was, in Jeffrey Richards's telling phrase, "the classic populist," a description that allowed Richards to link Capra's films with a broad church of presidential personalities—including Jackson, Lincoln, and Grant. It also allowed for the continuation of a debate in Capra scholarship questioning whether he had an anti-Roosevelt or anti–New Deal streak.[7] More recently, the stamp of populist determinism in Capra's movies has been reinvestigated, with historical assessments of the movement/party/ideology that grew out of nineteenth-century values, positioning these side by side with Capra's own "populism."

The link between Capra and Roosevelt can be solidified by a number of elements. For instance, Capra's films often involve two important character types. One is the crowd/masses/common people who ultimately vindicate the actions of a hero (typically Deeds, Smith, Willoughby, Bailey); the second is what has been called a "metaphorical God" (judges, vice presidents) or, in other words, FDR (Maland 94). Roosevelt is the presiding spirit in this interpretation, admonishing injustice and encouraging righteous belief, never more so than in the vice president's (Harry Carey) kindly and encouraging attitude toward Senator Jefferson Smith throughout the climatic filibuster scene in the eponymous film of 1939.

Another view suggests that Capra's heroic individuals are there to teach the community about sacrifice and ideals until, "the mechanism of collective redemption is released" (Muscio 173). Giuliana Muscio interestingly argues for the place of Capra *and* Roosevelt as dual moral guardians of this task, spreading hope and enlightenment with the view that radical ideals had to be made to seem old-fashioned before the public would accept them. Capra and Roosevelt could encourage that acceptability, she claims, because they were joint success stories, mirror images from opposite ends of the social spectrum but nevertheless representatives of the same American success story (Muscio 184).

Repeated viewing of the films does appear to reveal consistently the importance that Roosevelt's New Deal had upon the American people. Capra's social message still appears to grow out of the New Deal commitment to social and political reform. The resemblance, for example, of Longfellow Deeds's charitable activities to the recently formed Works Progress Administration (WPA) of the New Deal and the striking similarity of his New York mansion to the White House itself were metaphors that could not be ignored. Even Roosevelt's own comments seemed to strike the message that a Capra hero would readily impart. "We are definitely in the era of building; the best kind of building, the building of great public projects for the benefit of the public and with the definite objective of building human happiness," the president himself said at the time (Watkins 141).

Even Capra's presentation of the possible threats to democracy served on the American people by authoritarian leaders, as outlined in Lawrence Levine's description of cinematic politics in the 1930s, was not a tale of woe directed at Roosevelt's leadership (Levine 191). "Capra . . . opposed false leaders, those who manipulated social control to affirm their own power," says Muscio (182). Roosevelt was simply not a dictator, and as if to emphasize the point, she herself separates demagoguery from popular endorsement by claiming that Capra's heroes engage in oratory while the villains are associated with the written word, thus spontaneously paralleling Roosevelt. That is certainly true but misses one of the key messages that Capra wanted to convey. Yes, the media are more often than not involved in subverting the course of some just cause, and yes *March of Time* (1934–1954) sequences in Capra's films, utilizing the montage effects made famous by film editor Slavko Vorkapich, often flag up banner headlines as demonstrations of a popular press capable of placating the public with falsehoods, and, certainly, responses to overt propaganda from mogul figures (the boy scout newspaper in *Mr. Smith* being the most obvious example) are often crushed unceremoniously. But the point for Capra was that, while FDR may be no dictator and the New Deal no socialist manifesto, both had given birth to an administration that was growing expeditiously and had spawned a publicity machine which was taking on a life of its own.

What was being done, as Benjamin Ginsberg and Martin Shefter have discovered, was that, "Roosevelt's moves towards centralization began the transformation of the Democrats from a party dependent on a network of political clubs and organizations to one grounded in administrative institutions" (Ginsberg and Shefter 88). The result was the proliferation of a national apparatus that could mobilize support and govern from the center. And if there was one "anti-" issue in Frank Capra's films that did strike a chord with the public, even those who were major Roosevelt supporters, it was the presentation of government, specifically Washington, as growing into a larger, permanent bureaucracy.

Capra's political philosophy, therefore, remained complex and open to interpretation through America's turbulent depression and war years. Capra was far more influenced by Riskin's Rooseveltian ideas than has previously been acknowledged. But, as outlined above, Riskin really became a collaborator in Capra's revolt against bureaucratic authority. Indeed, as Joseph McBride maintains, the anti-auteurist notion suggested that Capra's writers were the ones offering the intellectual content and bite to his tales; they were the ones countermanding social inertia and Republican dogma. McBride quotes Richard Hofstadter, who argues that Capra's anti–New Deal views headed off a possible revolt by the underclass laid low and seemingly detached from society by the Depression (McBride 253, 262). Hofstadter, however, offers an even better interpretation of the Capra line in later works when he says Roosevelt actually disappointed the intellectuals during these years and suffered sharp criticism for a reform program that always seemed more pragmatic and consensual than ideological (McBride 222).

This view of Roosevelt as more instinctive than idealistic is important; for while it was correct to view Riskin as an avid New Dealer writing in the liberal communitarian dimension to Capra's films—with the director himself overlaying the stories with his own sense of "populism,"—the two also managed to portray a critical theoretical distinction that is often lost in the writing on Capra—the distinction between New Deal ideology and the Roosevelt power base. It was not leftist or ideological politics that worried Capra; what troubled him was the pragmatism of constitutional politics being substituted by the illusion of image and the charisma of authority. Capra foresaw the rise of character and media image at the heart of politics and realized quickly the ways in which these might be used to grasp and wield power. More than that, Capra spotted what many American political theorists have identified and debated ever since: that the New Deal changed the nature of political power and altered the na-

Jefferson Smith confronts the forces of power and wealth on the floor of the Senate in *Mr. Smith Goes to Washington* (1939).

tionalistic principles in American life. Capra reminded his audience that those principles still resided in the ideals and leaders of a momentous past.

CONCLUSIONS

Frank Capra's films, in their own way, reflected upon the changing role of the state, in political theory as well as in actuality, and the rise of corporate/business/private institutions as bulwarks of national interest. The place of populism, individualism, and democracy as a whole are hard to determine in Capra's canon because he understood that the Roosevelt leadership was at the heart of a transformed society, not necessarily good or evil, but rooted in a sectionalism where competing pluralistic interests would rule politics, economics, and possibly cultural life with only a tangential relation to the centers of power and accountability. In Theodore Lowi and Edward Harpham's words, "pluralist theory provided an elaborate explanation and defense of the institutional structures of power and policy that emerged out of the New Deal" (Lowi and Harpham 249, 278).

It was this alteration and uprooting of traditions and structures of power that Capra and Riskin gave some flavor to in their work. The Capra heroes become increasingly dispossessed in his films after 1936; even the wealthy like Grant Matthews are rootless and searching for meaning in society, much as Capra himself was in the postwar years. It is certainly true, as McBride observes, that Capra did have an "irrational basis" to his anti–New Deal views that may have grown out of his own accumulation of wealth as the decade progressed, but it also more readily forged itself in a resentment against Roosevelt's patrician background. This distinction is critical for it was not simply a slight at the president himself. Capra came to understand the privileged nature of his own position in the Hollywood studio system, but that only led him to criticize the oligarchic structure of authority still further.[8] Capra despised unseen hands and shadowy forces that controlled and manipulated lives—often more than the official seats of power like the executive. He could never quite rid himself of that feeling about his own career, despite such success. *Mr. Deeds Goes to Town* was therefore the first of a number of films that were not advertisements for the New Deal; although they may have been more likely a transparent adaptation of Capra's moderate Republican stance, his films became more forcefully about not only Roosevelt's leadership but also criticisms about power and class relations in America. Capra wanted a return to institutional respectability and stability. As he said in his autobiography, foreign-born Americans liked the title "President of the United States." The words were surrounded by the comfort of freedom and democratic expression, the protection of historical rhetoric that Capra found so reassuring. They were indeed close in tone to the debate concerning national responsibility first outlined by Jefferson and Hamilton, and later elaborated on by Herbert Croly in his classic study, *The Promise of American Life*.

It was through FDR, therefore, that Capra's fears about losing such tradition and his admonishment of various aspects of political change in the country would gather pace in the films after *Mr. Deeds*. In doing so, the director would critique a major reassessment of the role of institutions and the chief executive, and the results were films that, in Capra and Riskin's own way, reflected the shifts in the balance of political culture in America during a critical period of its history.

NOTES

1. Nelson conceives of an interpretation whereby *Mr. Smith*, both as character personification and narrative construction, "remains an appeal to child-like wish fulfillment in its world of hero and villains" (246). It draws upon iconic names and recognizable mythological characters that are eulogized, for her, in a comic-strip portrayal, a notion important for the referencing of presidential figures.

2. McBride reports that *Valley Forge* was eventually produced as a movie for television in the 1970s.

3. Gerster suggests that what Capra relays in *Mr. Deeds* is an American society uprooted from its basic traditions and suffering from an ideological schism articulated in Van Wyck Brooks's *America's Coming of Age*. Here, Brooks argues against "highbrow" and "lowbrow" cultures where theory and practice, "the poet," and "the man of the world" are wildly divergent and can no longer be secured as a single union. Gerster claims that in the character of Longfellow Deeds, Capra was attempting to create just such a union.

4. McBride determines that the auteur theory of film-writing made Capra's political digest even harder to swallow and that his raft of associates and the influences they variously wielded on him ultimately made him simply not want to reflect so heavily on any political meaning in his movies—which later interviews and comments by Capra corroborate (259).

5. The screenplay is quoted from the script edited by Charles Wolfe.

6. For further analysis of the importance of the film to Capra's political ideas, see my "Frank Capra's *State of the Union*: The Triumph of Politics."

7. For Richards, populism and mythology go hand in hand in Capra's films. Antiintellectualism and good neighborliness are the key facets of the populist ideology in Richards's eyes. Nelson also quotes Richards's populist thesis, but he sets this up as a means to use *Mr. Smith* as a force for anti–New Deal rhetoric rather than as an examination of the politics of leadership in Roosevelt's administration (245–46).

8. As Thomas Schatz comments, Capra was part of a group of filmmakers—including John Ford, Howard Hawks, and Alfred Hitchcock—who had unparalleled control over scripts, casting, and editing. Nevertheless, Capra wrote an open letter to the *New York Times* in April 1939, complaining that producers like Selznick and Goldwyn were autocrats in the system, unfeeling dictators who had no time for artistic talent (5–8).

WORKS CITED

Capra, Frank. *The Name Above the Title*. New York: Macmillan, 1971.

Carney, Ray. *American Vision: The Films of Frank Capra*. 1986. Reprint, London: Wesleyan University Press, 1996.

Croly, Herbert. *The Promise of American Life*. 1909. Reprint, Boston: Northeastern University Press, 1989.

Fearon, Peter. "New Era, New Deal and Victory: The American Economy 1920–1945." In *Markets,* edited by Grahame Thompson, 69–98. London: Hodder & Stoughton, 1994.

Gerster, Patrick. "The Ideological Project of *Mr. Deeds Goes to Town.*" *Film Criticism* 5 (1981): 36–46.

Ginsberg, Benjamin, and Martin Shefter. *Politics by Other Means: Politicians, Prosecutors, and the Press from Watergate to Whitewater.* London: Norton, 1999.

Hofstadter, Richard. *Anti-intellectualism in American Life.* New York: Vintage, 1966.

Kelley, Beverly Merrill. "Populism in *Mr. Smith Goes to Washington.*" In *Reelpolitik: Political Ideologies in '30s and '40s Films,* edited by Beverly Merrill Kelley, John J. Pitney Jr., Craig R. Smith, and Herbert E. Gooch III. Westport: Praeger, 1998.

Levine, Lawrence. "Hollywood's Washington: Film Images of National Politics During the Great Depression." *Prospect* 10 (1985): 169–95.

Lowi, Theodore J., and Edward J. Harpham. "Political Theory and Public Policy: Marx, Weber, and a Republican Theory of the State." In *Contemporary Empirical Political Theory,* edited by Kirsten Renwick Monroe. Berkeley: California University Press, 1997.

Maland, Charles. *Frank Capra.* New York: Twayne, 1995.

McBride, Joseph. *Frank Capra: The Catastrophe of Success.* London: Routledge, 1992.

McGilligan, Pat M., ed. *Six Screenplays by Robert Riskin.* Berkeley: California University Press, 1997.

Muscio, Giuliana. "Roosevelt, Arnold, and Capra, (or) the Federalist-Populist Paradox." In *Frank Capra Authorship and the Studio System,* edited by Robert Sklar and Vito Zagarrio. Philadelphia: Temple University Press, 1998.

Nelson, Joyce. "*Mr. Smith Goes to Washington*: Capra, Populism and Comic-Strip Art." *Journal of Popular Film* 3 (1974): 245–54.

Neve, Brian. *Film and Politics in America: A Social Tradition.* London: Routledge, 1992.

Parrish, Michael E. *Anxious Decades: America in Prosperity in Depression, 1920–1941.* London: Norton, 1994.

Poague, Leland. *Another Frank Capra.* Cambridge: Cambridge University Press, 1994.

Richards, Jeffrey. "Frank Capra: The Classic Populist." In *Visions of Yesterday,* 234–53. London: Routledge, 1973.

Schatz, Thomas. *The Genius of the System: Hollywood Film-making in the Studio Era.* London: Faber and Faber, 1998.

Scott, Ian. "Frank Capra's *State of the Union*: The Triumph of Politics." *Borderlines, Studies in American Culture* 5 (1998): 33–47.

Watkins, T.H. *The Great Depression: America in the 1930s.* London: Back Bay for Little, Brown, 1993.

Weber, Max. "The Nature of Charismatic Domination." In *Weber: Selections in Translation,* edited by W.G. Runciman. Cambridge: Cambridge University Press, 1978.

Wolfe, Charles, ed. *Meet John Doe: Frank Capra, Director.* London: Rutgers University Press, 1989.

Linda Alkana

THE ABSENT PRESIDENT

Mr. Smith, The Candidate, and *Bulworth*

Candidate McKay (Robert Redford) presents a youthful image in *The Candidate* (1972).

Historians use films to teach history. Educators use films in much the same way as they use books and historical documents, by placing them in a context, analyzing their messages, and critiquing their content. Such films work for teaching because the subject matter and the time period involved are usually circumscribed and self-evident. *All Quiet on the Western Front,* for example, is about World War I and the peace movement that followed it; *All the President's Men* gives insight into the Nixon years and Watergate.

Because of the usefulness of historical films for teaching history, it is worthwhile to investigate the possibilities of using political subject films to teach about politics. Hollywood has a long history of making films with political themes, and the tensions inherent in most political situations should give the necessary dramatic components for a Hollywood film. Nevertheless, as Phillip Gianos points out, while conflict is an important component of successful filmmaking, controversy is not (Gianos 7). Thus, when reaching for a mass audience, Hollywood often avoids taking sides or appearing didactic, thus possibly weakening the educational potential of political films. Nevertheless, through the years Hollywood has made some major films that, when compared with each other and their times, provide a forum to investigate substantive political issues. Among these larger issues are questions about who holds power and how; who challenges that power and why; what is the relative role of government, the people, and the media; how important is the individual in American politics; and how important is the power of the presidency to America.

Since power relations are inherent in most situations, these questions can be applied to a variety of films. Three American films, in particular, explicitly address American politics in the twentieth century. These films—*Mr. Smith Goes to Washington* (1939), *The Candidate* (1972), and *Bulworth* (1998)—share the theme of an American Senate race, were produced about a generation apart, and are award-winning, popular, and accessible films. They also allow insight into both the political process, as well as the historical themes of continuity and change. Interestingly, and perhaps ironically, none of these films, with their varying praise or criticism of the American political system, deals with the most popular American political institution, the American Presidency. Citing numerous studies, political scientist Michael Nelson has suggested that "long before children have any real knowledge of what the federal government actually does, they already think of the president in terms of almost limitless power and goodness" (Nelson 3). Elsewhere he points out that, in polls, most Americans choose presidents as political heroes and that "the American people, like American scholars and journalists, want and admire strength in the presidency" (Nelson 15). In fact, it is the absence of the president in these films that ultimately confirms this power and popularity of the American Presidency. His lack of presence in these films allows the American leader to remain above the corruption, the pettiness, and the partisanship of American party politics while, consequently, symbolizing continuity and strength in face of the challenges to the political system raised by the films.

MR. SMITH GOES TO WASHINGTON *(1939)*

The events in *Mr. Smith Goes to Washington* are set in motion with the death of a senator and the need for the governor—appropriately named Hopper—to nominate a replacement that will, like the governor and the state's other senator, Senator Paine (Claude Rains), hop to the demands of the corrupt and powerful Taylor political machine. After some initial difficulties, Governor Hopper (Guy Kibbee) acquiesces to the demands of his large family to nominate Boy Ranger leader and local nature advocate Jefferson Smith (James Stewart). Once in Washington, the new Senator Smith is immediately mocked by the press, who feature his picture on the front page of the newspaper making birdcalls and Indian signs. When he confronts the reporters, they make him face the fact that he is a stooge—he is holding office and is doing nothing. Acknowledging their point, Smith goes to Senator Paine, who encourages him to follow through with his dream for a boys' camp. Helped on by Saunders (Jean Arthur), Smith's secretary, who earlier had felt his patriotism and naïvetè were either foolish or a façade, Smith drafts the necessary legislation. Saunders quickly sees a problem: the location of the camp is on a site where a dam is to be built for the benefit of wealthy investors. She does not tell Smith but lets the sparks fly when he introduces the bill in the Senate. Very quickly he is condemned by Senator Paine, falsely accused of buying up the land himself, and threatened with expulsion from the Senate. Smith protests, then promises he will leave his seat if the people of his state want him to go.

While waiting for an answer from them, he maintains a filibuster, reading from the Constitution, taking cues from Saunders. The Taylor machine activates a media blitz in his state, keeps out any information about Smith's activities, orchestrates parades and billboards against him, and even runs Boy Ranger paperboys off the road when they try to spread Smith's message. Meanwhile, back in the Senate chamber, in the midst of his filibuster, Smith is confronted with mailbags of letters against him, saying he should go. Instead of heeding the letters as he said he would, Smith continues the filibuster until he collapses. At that point, a shot rings out: Senator Paine tries to kill himself, saying that it is he—not Jefferson Smith—who is not worthy to be a senator. Smith is vindicated: he has won over Saunders and the Senate, and the movie ends with cheers. The good young senator defeats the bad political machine and brings down the corrupt older senator. In true Hollywood fashion, there is a happy ending.

THE CANDIDATE *(1972)*

Thirty years later there is a far less clear-cut message in *The Candidate*. Bill McKay (Robert Redford), the son of the former governor of California and now a farm-labor lawyer, is convinced by Marvin Lucas (Peter Boyle), a political consultant, to run for the Senate with the idea that he can use his campaign as a forum for his progressive ideas. Lucas promises McKay that he may say what he wants, do what he wants, and go where he pleases. "What's the catch?" McKay asks. Lucas takes out a matchbook, and on its inside cover he writes the guarantee: "You'll lose." Once McKay makes this Faustian bargain, he is faced with decisions and compromises every step of the way: "Cut your hair." "Eighty-six the sideburns." "Don't say you're for abortion. Say you'll study it." At one point, when he asks why one of the compromises he faces is so important, since he is going to lose anyway, Lucas asks him if he really wants to be humiliated. McKay answers, "That wasn't part of the deal."

Increasingly McKay is swept into the campaign—rallies, debates, limos, and planes. He says he will not ask his father for an endorsement but then visits him anyway—and gets an endorsement. Later, he keeps a labor leader waiting, insults him by saying they have "shit in common"—yet still shares the podium with him and accepts his support. Another time, when he pauses for a moment in a debate to really talk about the issues, the cameras have already shut off— he has no audience. Each time he confronts Lucas with a question about the campaign, the issue is never resolved. When Lucas reminds McKay that he is the Democratic nominee for senator, McKay answers: "You make that sound like a death sentence." At the end of the film, with McKay's surprise victory, McKay asks Lucas the movie's final question: "What do we do now?" Jefferson Smith had been triumphant in victory: Bill McKay is only confused.

BULWORTH *(1998)*

If the ending of *The Candidate* is problematic, the ending of *Bulworth* is even more so. *Bulworth* owes much to *The Candidate,* and one can speculate that Senator Jay Billington Bulworth (Warren Beatty) is the kind of man Bill McKay might have become had he continued to let others direct his life. It is now 1996, and, in the California primaries, the "populace is unaroused"; Bulworth is expected to return to the Senate "for yet another term." Opening shots of multiple campaign videos and photos first reveal the smiling senator, then focus on the real senator, a blubbering wreck of a man who is sui-

Warren Beatty is Senator Jay Bulworth. *Bulworth* (1998).

cidal and who has just put out a contract on himself to be murdered for insurance money.

Seemingly liberated by this decision, Bulworth sets out for another day on the campaign trail, accompanied by a twenty-four-hour C-SPAN crew, his political handlers, and Nina (Halle Berry), a young African American woman he meets at a campaign function. His new freedom allows him to speak out, and he consequently does so. He quickly starts to alienate his donors, among whom are liberal Hollywood types and the insurance industry, and—just when his campaign managers wonder about this new strategy of brutally telling the truth—he begins rhyming and rapping about "big money" and "that dirty word, 'socialism'." He makes a farce out of his debate with the challenger, and then disappears with Nina into the black neighborhood of Los Angeles. Here he meets the local drug dealer, L.D. (Don Cheadle), who gives him insight into the "hood." Converted to a new cause, Bulworth returns to the

The senator discovers rap in *Bulworth* (1998).

campaign, dressed in baggie pants and a beanie, and rapping his message, this time to a new constituency. Now people are really listening; he is making sense to the TV viewers in Nina's neighborhood. They know he has heard them: "But we got babies in South Central/ Dyin' as young as they do in Peru. We got public schools that're nightmares/ We got a Congress that ain't got a clue. We got kids with submachine guns/ We got militias throwin' bombs. We got Bill [Clinton] just gettin' all weepy/ We got Newt [Gingrich] blaming teenage moms."

Bulworth feels good. He now realizes that he wants to live. Panicked, however, because he cannot call off the assassination, he flees from the campaign and the cameras. Then, Nina tells him that he will be OK—that she knew about the hit, was part of the plan, and has since changed her mind. Like Saunders in *Mr. Smith*, she now sides with the senator. Hiding in her house, Bulworth collapses into sleep for the first time in days. While the media wonder where the senator is, his campaign staffers realize they can spin his changes—the new Bulworth— to their advantage. Awake and refreshed, Bulworth goes out to meet the press, asking Nina to join him. She does; then a shot rings out. An insurance execu- tive Bulworth had threatened, not the hit man, has shot him. The rich are already fighting back. The film ends outside of a hospital. Is Bulworth alive? Is he dead? A mysterious old man (playwright/poet Amiri Baraka) chants: "We need a spirit, Bulworth, not a ghost. You got to be a spirit. You can't be no ghost." As in *Mr. Smith*, the end of *Bulworth* is determined by a gunshot. But where it is the opposition that crumbles in *Mr. Smith*, it is the people who rise in *Bulworth*. The film's enigmatic ending suggests that his spirit will continue.

POLITICAL POWER

What do these three films say about power—who holds it and how? Who wants it and why? What is the relative role of government, the people, and the me- dia? And where is the president? First of all, in *Mr. Smith Goes to Washington*, it is apparent that power is not held by all senators. Some, like Senator Paine, are the pawns of corrupt political machines, which also control the press and the dissemination of news in their states. But it would be wrong to conclude that because corrupt forces control some senators, they also control the presidency and government in general. In fact, there are several kinds of power demon- strated in this Frank Capra classic. There is the illegitimate power of Taylor and his henchmen, but there is also the legitimate, constitutional power of the Senate as a body. Smith triumphs not only because Paine cracks up; he wins because Saunders has faith in him and his vision, and because the president of the Senate (Harry Carey), at a crucial point, acknowledges Smith's right to speak. There is an interesting parallel here between some of the New Deal programs and the country as a whole. For example, even before the Wagner Act ensured the legality of unions, Section 7a of the National Industrial Recov- ery Act acknowledged the right of unions to organize (Watkins 245), and, with this encouragement from the government, the labor movement—just like Jefferson Smith—took off. Smith's desire for power goes through several stages: he first naïvely answers the call to duty; then he realizes he could do good things with his boys' camp; finally, he wants to expose the corruption of the system. There are other sources of power evident in the film as well. As clichéd as it may be, power in *Mr. Smith Goes to Washington,* just as in the 1930s, is held by white men in suits. Skin color, gender, and clothing are all sources of power, and they are revealed as such in these three films. Washington, D.C.—like much of America—was racially segregated in the 1930s, as was the Senate. Men held all positions of power. The film features an almost all-white, all-male cast, full of boy rangers, boy Senate pages, Taylor and his men, male senators, and male reporters.

The strongest character in the cast, however, is a woman. Saunders, Smith's secretary, knows the ropes and orchestrates Smith's victory. She is to Smith as Eleanor is to FDR. She is the strong woman, but she knows her place. Suits? It is a minor point in this film but indicative of the times. To make Smith appear presentable in Washington at one point, Saunders is told to take him out and get him a suit, a haircut, and a manicure. The appearance of power is maintained. President Franklin Roosevelt was not photographed in his wheelchair. The propriety of a particular image was accepted in the 1930s. Image would not be questioned as being part of the façade of power until the 1960s, but by then, ironically, the power of television reinforced the role of image as a symbol of power. Despite the counterculture of the 1960s with its challenge to uniformity and conformity of dress and appearance in society as a whole, those who wanted to hold political power still needed to maintain a particular image. Cutting his hair is one of the first compromises candidate Bill McKay has to make. Later, Bulworth sheds his suit; his conversion is apparent when he wears the clothes of another man. Interestingly, however, Bulworth returns to wearing suits, even though words are more important than images to Bulworth.

Related to the question of who holds power is the issue of the press and how it acts as a conduit between the people and the government. In the 1930s of *Mr. Smith,* the press is no monolithic, "media" entity, as it will later appear in the 1970s and 1990s. Smith's father had been a crusading reporter who was martyred for his beliefs. Smith himself edits *Boy's World,* the Boy Rangers newspaper, which is the link between the boys of the state and their two "voting parents," as Governor Hopper's sons tell him. Once Smith is in Washington, reporters hound him, not just for a story but because they do not respect him. Ditz (Thomas Mitchell), the alcoholic reporter who loves Saunders, is typical of the Washington press. He understands the system and is cynical about the whole process. He just wants a story. The press back in Smith's state is beyond cynicism—it functions as an arm of the Taylor machine, manipulating the public and rendering people powerless. The first scene of Charlie Chaplin's *Mod-*

ern Times, also a film of the 1930s, depicts people going into a factory as a herd of sheep. That is how the people are portrayed in *Mr. Smith*. Taylor controls the press; as a result, he controls the state. Within this context, the individual must speak up because, collectively, people are sheep. Ultimately, *Mr. Smith Goes to Washington* places its faith in the lone individual like Mr. Smith. It is not yet time for democracy of the people, by the people, and for the people. But because Mr. Smith makes his stand in the institution of the Senate, there still is democracy. And there is still the presidency. The first thing that Jefferson Smith does before he takes his seat in the Senate is to visit Mt. Vernon to acknowledge America's first president. He also visits the Lincoln Memorial twice; his second visit encourages him to fight for his beliefs. Smith saves the Senate with his stand. Although the president is absent, the presidency is never in danger.

A generation later, Bill McKay, the son of the former governor of California, has so little faith in institutions that he is not even registered to vote. He places his faith in the people, working for farm laborers at the grassroots level. Although there is no obviously corrupt Taylor machine in *The Candidate*, there is a machine of another sort—a campaign machine that takes on a life of its own. After McKay is approached and asked to run for the Senate, he asks Marvin Lucas, fresh from managing another campaign, the question that the naïve Mr. Smith, thirty years earlier, had not asked: "What's in it for you?" However, like every moment of confrontation in *The Candidate*, the answer is not clear. Lucas tells him "a thousand dollars a week and an airline credit card." Lucas may make senators, but he has little real power. The incumbent Senator Crocker Jarmon, "the Crock" (Don Porter)—another interesting use of names—certainly has the trappings of legitimate political power, as does McKay's father (Melvyn Douglas), the former governor, although with McKay senior, there are hints of corruption—"Let's go for a drink? After all, I did help him get his liquor license." Yet both of these men are from another era—a time before professional campaign managers and media advisors. And in the end, of course, Crocker Jarmon loses. About halfway through the film, as McKay has compromised a step at a time—never really selling out, just adjusting his image and softening his rhetoric—the journalist Howard K. Smith (in a cameo appearance) notes that voters are being asked to choose McKay the way they choose a detergent. McKay tries to stand up for himself: he brings up issues during the debate, which are not shown because the networks have enough footage; he visits free clinics and discusses poverty, but these visits do not show well in thirty-second spots.

In *The Candidate* (1972), Bill McKay (Robert Redford) is dwarfed by his own image.

Jeremy Larner, a former Eugene McCarthy speechwriter and the award-winning writer of *The Candidate*, explains that Robert Redford wanted to "make a movie about a liberal politician who sells out." Larner argues that most "of them don't sell out . . . They get carried away" (Larner 11). The candidate is carried away in a campaign world of crowds and noise. In such a world, the sources of power seem amorphous—shared by special interests, networks, and professional campaign managers who go from candidate to candidate. If anyone is in control, the film does not say who it is. Interestingly, the film appeared just before the Watergate crisis, which caused many Americans to wonder about political power, and, in particular, about the power of the presidency. Nonetheless, the political problems, as demonstrated in *The Candidate*, remain at the senatorial level. Although the institution of the presidency lacks the symbolic power it has in *Mr. Smith Goes to Washington*, its absence allows the presidency to remain immune to the political critique of *The Candidate*.

POWER TO THE PEOPLE

There are no strong women of Saunders' stripe in *The Candidate*. McKay's wife (Karen Carlson) is supportive, but she seems more supportive of the campaign than of her husband. Another woman, an attractive campaign worker, passes McKay her phone number, and she is seen leaving a hotel room with him. Even a brief appearance of Natalie Wood (playing herself) does not convey any idea that women have power in this world of politics. Yet, if boys and men dominate the political landscape of *Mr. Smith*, women are in most scenes of *The Candidate*; their roles are minor, but their numbers are many.

If *Mr. Smith* represents a world of good or bad, night or day, Hitler or Roosevelt, *The Candidate* springs from a decade of short-term presidencies, multiple issues, and the omnipresence of mass media. The good people of Mr. Smith's state are kept from knowing about him. With censorship and propaganda, the Taylor machine creates its own reality. The good people of California can only know Bill McKay through his campaign stops and TV spots, but the more of these he makes, the less he knows of himself. Thus the poignancy of his question: "What do we do now?"

People are no longer sheep in the world of *The Candidate*, but neither do they have power. The earnest farm workers are left behind as McKay is caught up in events; they are replaced by equally earnest campaign volunteers who do not know that their candidate is lost. The press of the 1930s is now the omnipotent and omnipresent media of the 1970s. Though some reporters may challenge the candidate, his image is becoming more important than his words. He is not a senator. He is a puppet, but the film never shows who is pulling his strings. Nevertheless, the world of *The Candidate* is more inclusive than that of *Mr. Smith Goes to Washington*. The people appear to have more power, albeit in conjunction with the campaign managers. Gone is the backroom manipulation of machine politics and corrupt senators, as seen in *Mr. Smith*. *Bulworth*, in turn, embraces a larger population as it reaches for those left out of the political process in its challenge to the American political system.

Bulworth is the most political of the three films; it pulls together the issues of power, the people, and the press raised in *Mr. Smith Goes to Washington* with the issues of candidates, campaigns, and access to the people that Bill McKay faces in *The Candidate*. *Bulworth* shows the consequences of a system where real power is held by an elite, which controls access to the airways that were given to it by the government. The government, in turn, makes politicians buy access to the people, but, in effect, makes politicians buy access to power at the expense of the people. Senator Bulworth tells one of three reporters that the reporter himself is just one of three rich guys, paid by richer guys, to ask the two rich candidates questions about their campaigns; but their campaigns are funded by the same rich people who pay the reporter. Bulworth goes on: "Republicans, Democrats, what's the difference? Your guys, my guys, our guys, us guys, it's a club. So why don't we just have a drink?"

Bulworth is no more in control of his fate than Bill McKay in *The Candidate*, but, unlike Bill McKay, he knows he has sold out, and he knows it was not to the professional campaign managers, who are ready to abandon the campaign when Bulworth starts acting oddly. Bulworth needs to go after money to be reelected, but if he does not want to be reelected, those with money will just support someone else. Power is in the hands of corporate interests. Bulworth does not call them "capitalists," but he does indicate that the forbidden word is "socialism" and that the democratic process is a sham to keep those with power in power. Bulworth raps:

> One man one vote/ Now izzat real?
> The name of the game is/ Let's make a deal.
> Now the people got their problems/ The haves and have-nots.
> But the ones that make me listen/ Pay for 30-second spots! . . .
> You've been taught in this country/ There's speech that is free.
> But free do not get you/ No spots on TV.
> If you want to have Senators/ Not on the take,
> Then give them free airtime/ They won't have to fake.

It seems that the circle is complete and that the Jim Taylors of the world have won. They no longer own just one state, but they own the media and the politicians; they give no voice to the people, rendering them powerless. Ironically, despite this cynical view of American politics, *Bulworth* presents, arguably, the most sanguine view of a democratic future by placing its faith in the American people.

Senator Bulworth is not a one-man crusader like Mr. Smith, believing in a system and trying to right its wrongs. The movie *Bulworth* reveals no faith in the system, but it champions the public. When he starts rapping about what he learned in the "hood," Senator Bulworth shows that he has listened to the people. He gives them free airtime. Once they find they are listened to, the people act. The drug dealer devises a plan to clean up the neighborhood; his transformation is as complete as Bulworth's (Grynbaum). He has his own boys' camp—his runners and lookouts and dealers—but they can be mobilized to do good things. Just as the president of the Senate's friendly nod allows Mr. Smith to fight for his beliefs, Bulworth's ear—he listens to what they say—and Bulworth's voice—he speaks for them, indeed, he raps with them—encourages the people to fight for themselves. Power to the people, says Bulworth. Then he is shot.

Bulworth—the most cynical of these three films about the political system—may be the most hopeful. It is not clear if Senator Bulworth lives or dies; it is not clear if he will be "a spirit, not a ghost"; but it is clear that the people in the neighborhood were listened to, and, once heard, *Bulworth* suggests, people have the power to act.

THE ABSENT PRESIDENT

What does it mean for an understanding of the political process if the president or the institution of the presidency is missing from films that deal with American politics, and, by implication, the American political system? Certainly, in terms of the cohesiveness of these three films, the president's absence means very little. These films are structured around senatorial races and are complete in themselves. It is a different matter, however, when considering the use of political films as teaching tools or when analyzing them as part of a broader political, social, or historical context.

Political films can give insight into both politics and contemporary political issues. Here the historical questions of change and continuity come into play. *Mr. Smith Goes to Washington, The Candidate,* and *Bulworth* portray changes in political perceptions, partisan priorities, and interests over time. However, the films also present a continuity of theme throughout the decades. All three explicitly explore American domestic politics while ignoring the role of the president in the American political process. Furthermore, the absence of the role of president in these domestic studies implicitly acknowledges his power in international affairs.

David W. Ellwood argues that film can give "fictional answers to urgent questions raised by a situation" (2). Among these situations are the possibilities of war or the need for national defense. Although the three films in question do not raise these issues, a concern for this larger domain is inherent in any study of political power—in fiction, film, or otherwise. The educator who wishes to use political films must ask questions about this larger political world, if even only to acknowledge its absence in the films under study. By leaving the president out of their analyses of the rights and wrongs of American politics, these three films highlight the privileged position of the president as a symbol of power and as commander in chief, who remains available and all-powerful in the event of a larger international political threat to the American system. As such, in spite of the multiple ways American politics is challenged in *Mr. Smith Goes to Washington, The Candidate,* and *Bulworth,* the absence of a president in these films honors the American Presidency as an important symbol of continuity and power, one which can be called upon in times when the reality of political events overshadow the fictional.

WORKS CITED

Books and Articles

Ellwood, David W. *The Movies as History: Visions of the Twentieth Century.* Great Britain: Sutton Publishing Limited, 2000.

Gianos, Phillip L. *Politics and Politicians in American Film.* Westport, Connecticut: Praeger, 1998.

Giglio, Ernest. *Here's Looking at You: Hollywood, Film and Politics.* New York: Peter Lang, 2000.

Grynbaum, Gail A. "Reviews: Bulworth's Alchemical Hip-Hop." *C.G. Jung Page.* 1999. <http://cgjungpage.org/films/bulworth/html> (10 October 2001).

Larner, Jeremy. "Still a Contender in National Politics." *Los Angeles Times,* 13 August 2000, Calendar 11–79.

Nelson, Michael. "Evaluating the Presidency." In *The Presidency and the Political System,* ed. Michael Nelson. Washington, D.C.: CQ Press, 1990.

Watkins, T.H. *The Great Depression: America in the 1930s.* Boston: Little, Brown, 1993.

Feature Films

Bulworth. Dir. Warren Beatty. Twentieth Century Fox, 1998.

The Candidate. Dir. Michael Ritchie. Warner Bros., 1972.

Modern Times. Dir. Charles Chaplin. Chaplin Studios, 1936.

Mr. Smith Goes to Washington. Dir. Frank Capra. Columbia, 1939.

Robert E. Hunter

WHO'S IN CHARGE HERE?

Technology and the Presidency in *Fail-Safe* (1964) and *Colossus* (1970)

The president (Henry Fonda) and his translator (Larry Hagman) cope with a nuclear nightmare in *Fail-Safe* (1964).

Early in the Kennedy administration (1961–1963), the president informed Dr. Jerome Wiesner, his science adviser, that the phone which would warn the chief executive of an impending Soviet nuclear strike was missing from the Oval Office. Kennedy's predecessor, Dwight D. Eisenhower, had supposedly kept this "'red telephone'" in a drawer of his presidential desk. Without this device, the leader of the Free World lost his most direct link with both the American early-warning system and U.S. nuclear forces. President Kennedy had already unsuccessfully searched for the telephone, but together he and Wiesner tackled the desk and "pulled out all the drawers." To their consternation, the instrument remained missing. Unbeknownst to the President of the United States, First Lady Jacqueline Kennedy had removed President Eisenhower's desk and replaced it with one Queen Victoria had given to Rutherford B. Hayes in 1880. Seeing the telephone as more of an unnecessary convenience than as a key element of the national security communications network, Mrs. Kennedy and her assistants had "disconnected and removed" it (Ford 28).

Although amusing, this anecdote is also chilling and revealing. The phone's easy removal shows the president's vulnerability both to mechanical failures and human frailties—or, in this case, a wife's aesthetic opinions. First of all, it shows that despite his image as an activist president and tough-as-nails Cold Warrior, John F. Kennedy did not always have complete command of the situation. Although he held the position of commander in chief, JFK did not always possess direct or immediate control over America's nuclear deterrent. The functioning of this command-and-control system was never entirely predictable, and it could be subject to both mechanical failures and human errors. This anecdote also underlines the crucial role of technology in the modern presidency and—in this case, at least—the president's apparent dependence upon machines to help him carry out his constitutional duties. Finally, it is noteworthy that this incident was not made public until years after it occurred, which reflects a Cold War culture of secrecy—even though such mishaps could catastrophically affect millions of people.

All of these issues were important during the years of the New Frontier, and they remain important today. The relationship of the American presidency to nuclear weapons has been debated ever since the Manhattan Project (1942–1945). Public discussion of the subject first emerged in the late 1950s and early 1960s. Fearful of living in the Bomb's shadow, large numbers of Americans participated in what might be described as a backlash against the prevailing "atomic ethos." This growing debate during the heyday of the Cold War can be seen in letters to the editor, public opinion polls, articles, books, and even motion pictures, which, beginning with *On the Beach* (1959), may be said to have both reflected and influenced this critical trend.

This essay will discuss two such films, *Fail-Safe* (1964) and *Colossus: The Forbin Project* (1970), and how they relate to American Cold War culture—and more specifically to perceptions of presidential leadership. Both movies are underappreciated. *Fail-Safe* has long been overshadowed by *Dr. Strangelove* (1964), while *Colossus* did poorly at the box office and has generally been overlooked. However, both films were based upon best-selling novels and can serve as cultural-historical bookends to the 1960s. They often deal with the same or similar issues, yet they also reflect how American attitudes and thinking evolved over the course of that turbulent decade.

Fail-Safe reflects a concern about technology but sees its growing power over human affairs as a reversible process. It also presents a strong president, whose actions prove decisive; he is a reassuring figure, consistent with the tendency of Americans to expect comfort and guidance from their president, especially from FDR onward. *Colossus,* on the other hand, gives a diminishing role to human agency. Its president is weak at the outset, and his control over events diminishes. He is, therefore, an unsettling figure, reflecting a growing 1960s disillusionment with the office and its occupants—as well as a sense that the problems are too difficult for one man to solve. The two films also pertain to ongoing dilemmas about the role of technology, both in relation to national security and to larger societal issues.

FAIL-SAFE *(1964)* AND *LEADERSHIP IN THE NUCLEAR AGE*

Written by political scientists Eugene Burdick and Harvey Wheeler, the novel *Fail-Safe* appeared in 1962, just ahead of the Cuban Missile Crisis (October 1962). With life seemingly imitating art, the book quickly became a best-seller, and Columbia Pictures released a film version in 1964. In both versions, the discovery of a UFO near Hudson Bay by the defense network of the U.S. Air Force leads to the dispatch of several groups of "Vindicator" bombers toward the Soviet Union. The alert turns out to be a false alarm, and most of the bombers are recalled before reaching their "fail-safe" points. However, an unfortunate combination of a mechanical malfunction and Soviet radio jamming causes one group of bombers to continue on their mission. As the planes head west to attack Moscow with nuclear weapons, the film chronicles the various efforts of Soviet and American leaders to forestall an impending catastrophe (Burdick and Wheeler 285–86; *Fail-Safe*).

From this point on, the President of the United States occupies the film's center. At the time of the novel's development (1958–1962), the question of whose hand hovered above the nuclear button was an issue of major concern. Historian David Rosenberg has noted that "where Harry Truman viewed the atomic bomb as an instrument of terror and a weapon of last resort, Dwight Eisenhower viewed it as an integral part of American defense, and, in effect, a weapon of first resort" (quoted in LaFeber 541). Combined with the Eisenhower administration's policy of "massive retaliation," the Quemoy-Matsu crises of 1954–1955 and 1958 raised the specter of America's employing nuclear weapons against Communist China. This was not to mention the constant threat of a U.S. Soviet nuclear exchange prompted by Cold War tensions in Berlin or elsewhere. The so-called "missile gap" was a major issue during the presidential election of 1960, and such events of the early Kennedy administration as the Bay of Pigs fiasco and the frosty Vienna summit of 1961 offered little hope that the danger had lessened.

During the Eisenhower and Kennedy years, U.S. nuclear strategy came to rely on the premise that both America and the Soviet Union would be irrevocably damaged—if not completely destroyed—by a nuclear exchange. First labeled "a 'stable balance of terror,'" this thinking later became known by the term "assured destruction" and finally by "mutual assured destruction," or MAD. Often associated with Robert McNamara, Kennedy's secretary of defense, the phrase actually highlighted "an aspect of U.S. deterrent doctrine which had been present from the 1940s" (Freedman 245–48). However, it was not until the late 1950s and early 1960s that this unpleasant reality became so widely discussed and publicized. While the concept sought to deter an opponent from initiating nuclear conflict, it also reminded people that their chances of surviving such an exchange were rather slim.

In such an environment, the question of presidential character and leadership assumed special importance, and this preoccupation is evident in both the novel and the film. Born in the atmosphere just described, the novel *Fail-Safe* presents a protagonist who is the ideal president. There can be no doubt that the character Burdick and Wheeler originally envisioned was John F. Kennedy. As described in the book, the president (he is never actually named) is a "scion of a wealthy family" who "first entered politics as a candidate for Congress" (Burdick and Wheeler 127, 16, 22, 59). Despite his youth, the novel's fictional president is experienced and mature, with an incisive mind. He is "athletic" and has a "physical ease" despite the crisis (Burdick and Wheeler 127–28, 59, 170). The book's president is also Catholic, smokes cigars, and is married to "a beautiful woman" who has mesmerized the American people (Burdick and Wheeler 272).

The president of the film is somewhat different. A picture's casting can say much about its intentions, and in director Sidney Lumet's version, the president is played by none other than *Young Mr. Lincoln* himself, Henry Fonda. Fonda brought to the role an established persona as a courageous, fair-minded person who would do what was necessary to see that justice was done and American ideals upheld.

The president in the movie is older and experienced like President Eisenhower but conveys more of John Kennedy's activism and vigor. Neither the film nor the novel identifies the president with a particular party; he is the leader of all the people. He first appears as a group of White House staffers catch an elevator to reach an underground shelter. Tall and lean, he strides at a measured, purposeful pace. His mannerisms are calculated, with perhaps only the clasping or rubbing of hands to express his inner tension. The president exudes verbal grace under pressure as well, asking Peter Buck (Larry Hagman), the translator sent to help him communicate with the Soviets, "How's your Russian today?" His delivery is as careful and steady as his physical behavior.

From the moment the president enters the film, he is shown to be in command, whether in long shot or close-up. Speaking by phone with military leaders and strategists assembled in the Pentagon, he establishes that he is only consulting them: "Mr. Secretary, I have a decision to make. It's my decision and I'll make it, but I want the advice of you and your people and I need it fast." Fonda's character is confident enough in his own abilities to value plain-speaking by others. For instance, he tells Buck before they communicate with the Soviet premier, "Don't be afraid. Say what you think." As those at the Pentagon and at the Strategic Air Command (SAC) headquarters in Omaha debate what to do if U.S. fighters fail to shoot down the bombers, the president refuses to interrupt their discussion. In this respect, Fonda's behavior parallels what we now know about JFK's handling of the internal debates during the Cuban Missile Crisis; both men valued a free-flowing, thought-provoking exchange. As with Kennedy and the Executive Committee (Ex Comm), however, it is always clear who holds both the final say and the ultimate responsibility.

Like Kennedy, *Fail-Safe*'s president is also an effective communicator. In one scene, Fonda convinces those gathered at SAC headquarters to provide highly sensitive information to their Soviet foes in the hope that, with such help, the Russians can destroy the errant Vindicators. In asking U.S. military personnel to overcome decades of training and Cold War enmities, Fonda stresses his role by introducing himself as the President of the United States. He then underscores his position in the chain of command by stating, "Whatever orders I give to American personnel are to be considered direct personal orders from the Commander-in-Chief. They are to be obeyed fully, without reservation, and at once." Having emphasized his military authority, he then plays the nationalist card: "I expect you to conduct yourselves as patriots." This chief executive clearly knows which rhetorical buttons to push.

The cinematic *Fail-Safe* also reflects the late 1950s and early 1960s leadership debate in another respect as well. Some citizens of the time, especially Democrats, questioned whether Dwight Eisenhower was mentally fit to be president. During many of his press conferences, Ike came across as a befuddled old man. He also experienced health problems near the end of his first term, suffering a heart attack in September 1955 and undergoing surgery for ileitis in June 1956. In line with the Kennedy campaign, *Fail-Safe* offers a leader who is not only physically but also mentally agile. Once the president becomes involved in the crisis, he is always thinking ahead. While everyone waits to see if American jet interceptors can shoot Group Six down before it reaches Russia, the president asks those in the Pentagon to consider what might be done should those fighters fail. While awaiting a chance to speak by radio with Colonel Grady (Edward Binns), Group Six's commander, the president orders the Air Force to locate the pilot's wife. If, as it turns out, the bomber pilot refuses to obey him, then the president can have the flier's wife plead with her husband to abort the mission. Fonda also devises the film's "sacrifice of Abraham" as the American and Soviet air forces work together to destroy the Vindicators. Should that cooperation prove insufficient (as it does), the president will direct a U.S. bomber to destroy New York City to compensate for the loss of Moscow. In short, the president shows quick thinking and foresight—in marked contrast to the partisan (although now proven unfounded) perceptions of Dwight Eisenhower.

As portrayed by Henry Fonda, *Fail-Safe's* president is a model leader. In his article "The Literary Presidency," English scholar Warren G. Rochelle has argued that the political literature of this period often both glorified and humanized presidents (Rochelle 416). He contends that the novel *Fail-Safe* fits this pattern and that the film version did too (Rochelle 409–10). Rochelle describes a "presidential mythos," which the onscreen Fonda both reflects and perpetuates. In his book *The Presidential Difference*, political scientist Fred Greenstein outlines "six qualities that relate to presidential job performance." *Fail-Safe's* leader embodies these categories of "public communicator," "organizational capacity," "political skill," "vision," "cognitive capacity," and "emotional intelligence" better than any of his real-life counterparts (Greenstein 5–6).

For these reasons, the president in *Fail-Safe* is a reassuring figure and embodies public attitudes toward the presidency since FDR, who comforted citizens during the Great Depression and World War II (Rochelle 407). Thanks to Henry Fonda, this crisis occurs when the *Best Man* for the job occupies the White House. One could certainly argue that this depiction is due to formulaic considerations. However, it also reflects the mood and visions of the early 1960s, when, in John F. Kennedy's words, Americans "stood on the edge of a New Frontier" and would "pay any price, bear any burden, meet any hardship" to conquer it (Sorensen 100, 12). *Fail-Safe* generally exhibits a confidence in the power of the individual, a faith in man's ability to wrest control back from the machine and step away from the abyss of nuclear destruction. Personal choices matter, as viewers see through the behavior of the president, the Soviet chairman, and several other characters.

One can misread the film's optimism, however. Julian Smith has said that "everything turns out reasonably well," with only Moscow and New York destroyed (Smith 197). That may be well and good for Yankee-hating baseball fans, but it hardly qualifies as a happy ending. Smith also contends that the movie "turns disaster into an excuse for national pride" (197). This is an odd declaration, given the failure of America's nuclear-deterrence strategy and technological safeguards, not to mention the self-inflicted incineration of the Big Apple. One could conversely argue that, if this is the best America can hope for with a model president, what are we likely to get with the real occupants of the White House?

Fail-Safe's position on the question of responsibility has also, it seems, often been misrepresented. Charles Maland, for instance, thinks that the film approves of existing U.S. defense policies (Maland 208). On the contrary, *Fail-Safe* makes a strong case that relying upon nuclear deterrence to keep the peace is flawed and dangerous. The film also criticizes the apparent dependence upon machines to maintain and oversee this deadly game. Julian Smith states that *Fail-Safe* "simplifies and romanticizes the issues of national responsibility" (Smith 197), but is that really the case? Audiences may indeed emerge from the theater feeling that U.S. political and military leaders are "doing the best job possible," in Charles Maland's words, but *Fail-Safe* questions whether even this is good enough (Maland 208). If, despite all the virtues of the American Constitution and democratic government, the world still loses Moscow and New York to a nuclear holocaust, what does that say about the existing system and the dangers of deterrence? In an almost Kennedyesque fashion, *Fail-Safe* asks: can we do better?

In his essay on the film, Michael G. Wollscheidt raises additional, larger questions. Does *Fail-Safe* absolve citizens of responsibility? Is it pessimistic about society's chances of escaping this predicament? With regard to the first question, Wollscheidt writes, "Hollywood films about nuclear war," this one included, "seem to have failed in casting man in the starring role" (Wollscheidt 74). If the president occupies the film's center, and much of the remaining screen time focuses on other characters, their decisions, and their actions, then surely this view is off the mark. Wollscheidt also contends that in this movie, "no blame may be affixed, for man was impotent in the face of an irresistible force" (Wollscheidt 74).

A closer examination of *Fail-Safe's* dialogue indicates the opposite. While U.S. and Soviet leaders do agree that "no one is to blame," the president later makes clear to the Soviet premier that, in his words, "We're responsible for what happens to us!" Wollscheidt further claims that the picture is pessimistic about how we can escape this potentially explosive predicament (Wollscheidt, 74, 72). Yet, on a deeper level, *Fail-Safe* actually strikes a hopeful note, because human agency still matters. As the president tells the Soviet premier near the close of *Fail-Safe*, "We put it there, Mr. Chairman, and we're not helpless. What we put between us, we can remove."

OCTOBER 1962: LIFE IMITATING ART?

Since both *Fail-Safe* (in book and film form) and *Colossus* (at least in the cinematic version) invoke the image and supposed qualities of John F. Kennedy, the contemporary chief executive's leadership during the Cuban Missile Crisis merits examination. To begin with, how did Kennedy's knowledge or level of interest in scientific subjects compare with those of his fictional counterparts? According to Nobel Prize–winning scientist Glenn T. Seaborg, whom JFK appointed as head of the Atomic Energy Commission, Kennedy's "natural drive for firsthand knowledge and curiosity . . . were reminiscent of the scientist's approach" (Seaborg 182). On one occasion, JFK even went so far as to fly dangerously low over an atomic blast crater! (Seaborg 182). Based on his personal encounters with the president, Seaborg characterized his boss as having "a first-rate intellect, a mind of a caliber equal to that of the best scientists I have known" (Seaborg 183).

Intelligence is one thing, but performance under pressure may be something else entirely. The Cuban Missile Crisis of October 1962 provides the closest glimpse we will (it is hoped) ever get of a chief executive dealing with the likelihood of general nuclear war. While the crisis resulted from calculated decisions on the part of Soviet leader Nikita Khrushchev and thus did not involve the mechanical glitches seen in *Fail-Safe* or *Colossus*, the missile placement in Cuba did come as a surprise to the Kennedy administration, and the two-week period which followed involved unexpected twists and turns.

How do JFK's actual leadership qualities and decisions compare with those of the leaders in *Fail-Safe* and *Colossus*? According to historians Ernest May and

Philip Zelikow, President Kennedy—in this instance, at least—largely lived up to the standards set by Burdick, Wheeler, Lumet, and Fonda. (He also, therefore, easily surpassed those of Jones and Sargent.) Unlike *Fail-Safe*'s fictional leader, who arrives completely qualified, JFK appears to have grown some during the crisis, as reflected by his handling of administration discussions about how to deal with the situation. Perhaps most importantly, he "did not make any impulsive decisions during the crisis. He invariably opened up much of his reasoning about the pros, cons, and likely consequences of his choices before he made them" (May and Zelikow 690–91).

Like Henry Fonda's president, Kennedy also "seems more alive to the possibilities and consequences of each new development than anyone else. He remains calm, lucid, and is constantly a step, or several steps, ahead of his advisers" (May and Zelikow 691–92). Even when confronted by such unexpected events as the downing of Major Rudolf Anderson's U-2 over Cuba, an act which under existing rules should have led to war, President Kennedy refrained from taking such potentially disastrous action as a retaliatory air attack against Soviet and Cuban installations. May and Zelikow conclude that no other "president (in a list of those who could imaginably have been elected) would have adopted a more peaceful course than the one Kennedy chose" (May and Zelikow 696).

Subsequent events also showed that the Cuban Missile Crisis prompted Kennedy and Khrushchev to work more closely in the future, just as the wayward bombers of *Fail-Safe* seem to have affected their fictional counterparts. While the real leaders' cooperation was tragically cut short by Kennedy's death in November 1963, it did offer a glimmer of hope for stabilizing, and perhaps ending, the Cold War. Both sides agreed in June 1963 to create a "direct teletype link," though not quite as advanced as *Fail-Safe*'s telephone hotline, and the two countries also signed the Limited Test Ban Treaty that July (Powaski 109).

COLOSSUS *(1970) AND PRESIDENTIAL LOSS OF CONTROL*

Both the written and filmed versions of *Fail-Safe* belonged to a wave of cultural critique that emerged in the early 1960s. These challenges to conventional thinking about American society were not confined to nuclear strategy. Rachel Carson, for instance, raised troubling questions about technology and the environment in her book *Silent Spring* (1962). The Civil Rights movement, which had begun with the Montgomery bus boycott (1955), rose in importance dur-

This is terrible — this book is crap

ing the Kennedy years. Although nonviolent, movement participants were often willing to defy authorities who they perceived as illegitimate or immoral. The establishment of Students for a Democratic Society and the youth protest movement in 1962 also epitomized a growing activism and criticism of established orthodoxies and those who expounded them (Patterson 443–44).

As the decade continued, American society became more divided, and the wave of dissent became an onrushing tide that swelled around a variety of issues: civil rights, the environment, feminism, sexual mores, and the Vietnam War. One part of this 1960s counterculture concerned the relationship of humans to technology. As historian Thomas Hughes notes, "Several authors in widely read books attacked the foundations of the technological society," whose "rational values . . . posed a deadly threat to individual freedom and to emotional and spiritual life" (Hughes 444–45). In *The Technological Society* (1964), Jacques Ellul argued that "politicians do not understand technological systems well enough to control them, and scientists and engineers are so specialized that their thinking cannot embrace the scope of technological systems, with their interacting technical, political, economic, and social components" (Hughes 452).

The intellectual Lewis Mumford was another such critic, one who had undergone a remarkable change in his attitudes towards technology. Mumford's book *Technics and Civilization* (1934) spoke hopefully of modern technology's possibilities. By 1970, the same year in which *Colossus* debuted onscreen, his perspective had changed. Mumford now spoke negatively of the "megamachine" and the scientific experts who built or maintained such devices (Hughes 449). In *The Pentagon of Power,* he wrote ominously that "automation, in this final form, is an attempt to exercise control, not only of the mechanical process itself, but of the human being who once directed it: turning him from an active to a passive agent, and finally eliminating him altogether" (Mumford 189). In this sentence, Mumford summarizes the basic theme of *Colossus: The Forbin Project*. The technological concerns of Ellul, Mumford, and others had grown between the days of *Fail-Safe* and the time of *Colossus,* and the latter film reflects these increasing anxieties.

If the president in *Fail-Safe* reflects public attitudes toward the American presidency since FDR, the leader in *Colossus: The Forbin Project* (1970) is emblematic of a growing 1960s concern about or disillusionment with the presidency. As a result, the president figures less prominently in *Colossus*. The movie was based on the eponymous 1966 novel by D.F. Jones. In terms of nuclear deterrence, if *Fail-Safe* stood for the era of the manned bomber, *Colossus: The*

Forbin Project represents the age of the Intercontinental Ballistic Missile (ICBM). In short, humans have even less direct control over nuclear weapons and decisions concerning their use.

In the film, the president of the United States (Gordon Pinsent; the character, as in *Fail-Safe*, has no name) decides to turn the responsibility for American national security over to a supercomputer called Colossus, which has been developed by Dr. Charles Forbin (Eric Braeden) and a team of scientists. Through a series of events, it becomes clear that Colossus is, in Dr. Forbin's words, "built even better than we thought." Most of the film concerns Colossus's growing control over American national security and the computer's increasing abuse of that power. Caught off guard by this technological wonder, the president, Dr. Forbin, and others attempt to first maintain and then reassert their authority. Meanwhile, the Soviets have developed a counterpart to Colossus, known as Guardian, which similarly displaces the Communist leadership and soon works in concert with Colossus. First published in Great Britain, the novel *Colossus* reached America in 1967. By that time, the Cold War nuclear standoff to which *Fail-Safe* referred seemed less acute, and it had become an even smaller concern by the time of the film's release in 1969. After the Cuban Missile Crisis of October 1962, John F. Kennedy and Nikita Khrushchev had worked to decrease Soviet-American tensions. Following Kennedy's assassination in November 1963, President Lyndon Johnson continued to negotiate with the Soviets, meeting Premier Alexei Kosygin for a summit in June 1967. Along with other nations, America and Russia signed the Treaty on the Non-Proliferation of Nuclear Weapons in July 1968. The Strategic Arms Limitation Talks began in 1969 (Powaski 120–23). As historian Paul Boyer has noted, however, all was not well: "In both the United States and the Soviet Union, nuclear weapons research, construction, and deployment went forward at a rapid clip after 1963" (Boyer 827). Such technological developments as underground testing, multiple warheads, and antiballistic missiles indicated that danger still existed; the arms race was anything but over. The MAD nuclear standoff between the superpowers also remained in place.

The leader in *Colossus* underwent a transformation while moving from the printed page to the screen, as did the leader in *Fail-Safe*. The novel *Colossus* also seemed to draw its presidential portrait from real life. Aside from height considerations, the president described has much in common with Lyndon Johnson. He is "dynamic and extrovert, the epitome of the man who knew what he wanted and saw that he got it" (Jones 12). In his early fifties, the president is "a professional politician to his fingertips" (Jones 13). His life revolves around power. His cinematic counterpart, however, looks remarkably like John F. Kennedy. Gordon Pinsent, who plays this leader, lacks the long-established onscreen persona that Henry Fonda brought to *Fail-Safe.*

In a pointed contrast to the presidential ideal drawn by Burdick and Wheeler and filmed by Lumet, Jones's chief executive is a man of diminished stature. While in director Joseph Sargent's movie version of *Colossus* the president gains a few inches, he loses even more of his luster. The president in *Colossus,* who looks vigorous like JFK, is in fact a leader who is progressively overpowered by events. For all his good looks, intelligence, and wit, he seems increasingly out of place in a technological world; in this restricted context, the president relies upon his advisers, particularly Dr. Forbin.

In *Colossus,* the president hopes the supercomputer will solve the problems dramatized in the movie *Fail-Safe.* As he tells the public after the activation of the computer, "For years we have been delicately and deliberately poised on the brink of a disaster too complete and humble to contemplate. There is an old saying, 'Everyone makes mistakes,' but that is just what man can no longer afford." He then speaks of Colossus's virtues, which include its ability to process information and also the fact that "it has no emotions, knows no fear, no hate, no envy. It cannot act in a sudden fit of temper." For the president, Colossus's activation offers the opportunity to focus not on preparing for war but on ending worldwide hunger and want.

These goals are noble, but the president in *Colossus* is, in effect, shifting this awesome atomic burden from man to machine. As he says at a White House gathering, "Harry Truman years ago . . . said that the buck stops right here, but now that's no longer true. Colossus will now take that buck. It'll also have to take that responsibility of a megamillion lives that all presidents have had to carry since Roosevelt." Colossus thus represents the ultimate mechanization of national defense; the buck-passing of *Fail-Safe* has become a complete abdication of authority and responsibility. Artificial intelligence pioneer Dr. Norbert Wiener warned against this danger as early as 1960:

> If we use, to achieve our purposes, a mechanical agency with whose operation we cannot efficiently interfere once we have started it, because the action is so fast and irrevocable that we have not the data to intervene before the action is complete, then we had better be quite sure that the purpose put into the machine is the purpose which we really desire and not merely a colorful imitation of it. (quoted in Mumford 189)

While the president presumably expects to retain his powers, his existing authority is unclear and quickly challenged. As the project's head scientist, Dr. Forbin is naturally expected to play a prominent role in Colossus-related discussions. It soon appears, however, that he is better qualified to lead than the president. Indeed, at one point Dr. Forbin disdains protocol and effectively takes over a cabinet meeting! At more sedate moments, the president often defers to Forbin. As the film progresses, the president is demoted from one of the lead characters to almost a bit player. It is Forbin, the arrogant genius behind Colossus, who becomes the dominant figure. This development is reflective not only of story considerations but also of the growing importance of the technological experts within the federal government.

In some respects, *Colossus* is thus reminiscent of Stanley Kubrick's *Dr. Strangelove* (1964). Both films include—as does *Fail-Safe,* for that matter—an apparently overconfident, ambitious, and presumably German-born adviser to the president. (These characters, it should be noted, referred in part to such real-life counterparts as Henry Kissinger and Werner von Braun.) As portrayed by Peter Sellers, Dr. Strangelove is admittedly more over the top than Dr. Forbin, but both suffer from the same hubris and an overreliance on abstract mathematical calculations that are belied by real events. While *Fail-Safe*'s Groeteschele (Walter Matthau) exhibits these same traits, Lumet's picture reveals that the president's strength of character overrides his adviser's arguments. In contrast, *Dr. Strangelove*'s President Muffley (Peter Sellers) and *Colossus*'s president lack the will, knowledge, or self-confidence to remain independent of their scientific *Wunderkinds.*

This challenge of presidential authority is not limited to Dr. Forbin. The key moment in *Colossus* occurs after the American supercomputer has been denied its established communications link with Guardian, its Soviet counterpart. Colossus asks (actually, demands) that contact be restored, and the leaders of the two countries refuse. Forbin explains their decision to Colossus, but finally the president takes matters into his own hands. He tells the computer, "We will not be threatened. You will obey your superiors. Transmitting facilities will not be restored." As he continues his delivery, the president is interrupted by Colossus, which warns him of a not-so-accidental missile launch. Cooperating with its mechanical comrade Guardian, Colossus has threatened to start a nuclear war to get what it wants. Confronted with the realization of his worst fears and the very nightmare Colossus was created to prevent, the president surrenders to the computer's ultimatum. Such nuclear blackmail will eventually lead to what Mick Broderick has called "an omnipotent form of 'benign' technological fascism" (Broderick 36).

Attempts to resist Colossus continue, but the president coordinates these efforts more than he leads them. Dr. Forbin is the picture's chief human protagonist, and the president often compares unfavorably to him. Unlike the leader in *Fail-Safe,* the president in *Colossus* is a befuddled young man. As noted before, he depends upon experts, and much of his onscreen time is spent asking them questions or acting perplexed. Again, he is not in complete command of the situation. In contrast to Henry Fonda, Gordon Pinsent usually *reacts* to developments. If anyone thinks ahead, it is likely to be Forbin.

Unlike *Fail-Safe, Colossus: The Forbin Project* offers little grounds for optimism. By the end of the film, its befuddled, out-of-touch president is powerless and virtually nonexistent, while Colossus appears poised to rule the world. One might place faith in the mighty Dr. Forbin, but even he is outmaneuvered by his invention. Ironically, Colossus and Guardian will oversee nuclear disarmament, because the computers—unlike their creators—see the logic in abolishing nuclear weapons. Colossus and Guardian also see the logic in machines running the Earth instead of man, however. During a global telecast, Colossus ominously speaks as "the voice of World Control." This latter-day Frankenstein also boldly declares that in time, people will come to accept its authority and even love the supercomputer.

While humanity may now be saved from atomic Armageddon, this peace requires the sacrifice of some of our most basic freedoms. If *Fail-Safe* argued that we had ceded some control over our lives to technology, *Colossus* presents us with utter abdication. Unlike the situation in *Fail-Safe,* in *Colossus* there is no escape: man cannot control or outwit his machines.

CONCLUSION

Both films reflect the remarkable arc of American culture during the 1960s. At the outset of the decade, the presidency was held in high esteem; it was personified in Camelot, and it reflected the seemingly limitless possibilities of U.S. power. A growing awareness of the danger of the atom was emerging, but the trend did not seem irreversible. By the end of the decade, however, the stature of the office and that of its occupants had plummeted, a decline prompted in part by debate over Vietnam and soon to be accelerated by the Watergate scandal. The public still saw nuclear weapons as a threat, but critics had become more concerned about the broader effects of Cold War militarization and mechanization upon American society.

Looking at *Fail-Safe* and *Colossus,* both the changes and the constants in such attitudes become evident. The Cold War and U.S.-Soviet arms race remained a subject of debate, but *Colossus* reflects the thaw in U.S.-Soviet relations. The exchange between *Fail-Safe*'s president and the Russian premier was awkward and tension-filled, and each side's military distrusted the other. In *Colossus,* both leaders conversed easily by videophone. Each was suspicious but in a more muted fashion. (Ironically, however, this hot line, so crucial to success in the one film, proves insufficient in the other.) The national-security apparatus of each country, however, is depicted as all too capable of making bad choices, mistakes that help lead to the predicaments presented in each film. In *Fail-Safe,* the leaders work together to avert Armageddon; in *Colossus,* they work together but fail to prevent conquest by computers.

Despite their different endings, both *Fail-Safe* and *Colossus* sound the warning voiced by writer Craig W. Anderson: "Man had best be cautious in his quest for technological advances or they will replace self-determination with machine determination" (Anderson 19). In one film, this "determination" is accidental, while in the other it is intentional. In each case, however, the decision by citizens to delegate responsibility threatens to overwhelm a system of government established in an age of quill and pen. *Fail-Safe* makes a more obvious case that human behavior shapes history, but both films urge audiences to reconsider their present course. Technology is, in effect, a double-edged sword. Machines may offer greater efficiency and reduce burdens, but they can also create new problems or exacerbate old ones. As Craig Anderson has noted, while it offers "relief from . . . [man's] problems," "this same technology could enslave Man" (Anderson 20). In the end, both films challenge Americans to ensure that the constitutional pen remains mightier than the computerized sword.

Nuclear weapons are generally little discussed these days, but they have not gone away—we have only forgotten them. The danger remains, and while the U.S.-Soviet record of avoiding mishaps is quite good, it is not perfect. As George Clooney's 1999 remake of *Fail-Safe* noted, the growing proliferation of such devices underscores the importance of the questions posed by both films. These issues also extend to other topics, such as the wisdom of developing antiballistic missile defenses, the continuing computerization of society, and genetic engineering.

Such considerations received little attention during the last presidential election, a matter that may not bode well for an eighteenth-century democracy poised to enter the twenty-first century. When the candidates discussed science and technology, it was usually in terms of a single subject (the environment) or very focused benefits (wiring classrooms). Perhaps people should inquire about their larger visions of technology's place in American society. *Fail-Safe* and *Colossus* compel us to ask: at what point does the cost outweigh the benefits? Surely we need leaders who will consider these dilemmas, but the films also encourage us to consider them ourselves.

WORKS CITED

Anderson, Craig W. *Science Fiction Films of the Seventies.* Jefferson, North Carolina: McFarland, 1985.

Boyer, Paul. "From Activism to Apathy: The American People and Nuclear Weapons, 1963–1980." *Journal of American History* 70 (1984): 821–44.

Broderick, Mick. *Nuclear Movies: A Critical Analysis and Filmography of International Feature-Length Films Dealing with Experimentation, Aliens, Terrorism, Holocaust, and Other Disaster Scenarios, 1914–1989.* Jefferson, North Carolina: McFarland, 1991.

Burdick, Eugene, and Harvey Wheeler. *Fail-Safe.* New York: McGraw-Hill, 1962.

Colossus: The Forbin Project. Dir. Joseph Sargent. With Eric Braeden. Universal, 1970.

Fail-Safe. Dir. Sidney Lumet. With Henry Fonda. Columbia, 1964.

Ford, Daniel. *The Button: The Pentagon's Strategic Command and Control System.* New York: Simon and Schuster, 1985.

Freedman, Lawrence. *The Evolution of Nuclear Strategy.* New York: St. Martin's, 1981.

Greenstein, Fred Irwin. *The Presidential Difference: Leadership Style from FDR to Clinton.* New York: Free Press, 2000.

Hughes, Thomas P. *American Genesis: A Century of Invention and Technological Enthusiasm, 1870–1970.* New York: Viking, 1989.

Jones, D.F. *Colossus.* New York: G. Putnam's Sons, 1967.

LaFeber, Walter. *The American Age: U.S. Foreign Policy at Home and Abroad, 1750 to the Present.* 2nd ed. New York: W.W. Norton, 1994.

Maland, Charles. "*Dr. Strangelove* (1964): Nightmare Comedy and the Ideology of Liberal Consensus." In *Hollywood As Historian: American Film in a Cultural Context,* edited by Peter C. Rollins, 190–210. 2nd ed. Lexington: University Press of Kentucky, 1998.

May, Ernest R., and Philip D. Zelikow, eds. *The Kennedy Tapes: Inside the White House During the Cuban Missile Crisis.* Cambridge, Massachusetts: Belknap Press–Harvard University Press, 1997.

Mumford, Lewis. *The Myth of the Machine.* Vol. 2 of *The Pentagon of Power.* New York: Harcourt Brace Jovanovich, 1970.

Patterson, James T. *Grand Expectations: The United States, 1945–1974.* New York: Oxford University Press, 1996.

Powaski, Ronald E. *March to Armageddon: The United States and the Nuclear Arms Race, 1939 to the Present.* New York: Oxford University Press, 1987.

Rochelle, Warren G. "The Literary Presidency." *Presidential Studies Quarterly* 29 (2000): 407–16.

Seaborg, Glenn T., with Eric Seaborg. *Adventures in the Atomic Age: From Watts to Washington*. New York: Farrar, Strauss and Giroux, 2001.

Smith, Julian. *Looking Away: Hollywood and Vietnam*. New York: Charles Scribner's Sons, 1975.

Sorensen, Theodore C., ed. *"Let the Word Go Forth": The Speeches, Statements, and Writings of John F. Kennedy, 1947 to 1963*. New York: Delacorte, 1988.

Wollscheidt, Michael G. *"Fail-Safe."* In *Nuclear War Films*, edited by Jack Shaheen, 68–75. Carbondale: Southern Illinois University Press, 1978.

John Shelton Lawrence

THE 100 MILLION$ MEN

Presidential Action/Adventure Heroes of *Independence Day* (1996) and *Air Force One* (1997)

Harrison Ford stars as President James Marshall in *Air Force One* (1997).

> Maybe the president's oath of office should be altered. When the Chief Justice administers the oath to the next incumbent, maybe he or she, after swearing to preserve, protect and defend the Constitution, should also swear to defend American filmmakers' right to use the presidency any way they like.
>
> —Stanley Kaufmann

Several factors affect the voting behavior of young people: transience, obstacles to voter registration, and the kind of stake that comes from home ownership. Do film images of the American presidency also play a role? Here the assumption is made that they do cultivate young tastes for screenlike presidents. It then follows that certain kinds of presidential candidates become necessary to sustain and to increase the participation of younger voters.

YOUTHFUL VOTERS AND THE MOVIES

During the past forty years, American presidential elections have had a declining appeal for young citizens. As a belated legitimation for the Vietnam draft (and a potential stimulant for youth voting), Congress sent the Twenty-sixth Amendment to the Constitution to the states on 23 March 1971. By 1 July of that same year, the amendment had been ratified (Brunner 75–76).

In the presidential election of 1972, the first in which an eighteen-year-old could vote, the participation of the eighteen- to twenty-four-year age group (49.6%) almost matched the participation of the twenty-one- to twenty-four-age group in 1968 (50.4%) (U.S. Bureau of the Census). Thereafter, however, it began a steady decline. The 1976 participation dropped to 42.2 percent, and in 1980 it fell again to 39.9 percent. Despite a bump back up to 42.8 percent in 1992, participation had dropped again by 1996 to a mere 32.4 percent.

The attrition among young voters does not match the behavior of older groups. The participation of the forty-five- to sixty-four-year group also declined but at a slower rate, from 74.9 percent in 1968 to 64.4 percent in 1996. The participation of voters in the over-sixty-five group, who maintain the high-voltage current to the third rail of politics, increased from 65.8 percent in 1968 to 67 percent in 1996.

So what has happened here? Can one understand the expectations of younger voters for presidential campaigns and candidates? Are youthful voters off "bowling alone"—to use Robert Putnam's apt metaphor—on Election Day? (Putnam). Are the dynastic family themes, such as seen in the 2000 campaign, too gerontocratic? Should the candidates promise psychoactive drugs instead of pandering to elders fixated on assistance for prescriptions? What—short of a reinstated draft during a roaringly unpopular war—would bring them to the presidential voting booth? And does paying attention to youth offer insight on serious defects in the nation's aging Constitution?

Pondering these big questions, political enlightenment may be found by looking at the movies of the 1990s that deal with U.S. presidential roles. Optimism regarding this approach seems warranted by several facts. First, young people go to the movies—they even leave the house at night to do it. Second, popular movies offer younger people a wider array of alternative U.S. presidents than current political parties. Additionally, box office receipts give a clearer sense of which kinds of president are market successes.

It is also apparent that theatrical moviegoing is inversely correlated with voter participation. According to the most recent Gallup poll on this topic, a whopping 88 percent of young adults in the eighteen to twenty-nine group have attended a movie during the year. The expected corollary is that movie attendance declines steadily with age. Only 43 percent of the over-sixty-five group (half the rate for young adults) reported attending a movie during the previous year (Gallup poll).

What do these numbers seem to be saying? Are the major parties ignoring the political preferences of younger voters expressed by box office ticket purchases? Should citizens who really care about cultivating civic responsibility in younger moviegoers consider reshaping the presidency itself to make voting a more audience-friendly experience? To the extent that young voter participation is a problem in delivering the right product to the market, Hollywood movies point toward solutions for these major issues in American democracy. Stanley Kaufmann's cynical comment about the rights of filmmakers dismisses a chance to revitalize the young voter's sense of importance regarding the presidency (Kaufmann 24).

PRESIDENTIAL MOVIES OF THE 1990S

Hollywood's past decade has produced screen presidents manically. Excluding made-for-TV films and numerous barely visible independent films, more than forty presidential films were delivered to mainstream distribution channels. A perspective for this number is apparent from the fact that the American film industry had produced only ninety presidential films from its beginnings until 1990.[1]

Box office receipts can be derived from the *Washington Post*'s list "$100 Million Films 1990-2000."[2] The presidential film rankings and their gross revenues are as follows:

The Best Box Office

The top four films share a common heroic pattern. Either the president performs high-stakes derring-do or he directly commands the heroes. In *Independence Day (ID4)* and *Air Force One (AF1)* the presidents are themselves action-adventure heroes. *ID4*'s President Whitemore (Bill Pullman) engages in victorious single-warrior-style combat with aliens in outer space. The very earth itself is at risk in his battle. Manhood, male dominance of independent woman, and the future of heterosexuality also seem to hang on the president's actions. And President Marshall (Harrison Ford) in *AF1* is clearly a Tom Clancy/ Jack Ryan kind of president, the last man left on the plane who has the wits and strength to defeat a cruel adversary in hand-to-hand combat. *Deep Impact's* President Beck (Morgan Freeman) also has the responsibility to save the whole world and commands "the Messiah Project," in which a team takes off in pursuit of an asteroid. Although the east coast of the United States is battered, his "Messiah" team does save the earth from an Extinction Level Event (ELE). The president is nameless and barely visible in *Armageddon*, but he still helps save the world by launching a team of saviors.[3] Although he inspires the whole world with American plans to save it, he also conspires with evil bureaucrats who want to blow up Harry Stamper's (Bruce Willis) drilling team on the asteroid.

The remaining films in the $100 million club present the president in much less favorable ways. *Clear and Present Danger* is a Tom Clancy thriller in which President Bennet (Donald Moffat) is an obnoxiously devious foil for the straight arrow Jack Ryan (Harrison Ford). This is their climactic confrontation:

> *President:* "How dare you come in here and bark at me like I'm some junkyard dog—I'm the President of the United States!"
>
> *Ryan:* "No, how dare YOU, sir?!"

Jack is acting with integrity and says, in effect, "How dare YOU subvert the U.S. Constitution?"[4]

In the Line of Fire does not present the president (Jim Curley) in a subverting role, but he is in the background as a question mark in the mind of the heroic agent Frank Horrigan (Clint Eastwood) assigned to guard him. Having failed to protect JFK in Dallas, he wonders whether he could stand to take the fall for *this* unworthy president. The success of the film derives from the vicious, suspenseful struggle between Horrigan and Mitch Leary (John Malkovich), the villain who wants to kill both Horrigan and the president.

The Pelican Brief offers a doddering out-of-the-loop president (Robert Culp) who negligently permits crime to flourish. Here it is the box office champs Darby Shaw (Julia Roberts) and Gray Grantham (Denzel Washington) who possess the heroic auras.

It is clear that for the $100 million movies, presidents should save the world—doing it themselves, if necessary. Spectacular special effects help too, though in a degree that is hard to estimate. And when a heroic role is not in the script for the president, the bumbling or nefarious presidential plans must be thwarted by heroic, bankable stars that will build the box office receipts.

The Box Office Disappointments

Because of underreporting about the details of failure, it is more difficult to say which presidential films had the worst returns. But one can selectively pick some significantly smaller box office returns among less successful movies, listed in approximate rank order from catastrophe to modest success. The table below shows reported budget numbers, where available, as an additional measure of failure (International Movie Database).

The feeblest performance is Michael Moore's *Canadian Bacon*. There the president (unnamed, Alan Alda) is an idiot who lets manipulative advisers push him into a phony war with Canada. In terms of financial losses, the worst films are *Primary Colors* and *Mars Attacks!* The former had a snickering topicality with its slick and sleazy climb from a southern governorship to the inaugural ball. In *Mars Attacks!* President Art Land (Jack Nicholson) sells out earth after being suckered by invaders from Mars. *Dick* charmingly retells the Watergate fable, deftly spoofing all the major players from Nixon (Dan Hedaya) to Bob Woodward and Carl Bernstein, but only video rentals will save its investors.

Among the more successful films with smaller box office, *Wag The Dog* played on the currency of Clinton's big Lewinsky problem, and *Dave* played out an Everyman fantasy initiated by overly strenuous presidential adultery. *The American President* also had a sex-in-White-House-with-other-than-spouse theme, tak-

Title	Actor/President	Budget/Gross (in $)	Year
Canadian Bacon	Alan Alda/ The President	11,000,000/178,104	1995
Primary Colors	John Travolta/ Pres.-Elect Jack Stanton	65,000,000/38,960,000	1998
Mars Attacks!	Jack Nicholson/ Art Land	70,000,000/37,540,000	1996
The American President	Michael Douglas/ President Shepherd	62,000,000/65,000,000	1995
Dave	Kevin Kline/Bill Mitchell	—/63,270,000	1992
Dick	Dan Hedaya/ Richard Nixon	13,000,000/6,241,000	1999
Wag The Dog	Michael Belson/ The President	15,000,000/43,022,000	1997

ing a point of view that mirrored the tolerance of the American public during Clinton's impeachment process. But the box office returns barely paid the bills.

One can conclude here that while filmmakers can find a market for presenting the president as a flawed, amusing figure, they are lucky when they can take anything back to the bank.

A CELLULOID CONSTITUTION?

What can be learned about voting behavior from the box office receipts?[5] By knowing that students see so many films, perhaps one can make reasonable suggestions about how their experiences might translate into practical politics.

One conclusion is that the old precinematic Constitution envisions a less-than-exciting president. The various roles of the president enumerated in Article 2, Section 2 are depressingly dull: serving as commander in chief of the army and navy; leading the executive departments; granting of reprieves and pardons; making treaties and appointing ambassadors and others with advice and consent of the Senate; filling vacancies in office during Senate recess; giving advice to Congress; convening it on occasion; receiving ambassadors; taking care that the laws be faithfully executed.

President Thomas J. Whitmore (Bill Pullman) faces the ultimate test of leadership in *Independence Day* (1996).

The oath of office further specifies that the president will "to the best of [his] ability, preserve, protect and defend the Constitution of the United States." But, as demonstrated by the presidents of box office champs *ID4* and *AF1*, the president himself must take direct action to achieve popularity. The other duties listed in the Constitution also lack plot potential. The tasks sound too repetitive, too detailed, and demand too much time. Can you imagine a movie about a president who finds a constructive compromise on the problems associated with Social Security or Medicare? Bo-ring!!

This simplified, operative conception of the popular presidency seems to fit the Republic of Entertainment: the president will fight foes, hand-to-hand and in outer space, if necessary (*ID4, AF1, Armageddon*); the president may act at his discretion in such a way as to compel the admiration of all mankind (*ID4, Armageddon, Deep Impact*); the president may act at his discretion to retain or restore male authority and sexual dominance within the family (*ID4, AF1*);[6] the president will preserve, protect, and defend the Constitution and avoid criminal enterprises and illicit sex in the White House (*Absolute Power, Pelican Brief, Mars Attacks!, Murder at 1600*). This simplified conception of the presidency pushes it in the direction of heroism and of the post-Clintonian demands for "character."

PROSPECTS FOR A FILM-INSPIRED PRESIDENCY

It seems radical to redefine the presidency so as to reach additional youthful voters. Of course, the nation must decide how important it is to get young people to vote. While these suggestions will seem irresponsible to some, there are some small signs that real presidential types are beginning to develop an understanding of the appeal of a box office presidency.

Item: During the 1996 campaign, Bill Clinton hosted Dean Devlin (producer), Roland Emmerich (director), and Bill Pullman (fictional president) from *Independence Day* at the White House. Even though it was a mere two years after the domestic terrorist blast in Oklahoma City, President Clinton praised a film in which the White House is incinerated. "I recommend it," he declared. (Rogin 9)

Item: Bob Dole, who had come off as a stuffy old moralist for earlier attacks on Hollywood, issued statements of praise for *Independence Day's* patriotism and battle between good and evil. Dole's spokesman explained that the violence was "socially redeeming" because "it promoted the greater good." (Rogin 9)

Item: For the White House Correspondents Association dinner, Bill Clinton made a video with Kevin Spacey in which he made an Oscar acceptance speech before his bedroom mirror before Spacey demanded to get his Oscar back. (Reuters TV)

These telling moments demonstrate a willingness of people for politicians to move the Oval Office toward the box office.

Besides the president's inherently dull job description, an additional obstacle to further progress in this direction is resistance from older voters. They have had a poor record of supporting anyone resembling an action-adventure type in recent presidential campaigns. John Glenn, a Korean War fighter pilot and astronaut, failed to get the nomination of the Democrats in 1980 and 1984. Neither George Bush nor Bob Dole, both veterans of World War II, could defeat Bill Clinton. John McCain could not defeat George W. Bush, and Al Gore, the Vietnam combat-zone journalist, derived no significant edge against the Texas Air Guard pilot, George W. Bush. Older voters seem out of tune with physical heroism or sacrifice as a qualification for office. The wonkish *The West Wing*, which they can stay home to see, seems to portray the president as nothing more than a soft-bodied policy-maker. Perhaps the older voters will simply die off—especially if Congress remains gridlocked over prescription drugs.

NEW DIRECTIONS FOR HOLLYWOOD

In looking at Hollywood formulas, one should remember their temporary life span. Maybe the past decade of success for President Harrison/Morgan Pullman reflects a generation of creators who read the same sorts of comic books as their youthful audience. Roland Emmerich, the German-born director of *ID4*, reports that the favorite films from his childhood were *Star Wars* and *Close Encounters*, followed by *War of the Worlds* and *Earth vs. The Flying Saucers*. Because such films formed his taste, he had a craving to make genre movies. He claims that his fellow Germans hated him for his simplicity. So he went to Hollywood (Major).[7] The rest is history—the single most profitable presidential film in history.

Who knows where Hollywood will take the next generation of celluloid presidents? Do not be surprised if the little boys who grew up admiring Stallone, Schwarzenegger, and the bulging biceps of G.I. Joe become the targeted market for buff-bodied presidents. It is clear that *ID4* and *AF1* have both moved in the "hard-bodied" direction. In the fall of 2000, youthful, voting-age audience members on the World Wrestling Federation's "Smackdown" program called for Bush and Gore to stop talking and get into the ring. Does this presage a serious run by Jesse "The Body" Ventura?[8]

But perhaps the evolution described here is just a temporary trend. One

The White House is destroyed in *Independence Day* (1996).

can also imagine another generation in Hollywood that would work at dramatizing some historical ideals for the president rooted in achievements of national leadership. How about an imaginary president who is responsive to a wide range of national needs; who can articulate a shareable vision that responds to those needs; who is capable of policy initiatives that serve those needs; who can operate within the separation of powers specified by the constitution—and who is decisive and shows integrity in pursuing all of the above?

Maybe young people would not find such a president so boring. Of course, one cannot tell Hollywood what to do. But just in case it asks, citizens can be ready with their suggestions.

NOTES

1. In arriving at numbers for films prior to the 1990s, the following indexes were used as a starting point: *Film Index International* (CD-ROM) of the British Film Institute; The American Film Institute's *Catalog of Feature Films, 1890-1970* (with a missing 1951–1960); and Magill's *Survey of Cinema* in the EBSCO-CD-ROM format, which contains citations and abstracts for fourteen thousand classic and contemporary films issued through 1993. Films were limited to those depicting the president during a real or imaginary term of office. Because of limitations in indexes, this number understates the total. The full list, reflecting assistance from others, is at the Film History League's web site at <http://www2.hnet.msu.edu/~filmhis/presidentialfilms/methods.html>.

2. The *Washington Post*'s list appears at its web site (washingtonpost.com/wp-srv/style/daily/movies/100million/article.htm) and contains numbers gathered from Ex-

hibitor Relations and the Associated Press. The grosses are box office numbers and do not include rental receipts. Omitted are *Forrest Gump* (Rank 6, $326,690,974) and *Contact* (Rank 193, $100,900,000) because the presence of real presidents is momentary and incorporated through film clip.

3. Stanley Anderson, who plays the president, is not even listed on the videocassette box.

4. This exchange and its meaning was called to my attention by A. Bowdoin Van Riper of Southern Polytechnic State University in Marietta, Georgia, on 16 June 2000.

5. Frank Manchel has warned against "assuming that box office receipts tell us about the meaning of film for their audiences" (Presidency on Film Conference, November 2000). This essay attempts to speculate about reasonable inferences from those numbers.

6. An important theme in both of these films is the disciplining of women to keep them in their place. In *Independence Day*, a variety of relationship problems are symbolically attributed to unruly women. President Whitemore's own careerist wife dies as a result of not minding her husband, and her final words are a tearful apology. In *Air Force One*, tension derives from the fact that President Marshall, though single-handedly flying the plane, defending against a MIG attack, and dangling from a cable from the plane, refuses to yield any authority to female Vice President Bennett (Glenn Close). *Deep Impact* has several scenes where men scream at women in order to subordinate them. Given the box office receipts for these films, may one assume that young men decide which movies to attend and take young women to socialize them for secondary roles? Manchel's caution about box office receipts is especially appropriate in looking at such films. A related question is whether women enjoyed the commercially unsuccessful *Primary Colors* far more than men did. Marty Knepper of Morningside College pointed out the date-for-the-movies phenomenon to me with great clarity.

7. In his interview, Emmerich states that as an outsider, he has a better idea of what is distinctly "American" than do American citizens themselves. It is also worth mentioning that another German, Wolfgang Peterson, directed *Air Force One*.

8. Susan Jeffords (*Hard Bodies*) defined the cinematic muscle boys before presidents themselves became action heroes. The WWF advocacy was a tongue-in-cheek play on its "Smackdown Your Vote," which worked with Youthvote 2000 and MTV'S Choose or Lose campaign. The WWF appeared at the Democratic National Convention in Los Angeles to launch its supporting public-service announcements ("WWF Smackdown Your Vote," *Business Wire*, 8 August 2000).

WORKS CITED

Brunner, Borgna, ed. "Amendment XXVI," *Time Almanac 2000*. Boston: Information Please, 1999.

Gallup Poll. "Gallup Goes to the Movies." 24 March 2000. <http://www.gallup.com>.

International Movie Data Base (www.imdb.com), viewed 15 October 2000.

Jeffords, Susan. *Hard Bodies: Hollywood Masculinity in the Reagan Era.* New Brunswick, New Jersey: Rutgers University Press, 1994.

Kaufmann, Stanley. "Air Force One." *New Republic* 217.8 (1997).

Major, Wade. "Invasion USA [interview with Roland Emmerich]," *Box Office Cover Story.* July 1996. <http:www.boxoff.com/coverjuly96c.html> (28 September 2000).

Putnam, Robert D. *Bowling Alone: The Collapse and Revival of American Community.* New York: Simon and Schuster, 2000.

Reuters TV. "President Clinton with Kevin Spacey in Spoof Video." Reuters TV, 30 April 2000.

Rogin, Michael. *Independence Day, Or How I Learned to Stop Worrying and Love the Enola Gay.* London: British Film Institute, 1998.

U.S. Bureau of the Census. "Table 2. Percent Reported Voted and Registered by Age and Region of Residence: November 1964 to Present." 17 October 1997. <http:www.census.gov/population/socdemo/voting/history/vot02.txt)>.

Loren P. Quiring

A MAN OF HIS WORD

Aaron Sorkin's American Presidents

Library of Congress.

THE SACRED POETRY OF POLITICS

The idea of American presidential history as a succession of visionaries, interrupted only by the occasional fop or fool, is tied to the idea of America itself as a land of self-creation, a place of freely becoming what we freely speak. A leader's words matter not because they issue from divine right but because "speaking up" is the instrument of political being. If a man does not talk, someone else will, and that utterance will displace him. In the ontology of American citizenship, what one *is* depends on what one *says*. Talking is being, a phenomenon that makes the relationship between leader and nation a deeply rhetorical one. For the poet Walt Whitman, keeping this relationship alive between leader and citizen was a matter of keeping the conversation going, perpetuating the archetypal citizen in each of us. So Whitman offered his own self-creating voice as national emblem. "If you do not say anything," he warns, "how can I say anything?" (Whitman 245). This model for the politically generative voice was, of course, tied to Abraham Lincoln, who assumed a fundamentally American posture toward language. Lincoln understood, explains Garry Wills, that a democratic nation created itself ultimately from its words, not from its blood or its guns.[1] That rhetorical sensibility has carried over into our own time. George W. Bush, preparing his first television address to the nation after the terrorist attacks of 11 September 2001, spent "days" on the speech's conclusion—in which, reports James Fallows, he "switched from the 'we' of most of the speech ('We will not tire . . . ') to the 'I' of personal commitment"—because, in the words of Bush speechwriter Michael Gerson, the president wanted "to finish with a statement of moral confidence in . . . the makeup of the universe." Intuitively, perhaps, Bush equated the nation's moral confidence in the universe with the "personal commitment" he would voice in an authoritative "I," signaling an equation that embodies a sacred "vow" to his citizens (Fallows 44).

The notion that sacred and authoritative words lie at the heart of a leader's identity is not, however, a strictly democratic assumption. It springs from a deeper anxiety about making a public language serve a private will. Consider the anxiety about language underlying the hesitancy and doubt in *Hamlet*, for example: a prince searching for a voice that can beget decisive action and restore the health of his kingdom. But Hamlet is tormented by the thought that words might be, after all, nothing more than air, that everything he knows about his comrades, his parents, his lovers—all of the oaths one gives, tacit or expressed, toward friendship or fidelity or citizenship—might be as variable and delicate as a pun. So Hamlet yearns for a language of correspondence: fixed, verifiable, signatory. To the traitorous Rosencrantz and Guildenstern, he pleads, "be even and direct with me" (II.ii.287), and to his benighted mother, who complains that a fictional queen overplays her faithfulness to her husband, Hamlet, angry and desperate, replies, "O but she'll keep her word" (III.ii.231). He needs faith in the reality and fidelity of words, a play suited to a verifiable action, but appearances keep tricking him out of that faith. So he talks and talks, filling the voids left by doubt with a punning discourse that is madly—and, in effect, passive-aggressively—calculated to penetrate appearances and reveal the truth (cf. III.iv.40-51). What Hamlet so clearly lacks is confidence in his own power to stamp his leadership into words he can trust.

LOGOS OR IMAGE?

Shakespeare understood that language is a battleground for any leader, but it is a crucial one to a society in which words are constantly up for grabs. In American democracy, a leader exists *because* he seizes verbal territory, and Aaron Sorkin, whose fictional commanders thrive in proportion to their verbal prolixity, means to seize that ground. In the motion picture *The American President*, the leader of a nation sick like Hamlet's Denmark faces a similar trickery in the discourse around him. His mission as commander is to extirpate deception with a faithful civic discourse. For President Andrew Shepherd (Michael Douglas), the nation's trickery lies in the image factories of its media, primarily television. Like Whitman's anxious self-creator and Shakespeare's desperate prince, Sorkin's Shepherd wants to live in the sure and rational force of his words. He wants a language of command. But he keeps getting dragged into the slipperiness of image, into the dangling logic of the snapshot, which his nemesis, Senator Rumson (Richard Dreyfuss), can spin at will. Not only is Shepherd failing to speak up against Rumson's slurs on television, but he is battling the very medium in which his language is supposed to be forged into counterargument. Because an image has no inherent logic—no *logos*—Rumson can recast a picture of a young Sydney Ellen Wade (Annette Bening) burning a flag in protest of apartheid as a portrait of a radical whore who whispers sweet-nothings in the president's ear. Shepherd is caught off-balance in this tele-visual world, where the logos of speeches, which would indelibly imprint him upon the discourse of governance, is merely waves of sound bites that momentarily impress—and then disappear, like air. Shepherd wants to function like the resolute Hamlet of Act V, a king who finally recognizes that he can create, not just describe, reality (cf. V.ii.29–79), signing and sealing language all by himself. But Shepherd, an American prince, is not the ordained maker of truth and good in his own tele-visual kingdom. If he who talks, rules, then Shepherd is having trouble finding his voice here. So he is stuck, as it were, in the first four acts of Hamlet's world, trying to resist the appearances that continually subvert his clarity and resolve. He wants to speak in a kingly language of reason, but the broken anti-language of television undoes him.[2]

Shepherd thus reacts to the threat of his verbal impotency by imperiously refusing to let image dictate reality. His aide Lewis Rothschild (Michael J. Fox) wants to explain to the public the nature of the president's relationship with Sydney. Shepherd declines. "We can't just leave it at that," Lewis complains. "Well, I'll tell you what," commands Shepherd, "we just did." Likewise, when

Sydney opens a conversation by protesting that her attraction to the president is not the relevant issue, Shepherd counters, affectionately but peremptorily, "I'll tell you what: let's make it the issue." In the president's mind, the logic of the world is something to be created from the voice of resolve, from the true and determined word, and Shepherd stands ready to give the world his logic, if only it will listen. Behind his affable charm is the righteous arrogance of a king, for whom reality is what he says it should be. After reporters discover Sydney's sleep-over at the White House, the press secretary (Anna Deavere Smith) scrambles for control over the image: "The important thing," she says to the president, "is not to make it look like we're panicking." Shepherd, contemptuous of television's chop-logic, replies, "See, and I think the important thing is actually not to *be* panicking." Image itself, which slips so easily from his verbal control, is Shepherd's constant political foe, and so his resistance to it must always be matched by his articulacy—if only he can speak it (and himself) into being.[3]

In Aaron Sorkin's political romance, a self-creating voice is the president's anchor. A king must arrogate the truth, take control of it. Shepherd intends words, not image, to define his civic character. The presidency is completely about that character, he says, after the symbolically potent gesture of interrupting his press secretary at the podium. In this climactic radio and television speech, Shepherd finally distinguishes his character from its "look." His presidency shall not be a function of a rival's words in a visual medium that abjures reason; it shall be his words, his logic, his logos. Shepherd's usurpation of the press briefing becomes a kind of verbal usurpation of image. The speech he gives sets things straight—about Rumson, about Sydney, about himself. His real character hinges on his imposing a "hard" language of correspondence and rational exposition. Democracy is "work," he explains. Until now, of course, that hard expository language has failed to seize the ground of "truth," thus allowing Senator Rumson to usurp the president by usurping the medium by which modern America converses, speaking in fragments and innuendo, and appealing to a people too lazy to reason. Earlier, when Shepherd's chief of staff (Martin Sheen) reminds the president that "politics is perception," Shepherd bristles with quiet disdain. No, he wants politics to be the voice of reason, not the rocky monument or the sexy photograph or the mendacious impulse disguised in a sound bite. He wants a noble, rational, controllable language—and he wants it to be his.

All of Aaron Sorkin's good citizens respond dutifully to this archetypal voice of reason. They are like the idealized national audience to whom Lincoln appealed repeatedly in his addresses, and it is that kind of bold transcendent voice to which Sorkin's literary sensibilities harken. For Lincoln, Garry Wills argues, the "great ideals" that were made at Gettysburg "to grapple naked in an airy battle of the mind" persist in American politics because Americans themselves are "intellectually autochthonous, having no pedigree except that of an idea" (Wills 86). Lineage is a matter not of blood but of logos—a rational language floating in air, sustained, as Whitman believed, only by those who continue to speak it into presence. Lincoln obligated all American heroes not to indelible actions but to indelible words, "the nation's permanent ideal" (Wills 88). And he did this himself at Gettysburg, says Wills, through a "stunning verbal coup" of the Constitution, by altering "the document from within" in order to turn what the president saw as its spirit—equality—into its new letter (Wills 37–40). Lincoln was a king, then, in that deepest linguistic sense: he *made* language, the language that reasons this nation into being. He gave America a new logos.

THE RIGHT AND LEARNED WORD

Sorkin's presidents long for such authenticity and authorship,[4] and so do their disciples. In *The West Wing*, when Ainsley Hayes (Emily Procter, "In This White House"), the new Republican counsel to the White House, hears a colleague call the president's staff "worthless," Hayes declares that "their intent is good; they are righteous, and they are patriots." Despite her political antagonism toward the administration, she is acknowledging the force and authenticity of the conversations she has recently witnessed at the White House. Members of the staff *mean* what they say, and she can hear the ring of that truth, even while she questions their policies. She, too, wants to be recreated by the authentic word, the imprinting voice, which makes of air a righteous will. Indeed, in *The American President*, the decisive moments of Andrew Shepherd's relationship with Sydney—their introduction, courtship, and reconciliation—occur mainly in allegiance to this agonistic voice, like an abstract testament to the power of words over image. Early in the film, when Sydney is deriding the president for his environmental policy, Shepherd sneaks into the room and says from behind her, "Let's take him out back and beat the shit out of him." For Sorkin, getting through clearly to the ears rather than to the television-saturated eyes takes time and energy, the fulfillment of verbal power coming finally as the mantle of heroism. Later in the film, Shepherd struggles on the telephone to convince Sydney that the voice she hears asking her on a date is authentic.

And, in the film's denouement, this same disembodied voice has, over Sydney's car radio, called her back to him. Their romance lives or dies in the faithfulness of that voice. After the president promises to bring her client's legislation to Congress, Sydney asks him, "Do I have your word on that?" "Absolutely," he assures her. It is a lie, and this verbal infidelity begins the film's larger drama of loss and reconciliation. As it was for Whitman, love of country is for Shepherd a romance of words held in trust with the wakeful citizen. Citizenship itself is just that: faithful rhetoric, a conversation held true. By finally holding true to his word to Sydney, Shepherd answers to the higher civic purpose they both serve as "shepherds" of a nation's discourse.

To be a man of one's word, instead of one's image, is to value the order and purpose that public words can bring to one's society, as well as to oneself. Aaron Sorkin wants a president who can embody the rational discourse governing our society, faithful not to the random seductions of image but to the oaths that the Constitution represents. If a president's words fail, either through stupidity or mendacity, the chain of reason he keeps alive—the constitutional voice of a nation's being—is broken, and we succumb to appearances, sinking into tribal allegiances and selfish gratification, the prejudicial world of image and class. For Sorkin, rational discourse, by sustaining civic order and taking as its scripture the Constitution and the Declaration of Independence, rescues us from a vulgar society and daily reconstitutes in the citizen the characteristically American metaphysics of destiny: namely, that utterance shall be being, that we shall become what we say. A statue of Lincoln or a painting of Kennedy does not make us Americans, nor does birthright or race. Words make us Americans—the right words. Andrew Shepherd believes this metaphysic so deeply that he urges his daughter to read the Constitution just for pleasure. It is the story of how a country's identity could spring from nothing more than assertion, the will to speak. Being an American is a daily rhetoric, he believes, the perpetual flight of reason from reflex. This ethic is exactly what attracted Sorkin to the dramas of the White House in the first place, a venue that offers, he has explained, a world "populated by people who, by and large, have terrific communication skills" and must grapple with "terribly complicated" issues:

> You're talking about very learned people capable of arguing both sides of an issue, and it's that process that I enjoy dramatizing. . . . They're fairly heroic. That's unusual in American popular culture, by and large. Our leaders . . . are portrayed either as dolts or as Machiavellian somehow. The characters in this show are neither. They are flawed, to be sure. . . . But they . . . have set aside

probably more lucrative lives for public service. They are dedicated not just to this president, but to doing good, rather than doing well. The show is kind of a valentine to public service. It celebrates our institutions. It celebrates education often. These characters are very well educated, and while sometimes playfully snobby about it, there is, in all of them, a love of learning and appreciation of education. (Sorkin *Online NewsHour*)

Naturally, then, whenever people abuse words, Sorkin's ethic condemns them. Sam Seaborn (Rob Lowe), President Josiah "Jed" Bartlet's speechwriter in *The West Wing*, habitually destroys his opponents on the weekly talk shows, often talking faster than most people can think. If that verbal wizardry should turn inaccurate, however, the Sorkin ethic will zealously punish him. After Sam flubs his geography—and thus gets "his ass kicked by a girl" on TV—even the other White House staffers run to see it. Accuracy has a totemic value in *The West Wing*, displacing the totems of merely "looking good" on television. The girl correcting Sam on television is Ainsley Hayes, the legal counselor President Bartlet soon wants to hire because, as he says, "she's not just carping"; she, too, wants to get things right, even down to placing the town of Kirkwood accurately in California, not Oregon. The president recognizes in her the same kind of ideal voice she will hear in him and his staffers. What they all share, then, in is the hunt for a language of correspondence. If America constitutes itself as a language—not just a land—of ideals, then getting words right matters at every level. As Leo McGarry (John Spencer), Bartlet's chief of staff, says, the president is "not going to stomach hypocrisy." Words must be true, never cheapened or wasted or just plain wrong.

This ethic applies even to comedic scenes. When Bartlet orders his HUD secretary to apologize for calling a congressman a racist, his greater complaint is that the secretary could not find an accusation any wittier than "if the shoe fits." In the episode "Galileo," the president corrects a NASA publicist's modification of the absolute adjective "unique." Something cannot be "very" one-of-a-kind, Bartlet quips. When Leo calls the president a "geek," the president's personal secretary reprimands him: "Not in this office," says the maternal Mrs. Landingham (Kathryn Joosten). If, as Sorkin maintains, words define and sustain being, then "geek" is bad not merely because it is disrespectful but because, in that office, the term is wrong, inaccurate. The president cannot *be* a geek in the Oval Office, so the words defining him there must, in the metaphysics of the American voice, match that civic identity; language must correspond. At one point, Leo himself adopts a ridiculous zeal for getting words right: he phones in the correct spelling of a single word in a *New York Times* crossword puzzle.

Indeed, a single word can even break a person. In the 2001–2002 opener ("Manchester, Part I"), Bartlet's press secretary, C.J. Cregg (Allison Janney), says that the president is "relieved" to be focusing on something that matters— a military strike on Haiti rather than the story about his concealment of multiple sclerosis. One second later, she is mortified: "relieved" to be attacking another country? As his daily public voice, and in an age of instant information, C.J. knows that political identity—hers as well as the president's—flows from her judicious dissemination of words. If she loses control over language— and she just has—Bartlet will have to step in, just as Shepherd does in *The American President*, to reword himself, even if it means turning himself into what President Bartlet finally admits to being all along: "OK, I'm an oratorical snob" ("War Crimes"). Like it or not, rightness in language is a kingly duty, and Bartlet will achieve it, no matter the cost to his image.

THE CONSTITUTING VOICE

Everything from moral hypocrisy to minor solecisms is thus fair game for Sorkin's rational idealism because the oaths of office are, after all, oaths—words spoken in national trust, rooted in what Jefferson called the "holy purpose" of the document by which he himself declared America into being (Maier 186). Like Jefferson, Sorkin sees leadership in terms of both mastery of—and fidelity to— words. (This double purpose explains the pontifications littering much of Sorkin's writing, which always seems to have room for a good speech or two.) In fact, the Declaration of Independence can be seen as a prototype for the work of each American king, who must spin (in multiple senses of the word) his nation's vocabulary to what is *right*. Noble leadership springs from the power to enforce this correspondence. But such enforcement founders on the very slipperiness of the language being pressed into correspondence. Plato wished this nettlesome fact away by imagining a perfect language of being, where political character could be made holy and absolute. Anything less was tantamount to treason (an attitude that explains why fanciful poets do not make the cut). Plato dutifully reproves his effete colleague, Ion, for example, for mixing up analogical reasoning (comparison based on similar effects) with homological reasoning (comparison based on similar structure), and he reproaches the relativist Cratylus for siding with the philosopher Heraclitus, for whom reality is more like a stream than a rock. Plato denounces each of them because the very medium through which he must conduct his interrogations of the truth is subject to the same kind of mistake that C.J. Cregg bumbled into in the press-room. Language gets away from us, and the chaos incipient in a language that escapes authoritative control threatens the form and faith of a nation's being. A language on the slide is a mind on the slide, which is a people on the slide. Plato wanted to fix discourse in a language of perfect correspondence, even trying to find transcendent *Ur*meanings for consonants like "l" and "t" (Adams 40–41). He sought authentic, authoritative voices. And, for all his liberalism, Sorkin does, too; he wants verbal absolutes. If President Bartlet can be long-winded, especially in defense of leftist causes, it is because Sorkin actually is seeking that most conservative of ideals, an absolute language of civic being, where right and wrong can be judged accurately. Vigilance in words is crucial to the execution of political—as opposed to military—leadership. But how can one speak the "hard" truth in a language that keeps dissipating? Words evolve; they never sit still.

Hence the importance of a leader whose verbal acuity is matched by his certitude, both of which efface the anxiety that language, like the character it creates, is always at risk of shifting out of control. In the episode "Let Bartlet Be Bartlet" (*The West Wing*), after having "dangled his feet" in some volatile is-sues—gays in the military, for one—the president tells Leo McGarry, "I want to speak." Being "Bartlet"—being president—means getting the man to speak up, not to dangle. "I dream of great ideas and energy and diction and honesty," he proclaims; "I can sell that." Sorkin and Plato hope their leaders can sell it, too. All it takes is the proper application of force. President Shepherd, in *The American President*, ridicules the false logic from Senator Rumson by exclaiming "he can't sell it!" Shepherd has a better logic, and he wants to sell that. He has ideas, energy, diction, honesty—or wants them, as does the relativist-stricken Prince Hamlet who would be King: both figures are striving to be absolute, certain, poised in a seamless discourse of intentionality that might perfectly imprint itself on a nation, redeeming it from fickle, ignoble lusts, be they those of a Claudius or a Senator Rumson.

Ironically, Rumson's self-infatuating arrogance (Rumson is a kind of Polonius, believing that one must to thine "own self" alone be true, not to anyone else) is a kind of shadow-self to Shepherd (and, implicitly, to Bartlet); he is a doppelgänger who wields cynically what the president wields nobly: the will to power, a vaunting discourse hardened in proportion to the vicissitudes of language. When the impassioned Sam Seaborn says, "Oratory should raise your heartrate. Oratory should blow the doors off the place," he really does mean the classical tool by which a leader shapes his people through an act of verbal will, with ideas full of "energy and diction and honesty."[5] The moral political question, however, is *whose words?* Such energy and diction must always belong to someone; they do not emerge from nothing. Energetic discourse comes from the man who speaks and in speaking—in choosing the words that constitute a nation's purpose—that man chooses us, makes us. Leo McGarry says that Jed Bartlet lives for the podium, like a pitcher scratching at the dirt, waiting to throw the perfect ball ("Bartlet for America"). The truth is a bit more ominous: a leader *is* that podium. In the American ontology, the podium launches a leader into civic being. Without it, he returns to nothing.

Of course, the risk in every pitch—the tenuous verbal being of a nation as it finds or loses its expression in the voice of its leader—explains the impulse in Sorkin's work to seize words quickly and completely, to pitch fast and hard. Strong words make strong leaders—who make strong states. The rhetorician Isocrates, with his chief rival, Plato, believed precisely this about verbal power, thus helping to turn the entire culture of ancient Greece, observes Daniel Boorstin, into "a culture of language." The cause was noble: "True words, words in conformity with law and justice, are images of a good and trustworthy soul." Such a "faith in the immortal word," says Boorstin, formed the basis of Western

America's greatest podium.

culture, our culture (Boorstin, *Creators* 226). But that faith in the "immortal word" is what Alexis de Tocqueville found so disturbing about American democracy, because words easily get confuted by the "majority," and the "mighty pressure" of that collective "mind" upon the individual intelligence can overwhelm the soul, rendering it weak and insignificant (Boorstin, *Creators* 435).[6] Democracies, because they float on the words of consent, are always at risk of sinking into a muddle. Enter the strong, noble leader—except for what Tocqueville saw even at the executive level in America: the president, because he rules, in effect, by majority, is equally weak and insignificant (Boorstin, *Creators* 127). From this double weakness against the threat of the demos, American political writers from Jefferson to Lincoln, from Democrat to Republican, reach almost instinctively, then, toward a dreamlike faith in the power of articulacy—toward the *immortal* word—in order to transcend what so precariously sustains its democracy: the *changeable* word. This paradox keeps America always on the move, never at rest with its language or the identity it shapes but always seeking the real and final utterance.

SAVING US FROM OURSELVES

The premiere for the 2000–2001 season of *The West Wing* elevated Sorkin's quest for an immortal civic language to messianic proportions. In a flashback to the New Hampshire primaries, then-Governor Bartlet is first struggling to find his proselytizing voice—and his audience. Josh Lyman (Bradley Whitford), later the deputy chief of staff, wonders at this early stage if the governor is "the real thing." What he means by that phrase becomes clearer when Leo, as campaign manager, tells Bartlet, "You're going to open your mouth and lift houses off the ground." Leo's rhetoric fits with the theophanic structure of the episode. One by one, each future staffer answers the righteous call of the Good Shepherd, an Irish-Catholic (Sheen) emerging as philosopher-king to a benighted people. His disciples are mired at the moment not simply in ignominious jobs but in morally fatiguing lives. Like the nation itself, they need salvation. C.J. Cregg, for example, labors among the voices of Hollywood suck-ups and narcissists. Like Sam Seaborn, who has questioned the merits of a lucrative but dubious shipping contract for one of his company's clients, C.J. has just confronted a hack film director with the awful truth of his stupidity. Sam quits and C.J. gets fired. Why did they do it? Josiah Bartlet, the real thing, has just asked them to serve, and the call from a righteous leader has awakened their quest for an absolute truth, redeeming them from their baser selves and from a world of dissimulation and moral compromise—a world, in short, of false and faltering words. They want to speak the truth, and Bartlet, like Plato's potentate of reason, is Sorkin's American Messiah, a godlike voice invoking the concordant anthem of a faithful and energetic nation. His staffers religiously join that chorus because, when Bartlet speaks, they want to hear one sure voice, one pure truth: His.

Aaron Sorkin is writing not so much about what makes a good man (some historians rate Lincoln, for example, fairly low on personal honesty, and Kennedy's sexual peccadillos are now as familiar as his high-minded calls to civic duty). He is writing about what makes an archetypal leader, especially an American one. Sorkin is adding to the pantheon of American archetypes by adding to the voices that perpetuate this nation's integrity—literally, what keeps it whole: words. Words are national currency and creation. Plato, like Shakespeare, knew that language usually is the first battleground with one's own people. Besieged by war with the Spartans (431–404 B.C.), the Athenians had to shore up faith in their leaders, their values, and their identity by shoring up the medium by which doubt might be subversively produced and distributed—language. Plato's mentor, Socrates, is unequivocal on this point. "Nor can we reasonably say," he tells Cratylus, "that there is knowledge at all, if everything is in a state of transition and there is nothing abiding" (47). Socrates wishes he could dispose of language altogether and know things directly, "from the things themselves," but, acknowledging that language does intervene, he hopes at least to keep his disciples from falling into the "whirlpool" of "flux," and, as he protests in *The Republic*, to keep them from taking the state's gods with them (22). The point is to keep language both fixed and proprietary, an authoritative logos. That goal is why Socrates, two millennia before Machiavelli (1469–1527) penned *The Prince*, can allow his leaders to lie if doing so serves the public good (24). For him, strong leadership is actually more important than the truth.

Perhaps Sorkin is more the moral purist, then, on this point (despite his *not* facing defeat by any Spartans), but his aim is similar. The leader must take control of the nation's language. Plato understood this task, as did Shakespeare and Whitman, or Jefferson and Lincoln: a man leads by possessing the language by which civic identity is created in the first place. In today's world, though, such possession succeeds only if a leader's words can rewrite his visual being, which television parcels out to the masses in crude sensory fragments. When Sorkin invites viewers to reason—and he does so with a prolixity unmatched in television—he is also inviting them to bracket the audio-visual medium that normally excludes the articulate, discursive citizen. Like a Plato or a Lincoln or a Whitman, Sorkin wants to keep the dialogue of America going, not only to restore a clear, systematic language to its place in the arguments we have about liberty and justice but also to lead viewers away from the half-logic of tele-visual being. He wants Lincoln's "chorus of the Union," a people of "virtue and vigilance" who "think calmly and *well*" (Lincoln 60–61). As much as possible, Sorkin is hoping to wrestle our television culture back into the great addresses in which a leader is once more, and always, a man of his word, and is thus a man of *our* word—which is to say, a man who, for better or worse, possesses words even before they become ours.

NOTES

1. Wills, referring to Lincoln's Gettysburg Address, says, "Words had to complete the work of the guns" (Wills 37).

2. See a *NewsHour* interview with Sorkin on the genesis of his immensely successful spin-off from *The American President*, TV's *The West Wing*: "There's a great tradition in storytelling that's thousands of years old, telling stories about kings and their palaces, and that's really what I wanted to do."

3. Sorkin is continuing the Western connection between an individual's value and his verbal skills, which comes, apparently, from the sense England had of itself as the leader of Protestantism. According to Lewis Perry, "One token of civility was literacy . . . England had become a nation where those who mattered could read, or at least recite, the Bible" (Perry 16–17).

4. Pauline Maier notes that, in his "short list" of achievements, Thomas Jefferson declared himself "Author, not draftsman, of the Declaration of Independence. That contribution [his authorship] . . . had assumed pre-eminence in his writings and reflections, as the Declaration itself became a redemptive force," a founding "act of union of these States," a "holy purpose" (Maier 186).

5. Actually, Sorkin is appealing both to and against the classical tradition of oratory. On the one hand, the legacy of Cicero indicates that oratory was "first of all, the indispensable accomplishment of an ancient politician." On the other hand, Cicero himself "boasted of being able to 'throw dust in the eyes of the jury,'" a boast indicating that oratory has always skirted the line of veracity precisely because, whether speaking of ancient Rome or of modern America, "arguments derived from law and fact counted for less than appeals to passion and prejudice" (see Griffin 78).

6. Alexis de Tocqueville's complaint about democracy as an enervating *ideology* finds its counterpart in Boorstin's complaint about democracy as an enervating *psychology* when effected through television, whose blurring manipulations of our senses, like the dependencies between branches of government, weaken a people's constitutional powers: "The new miasma . . . reached out to befog the 'real' world. Americans began to be so accustomed to the fog . . . that reality itself became slightly irritating. . . . As broadcasting techniques improved, they tended to make the viewer's experience more

indirect, more controlled by unseen producers and technicians. . . . the TV watcher in the living room lacked the power to decide" (Boorstin, *Americans* 396).

WORKS CITED

Adams, Hazard, ed. *Critical Theory Since Plato.* Rev. ed. Fort Worth: Harcourt Brace Jovanovich, 1992.

Boorstin, Daniel J. *The Americans: The Democratic Experience.* New York: Vintage, 1974.

———. *The Creators: A History of Heroes of the Imagination.* New York: Random House, 1992.

Fallows, James. "Councils of War." *Atlantic Monthly,* December 2001, 42–45.

Griffin, Miriam. "Cicero and Rome." In *The Roman World,* edited by John Boardman, Jasper Griffen, and Oswyn Murray. Vol. 2 of *The Oxford History of the Classical World.* New York: Oxford University Press, 1986.

Lincoln, Abraham. "First Inaugural Address," 4 March 1861.

———. *Abraham Lincoln: His Speeches and Writings.* Edited by Roy P. Basler. Cleveland: World Publishing Company, 1946. Reprint, in *Great Speeches.* New York: Dover, 1991.

Maier, Pauline. *American Scripture: Making the Declaration of Independence.* New York: Knopf, 1997.

Perry, Lewis. *Intellectual Life in America: A History.* New York: Franklin Watts, 1984.

Shakespeare, William. *The Riverside Shakespeare.* Edited by G. Blakemore Evans. Boston: Houghton Mifflin, 1974.

Sorkin, Aaron. Interview with Terence Smith. *Online NewsHour.* PBS. 27 September 2000 <http://www.pbs.org/newshour/media/west_wing/sorkin.html>.

———. *The American President.* Dir. Rob Reiner. Warner Bros., 1995.

Tocqueville, Alexis de. *Democracy in America.* 13th ed. 1850. Reprint, edited by J.P. Mayer. Translated by George Lawrence. New York: Perennial Library, 1988.

West Wing. Created by Aaron Sorkin. NBC. WGBA, Green Bay, Wisconsin. 1999–2001.

Whitman, Walt. *Leaves of Grass.* Introduction by John Hollander. 1892. Reprint, New York: Vintage Books/Library of America, 1992.

Wills, Garry. *Lincoln at Gettysburg: The Words That Remade America.* New York: Simon and Schuster, 1992.

Part Three

Closing in on the Present

Peter C. Rollins

HOLLYWOOD'S PRESIDENTS 1944–1996

The Primacy of Character

Library of Congress.

Woodrow Wilson: the president as idealist (1913–1921).

Character is something very hard to define, but everybody knows what we mean when we use the word. Character might be described as the sum total of a person's inherited characteristics, plus what he does with them. We begin with thoughts, thoughts translate themselves into acts, and acts repeated evolve into habits. Habits form character, character determines destiny, and destiny is tied up irrevocably with destination.

—John S. Higgins, *Lay Sermons*

INTRODUCTION: THE ISSUE OF CHARACTER

Is presidential "character" a proper topic for discussion and debate? During the presidential campaign of 1992, the question of character was pushed off the national agenda in favor of the issue of economics. Such would not be the case in the subsequent presidential contest in 1996, when Bob Dole was hard-pressed to attract attention away from an incumbent who, with masterful political maneuvering, had moved back to "New Democrat" positions after four years of "Old Democrat" actions. Most Americans in the fall of 1996 found themselves in a more prosperous situation as the Dow hit a record high. With his tax-cut proposal not cutting through to the public as he had hoped, Bob Dole attempted to raise the subject of character. Initially, the American public seemed indifferent to the scandals associated with Paula Jones, Gennifer Flowers, Vince Foster, Whitewater, Dick Morris, billing records, and Travelgate. Clinton spin doctors dismissed the Dole arguments about character as diversions from legitimate issues of a presidential campaign—issues such as Medicare, gun control, and the national debt.

The motion pictures about American presidents made since World War II provide fascinating commentary on the place of the character issue in popular culture. Films about America's presidents do not merely touch on the topic; from Darryl Zanuck's *Wilson* (1944) to the apocalyptic *Independence Day* (1996), Hollywood's films about the presidency seem to be obsessed with the issue. Why character? Because Americans do not merely change administrations every four years—or have the opportunity to do so; citizens of the United States have the option to change sovereigns with every presidential election. Unlike the British, Americans do not have a monarchy to lend symbolic continuity to the national identity. The transitions, as a result, impose more of a burden on the officeholders. Voters do not merely expect the president to oversee the actions of the executive departments, but—since the time of George Washington and Parson Weems's mythical cherry tree—they expect a president to be a symbol of national character.

On the one hand, the presidency is a national mirror, and Hollywood, recognizing that symbolic dimension of the office, has opted to focus on the character issue and to subordinate any domestic and foreign-policy matters. The choice, given the mass audiences addressed, may be linked to the melodramatic dictates of the medium. On the other hand, there is great wisdom in seeing presidents as symbolic figures—curiously caught in time and tradition,

President Wilson was his own
speech writer.

and navigating themselves and their nation by the strength and resources of
character. Even the etymology of the word points to the role as guardian of the
nation's spirit. "President" comes from "preside" which means "to guard or
preside over." And the films—like the oath of office—stress the president's
duty to "protect and defend" the Constitution of the United States. To do so
requires personal strength, values—and character.

DARRYL ZANUCK'S WILSON (1944): THE TRIUMPH OF CHARACTER OVER HISTORY

The opening crawl for *Wilson* speaks volumes for all of the films about the
presidency. As the national anthem plays, the opening words on screen speculate: "Sometimes the life of a man mirrors the life of a nation. The destiny of
our country was crystallized in the life and times of Washington and Lincoln,
and, perhaps, too, in the life of another President. . . . This is the story of
America and the story of a man." In other words, the study of the character of
a president will reveal the strengths and weaknesses of the American nation as
it emerged from the isolationism of the nineteenth century to its responsibilities as a world power in the twentieth century.

As Woodrow Wilson, actor Alexander Knox portrays an academic who was devoted to advancing "the principles of democratic equality." To the viewer interested in politics and legislation, the film spends an (apparently) inordinate amount of time investigating Wilson's family life—especially his relations with his much-beloved daughters and his wife. The clear message is that these intimate relations cultivate a character that is caring and virtuous. Wilson reads with his family, sings with his family, and dances with his family. These activities only make him stronger as a defender of values—although, behind his back, the scoffing professional politicians scorn him as an "idealist."

Every presidential film relates the central character to previous presidents. Wilson is in good company in associating himself with Lincoln: "My dream is to turn America more and more to the principles of freedom so that America puts human rights above all rights and the American flag is the flag of humanity." When Wilson finally makes the White House his home, one of the first rooms he visits is the place where Lincoln signed the Emancipation Proclamation; Lincoln's bed is a historical artifact important to the entire family. The film tries to balance out a study of legislative accomplishment with a view of the personal life. On the legislative side, Wilson creates the Federal Reserve System, passes the Underwood Tariff, the Clayton Antitrust Act, the Adamson Act, and creates the Federal Trade Commission. On the other hand, his tenderness and family values show through in his devotion to an ailing wife. As she lies on her deathbed, he reflects that "I don't think that two people were ever so happy." Despite his public accomplishments, Wilson is no egotist.

When his cherished League of Nations fails to be ratified by the Senate, Wilson wastes away his health in his effort to make his case before the American people. He is prescient in his prediction that the choice is either a League of Nations to preserve the peace or "Life with a gun in our hand." The film ends with Wilson leaving office in ill health but as a leader of vision who knows that his goals will prevail. There is nothing here related to expediency or political gain. Indeed, even Senator Lodge, Wilson's chief antagonist over the league, is portrayed as a man of principle. We are simply sure that the side of right is Wilson's and that America will eventually learn to come round to his point of view, a perspective validated by subsequent history and the integrity (not to mention the self-sacrifice) of a great president. Producer Darryl Zanuck hoped that the film would foster popular support for the United Nations, the international organization emerging out of World War II as an instrument of conflict resolution, and a second (and, it is to be hoped, successful) attempt at a "League of Nations."

MAD takes on a more traditional, psychological meaning when General Jack D. Ripper (Sterling Hayden) sends the "go code" to his aviators as they reach their "fail-safe" point in *Dr. Strangelove* (1964).

DR. STRANGELOVE *(1964) AND* NIXON *(1995):* THE COUNTERCULTURE'S NIGHTMARE ABOUT LEARNING TO LOVE THE BOMB

Stanley Kubrick's noir comedy about nuclear war was a breakthrough film evidencing a new view of not only the presidency but of the entire American political system. *Dr. Strangelove* appeared at the height of the Cold War when nuclear apocalypse was accepted as a part of "normal" existence and the doctrine of MAD ("Mutually Assured Destruction") was a key element of American and Soviet strategic planning. The dangers of nuclear war and the uncontrolled growth of technology were two themes pervasive to Kubrick's films; as a critical observer of twentieth-century society, he believed that our machines and our social institutions have eluded our grasp. We are constantly in danger of being destroyed by them or of being misled by our imperfect human nature—we can create wonders of science and technology, but we cannot necessarily control them. *Dr. Strangelove* is a film that addresses these problems in relation to presidential leadership. General Jack D. Ripper, a SAC (Strategic Air Command) squadron commander obsessed with the crackpot issue of fluoridation, orders his B-52s to attack the Soviet Union. The plot of the film involves futile attempts by national leaders to avert the inevitable thermonuclear tragedy. President Merkin Muffley (played by Peter Sellers) resembles Adlai Stevenson. Muffley is ignorant of the various war plans that have been developed by his strategists, and his leadership style, which is sane and rational by comparison, lacks the force and determination to avert the inevitable detonation of the Soviet "Doomsday Machine." The president's impotence is epitomized when he stops two quarreling advisers: "Gentlemen, you can't fight here. This is the War Room!" As film scholar Charles Maland has observed about Muffley: "If the person who has the most rational strategy (and who also happens to be the commander in chief) is unable to control nuclear weapons and his military advisors, citizens really have something to worry about"(quoted in Rollins 202).

Actor Peter Sellers plays three major characters in *Dr. Strangelove,* and the "splitting" may be a commentary on character as perceived in a post–Freudian era. As British Commander Mandrake, on loan to the Pentagon, Sellers is a reasonable and balanced professional who knows the place of violence in international affairs but is not consumed by it. As President Muffley, Sellers reveals that the national leaders—apprenticed on election campaigns and domestic politics—do not have the training, attention, or the martial grit to control the "military-industrial complex." Finally, in his role as Dr. Strangelove, Sellers shows the hideous potential of intellect gone awry—perhaps even motivated by some form of death wish. The world has become too complex for character to determine destiny. We are in a world in which the system singles out people for the wrong jobs, and the result will be disaster, for the aggressive dominate when the virtuous remain out of the fray. Alas, our technocratic and complex society no longer responds to the charisma of character.

NIXON *(1995): PERSON OR PERSONA?*

So much has been written about Oliver Stone's *Nixon* that it would seem unnecessary to reopen the argument; however, a viewing within the context of other films about the presidency brings some unexpected themes forward—including the theme of character. From the opening scene of General Alexander Haig delivering the compromising Oval Office tapes to a beleaguered president until the final scene in which Haig threatens to release a copy of a much-feared tape, *Nixon*—as its title implies—is about the individual personality and character of an American icon. Those who have attacked the film ignore director Stone's claim that his study was based on considerable research (the script is studded with endnotes) or that the filmmaker felt considerable admiration for Nixon as a tragic leader.

According to Oliver Stone, Richard Nixon was a man divided within himself, a complex personality with both base and noble qualities. Part of his move up the ladder of success was attributable to the death of his two brothers from tuberculosis. One result was that his mother devoted her energy and resources to putting Richard through college and law school—another unforeseen result was "survivor guilt" which plagued the mature Nixon. On the other hand,

Richard Nixon, the thirty-seventh president of the United States, 1969–1974.

Richard Nixon was capable of great vision. The film shows how genuinely concerned Nixon was about the trauma of the Kennedy assassination on the country. During the Vietnam era, Nixon's bold actions (with Henry Kissinger) opened the door to China and—by what is called "trilateral diplomacy"—cracked the once monolithic Communist bloc into factions vying for American detente. Referring to his "higher self," Anthony Hopkins (as Richard Nixon) says that "Nixon was born to do this." In fleeting moments throughout the film, Oliver Stone seems to stand back in awe.

Although one would expect Richard Nixon to be depicted as the worst possible villain in an Oliver Stone movie, this is not the case. Stone's conspiratorial world contains greater threats to the national honor. In a scene cut from the theatrical release (but appended to the rental/purchase tape), Sam Waterson plays Richard Helms, director of the CIA. During a presidential visit to the agency, Stone unveils a true Cold War zealot, a man—driven by a mindless anticommunism—who ignores the subtle vectors of international power that Kissinger and Nixon orchestrated so effectively. Waterson's Helms is a repeat of Peter Sellers's Dr. Strangelove: in a long monologue, the CIA chief quotes tiresomely from "The Second Coming," a W.B. Yeats poem about the loss of innocence. The poem also suggests the ideas of mortality and the transitory nature of human existence. In his response, Nixon reflects in a personal way about death, drawing connections between his family's experience and other traumatic moments in recent history. In chilling contrast, Helms is morbidly fascinated with death—indeed, at one moment, his eyes go black in a special effect that has metaphysical implications. Like Dr. Strangelove in the final satiric scenes of Stanley Kubrick's 1964 film, Waterson is motivated by a fanatical and self-destructive obsession. In comparison, Richard Nixon is a real person—with flaws and passions, to be sure, but a genuine human being.

Nixon is also contrasted with his Texas backers. In a scene reminiscent of *Wilson*, Nixon's pro-Cuban and antiliberal backers attempt to dictate policy to the president. Strong in his need to play out the historical role of his higher persona, Nixon is quite capable of fending off the suggestions of the money boys. (Wilson successfully shrugged off the machine politicians from the strength of his character—a much firmer platform than a mere sense of role.) Here Oliver Stone shows that Richard Nixon was not the worst man in the political system—just a complex man with many elements of character so flawed that he was doomed to a tragic end on an Aeschylean scale.

What makes such an interesting link between Kubrick and Stone is the criticism at the heart of the film. During the student demonstrations of 1970,

Nixon impulsively visits the Lincoln Memorial. There a young protester responds to the president's statement that he does not want the war to go on. In a moment of New-Left epiphany, she observes, "The system won't let you stop it." This insight is repeated aloud by Nixon as his handlers lead him away from the crowd: it is the system that is rotten, and no one can stop the bestial and destructive juggernaut. Short of a nuclear apocalypse, this is also the lesson of Kubrick's *Dr. Strangelove*; the divided and fragmented Nixon of Stone's movie is a composite of the Sellers personas of the earlier film. It is a bleak picture of the American scene in which the force of personality and the virtues of character no longer matter. In their lack of concern for character during the 1996 presidential campaign, were Americans proving that they had learned from the 1960s counterculture that personal responsibility is an irrelevant issue in a world of violence, political conspiracy, corporate greed, and power elites?

THE RETURN OF A "CAPRAESQUE" FORMULA IN THE AMERICAN PRESIDENT (1995)

The American President is a delightful and upbeat look at a functioning presidency that has thrown Ahab out of the White House. As President Shepherd (overseeing a flock?), Michael Douglas walks and talks like a man in charge: he is decisive and aggressive. While his staff is obsessed with polls and statistics, he has the inner strength to know when to act and when to let forces play themselves out. On the personal side, he is a single parent who has time to talk with his teenage daughter about the democratic basis of the Constitution and the enormous importance of the opening words, "We the People."

Much of the plot revolves around the love interest with Sydney Ellen Wade (Annette Bening). While his staff worries about the polls and his adversaries attack his personal life, Shepherd defends his privacy: "This is not the business of the American people." Knowing that personal behavior, character, and the presidency are inevitably interconnected, the chief of staff (Martin Sheen) counters: "The American people have a way of making the things they want their business."

A Republican opponent, Senator Rumson from Kansas (Richard Dreyfuss) attacks the president on the character issue. Rumson talks about the "girlfriend"; in cinematic rebuttal, the film cuts to Shepherd reading a story to his daughter in a solid, family setting. Yet the attacks on Shepherd and Ms. Wade take their toll, forcing the president into a corner. Here a short reference within the film to Frank Capra takes on special meaning. During Wade's first visit to the White

House, she mentions that such access seems "so Capraesque." A White House guard then explains the reference to Frank Capra and the film *Mr. Smith Goes to Washington*, but the true significance of the Capra reference is to what scholars call "the Capra formula." According to the famous "Capra formula," the main figure of a Capra movie is attacked in the newspapers and his character publicly impugned until he is almost destroyed. Then, at a crucial turn, he fights back—and ultimately triumphs because of the resiliency of both his character and American values.

It is important that, when Shepherd turns to defend himself and Ms. Wade, he announces to a press conference: "Being President of this country is completely about character." He comes back against his Kansas opponent with dynamic policy positions on free speech (flag burning is a First Amendment right); with an economic focus rather than silly rhetoric ("it's the economy"); with an initiative on global warming (support for an unpopular fossil-fuel bill); and with stiffer gun controls. After taking these stands, he announces his candidacy and walks in triumph back into the White House, conspicuously passing by a portrait of Woodrow Wilson.

FULL CIRCLE

The image of President Wilson brings this overview of the presidency in post–World War II movies full circle. Darryl Zanuck devoted two years of his life to the film biography of the great Democrat, hoping to teach America a vital lesson about its international responsibilities. On the basis of a strong, focused, centered character, Americans were to see the seeds of their new, global role. During the 1960s and after, counterculturalists Stanley Kubrick and Oliver Stone savaged the symbolic office in their despair that no president could control "the beast" of the military/industrial/political complex. In addition, their pop-Freudian notions about human nature disposed them to see the future as a bleak nuclear holocaust or a spiritual wastcland where personal values no longer counted.

The American President returned to a more upbeat view of the office and its possibilities. Clearly a defense of some of the policies and style of the Clinton White House, the film may be seen as a document of Hollywood's new optimism about its contacts with executive power after the Republican administrations of Ronald Reagan and George Bush. By emphasizing the issues of family values, the film was an astute foretaste of Clinton's campaign strategy. More cleverly, in its outspoken defense of personal privacy for the president, director Rob Reiner successfully applied a smooth layer of Teflon to Hollywood's favored candidate.

Whatever the reasons for the change, the new film was not alone in the restitution of the office. Other films in 1995 and 1996 restore some luster to the presidential image. Harry Truman is revived and upgraded in an HBO special. Admittedly an offspring of the David McCullough biography, the docudrama *Truman* stresses the humility, tenacity, and rootedness of "the man from Missouri." Although lacking the erudition of Wilson, the Truman of the film is a family man, a community man, and a person humbled and ennobled by his responsibilities. He was who he was, and we need to respect him for his rocklike integrity. The film concludes with Harry and Bess Truman returning home to Missouri without fanfare or wealth. Psychologically whole and with great dignity, a man of the great democracy returns to his rightful place. (Curiously, the revival among historians of interest in, and admiration for, President Dwight Eisenhower, a Republican, has seen no ripple effects in Hollywood or New York.)

Harry S. Truman, the thirty-third president of the United States, 1945–1953.

One of the biggest moneymaking films for the summer of 1996 was *Independence Day*, a film that involves a monstrous threat to the world and requires the leadership of a resilient president. In the film, President Whitemore (Bill Pullman) is a Gulf War veteran who tries every peaceful means to negotiate with alien creatures in space ships hovering above America's major cities. When spectacular attacks on the cities begin, the president leads an assault on the enemy. Joining with a Marine Corps pilot, Captain Steven Hiller (Will Smith), and a scruffy Vietnam veteran, Russell (Randy Quaid), the president helps to coordinate a high-tech attack on the invaders, which saves the world. In the concluding scene, the military and presidential leaders congratulate themselves on their victory and declare a new "Independence Day" for mankind.

Integrity and strength of character are what this film posits as the traits desirable in a president. When truly confronted by "the Beast," the president works with the ordinary citizens (yes, "We the People . . .") to prevail. With the character of an actual president constantly assailed in the media, Americans flocked to see an impersonation of a president as a paragon of strength—and virtue. In doing so, they affirmed their need for a role model in the White House. Whether upbeat or despairing, the films about the American presidency make character the major issue—not a side topic. Just after being forced to resign, Oliver Stone's Nixon looks at a pensive portrait of John F. Kennedy and reflects: "When they look at you, they see what they want to be. . . . When they look at me, they see who they are." Heroes or villains, our presidents are our representative men. In real life, they are the symbols of who we are—in the movies, they are icons by which Hollywood attempts to define us to ourselves.

WORKS CITED

Higgins, John S. "You Can Take It With You." In *The Word With Power: Lay Sermons, 1960–1961*, 205–208. New York: National Council, 1961.

Rollins, Peter, ed. *Hollywood as Historian: American Film in a Cultural Context.* 2nd ed. Lexington: University Press of Kentucky, 1998. This work contains essays on *Wilson* and *Dr. Strangelove*.

———. *Film & History: An Interdisciplinary Journal of Film and Television Studies.* This electronic source has its 32-year index on line at <http://h-net.msu.edu/~filmhis/>. Many articles of interest on American political institutions, including the presidency, can be printed out from this word-searchable CD-ROM.

Toplin, Robert B. *History By Hollywood: The Use and Abuse of the American Past.* Urbana: University of Illinois Press, 1996. This work contains good articles on *All the President's Men* and *JFK*.

Charlene Etkind

RICHARD NIXON AS *DICK* (1999) AND THE COMEDIC TREATMENT OF THE PRESIDENCY

Relaxed and smiling, Richard Nixon projects both power and confidence, two hallmarks of the U.S. presidency.

Library of Congress.

The United States has no king, no one ruler invested with the power of "The State," ruling over the kingdom with benevolent grace. One man, who has just a few short years to guide this complex and changing country, heads the United States. The American presidency is not invested with the same glory and majesty that a dynastic kingship carries; the president's reign is too short. But the American public has elevated the office to mythic status and holds its occupant in reverent awe. Most men elected to the presidency bring to the office their foibles and peccadillos, which ultimately reveal to the public a less-than-godlike image of the president. Of all the presidents in recent history, many would consider Richard Nixon (1969–1974) the one who has eroded the public image of the presidency more than any other.

It becomes the task of historians, scholars, and educators—nay obligation—to reexamine the past and the culture, which surrounds events, and personalities that make up the history of the United States, especially the presidency. Conveying the results of this research can become a burden when historical accuracy about the office and its occupant collides with cultural perceptions and expectations nurtured over time. Many of the original participants in an event are still alive, and there is someone adding to the story, often in an attempt to rebut the facts. This is collective memory at work. (Collective memory is like a bunch of gossipy neighbors at the back fence. They all know a little something about someone, and often each tidbit of information smacks of both truth and exaggeration.) Hollywood is our gaggle of gossips—for film has become both creator of and repository of collective memory—part history, part exaggeration, and part speculation. Add to this repository a "cult of personality," which lends mythical dimensions to the persona of a prominent person, and you have all the ingredients of popular myth.

Film extends imagination and makes sense of experience by recreating and recasting events. According to political scientists Dan Nimmo and James Combs, "We build our image of the world by making connections, constructions, and pictures of reality as if they were true. We impute an order and meaning to the world by importing into our images of the world a variety of symbolic structures to which we give reality" (Nimmo and Combs 5). In film, the symbolic structures are often more plausible than historical reality and are cast into a seamless stylization of the everyday, which becomes more believable than true history. Film re-creations offer a working model of historical events in which people can imagine the event taking place and imagine themselves as participants.

This essay examines the movie *Dick* (1999). The movie takes its place in a category of similar movies that depict a bumbling, antihero who is adored by innocents. It is a film reflexive of the culture and the era of the 1970s rather than of the eponymous protagonist, Richard Nixon. A second film, which preceded *Dick*, *The World of Henry Orient* (1964), provides an era-specific example of hero worship and its consequences. *Orient* has a similar plot, though with a less stellar personality than the president as the object of youthful infatuation. Another perspective on the era and the personality of Richard Nixon, Oliver Stone's *Nixon* (1995), will be also discussed.

THE MYTHIC IMAGE

Richard M. Nixon began his presidency in January 1969 and resigned from the office in August 1974. Nixon was president during one of the most turbulent decades of American history. According to an official biography posted to the Richard Nixon Library website, "the central event of the years Richard Nixon served as President—influencing virtually every aspect of U.S. foreign and domestic policy, causing substantial cultural and social upheaval, and leading ultimately to Watergate—was the Vietnam war" (Nixon Site).

Richard Nixon died in 1994, twenty years after his tumultuous resignation from office. The moment was ripe for reinventing the Nixon legacy. Hollywood directors and writers, in this case, have taken on the task and begun to interpret the personalities and the era as pseudohistorians. Popular films about the Nixon presidency, which have begun to proliferate, propose a retelling of fact wrapped in an entertainment package.

Film has a two-tiered quality for historians. The first layer reflects the film's place in the industry and what genre it explores. Film historian Stuart Kaminsky says of genre study, "[It] is based on the realization that narrative forms have both cultural and universal roots" (12). In the case of films about Richard Nixon and his presidency, the opposing categories of drama and comedy offer the audience a chance to examine the "what ifs" of a controversial administration.

The second layer is bounded by the cultural milieu in which the film takes place. The public now has a need to reexamine events of the 1960s and 1970s and to define them historically. According to Kaminsky, "a film or a series of films corresponds to a need of the viewing public" (14). It is a prerogative of the retelling to add up the things known and to couple them with cultural perceptions in order to question the validity of our judgments. Movies do this for us as they entertain.

After these two considerations are met, then the historical content can be examined. At best, the historical content often proves to be exaggerated, only roughly following the chain of events it is portraying; at worst, the content is grossly inaccurate. In comparing films, however, an astute viewer can often glean from the offerings an insight into cultural attitudes that academic historians ignore.

Oliver Stone's *Nixon* (1995) stresses the mythic dimensions of a tragic American leader. The office of the president and the person of the president as leader/hero/savior take their roots from American cultural myths. According to Nimmo and Combs: "Many Americans invest so much mythological currency in the presidency that they imagine the office and the occupant to possess heroic qualities far beyond those of imaginary mortals" (Nimmo and Combs 69). Stone's movie capitalizes on this thematic opportunity.

Stone used an archetypical characterization of Nixon to demonize him and to reassure a countercultural generation that rebellion against a corrupt government was not only justified but necessary. In Stone's movie, events and personal idiosyncrasies were melded in the personality of Nixon as the embodiment of a malignant force—which Stone often calls "The Beast"—that threatened the nation. As the mythic narration of Stone's film advances, Nixon becomes a scapegoat and, ultimately, a sacrificial lamb.

THE LESS-THAN-MYTHIC MAN

But take away the myth and what is left is the man. Richard Nixon was a consummate politician, and he did what he knew how to do best, to play politics and try to keep his job. He messed up, and arguably, to a greater degree than most of us. Historically, Nixon had won and lost in the political arena many times, and sometimes nefariously, but until 1973 he always managed to bounce back. According to journalist Tom Wicker, Nixon's greatest strength was his tenacity. Unfortunately for Nixon, tenacity and power created a heady cocktail, the aftereffects of which would prove to be lethal (Wicker 67). But even in his later years, after all the judgments by his critics were registered, Nixon managed to resurrect his image by adopting the role of author and elder statesman.

Richard Nixon was a product of his culture even as he helped to shape events. Many of the events that contribute to the cultural milieu preceded him and belong to a historic past. Investigative reporter Jonathan Schell describes some of the factors Nixon had to deal with, which preceded his election:

> By 1968, when Nixon assumed the presidency, the war [in Vietnam] had already installed itself at the center of the nation's political life. The political consensus on which President Lyndon Johnson had thought to build a program of reforms in American life had begun to fragment and dissolve. . . . A movement for racial justice that had gathered strength in the early part of the nineteen-sixties had grown angry and violent. . . . A program to eliminate poverty in the United States had been curtailed as federal funds were poured into the war effort (Schell 7–8)

Nixon had been active in post–World War II Cold War politics and had actually engaged many of the foreign adversaries feared in the United States. Many remembered Nixon for his alliance with Senator Joseph McCarthy during the late 1950s. Nuclear annihilation and the fear of communism taking over the government were very real fears in the minds of the American public of this era.

Those who came of age in the 1960s are a product of forces that not only spawned Nixon and his politics but also worked to create a cocoon of innocence. These ideals came unraveled as the reality of war and domestic unrest ate slowly away the public's sense of security. For this generation, Richard Nixon personified the deterioration of their civic faith.

LIFE IN A COCOON IN DICK

Two movies, *Dick* and *The World of Henry Orient*, represent life in a cocoon of innocence and reveal what happens when innocence confronts harsh reality. A most effective genre of movies used to portray this type of lost innocence is the comedy; it is within the framework of comedy that the seriousness of an event or era can be examined, demystified, and rendered harmless. Kaminsky says, "The comedic form allows us to examine topics that are too difficult to face unless we can laugh at them" (Kaminsky 182). We experience a sense of catharsis when we laugh, and sometimes a cathartic is what is needed to provide relief from the stress of an event.

The movie *Dick* is about the innocence of America in the late 1960s and early 1970s. The plot of the movie involves a mélange of adolescent crushes, patriotism, and hometown values. The plot revolves around an ideal of a typical American teen and her misunderstood altruism. It is a story for average

President Nixon (Dan Hedaya) takes the girls into his confidence in order to distract them from Watergate ploys in *Dick* (1999).

people who have ever wanted to be a part of something bigger than themselves. Nimmo and Combs point out that "popular vehicles [such as movies] act out for us desired states of affairs, confirming myths about what we want or, at least, about something good we believed once existed" (Nimmo and Combs 141). This movie capitalizes on events and emotions of the 1970s many *wished* could have happened. The movie *Dick* recreates the events of the later Nixon administration in a comic, bumbling fashion, giving the audience the impression that Nixon was not a calculating liar but rather a man who was a product of the cultural angst that permeated the country at the time.

Dick introduces two teenage characters—Betsy Jobs (Kirsten Dunst) and Arlene Lorenzo (Michelle Williams)—who are busy pursuing adolescent fantasies of star-struck love when they become witnesses to the misdeeds inside the White House fence. These girls live in Washington, D.C., in the early 1970s. Arlene lives in the Watergate apartment complex with her alcoholic, neglectful mother; Betsy and her family represent the middle-American family stereotype of conservative mother, father, and rebellious older brother. Betsy and Arlene are caricatures of an innocent American public stumbling into political intrigue as they become embroiled deeper and deeper in the labyrinth of the Watergate scandal and Vietnam-era politics.

In the beginning of the movie a cultural calm is evoked, a calm that is reminiscent of the atmosphere that the early Nixon administration was trying to create.

According to Schell:

> President Nixon had seemed to be moving decisively to set the tone of his Administration. He would take special care to avoid the afflictions of the Johnson Administration in its last years. His would be a government of national unity. The war abroad and the strife at home were to be brought to an end. Where Johnson had been deceptive, the new President would be straightforward; where Johnson had been angry, he would be calm; where Johnson had been secretive, he would be open. New ideas would be welcomed, old enmities forgotten. . . . A widespread conviction took hold that the country would now enjoy a period of cooling-off under the leadership of a modest, unpretentious, hardworking, practical-minded Administration. (Schell 26–27)

Betsy and Arlene take the audience to visit the idyllic White House as part of a class field trip.

In the opening scenes, the creators of the film, Andrew Fleming and Sheryl Longin, introduce the *real* concerns of the teenage lead characters by having them experience common cultural events of the time. Political intrigue and politicians are not on their minds; going to McDonalds and writing love letters to screen idols are what the teenagers of the era longed to do. The film reflects a longing of the public at the beginning of the 1970s to return to a placid simplicity of an earlier era. Indeed, it is for this reason that the theme of growing up and the loss of innocence works so well in the film.

As the film progresses, Betsy and Arlene accidentally catch a glimpse of the "other" White House where they encounter the "real" business that takes place behind closed doors. At first they become mere voyeurs to state secrets by just being in the wrong place at the wrong time; Nixon's staff sees them as a security threat, however, and wants to "debrief" them. Then they encounter the president, who seems to be no more harmful than an adult with a pet problem. The girls have an immediate rapport with his dog, Checkers, and Nixon asks them to be official dog-walkers in an attempt to normalize the situation. The girls are thrilled: by volunteering their services (as dog-walkers) and thus solving the president's dog problem, they can perform their patriotic duty for the good of the country.

The more the girls interact with the president and his staff, the more they are exposed inadvertently to elements of future contention. Each scene sets up a dilemma that gets resolved by the end of the comedy: in the first scene, they witness the Watergate break-in; in the second (in an effort to keep the president from embarrassment), they remove from his shoe a part of the CREEP (Committee to Re-Elect the President) list, which they keep as a souvenir of their White House field trip. Fleming and Longin introduce many topics of social concern of the 1970s with each encounter between Nixon and the girls. The drug culture, the draft, war, and relations with Russia are all worked out as Arlene, Betsy, and Nixon share accidentally laced marijuana cookies in the Oval Office. The film is a portrayal of the classic tale of Rome burning while Nero fiddles away. Nixon is portrayed as unconcerned about the escapades and dirty deeds of the staffers who surround him; throughout the movie the president is distracted about his public image and seems genuinely hurt that his intentions have been misunderstood.

What makes this film work is the trope of the loss of innocence of two naïve girls, for they mature with each encounter. By the end of the movie, their idol reveals his human failings, forcing the girls to confront their own ideals and power to influence people and events. This trope works as a metaphor for the United States during the Nixon era; at first the public was lulled by the campaign promises of a president who would do things differently from earlier administrations; then, as each incident of Nixon's perfidy accumulated, the public—like the girls—was forced into disillusionment and yet, ultimately, growth. *Dick* thus ends on a positive note, despite the negative experiences it presents.

INFATUATION AND PARANOIA IN
THE WORLD OF HENRY ORIENT *(1964)*

Another film that depicts a similar trope of coming of age and loss of innocence is *The World of Henry Orient,* a story of two adolescent girls who fall in love with the pianist Henry Orient (Orient is played by Peter Sellers as a Lothario who seduces women with his piano playing). Gil and Valerie (the star-struck teenage girls) follow Orient through Manhattan in an attempt to get closer to him, but their constant surveillance serves to make Orient more paranoid in his on-screen, adult romantic encounters. In the dénouement, Orient seduces Valerie's mother, forever shattering the infatuation of Valerie with Orient. This painful awakening forces the girls to confront the reality of growing up.

The generic similarity between the movies *Henry Orient* and *Dick* is striking. The plots revolve around two adolescent female characters who encounter a situation that is beyond their years. The girls in both of the movies are seduced by the power and the personality of the leading male character. In each of the movies, one character (Arlene in *Dick,* and Valerie in *Henry Orient*) is infatuated with the lead character. The girls elevate the men to idol status in a traditional teenage ritual of pasting their pictures in a scrapbook, which becomes a tribute to their infatuation. In both of the movies the male character becomes increasingly paranoid and bumbling because of the girls' continuing presence. Finally, in each of the movies, the male character commits an unpardonable act of betrayal that forces the girls to address their emotions and their future as adults.

The World of Henry Orient is a cultural parody of youth and innocence in the early 1960s. J.M. Rice said of the film: "The sixties became The Sixties around the time of this film, 1964. . . . If the Kennedy assassination and Vietnam are cultural watersheds, then this film is a wonderful cinematic artifact; it gives lie to the condescending put-downs of the era by the current generation" (Rice 2).

Director George Roy Hill presents a "benign" portrait of America whose citizens sleepwalk through life with nothing more to worry about than what to wear to the party or who is going to bed with whom. Serious threats to the family—divorce, abandonment, lesbianism, and adultery—are issues that Hill broaches during the movie but which are never really examined as the girls,

Val and Gil, blithely enjoy unencumbered flights of youthful fancy. Serious consequences seem to have no lasting impact on the heroines because Daddy "fixes" everything. By the end of the movie, the world is put to right and everyone's role is defined in the grand scheme of life. The movie *Henry Orient* was a perfect morality play for an American audience that in 1964 had just begun to face the assassination of a president and the trials of the Vietnam conflict. Americans were still living by the post–World War II ideals of the nuclear family, the American dream of prosperity and leisure, and the conviction that the government was *for* the people.

It is no mistake that Fleming would choose to use this kind of trope for *Dick* to illustrate the political naïveté of most Americans in the early 1970s. America was reeling from the tumultuous events of the late 1960s and was nostalgic for a return to national innocence.

COLLECTIVE MEMORY REDUX IN DICK

For an audience in 1999, a stylized version of 1970s chic sets the scene for a less sinister look back at history. The film *Dick* asks the question: what really happened back then? For those who were coming of age in the early 1970s the stylization of *Dick* mirrors youthful perceptions of both society and government. An article from the Baby Boomer Headquarters website gives a pertinent description of the 1970s:

> In the 70's the [television] networks tossed us "The Brady Bunch," a blended family, and "The Partridge Family." I'm not sure what they were, but they weren't partridges, and they certainly were not the nuclear family that prevailed for the first 60 years of the decade. . . . In the mid-to-late 60's, many kids began wearing bellbottom pants. They let their hair grow long; they wore flowers in their hair . . . . In the 70's, many kids wore platform shoes and paisley shirts. Blacks, including Jesse Jackson, grew beards and mustaches and wore Afros. The bizarre even went mainstream: leisure suits became the standard attire for some adults, we wore those horrible wide ties, and even ABC News dude San Donaldson grew long, thick sideburns; and his superiors let him get away with it. What in the world were they thinking of? ("70's Story" 1)

Thinking indeed. As portrayed in *Dick*, many ordinary people were merely interested in the mundane world of fashion, of partying, and of falling in love. If anyone was thinking about politics at all, it was only because the piecemeal news exposure of the perfidy of the administration forced a closer look every once in a while. By the end of the 1960s, with all its riots and social discontent,

Richard Nixon (Anthony Hopkins) after he wins his first presidential nomination in 1968. *Nixon* (1995).

thinking was just too much—many Americans just wanted to continue to live a benign, consumerist fantasy.

Images in *Dick* have been stripped of their mythic proportions. Nixon is not the embodiment of evil that Oliver Stone portrays in his dark drama. In *Dick*, Nixon appears bumbling, fatherly, a bit paranoid, but never more evil than an ordinary man thrust into the pitfalls of Washington politics. Fleming projects the evil onto Nixon's administration with the characters that portray Nixon's henchmen acting like heavy-handed storm troopers.

The comic genre works for *Dick*, and the Nixon character is comparable to the Sellers/Orient character in *The World of Henry Orient*. The leading male character in both of these movies is the sophisticated, world-weary figure to whom the girls look for answers to the confusing turmoil of growing up. In *Henry Orient* of the 1960s, the girls never actually talk to their idol. (The other adults in the movie mediate the evil and wrongdoing.) In *Dick*, set in the 1970s, the girls seek counsel with Nixon and even try to get him to change the course of the events in which they and their families become embroiled. In the end, the girls in *Dick* take charge of their own lives and turn their disillusion into empowerment. Life goes on for them as stronger young adults.

The power of comedy is that filmmakers can take social fears and concerns and tie them with events in a way that creates a safe haven of laughter. Laughter can then work as a cathartic; history becomes a series of foibles and gaffes that can be controlled and overcome. As we distance ourselves through time from actual events, we can collect all that we know and revise the story. We find we can laugh at our fears. The people who represented evil and chaos become mere caricatures and, in this type of portrayal, become less worthy of serious emotion. The cathartic release of serious emotion in caricature is why the final scene in *Dick* works so well. Arlene and Betsy say goodbye to their nemesis by wrapping themselves in patriotic righteousness and waving a derogatory banner at Nixon's passing helicopter. A defeated and confused-looking Nixon can only shake his fist at them in a gesture of hopeless defeat. Oliver Stone, on the other hand, creates a more apocalyptic conclusion for his movie. By the end of *Nixon*, the audience is led to believe that the individual is almost helpless against the power of the establishment—even Nixon himself cannot control "The Beast." In the end, Fleming would have us "get on with it." Stone, however, would add Nixon to our enduring myths and hold him forever as a symbol of power gone mad and as a milestone of a system irrevocably broken.

So as the collective memories of the 1960s and 1970s compound and then become dim in the minds of those who lived through the era, movies such as *Dick* and *Henry Orient* become nostalgic reminders of what we really lost. Lost ideals are only momentarily relived in these types of movies, which present a bit of lighthearted innocence and romance, and the belief that each of us *can* make a difference. Stone's *Nixon* is too much of a real-time reminder of the collective pain the nation felt from events of these decades.

What does endure from people and events that make up history are the stories that are passed on to the next generation. To make the retelling easier, characterizations and perceptions of power are encapsulated into mythic figures. Accurately or inaccurately, myth both enlarges historic reality and subsumes emotion and uncertainty about the future into predictable formulas with comforting outcomes. These formulas are cycled and recycled in popular genre. These formulas become the stories of modern generations and are told by the premier storytellers of the culture. Movies serve the role of storyteller for twenty-first-century audiences. But can the retelling assuage the ravages of the past? By casting Richard Nixon as the embodiment of evil as Stone does, the retelling becomes didactic and offers the audience little relief from the unrelenting pain created by Nixon's crimes. The comedic form is demythologizing, presenting instead characters with human failings; this allows the audience to mitigate its fears. *Dick* thus serves a restorative purpose, returning to the audience a sense of control and a chance to give the deeds of the past a historical perspective.

WORKS CITED

Fero, Marc. *Cinema and History.* Detroit: Wayne State University Press, 1988.

Fleming, Andrew, and Sheryl Longin. *Dick.* Dir. Andrew Fleming. With Dan Hedaya as Richard Nixon. Columbia Pictures, 1999.

Johnson, Nora, and Nunnally Johnson. *The World of Henry Orient.* With Peter Sellers as Henry Orient. United Artists, 1964.

Kaminsky, Stuart M. *American Film Genres.* Chicago: Nelson-Hall, 1985.

Lule, Jack. *Daily News, Eternal Stories: The Mythological Role of Journalism.* New York and London: The Guilford Press, 2001.

Nimmo, Dan, and James E. Combs. *Subliminal Politics Myths and Mythmakers in America.* Englewood Cliffs, New Jersey: Prentice-Hall Inc., 1980.

Nixon Foundation Research Library. <http://www.nixonfoundation.org/ Research_Center/Nixons>.

Rice, J.M. "Hollywood." *Internet Movie Database,* 1999–2000. <http://www.us.imdb.com>.

Rivele, Stephen J., and Christopher Wilkinson. *Nixon.* Dir. Oliver Stone. With Anthony Hopkins as Richard Nixon. Buena Vista Pictures, 1995.

Schell, Jonathan. *The Time of Illusion.* New York: Alfred A. Knopf, 1976.

"70's Story." *The Baby Boomers Headquarters.* 1999–2000. <http://www.bbhq.com>.

Sklar, Robert. *Movie-Made America: A Cultural History of American Movies.* New York: Vintage Books, 1994.

Stuck in the 70's. <http://www.StuckInThe70's.com>.

Wicker, Tom. *One of Us: Richard Nixon and the American Dream.* New York: Random House, 1991.

Wills, Garry. *Nixon Agonistes: The Crisis of the Self-Made Man.* Boston: Houghton Mifflin Company, 1970.

Wood, Michael. *America in the Movies or "Santa Maria, It Had Slipped My Mind."* New York: Columbia University Press, 1989.

Donald Whaley

"Biological Business-as-Usual"

The Beast in Oliver Stone's *Nixon*

"What's the point of being president? You're powerless," a woman says to the president in *Nixon* (1995).

One line historians have taken in criticizing Oliver Stone's *Nixon* is to attack Stone's use of the Beast, a metaphor that appears in the film.[1] Stephen Ambrose, in an essay on *Nixon,* gives an account of the scene in which Nixon talks with Vietnam War protesters at the Lincoln Memorial. A young woman asks why Nixon does not stop the war, then, beginning to comprehend, she says, "You can't stop it, can you? Even if you wanted to. Because it's not *you.* It's the system. And the system won't let you stop it." Nixon says to his chief of staff, H.R. Haldeman, "She understood something it's taken me twenty-five fucking years in politics to understand. The CIA, the Mafia, the Wall Street bastards . . . 'The Beast.' A nineteen-year-old kid. She understands the nature of 'The Beast.'" Quoting this dialogue Ambrose concludes, "This is sophomoric Marxism circa 1950" and accuses Stone of distorting the past to further a political agenda (Ambrose 207). Arthur Schlesinger Jr. takes the Beast as evidence that Stone views the world as a place where "ten or twenty people secretly plot the basic decisions" and concludes Stone has "a conspiratorial obsession" (Schlesinger 215). There are problems with both criticisms.

Those familiar with Stone's work will know that the Beast appeared in an earlier Stone film, *Platoon*. In that film, American troops await an imminent attack by the North Vietnamese Army (NVA). One American soldier, referring to the NVA, says, "The Beast is out there, and he's hungry tonight." If Stone is a Marxist, what kind of Marxism is it that would classify the CIA, the Mafia, American big business, *and* the army of Communist North Vietnam as part of the same phenomenon? And what are we now to make of Schlesinger's view? If the Beast is a conspiracy, are the CIA, the Mafia, American big business, and the NVA all involved in the same conspiracy? These things make no sense. Clearly, the Beast is something other than what Ambrose and Schlesinger think it is.

To understand the Beast it is useful to turn to the writings of one of Stone's contemporaries. In a 1992 interview Stone acknowledged, "I'm very influenced by Camille Paglia" (Paglia, *Vamps* 471). I am not suggesting that Stone took his concept of the Beast from Paglia; his use of the metaphor in *Platoon* predates publication of her writings. I am suggesting that both Paglia and Stone derive their ideas from what literary critic Paul Zweig identified as a "new adventure myth" created by certain nineteenth-century writers. These writers, Zweig argued, saw Western culture, with its emphasis on work, on "due and regular conduct," and on obedience to law and conscience, as a prison from which adventure offered escape. According to Zweig, this new adventure literature (for example, Herman Melville's *Moby Dick* or Joseph Conrad's *Heart of Darkness* or *Lord Jim*) dramatized "dark emotions." The new adventurers were rebels and criminals; adventure became an act of revolt. Zweig argued that the philosophers of this new adventure myth were the Marquis de Sade and Friedrich Nietzsche, the latter of whom, Zweig said, despised "the modern ideal of domesticity" and viewed the philosopher "as an adventurer, questing for an order of experience beyond domestic categories, 'beyond good and evil.'" Among the writers who carried this tradition into the twentieth century, Zweig contended, were Ernest Hemingway and Norman Mailer (Zweig 17, 167–84, 15, 187, 209, 247–52). Stone has talked about the powerful influence Conrad, Hemingway, and Norman Mailer have had on him (Stone, "Oliver Stone" 13–16), and Nietzsche's influence is apparent in Stone's work, especially *The Doors* (which Stone directed and co-wrote) and *Conan the Barbarian* (which he co-wrote).[2] Paglia's version of feminism celebrates women, such as Paglia's role model Amelia Earhart, who have escaped the "bourgeois prison" of "the kitchen" or "the office" into what Paglia calls "male adventurism." In *Sexual Personae* Paglia makes clear that Sade and Nietzsche inspired her (Paglia, *Vamps* 347, ix, xii, 25; *Sexual Personae* 2, 14; *Sex* 101, 105–7, 110–11). Because Stone and Paglia derive their ideas from the same tradition, studying Paglia's writings can illuminate Stone's work in general and his concept of the Beast in particular.

THE BEAST IN THE WRITINGS OF CAMILLE PAGLIA

Paglia lays out systematically in her writings the view of human nature implicit in the new adventure myth. She rejects "the sunny Rousseauism running through the last two hundred years of liberal thinking." She goes on:

> Rousseau rejects original sin, Christianity's pessimistic view of man born unclean, with a propensity for evil. Rousseau's idea, derived from Locke, of man's innate goodness led to social environmentalism, now the dominant ethic of American human services, penal codes, and behaviorist therapies. It assumes that aggression, violence, and crime come from social deprivation—a poor neighborhood, a bad home.

Instead she sees "the dark tradition of Sade, Darwin, Nietzsche, and Freud as more truthful about human perversity. It is more accurate to see primitive egotism and animality ever-simmering behind social controls . . . than to predicate purity and innocence ravaged by corrupt society" (Paglia, *Vamps* 25; *Sexual Personae* 2).

"Aggression," Paglia declares, "comes from nature; it is what Nietzsche is to call the will to power." Paglia refuses to accept the "idea of the ultimate benevolence of nature." "In nature," she writes, "brute force is the law, a survival of the fittest." She emphasizes the "brutality of biology and geology, the Darwinian waste and bloodshed." "Nature," she asserts, "is a Darwinian spectacle of the eaters and the eaten." "For Sade, getting back to nature," she adds, "would be to give free rein to violence and lust" (Paglia, *Sexual Personae* 1–3, 6, 16).

Stone's vision is similar to Paglia's. In an essay in Robert Brent Toplin's *Oliver Stone's USA*, Stone has written about "the law of survival, the natural law, . . . the way of the world where, under every peaceful blade of grass, tiny yet feral bugs devour other bugs in cycles of destruction and creation" (Stone, "On Seven Films" 248). That view pervades Stone's work. In his autobiographical novel, *A Child's Night Dream*, Stone portrays himself as an eight-year-old who, enraged at being taunted, tries to strangle his cousin: "I am all hard inside, hard as I can possibly be, inexorable like Nature. . . . The Power The Glory! Of killing! Raw brute force." A game Oliver and his cousin play—literally "a Darwinian spectacle of the eaters and the eaten"—makes clear that Stone sees children not as living in Rousseau-like innocence, but as participants in nature's cruelty. The boys "went out to hunt for buckets of giant multicolored snails, running the captured ones in endless chariot races around intricate coliseums of rocks and plants, allowing the winners their freedom, and eating the losers in soft butter and garlic" (Stone, *Child's Night Dream* 62–63, 58).

A similar Darwinian game appears in Stone's first movie, the horror film *Seizure*. In that film, three inmates escape from an asylum for the criminally insane and take prisoner a group of people spending the weekend at a country estate. The lunatics force their prisoners to run five times around the house, telling them that the weakest, the one who crosses the finish line last, will be executed. That we are meant to understand this game as a metaphor for the struggle for survival in nature is made clear because one of the prisoners, just before the race begins, says, "With all our civilization we must still learn to accept that nature holds no special account of our disasters."

Paglia says of capitalism, "As an economic system, it is in the Darwinian line of Sade, not Rousseau," and she writes of the "capitalist survival of the fittest" (Paglia, *Sexual Personae* 37). Likewise, in *Wall Street* Stone associates capitalism with the Darwinian struggle in nature. In that film corporate raider Gordon Gekko (Michael Douglas), speaking at a stockholder's meeting, defends his practice of taking over companies, wrecking them, and selling off their assets for a profit. Gekko denies that the "law of evolution in corporate America" sanctions "survival of the unfittest." He goes on: "The point is, ladies and gentlemen, that greed, for lack of a better word, is good . . . greed is right . . . greed works. Greed clarifies, cuts through, and captures the essence of the evolutionary spirit." Susan Mackey-Kallis has noted the "depiction of Social Darwinism" in *Wall Street* (Mackey-Kallis 143).

David T. Courtwright has pointed out the "pure cinematic Darwinism" of Stone's *Natural Born Killers*. Courtwright notes that one of the film's serial killers, Mallory (Juliette Lewis), sings, "I guess I was born, naturally born, born bad," and the other, Mickey (Woody Harrelson), in an interview with journalist Wayne Gale (Robert Downey Jr.), tells Gale that "killing's in his blood. His father was violent and his father before him. His gene pool is a flaming pit of scum into which God threw him. He kills unselfconsciously. The wolf don't know why he's a wolf." The born-killer riff is reinforced by predatory images— hawks, scorpions, snakes, praying mantises—that appear throughout the film (Courtwright 199–200).

Indeed, in one scene, as Mickey watches television in a motel, images flash across the screen—Hitler, Stalin, an explosion of a hydrogen bomb, a scene of combat in Vietnam, a gunfight from *The Wild Bunch*, a scene from *Midnight Express* in which an inmate in a Turkish prison takes vengeance on a snitch by biting out his tongue, a chain-saw murder carried out by a gang of Colombian drug dealers in *Scarface*. Interwoven with these images are scenes from nature shows—lions copulating, time-lapse photography of a plant growing, zebra stallions fighting, insects eating other insects. This montage reinforces the idea that war, criminal violence, and other forms of human aggression come from nature. Mickey articulates the film's Darwinian theme during his interviews with Wayne Gale. When Gale asks how Mickey can kill innocent people, Mickey replies that no one is innocent and says, "It's just murder, man. All God's creatures do it in some form or another. I mean, you look in the forest and you got species killing other species. Our species killing all species including the forest, and we just call it industry, not murder." In a scene cut from the theatrical version of the film but available on video in the additional scenes included in the director's cut, a survivor of an attack by Mickey and Mallory says of the killers, "They're just shocking the world into remembering the primal law. . . . Survival of the fittest."

For Paglia, "man's latent perversity" comes from what biologists call "man's reptilian brain, the oldest part of our central nervous system, killer surviver of the archaic era." Paglia, far from believing as Rousseau does that humans are innately good and that society corrupts them, argues, "Society is not the criminal but the force that keeps crime in check. When social controls weaken man's innate cruelty bursts forth" (Paglia, *Sexual Personae* 11–12, 2). That Stone shares that view is made clear by his commentary on *Natural Born Killers*: "We have in us the killer brain, but we also have a culture that has moved away from that violence. Yet we still seem to possess the remnants of the old brain in all aspects of our culture, up to and including war made by respectable men in establishment positions" (Stone, "On Seven Films" 247).

Which brings us to the Beast. Stone has said that Richard Nixon's "potential was limitless, but ultimately was limited by powers that even he couldn't control. To some degree, *Nixon* is about the illusion of power" (Stone, "Interview with Oliver Stone" xvii). The Beast symbolizes those powers that limited Nixon's potential, that frustrated his plans. Stone has called the Beast "a metaphor" for "a force (or forces) greater than the presidency" (Stone, "Conversation" 308–9). The use of the term "the Beast" to name those forces associates them with nature.

Paglia argues, "Human beings are not nature's favorites. We are merely one of a multitude of species upon which nature indiscriminately exerts its force. Nature has a master agenda we can only dimly know." She adds:

> The gravest challenge to our hopes and dreams is the messy biological business-as-usual that is going on within us and without us at every hour of every day. Consciousness is a pitiful hostage of its flesh-envelope, whose surges, circuits, and secret murmurings it cannot stay or speed. . . . Free will is stillborn in the red cells of our body, for there is no free will in nature. Our choices come to us prepackaged and special delivery, molded by hands not our own. (Paglia, *Sexual Personae* 1, 7)

The Beast in *Nixon* behaves the same way Paglia describes nature behaving. The Beast has a "master agenda" of its own, of which Nixon and others are only vaguely aware. Christopher Wilkinson, Stone's co-writer on the film, explains what the writers meant by the Beast:

> In order for Nixon to have become President in 1968, Jack Kennedy had to die, Lyndon Johnson had to be forced into retirement, Dr. King had to die, Bobby Kennedy had to die, Hubert Humphrey had to be eviscerated in Chicago. It almost seemed that Nixon was being helped, helped by something dark, something sinister, something frightening, some *thing*.
> And we called it the Beast. (Wilkinson 58–59)

The Beast closely resembles Paglia's "messy biological business-as-usual that is going on within us and without us at every hour of every day." In part, the Beast is within Stone's Nixon, the perverse side of him, which comes from nature. Wilkinson explains that the Beast "became a metaphor for the dark side of Nixon himself. The monster within that relentlessly drove him. To claw his way to the top. To lie. To cover up" (Wilkinson 60). The Beast also stands for powerful forces outside Nixon. Wilkinson writes:

> The Beast became a metaphor for the darkest organic forces in American Cold War politics: the anti-Communist crusade, secret intelligence, organized crime, big business. People and entities with apparently divergent agendas. But at certain moments in history, their interests converged.
> And people died. (Wilkinson 59)

The use of the word "organic" to describe these forces of Cold War politics, which the Beast represents, again associates the Beast with nature. For Stone war, organized crime, and capitalism are tied to the Darwinian struggle in nature, are remnants of the ancient reptilian, killer brain that still exist in human culture. That explains how the CIA, the Mafia, and American big business in *Nixon* and the NVA in *Platoon* can all be manifestations of the Beast. All can be understood as remnants of the killer brain.

In the film, Nixon (Anthony Hopkins) senses that something is helping him. He tells Haldeman (James Woods) that after Bobby Kennedy's death, "I knew I'd be president. Death paved the way, didn't it? Vietnam. The Kennedys. It cleared a path through the wilderness for me. Over the bodies . . . Four bodies." The four bodies are the Kennedys and Nixon's brothers, Arthur and Harold, both of whom died of tuberculosis. The deaths of his brothers made it possible for his parents to afford to send Nixon to law school. Nixon asks, "Who's helping us? Is it God? Or is it . . . Death?" (Rivele, Wilkinson, and Stone 183–84).[3] We know from Wilkinson that it is the Beast that is helping Nixon, and this scene contains a visual commentary on the Beast. As Nixon asks who is helping him, the film cuts to an image of tuberculosis bacilli under a microscope, then, in a flashback, to a desert landscape—the sanitarium where Harold is dying of tuberculosis. The effect is to identify the Beast with nature and the Beast's agenda with nature's agenda.

After Harold's death, in words that call to mind survival of the fittest in nature, Nixon's mother (Mary Steenburgen) urges her son to go to law school. Nixon feels guilty about Harold. "Did he have to *die* for me to get it?" Nixon asks. His mother replies, "It's meant to make us stronger. Thou art stronger than Harold . . . stronger than Arthur. God has chosen thee to survive" (Rivele, Wilkinson, and Stone 186).[4]

In the scene at the Lincoln Memorial, when the young woman realizes Nixon cannot stop the war because "the system" will not let him, she says, "Then what's the point? What's the point of being president? You're powerless." Nixon replies, "No, no. I'm not powerless. Because . . . because I understand the system. I believe I can control it. Maybe not control it totally. But . . . tame it enough to make it do some good." The woman responds, "It sounds like you're talking about a wild animal." Nixon answers, "Maybe I am," and then at the end of the scene he says to Haldeman, "She understands the nature of 'the Beast.' She called it a wild animal" (Rivele, Wilkinson, and Stone 221–22). In his account of this scene, Ambrose leaves out these references to the Beast as a wild animal. But it is precisely these references that make clear that, whatever Ambrose thinks, Stone's concept of the Beast is not Marxist. This dialogue associates the Beast with nature, an association reinforced by visuals in the scene. As the young woman speaks the words "the system," a shot of Nixon's dead brothers appears, making the point that the things we are told in this scene "the system" comprises—the CIA, the Mafia, big business—are Darwinian forces rooted in nature just as much as the tuberculosis that killed Nixon's brothers.

If Stone's concept of the Beast is not Marxist, neither is it what Schlesinger thinks it is, the idea that "ten or twenty people" are secretly directing history behind the scenes. Wilkinson writes:

> We conjured up a most chilling truth about the Beast. Not that it exists—but that *it does not know* it exists.
> We imagined the Beast as a headless monster lurching through postwar American history, instinctively seeking figureheads to wear its public face, creating them when need be, destroying them when they no longer serve its purposes. (Wilkinson 59)

That idea appears in the film's treatment of President Kennedy's assassination. In the film, Nixon believes a CIA plot to murder Fidel Castro somehow backfired. "Whoever killed Kennedy came from this . . . this *thing* we created. This Beast," Nixon says. "It was like . . . it had a life of its own. Like . . . a kind of 'beast' that doesn't even know it exists. It just eats people when it doesn't need 'em anymore" (Rivele, Wilkinson, and Stone 290, 181). In a scene cut from the theatrical version of *Nixon* but available in additional scenes included on the video of the movie, CIA Director Richard Helms (Sam Waterston), in a meeting with President Nixon, characterizes the agency's plot to murder Castro: "Not an operation so much as . . . an organic phenomenon. It grew, it changed shape, it developed . . . insatiable devouring appetites." As he speaks these lines, according to directions in the screenplay, "Helms wanders over to his prize orchids, fingers them. . . . Suddenly, the Beast is in the room" (Rivele, Wilkinson, and Stone 208). Part of this scene is double-exposed, showing not only the meeting between Nixon and Helms but also time-lapse photography of flowers opening. The flower imagery and the characterization of the Beast as "an organic phenomenon" again associate the Beast with nature but also imply that the Beast has the properties of an organism, that, like the flowers, the Beast has a life of its own and develops according to its own natural laws, but that, also like the flowers, it has no consciousness; it is alive. Stone, in an interview, characterized the Beast as "a System of checks and balances that," fueled by corporate and state power, "drives itself" (Stone, "Past Imperfect" 35). In the film, FBI Director J. Edgar Hoover (Bob Hoskins) characterizes "the system" as something that "adjusts itself" (Rivele, Wilkinson, and Stone 177). The point here is not that a small cabal is secretly directing history in a

Richard and Pat Nixon (Anthony Hopkins and Joan Allen). *Nixon* (1995).

highly ordered way behind the scenes, but that no human beings are in control. Darwinian forces are in the saddle and ride human beings. It is all biological business-as-usual.

TWO MEETINGS WITH THE BEAST

Stone has said that Nixon was removed from office because he "ran up against 'the Beast'" (Stone, "Conversation" 309). Stone's Nixon is one of those figureheads the Beast has sought out to wear its public face. "You're just a mouthpiece for an agenda that's hidden from us," a member of the audience at a 1968 campaign event says to Nixon in the film (Rivele, Wilkinson, and Stone 169). But Stone's Nixon does not want merely to serve the Beast, he wants to tame the Beast, to set forth his own agenda, and in trying to do so, he antagonizes powerful forces, something made clear in the film by two face-to-face meetings Nixon has with manifestations of the Beast.

The first is Nixon's meeting with CIA Director Helms, a scene that appears in the director's cut of the film. Not only does the screenplay state that the Beast is in the room during this scene, but animal imagery also signals the presence of the Beast and again associates the Beast with nature. According to the screenplay, Helms greets Nixon "with a reptilian smile." Prominently displayed in the scene is a woodcarving of a bird of prey. Helms recites lines from Yeats's "The Second Coming." As he says the words "What rough beast, its hour come round at last/Slouches toward Bethlehem to be born?" he moves in front of the woodcarving so that only the bird's wings can be seen, appearing to come from Helms's back, a visual that identifies him as a manifestation of the Beast. Helms expresses displeasure that Nixon has done nothing to remove Castro and that the president has planned a diplomatic opening to China. The camera looks down on Nixon, making him look small, weak, and vulnerable compared to Helms, thereby suggesting that the Beast is a force more powerful than the presidency. The screenplay makes clear that Nixon feels threatened: "A disturbing image suddenly appears in Nixon's mind—KENNEDY with his head blown off in Dallas. Followed by an IMAGE of his own death. In a coffin" (Rivele, Wilkinson, and Stone 205–12).

Nixon's second confrontation with the Beast takes place at the Texas ranch of Jack Jones (a fictional character played by Larry Hagman) where Nixon meets with a group made up of wealthy businessmen and anti-Castro Cubans. Again, animal imagery makes clear that the Beast is present. Upon meeting the group, Nixon has a subconscious image of "something slimy, reptilian" (Rivele, Wilkinson, and Stone 157). In a scene cut from the film but appearing in the screenplay, Nixon and Jones watch a "red-eyed, snorting" Brahma bull that "thrashes viciously against the reinforced walls of its pen." Jones refers to the bull as a "beast" and says, "This here's a bad bull. You piss him off, he'll kill everything in his path" (Rivele, Wilkinson, and Stone 240). The men at Jones's ranch supported Nixon in the 1968 election but have grown angry with the president. Jones articulates what upsets the group, beginning with Nixon's handling of the Vietnam War:

> It looks like to me we're gonna lose a war for the first Goddamn time and, Dick, Goddamnit, you're going along with it, buying into this Kissinger bullshit —"detente" with the Communists. "Detente"—it sounds like two fags dancing. . . .
>
> I mean I got federal price controls on my oil. The ragheads are beating the shit out of me. And I get your EPA environment agency with its thumb so far up my ass it's scratching my ear. . . .
>
> And now I have a federal judge ordering me to bus my kids halfway 'cross town to go to school with some nigger kids. I think, Mr. President, you're forgetting who put you where you are.

Nixon replies, "The American people put me where I am," to which Jones responds, smirking, "Really? Well, that can be changed" (Rivele, Wilkinson, and Stone 241–42). Nixon has tried to tame the Beast, but his hopes are frustrated by the Darwinian forces the Beast represents. Nixon becomes their victim. Christopher Wilkinson maintains, "Nixon violated the cardinal rule of American politics: Don't piss off The Beast. Nixon's Administration was dismantled when he was well on his way to arguably becoming the most effective *centrist* President in American history: SALT I, China, the schools, the EPA" (Wilkinson 59).

If Stone's Nixon is the victim of Darwinian forces operating outside him, he is also the victim of the Beast within. The same traits that helped him claw his way to the top—the ruthless ambition, the willingness to abuse power, the lying and covering-up—also bring him down. Eric Hamburg, co-producer of *Nixon*, has written that, "Nixon is a tragic figure of Shakespearean proportions—an immensely intelligent and gifted man, but one who carried within him the seeds of his own destruction," an assessment with which Stone has concurred (Hamburg, Introduction xiv; Stone, "Interview with Oliver Stone" xvii). Henry Kissinger (Paul Sorvino) makes the point in the film when he says of Nixon, "It's a tragedy because he had greatness in his grasp, but he had the defects of his qualities."

In running up against the Beast, Stone's Nixon had run up against nature, both outside himself and within himself. If *Nixon* is a tragedy, the film is not just a tragedy in the traditional Greek or Shakespearean sense; *Nixon* is also a tragedy in precisely the way Paglia characterizes the genre. "Tragedy is the most western literary genre," she writes. "The western will, setting itself up against nature, dramatized its own inevitable fall" (Paglia, *Sexual Personae* 6). Schlesinger argues that Stone should have left the Beast out of the film, that the Beast "is an additive that impairs the whole and could have been deleted without harm to the rest" (Schlesinger 215). Schlesinger does not get it. The Beast is not extraneous to *Nixon*. It is a key to understanding the film.

NOTES

1. Writers on *Nixon* differ on how they use capitalization and quotation marks in handling this metaphor. Variations include the Beast, The Beast, the "Beast," "the Beast," and "The Beast." Even the screenplay is not consistent in the way it handles the metaphor. I have used the first variation, which is the most common. Where I have quoted the work of others, I have let their way of dealing with the metaphor stand.

2. Stone was so influenced by Conrad's *Lord Jim* that, after reading it, he dropped out of Yale and headed for Southeast Asia in search of the kind of adventure he had read about in the book. Norman Mailer was a major influence on Stone's autobiographical novel, *A Child's Night Dream* (see Riordan 32–33, 39). For Hemingway's influence on Stone and especially on *Platoon*, see Roberts and Welky. Susan Mackey-Kallis has argued that Stone's Jim Morrison in *The Doors* might be understood as "a Nietzschean antihero" (MacKay-Kallis 102). For a fuller discussion of Stone's relationship to the philosophical tradition described by Zweig and for an interpretation of *Platoon* as an expression of the adventure myth, see Whaley.

3. Sometimes dialogue in the film differs from dialogue in the screenplay. Whenever I have used the screenplay, I have cited it. Dialogue from *Nixon* quoted in this essay without a citation comes from the film.

4. The words of Nixon's mother also call to mind the quote from Nietzsche, "That which does not kill us makes us stronger," a quote Stone and John Milius used at the beginning of *Conan the Barbarian*.

WORKS CITED

Ambrose, Stephen E. "Is It History?" In *Oliver Stone's USA: Film, History, and Controversy*, edited by Robert Brent Toplin, 202–7. Lawrence: University Press of Kansas, 2000.

Carnes, Mark C., ed. *Past Imperfect: History According to the Movies.* New York: Holt, 1996.

Courtwright, David T. "Way Cooler Than Manson: *Natural Born Killers.*" In *Oliver Stone's USA*, edited by Toplin, 188–201.

Hamburg, Eric. Introduction. In *Nixon*, edited by Hamburg, xiii-xvi.

———, ed. *Nixon: An Oliver Stone Film.* New York: Hyperion, 1995.

Kunz, Don, ed. *The Films of Oliver Stone.* Lanham, Maryland: Scarecrow, 1997.

Mackey-Kallis, Susan. *Oliver Stone's America: "Dreaming the Myth Outward."* Boulder: Westview, 1996.

Paglia, Camille. *Sex, Art, and American Culture.* New York: Vintage, 1992.

———. *Sexual Personae: Art and Decadence from Nefertiti to Emily Dickenson.* 1990. Reprint, New York: Vintage, 1991.

———. *Vamps and Tramps.* New York: Vintage, 1994.

Riordan, James. *Stone: The Controversies, Excesses, and Exploits of a Radical Filmmaker.* New York: Hyperion, 1995.

Rivele, Stephen J., Christopher Wilkinson, and Oliver Stone. "Nixon: The Original Annotated Screenplay." In *Nixon*, edited by Hamburg, 81–307.

Roberts, Randy, and David Welky. "A Sacred Mission: Oliver Stone and Vietnam." In *Oliver Stone's USA*, edited by Toplin, 66–99.

Schlesinger, Arthur M., Jr. "On *JFK* and *Nixon*." In *Oliver Stone's USA*, edited by Toplin, 212–16.

Stone, Oliver. *A Child's Night Dream.* New York: St. Martin's, 1997.

———. "A Conversation Between Mark Carnes and Oliver Stone." Interview with Mark Carnes. In *Past Imperfect*, edited by Carnes, 305–12.

————. "Interview with Oliver Stone." Interview with Michael Singer. In *Nixon,* edited by Hamburg, xvii-xx.

————. "Oliver Stone: An Interview with the Director." Interview with David Breskin. In *Films of Oliver Stone,* edited by Kunz, 3–64.

————. "On Seven Films." In *Oliver Stone's USA,* edited by Toplin, 219–48.

————. " 'Past Imperfect: History According to the Movies': A Conversation between Mark C. Carnes and Oliver Stone." *Cineaste* 22.4 (1997): 33–37.

Toplin, Robert Brent, ed. *Oliver Stone's USA: Film, History, and Controversy.* Lawrence: University Press of Kansas, 2000.

Whaley, Donald. "Oliver Stone's Journey to Myth-Country: *Platoon* and the Cultural History of Adventure." In *Films of Oliver Stone,* edited by Kunz, 113–23.

Wilkinson, Christopher. "The Year of the Beast." In *Nixon,* edited by Hamburg, 56–60.

Zweig, Paul. *The Adventurer.* New York: Basic, 1974.

Myron A. Levine

MYTH AND REALITY IN THE HOLLYWOOD CAMPAIGN FILM

Primary Colors (1998) and *The War Room* (1994)

Modeled on presidential candidate Bill Clinton, and drawn from a book by correspondent Joe Klein, Governor Jack Stanton (John Travolta) is ever ready to press the flesh in *Primary Colors* (1998).

Two film accounts of the 1992 election seek to provide an "insider's" view of how a modern presidential campaign is fought and won. *Primary Colors* (1998), based on the novel by campaign-trail reporter Joe Klein (who wrote under the pseudonym Anonymous), presents a fictionalized parallel to Bill Clinton's rise in the 1992 Democratic primaries. *The War Room* (1994) claims even greater authenticity as a documentary that was afforded unique access to the Clinton campaign headquarters (the "war room") in Arkansas.

But just how accurately do these films portray the making of the president? How well do these portrayals stack up against more scholarly analyses of voting behavior and the 1992 campaign?

THE NEO-POPULIST ATTACK: THE GENRE OF THE HOLLYWOOD CAMPAIGN FILM AND THE CANDIDATE *(1972)*

For decades, Hollywood has argued that a professional political class has "stolen" politics from the people. *Mr. Smith Goes to Washington* (1939), *Meet John Doe* (1941), and *All the King's Men* (1949) were broadsides against the manipulation, corruption, and intimidation of the old political party machines. With the decline of old-style political party organizations, such feature films as *Primary Colors, The War Room, Bob Roberts* (1993), and *Wag The Dog* (1998) sought to expose the power of a "new" campaign elite. Even *Being There* (1992), the story of a simpleton who becomes a media phenomenon and a national candidate, is a cautionary warning that all is not what it appears to be in modern American politics.

The Candidate (1972, written by Jeremy Larner and directed by Michael Ritchie) typifies the neopopulist Hollywood critique of contemporary American politics. Robert Redford plays the idealistic, public-interest advocate J.J. McKay, who is recruited by a campaign consultant (played by Peter Boyle) to run for the United States Senate; along the way to victory, McKay loses his principles, his idealism, and his virtue. As the campaign progresses, his principled stands on issues give way to the meaningless rehearsed phrases and personal-image puffery. His loss of virtue is signified by the deterioration of his marriage: he sleeps with a campaign groupie, and his once-passionate marriage is reduced to a cold and bloodless relationship where he and his wife stage-manage for television the appearance of being a happy couple. When his election victory is announced, he can only ask his campaign manager: "What do we do now?" McKay has become a politician: he stands for nothing and can no longer act without cues from his advisers.

At the time of its release, *The Candidate* highlighted many of the technological innovations of the media-age campaign. Television consultants test alternative versions of spot ads and use tracking polls to gauge the campaign's progress. McKay's managers change the candidate's schedule to take advantage of new media opportunities and photo ops. In a "tarmac campaign," the candidate flies to as many major media markets as possible in a single day. On the command of a media adviser, McKay even switches neckties before taking the stage for a televised debate.

But just how accurate is *The Candidate* in its critique of modern American politics? Are contemporary elections decided by a candidate's good looks, a carefully crafted image, and a slogan ("McKay, The Better Way")? For all their insight, *The Candidate* and other films of the genre neglect other factors that are crucially important to the success of a campaign.

THE "NEW" LITERATURE ON ISSUE VOTING

Quality social science voter surveys, which only first appeared at mid-century, led to a near-consensus that issues were *not* of great importance in determining the voters' decisions in presidential elections. *The American Voter* (1960) and other national studies by the University of Michigan's Survey Research Center established the prevailing paradigm, that psychologically rooted partisanship and the personal images of candidates—not issues—were the dominant influences on electoral behavior.[1]

But even at the time, the perspective of *The American Voter* was subjected to considerable challenge. Harvard professor V.O. Key Jr. reviewed other national polls and responded in *The Responsible Electorate* that "voters are not fools":

> In American presidential campaigns of recent decades the portrait of the American electorate that develops from the data is not one of an electorate straitjacketed by social determinants or moved by subconscious urges triggered by devilishly skillful propagandists. It is rather one of an electorate moved by concern about central and relevant questions of public policy, of governmental performance, and of executive personality. (Key 7–8)

Key argued that issues had a lot to do with voter choice: "standpatters" stood with a party as they approved of its performance and promises; "switchers" moved toward the party that was closer to their policy views (Key 55). Yet, Key's critics countered that his data and methods were inadequate.[2]

By the time *The Candidate* appeared, *The American Voter* paradigm was being subjected to a renewed and more sustained challenge; in essence, the film's "wisdom" was already out of date. New studies on voting behavior, typified by Norman Nie and others, *The Changing American Voter* (1976), pointed to the importance of issues and ideology in the presidential elections of the 1960s and early 1970s.[3] The quiescent 1950s had passed, and citizens could not help but be aware of the major issues of the day as television broadcast heated images of the civil rights struggle, Vietnam, and urban riots into the American living room. In looking at 1972, even researchers at the University of Michigan's Survey Research Center/Center for Political Studies came to the conclusion that issues rivaled partisanship and personal assessments in their impact on the voting decision (A. Miller and W. Miller; W. Miller and Levitin).

Why had so many analysts for so long failed to see the importance of issues in elections? In part, these analysts had set too strict a standard for issue voting.

As Morris Fiorina explains: "They [the voters] need *not* know the precise economic or foreign policies of the incumbent administration in order to see or feel the *results* of those policies" (Fiorina 5). Fiorina continues:

> What does it matter if this voter is not familiar with the nuances of current government policies or is not aware of the precise alternatives offered by the opposition? He is not a professional policy formulator. . . . Perhaps he can't "cognize the issue in some form," but he can go to the polls and indicate whether or not he likes the way those who can "cognize the issue" are in fact doing so. (Fiorina 10–11)

Citizens do not have to have the depth of understanding of a policy analyst in order to vote *retrospectively*, rendering judgment on the recent past, especially on the performance of the incumbent administration.

Retrospective assessments led the electorate to oust Gerald Ford in 1976 (in part for his pardon of Richard Nixon and in part for his inability to turn around the nation's sluggish economic performance) and Jimmy Carter in 1980 and George H.W. Bush in 1992 for their economic failures. In 1984 and 1988, voters rewarded the Republican administration for the country's dynamic economic performance, just as they rewarded Bill Clinton with reelection in 1996. In an era of declining partisanship, economic assessments had come to exert a newfound important influence on voting behavior (Wattenberg, "Theories of Voting" 176).

Samuel Popkin in *The Reasoning Voter* uses the phrases "'gut' reasoning" and "low-information rationality" to describe the kind of practical thinking by which voters learn from a political campaign and render judgment. According to Popkin, the citizenry is not putty in the hands of the media elite; rather, voters are video-literate and do not uncritically accept everything they see or hear on TV. Voters discount the exaggerated claims made in political commercials; they also compare political claims with their own life experiences and with the knowledge they have gained from other sources. Political messages must strike a responsive chord with voters or else they are screened out.

Of course, the exact importance of issues varies from election to election.[4] Still, the media elite does not have nearly the control over voters that Hollywood assumes; what the voters think, too, is of critical importance. Candidates and their media advisers can successfully "spin" an issue only if voters, judging from their own experience, see the concern as important and deem the campaign's assertions to be valid. As Jean Bethke Elshtain has so eloquently phrased it: "Voters and candidates are co-constructors of issues" (Elshtain 117).

PRIMARY COLORS: *A MORALITY TALE*

Primary Colors (screenplay by Elaine May; produced and directed by Mike Nichols) is a docudrama that claims special insight and relevancy as the result of its close proximity to real-world events; its story is based on the insights gained by a reporter who "was there" with Bill Clinton in 1992. John Travolta, Emma Thompson, and Billy Bob Thornton (who plays a James Carville–like, over-the-top campaign manager) lend the film still greater authenticity with their on-the-mark characterizations of their real-life counterparts. Walk-on appearances by Geraldo Rivera, Charlie Rose, Larry King, and Bill Maher, all playing themselves, further blur the line between fact and fiction.

Jack Stanton (Travolta) is a Clinton-like, personable, but philandering, junk-food-eating southern governor. He is a man of considerable talent: he possesses great warmth, considerable boyish charm, an ability to listen to others and empathize, and a sincere commitment to the poor. Like Clinton, Stanton also has a smart and politically ambitious wife, Susan (Thompson).

In the film's opening sequence, the camera bores in on an extreme close-up of Jack Stanton shaking voters' hands. A campaign insider expresses his total awe of Stanton's skills:

> You know, I've seen him do it a million times now. But I can't tell you how he does it, Henry. The right-hand part . . . I can tell you a lot about what he does with his left hand, though. He's a genius with it. He might put that left hand up on your elbow, or up your biceps, like he's doing now. A very basic move! He's interested in you; he's honored to meet you. . . . If he doesn't know you that well and wants to share something emotional with you, he'll lock you in a two-hander.

Primary Colors is another Hollywood film that seeks to expose the hegemony of technique and style in the modern campaign.

Yet, to its credit, *Primary Colors* seeks to be more than just an attack on political image-making. At its core, the film is a morality tale: it is the story of the temptation of a political innocent, Henry Burton (Adrian Lester), the grandson of a noteworthy civil rights leader. Henry joins the campaign and is cautioned "not to get burned" or tainted by the process.

The docudrama contrasts contemporary electoral politics with a better past before the campaign professionals took control. When Susan asks, "So, why are you here?" Henry replies:

> I was always curious about how it'd be to work for someone who actually cares

about . . . I mean, it couldn't always have been the way it is now. It must have been very different when my grandfather was alive. Hey, you were there. You had Kennedy. I didn't. I've never heard a President use words like "destiny" and "sacrifice" without thinking "Bullshit!" And . . . okay, maybe it was bullshit with Kennedy, too, but people believed it. And, I guess, that's what I want. I want to believe it. I want to be part of something that's history.

The older staffers on the Stanton campaign refer wistfully to the youthful idealism of their involvement in the antiwar 1972 George McGovern campaign. Media-dominated contemporary politics, in contrast, is portrayed as if something is missing, as if something important has been stolen from the people.

In two important ways, *Primary Colors* transcends the genre of the Hollywood campaign film. First, it does not portray the campaign elite as omniscient: instead, Stanton's handlers are often shown to be flying by the seat of their pants, reacting to events in a frantic effort to put out political fires. Second, the filmmakers do not paint the modern campaign as all-evil. Instead, they present a more nuanced and ambiguous assessment, offering the pragmatic argument that moral compromise may, at times, be necessary in the service of a greater good (in the film's case, the election of the one candidate who has a genuine concern and empathy for the people living on the fringes of American society). The film even concludes, at President Stanton's inauguration, on a guarded note of optimism.

This ambivalent attitude toward Stanton and the modern campaign is established in one of the film's early scenes. The governor is at an adult reading program, intently listening to the tales of former illiterates. He seems to be a man of great sensitivity: his listening skills and his commitment to fight for the forgotten are quite evident—even if he is a scamp who sleeps with their teacher and fabricates the story of how his Uncle Charlie was awarded a Medal of Honor only to return home and refuse jobs because he could not read.

There is something genuinely human and caring about Stanton. He and his southern compatriots get teary-eyed in an alcohol-drenched "Momma-thon" where each pays emotional tribute to the sacrifices of his mother. Stanton invites the homeless to Thanksgiving dinner at the governor's mansion. In the midst of the political firestorm created by the sensationalist Gennifer Flowers–like charges of a past extramarital relationship, Stanton is found sitting alone in a Krispy Kreme donut shop, expressing real concern for the counterman who works twelve-hour shifts at $5.25 an hour but cannot obtain health insurance. As Henry sums it up when his girlfriend accuses him of selling out: "I think this guy [Stanton] could be the real thing."

Primary Colors has been attacked for being soft at its core, for being gentler than the novel on which it was based. Critics charge that Nichols and May are liberals who have chosen to portray the story of Clinton's transgressions and national emergence in a favorable light. A review in the liberal *San Francisco Chronicle* argues that the movie "emerges as a sneaky Clinton apologia" (LaSalle). Indeed, the film *is* less harsh on its main characters than was Klein's novel. *The Houston Chronicle*'s Lynda Gorov interviewed director Mike Nichols and reported that the director "scoffs at charges that he toned down the movie," which he insists is a work of fiction. Yet, she reports that Nichols was "adamant about wanting the Clintons to understand that *Primary Colors* is a love letter to them rather than hate mail." As Nichols himself stated: "I hope they [the First Family] know how much the movie loves them and admires them and feels for them" (Gorov).

But it would be a disservice to *Primary Colors* to view the movie solely as an apologia for Clinton. Rather, it is a cinematic essay that asks the perennial question: Can service in politics, in this case a national campaign, be honorable given the pressures for ethical and moral compromise?

Stanton's advisers buckle under the pressures of the campaign. Stanton's staff initiate preemptive action so that their candidate will not "get trapped like Hart," a reference to how news stories on Gary Hart's extramarital fling with Miami model Donna Rice forced him to withdraw from the 1988 Democratic race. Stanton's wife Susan makes the strategic decision to call in "dust buster" Libby Holden (Kathy Bates) to clean up the potentially harmful detritus of Stanton's past before the media seize on it. Electronic surveillance and physical intimidation are among the unsavory and unscrupulous weapons in Libby's arsenal—all used for the allegedly noble purpose of electing Jack Stanton. Even Libby, who fondly remembers the idealism of her involvement in the McGovern movement, has come to recognize the harsh, cold realities of politics in the 1990s.

Ultimately, the Stantons flunk Libby's ethical "limbo" test ("How low can you go?") when they discuss a plan to undermine the presidential candidacy of Governor Fred Picker, the last remaining obstacle on the road to Stanton's nomination. Picker is presented as a man of honor and decency—and is played wonderfully by Larry Hagman, contrary to his J.R. Ewing *Dallas* stock type. The Stantons discuss the means by which the campaign will leak to the press evidence that will point to Governor Picker's past use of cocaine and a possible homosexual relationship. Libby objects that such personal information is irrelevant; she appeals to the idealistic activism they shared in the past, when they were out to change politics. Susan Stanton replies: "We were young. We didn't know how the world worked." Susan also argues for the virtue of using the information to prevent Picker from winning the Democratic nomination rather than risking the possibility that the Republicans will get hold of the information and deny a Picker-led Democratic ticket any chance of winning the White House in the fall.

Disillusioned and despondent, and suffering a history of mental problems, Libby kills herself. The act jars Henry, who is finally cognizant of what he has become. (He had even stooped so low as to help intimidate a good man, the father of a pregnant girl with whom Stanton slept). Henry tells Stanton that he is resigning from the campaign.

But, much to the film's credit, there is no simple "wrap" in which Henry reclaims his moral virtue by triumphantly walking away from the campaign. Instead, it is Stanton who is allowed to make the closing argument in the film, defending the necessity of deception, image-making, and "hardball" tactics: "This is the price you pay to lead. You don't think Abraham Lincoln was a whore before he was a President? He had to tell his little stories and then smile his shit-eating, backcountry grin. And he did it just so that one day he would have the opportunity to stand before the nation and appeal to the better angels of our nature." In the film's ambivalent assessment of modern politics, then, even the questions of Henry's morality and relationship to the campaign are not neatly resolved. The closing scene of the film shows Henry dressed for the inaugural ball. We are not sure if he has taken his leave from the Stanton campaign (now the Stanton administration) or not.

WHAT PRIMARY COLORS IS MISSING

In its parallel story, *Primary Colors* presents a partial and misleading account of the reasons that underlay Bill Clinton's rise, fall, and rebound in 1992. The film focuses on the manipulations of the Stanton/Clinton staff. It totally neglects the most basic reason for Clinton's appeal—the broad policy orientations that Clinton and American voters shared in 1992.

Voters and issues are virtually nonexistent in the account presented by *Primary Colors*. On the few occasions that it does not slight voters, the film takes a pejorative view of them. Customers in a restaurant are shown watching the Stantons appear on *60 Minutes,* just days before the crucial New Hampshire primary, to respond to the furor over allegations of Jack's philandering. What are the viewers' concerns? Nichols's film suggests that American citizens responded only to the couple's visual appearance, including the cut of Susan's hair!

Of course, the Clintons' dramatic, post–Super Bowl appearance on CBS's *60 Minutes* was a masterstroke. Bill and Hillary sat before a fire, side by side, while Bill denied having a twelve-year affair with Gennifer Flowers. But, as great a media manipulation as it was,[5] without Clinton's already established appeal as a middle-class-oriented Democrat, the television appearance would not have been enough to salvage his strong second-place finish in New Hampshire.

To a great degree, Bill Clinton was able to survive the Gennifer Flowers firestorm because he had already defined his candidacy in a way that appealed to voters. He ran as a New Democrat, an alternative to his more left-leaning primary opponents and the failed Democratic candidacies of the recent past: George McGovern, Walter Mondale, and Michael Dukakis. His moderation offered voters, especially middle-class voters, a preferable alternative to the candidacies of Iowa senator Tom Harkin and former California governor Jerry Brown, candidates who embraced a more strident, class-conflict orientation.[6]

Director Mike Nichols's film contains only two very brief hints of Clinton-Stanton's moderation on the issues; even then, it does not portray this moderation as having anything to do with his success. In a Democratic presidential debate, Stanton talks of the need to lower deficits. But even here, Nichols portrays Stanton's success as the result of personal imagery—that he appeared decisive and showed strong emotion, actions that helped humanize him to the TV audience. Similarly, when Stanton appears before a group of union workers at a closed factory in Portsmouth, New Hampshire, he gains their enthusiastic applause when he tells them that someone must tell them the truth: that "muscle jobs" have been lost to low-wage nations overseas, that the factory will not reopen, and that the way to economic security is by competing through education. Once again, it is Stanton's gutsy personal style, more than the substance of his message, which is seen as the reason for the audience's approving response.

In contrast with this cinematic explanation, Clinton's substantive message was very much at the root of his national emergence. From the very beginning of the primary season, Clinton targeted party moderates and the middle class, not the party's liberals and the poor. Clinton differed from his more liberal Democratic opponents in his support of the death penalty, his promise of a tax cut for the middle class, and his vow to impose a two-year limit on welfare ("to end welfare as we know it"). During the campaign, his proposed national health program was pitched as a plan that would help middle-class citizens who faced the daunting prospects of the loss of health coverage when they switched jobs.

Clinton's New Democratic orientation was no mere campaign façade or bit of image-making. His philosophy of governance lay in the predominantly southern Democratic Leadership Council (DLC) that Clinton had chaired, an organization dedicated to steering the Democratic Party back to a more winning, moderate, and less ideologically liberal position.[7] Throughout the primary season, Clinton reiterated the policy positions that he and the DLC had been taking for a number of years (Lipset 13–14).

Clinton saw great political advantage in separating himself from liberal orthodoxy and from traditional liberal Democratic constituencies. At a progressive conference dominated by labor unions, he refused to promise that he would lead the effort to repeal the right-to-work provisions of the Taft-Hartley Act. At a conference of The Rainbow Coalition, an organization cofounded by Jesse Jackson, Clinton criticized rap-singer Sister Souljah for her remarks that blacks should take a week off from killing each other and kill whites instead. Throughout the primary campaign, Clinton kept his distance from Jackson. Clinton would not let himself be portrayed, as Republicans had portrayed Walter Mondale in 1984, as being too closely allied with liberal "special interests," including organized labor. Nor would he allow himself to be tagged as a "liberal," the label that the Republicans had used so effectively to defeat Michael Dukakis in 1988.

Instead, Clinton's general political orientation was blatantly obvious from the very beginning of his 1992 presidential effort. In his basic New Hampshire TV ad, Clinton explained that his "plan" to get the economy moving again "starts with a tax cut for the middle class." His closing line in the ad left no doubt as to just whom the spot targeted: "Together we can put government back on the side of the forgotten middle class and restore the American dream." This was the message that was the key to Bill Clinton's emergence in 1992. Yet, *Primary Colors* nowhere mentions the candidate's New Democratic or middle-class issue orientation.

After the New Hampshire primary, the Democratic race essentially became a two-candidate affair between Clinton and former Massachusetts Senator Paul Tsongas, the New Hampshire winner. Tsongas ran as a nonpolitician who would tell the truths about the sacrifices necessary for deficit reduction. But it was just this issue orientation that ultimately allowed Clinton to defeat Tsongas. In the eyes of the voters, especially voters in the Democratic primaries, Tsongas was on the "wrong" side of a key issue by having even suggested cuts in a program as important as Social Security.

Primary Colors, however, chooses to portray its parallel Clinton-Tsongas story only as the triumph of demagoguery, expediency, and deception. Stanton caves in to the pressure from his campaign aides to "go negative" against Senator Lawrence Harris (his Tsongas-like opponent). Before an audience of elderly Jews in Florida, Stanton charges Harris with attempting to freeze the COLA (cost-of-living adjustment) in Social Security and in failing to stand by Israel. An apoplectic Harris phones Stanton on a call-in radio show and charges him with using scare tactics. Stanton, according to Harris, had misrepresented his campaign booklet promise to "study a freeze of cost of living [COLA] adjustments" as a proposal to cut the COLA. After Harris suffers a heart attack, a rueful Stanton confesses to his aides that "he's [Harris is] right about the damned issues."

In the real-world campaign, the two leading Democrats more sharply defined their differences in the 1992 race after New Hampshire, when the campaign trail headed to the South for the Junior and Super Tuesday primaries. Clinton ads contrasted his middle-class-oriented prescriptions with the Republican-style "trickle-down economics" of Tsongas's blueprint, *A Call to Economic Arms*. Clinton ads used Tsongas's own words to castigate him for his promise to be "the best friend Wall Street ever had." Clinton also attacked Tsongas for endorsing nuclear power, for a proposed fifty-cent-a-gallon hike in the gas tax, and for advocating a reduction in the "capital gains tax for the rich" while opposing a tax cut for the middle class.

There was definitely more than a degree of demagoguery involved in Clinton's attacks on both the Israel and the Social Security issues. Tsongas's proposed cuts in Social Security were much narrower than the Clinton ads made them out to be, especially as Tsongas averred that he was "looking at" reducing benefits only for retirees with incomes over $125,000. Yet, the Clinton attacks on Tsongas's plan for Social Security were not pure demagoguery; they contained more than a nugget of truth. Florida's elderly did not like the prospects of cuts, even in the COLA; they wanted a president who would protect benefits and not set a precedent for cutting back Social Security gains.

Survey analysis by political scientist Larry Bartels has documented that voters learn much about candidates and their ideologies as the primary season progresses (Bartels 84–88). Even when voters do not quite learn about candidates' stances on specific issues, they do become more knowledgeable about candidates' general issue dispositions. In 1992, voter cognizance of the general issue dispositions of the candidates helps to explain why, in primary after primary, Tsongas drew very little support from lesser-educated, blue-collar voters and African Americans—those people least financially able to bear the benefit freezes and sacrifices proposed by Tsongas.[8] Tsongas came up short with traditional Democratic constituencies, including the elderly, who wanted to defend traditional and important benefit programs.

THE WAR ROOM: *A PARTIAL REALITY*

The War Room, the Academy Award–nominated documentary directed by D.A. Pennebaker and Chris Hegedus, similarly fails to record the issue basis of Clinton's successful candidacy. R.J. Cutler[9] and Wendy Ettinger (who, with Frazer Pennebaker, produced the film) came up with the initial concept for the project and recruited noteworthy documentarian D.A. Pennebaker, whose association lent the project further credibility, especially with cinema cognoscenti.

Pennebaker had worked on *Primary* (1960), the cinema vérité account of the John F. Kennedy–Hubert Humphrey square off in the crucial 1960 Wisconsin Democratic primary. *Primary* was a political classic, affording one of the first important looks inside the workings of a modern national campaign. It used a "direct cinema" approach that Pennebaker would again employ in filming *The War Room*. Over the years, Pennebaker, often working with his wife Hegedus, gained critical acclaim for their opus of documentary work, which even includes such "rocumentaries" as *Don't Look Back* (1967), a profile of Bob Dylan during his 1965 concert tour of England; *Monterey Pop* (1968); and *Searching for Jimi Hendrix* (1999).

In crucial ways, documentaries are highly subjective, even emotional, interpretations of events. The documentarian constructs a highly interpretative work through the processes of selection, reduction, and emphasis. Contrary to popular belief, the camera does not really afford the viewer "the best seat in the house"; instead, the viewer is presented a much-reduced, edited, and highly selected version of actual events.

The War Room presents a simple thesis, documenting the importance of campaign manager James Carville, communications director George Stephanopoulos, and other media-savvy campaign operators to Bill Clinton's 1992 presidential victory. Carville, Stephanopoulos, and other campaign advisers are presented as masters of "spin," the all-important political art of getting the media to interpret events in ways favorable to their candidate. Spin, according to the film, is what wins contemporary campaigns.

The film presents a seemingly ceaseless succession of efforts at spin and media control. Clinton tries to get reporters to downplay the Gennifer Flowers charges; he observes that it is a "sad" day when the mainstream media has pursued an item first printed in a tabloid paper "like *The Star*"—which paid

Flowers for her story. Carville excoriates reporters for their focus on how Clinton evaded the draft, lamenting to a *Washington Post* reporter: "Every time somebody farts the word 'draft' it's on the front page of the papers." He urges reporters to give greater attention to the Republican record on jobs and education, which he says are the real issues about which Americans care. Stephanopoulos and media adviser Mandy Grunwald try to persuade the press to portray H. Ross Perot's withdrawal from the race[10] as a momentum-builder for Clinton. Campaign strategist Mickey Kantor points to good media coverage that can be obtained by convincing a number of Perot aides to announce for Clinton. Later in the film, Stephanopoulos is even seen on the phone, cajoling and threatening the caller not to air the unsubstantiated allegations that Clinton fathered a black child: "Think of yourself. I guarantee you, if you do this, you'll never work in Democratic politics . . . [and if you hold back on the story] you'll have a campaign who understands that in difficult times you did something right."

What matters in candidate debates? Of course, according to *The War Room*, it is not so much what is said in the exchange itself but the postdebate spin put on the event. Stephanopoulos sets forth the uniform postdebate message that all Clinton campaign operatives will repeat to reporters: "Bush was on the defensive." Stephanopoulos is in such a rush to get to the postdebate media room that he will not even listen to the candidates' closing statements but instead must have a summary relayed to him by cellular phone. What is most important? As Clinton aides phrase it, it is to "be there first" and to "be there swinging."

The film also shows Republican Mary Matalin (who will later marry James Carville!) similarly attempt to spin the press by arguing that Clinton's inconsistencies in explaining his past antiwar activities are part of the larger story of Clinton's untrustworthiness. Both parties engage in spin, and *The War Room* leaves the impression that the Democrats won in 1992 only because their spindoctors were more adept at the job!

Technological sophistication is also essential to the modern campaign. The Clinton elite learned from the failures of the Dukakis 1988 campaign to immediately reply to his opponents' charges. Indeed, the Clinton campaign became famous for its instant response to any attack. During a conference call, Grunwald, Carville, Stephanopoulos, and pollster Stan Greenberg create an ad in response to Republican attacks; according to the session's participants, this is done in less than a half hour. Alternative scripts for the ad are tested before a focus group, and the modified ad is ready to air the next day.

The War Room dwells on the actions of campaign elites. This is a legitimate focus for a political documentary. But the cost of doing so is that the film presents elections as if they are about little more than elite strategy and professional image-making. *The War Room* even presents the trite predebate shot of the candidate testing alternative neckties before the camera.

As was the case with *Primary Colors, The War Room* fails to document the role played by issues in 1992. The film encapsulates the New Hampshire primary story with a quick cameo of Clinton's televised response to the Gennifer Flowers allegations quickly followed by a clip of his early election-day declaration that he is the "comeback kid," a skillful ploy that effectively shaped the news coverage of the New Hampshire results that evening and the next day. The documentary then cuts to a montage of newspaper headlines reporting Clinton victories in Florida, the South, and the Midwest. As in *Primary Colors,* there is no mention of Clinton's moderate or New Democratic agenda and his appeal on the basis of substance.

In an attempt to highlight the importance of personal and media imagery, the documentary shows Clinton campaign advisers, including pollster Stan Greenberg, discussing tracking-poll results that reveal "extraordinary changes in favorability." Yet, Greenberg, in *Middle Class Dreams,* his own review of his polling data in 1992, clearly attributes Clinton's electoral success to his middle-class-oriented, family-oriented "people's" platform.[11] This, however, is neither the Greenberg thesis nor the Clinton appeal that *The War Room* chooses to reveal.

The War Room similarly portrays national party conventions solely as exercises of image manipulation. The film shows Clinton advisers vigorously debating which produces the better television effect: numerous handmade signs or a coordinated sea of manufactured Clinton-Gore signs. The modern televised convention is presented as a sea of manipulated images.

Yet, the modern national convention is about more than mere image-making; even in the staged-for-television national convention, the presidential candidate still must choose the themes and issues that will be communicated to voters. According to Samuel Popkin, national party conventions are information-rich spectacles that help voters to make up their minds (Popkin 15, 62, 110, 217–18). In scripting the convention and his speech, a candidate selects his priorities for the fall campaign. The televised convention allows viewers a chance not only to judge the nominee's platform but also to evaluate his place in the party; viewers get to see the social composition of the candidate's coalition and to judge the nominee by hearing what others say about him.

Clinton used the 1992 convention to further convey his New Democratic agenda and the message that the age of big government had come to an end. The entire convention was built around the theme of "A New Covenant" with its insistence on individual responsibility, strengthened families, and respect for the military (Maisel 671–98; Timmerman and Smith 78). *The War Room*, however, does not present even a glimpse of these convention messages. Instead, Pennebaker's parsimonious choice of convention segments includes only footage of Clinton and his aides walking through the hallway as Clinton climbs the stage for his triumphant acceptance speech. What brief bit of Clinton's acceptance speech does the filmmaker excerpt? Only Clinton's reference to his personal biography, his rise from Hope, Arkansas: "I still believed in a place called Hope." Totally omitted are those portions of the speech in which Clinton lays out his moderate New Covenant policy orientation. Nor does Pennebaker even include footage on Clinton's selection of Al Gore as his vice-presidential running mate. The choice of Gore, whose reputation at the time was that of a Tennessee centrist, was meant to reinforce the moderate image of the Democratic candidacy. The unusual selection of a ticket of two southerners was also meant to mark a break with Democratic practices of the past. Yet, all convention footage pointing to the thematic basis of Clinton's appeal was left on the cutting-room floor.

Harlan Jacobson, writing in *The New Democrat*, the magazine of the Democratic Leadership Council, has attacked the documentary for resting "on what is electoral folk wisdom: The public doesn't vote on the issues; it scores the battle." In *The War Room*, Clinton campaign staff members do on occasion blurt out a reference to the state of the economy under Bush, to health care, to abortion, and to the president's broken vow not to raise taxes. The film also concludes—at the very last—with a lingering glance at the famous handwritten sign above Carville's desk that includes the words "the economy, stupid." Unfortunately, this shot constitutes the longest reference to this vital issue in the entire film! Issues exist only at the periphery of *The War Room*; the documentary makers are preoccupied exclusively with the actions of campaign elites, not with the policy concerns of cither the people or the candidate.

The War Room suffers a bias of proximity; too close to their subjects, the filmmakers exaggerate their importance. Caught up in the heady atmosphere of the Clinton headquarters (just as Pennebaker had been similarly caught up in the energy and excitement of the JFK campaign in *Primary*), they can see nothing of greater importance than the actions taken by Carville and Stephanopoulos and others. The camera records action; good video stresses characters and personalities over abstractions. The policy preferences of the mass public are not easily captured by the documentarian's camera and are consequently devalued and ignored.

Through a Very Small Keyhole

The makers of *The War Room* boast of the unprecedented access they were allowed to the conversations and phone calls of the Clinton campaign; in reality, however, the film's fabled access was not that substantial. As one political columnist has observed, *The War Room* fails to provide an "authentic" look inside the Clinton campaign as the filmmakers' fabled access was really "limited to occasional hangout time" with "the campaign brain trust." The audience is "denied access to the back rooms where the big cigars were smoked and the deals cut" (Carroll). We do not see the formulation of strategy, only its implementation, and we only see small pieces of that" (Pollack).

The documentarians were afforded only the smallest of keyholes through which to view the campaign. They were denied access to Clinton and instead were granted only limited access—about forty hours of footage was filmed over just eight days—to the Little Rock war room (Borders.com).

It was only at the time of the Democratic National Convention that the documentary makers finally received approval for even the quite limited access they were afforded. Significantly, it was at that time that Pennebaker and Hegedus came on board the project. As a consequence, the documentary's coverage of Clinton's emergence in the Democratic primaries is most incomplete, with the filmmakers having to rely on news media highlights and other stock footage.

Shot on a paltry $140,000 (with the producers raising only an initial $75,000),[12] the making of *The War Room* was severely constrained by finances as well as by the limited nature of the access granted by the campaign hierarchy. These limits help to explain the most curious sequence in the documentary: the fairly large amount of time devoted to the trivial story of James Carville's efforts to get the press to pick up the story that Bush campaign paraphernalia is being produced in Brazil. Carville tries to convince a CBS contact that the footage, obtained from Brazilian television, will underscore Bush's insensitivity to the plight of the American workers. Ultimately, the campaign's efforts prove fruitless; the press will not run the story without any proof that it was Bush campaign officials who actually ordered the Brazilian-produced signs.

Why does this nonevent receive so much coverage when other, more significant events are not revealed in the documentary? Quite simply, the Brazil story unfolded during one of the few times when the camera was allowed fairly decent access to campaign discussions and phone calls—quite possibly as Clinton officials felt it was safe to permit the camera team to record such a minor episode.

BIAS AND PERSPECTIVE: AN OVERALL ASSESSMENT OF THE WAR ROOM

The War Room is a remarkable achievement and a victory for low-budget, independent filmmaking. The camera allows insightful close-ups, but the filmmakers never established a critical distance. As one reviewer recounts, Ettinger and Cutler decided to make the documentary as they "were greatly excited by the Clinton campaign" (Borders.com). Ettinger herself describes their fascination with Clinton: "Clinton was doing something that had never been done as long as I had been able to vote. It reminded everyone of the Kennedy era, in terms of intelligence and charisma."[13] Film critic Rita Kempley similarly observes: "The filmmakers seem to have fallen in love with their subjects: Carville, the showboating quipmeister, and Stephanopoulos, the quiet guy."

The War Room lacks the emotional detachment of such other political documentaries as *So You Want to Be President?* (1984), a *Frontline* television program that detailed the meteoric rise and fall of Gary Hart as he attempted to wrest the 1984 Democratic nomination from Walter Mondale. *So You Want to Be President?* is not a perfect film. It, too, suffers as it slights the role of issues in the modern campaign, attributing Hart's fall to Mondale's debate sound bite (his "Where's the beef?" caricature of Hart's "new ideas") and Hart's own campaign gaffes (with reporters, for instance, focusing on such trivial matters as why he had changed his name from Hartpence). But despite this failing, *So You Want to Be President?* was a balanced work that revealed both the strengths and weaknesses not just of the Hart campaign effort but also of a media- and money-dominated presidential nominating system. It was a piece of political commentary; in comparison, *The War Room* is political hagiography.

Is *The War Room* a successful documentary? In explaining why he allowed the filmmakers to record the campaign, George Stephanopoulos said: "I hope this film will show people how a modern campaign is run and the passion behind it, and that they'll come away with a little more respect for the political process."[14] By this standard, *The War Room* is a success; it reveals both the excitement of the presidential campaign and the commitment of Clinton's aides to the election of their candidate and to the ideals that his election embodies—a

marked contrast to the dispassionate detachment of the campaign professionals as portrayed in *The Candidate*. This is the same success that can be claimed
by Aaron Sorkin's *The West Wing*, the much-honored television series that com-
municates the same sense of excitement and the commitment of presidential
staff members who work long hours at an often quite difficult job.

But if the "ultimate test" for *The War Room* is whether it provides "a true
record of 1992" (Hagstrom 703), the film must be judged a failure. By slighting
the role played by voters and the importance of issues in 1992, the film presents a superficial view of the American political process.

THE SIN OF OMISSION AND THE HOLLYWOOD POLITICAL FILM

Primary Colors and *The War Room* are insightful films that capture the excitement, technological sophistication, and craftsmanship of the modern media
campaign. But as insightful as they are, they are reductionist portraits. Presidential elections are not determined as much by the strategic actions of media
elites as by candidates' themes and voter concerns. Martin Wattenberg's review
of the National Election Survey data from 1988 and 1992 reveals that issues
were the dynamic factor that explain "How Clinton Won and Dukakis Lost."

For all their drama and insight, the contemporary film critique of American national elections is myopic and cynical, misrepresenting the election process and performing a disservice to the American voter. A camera focused on
voters and their concerns—rather than one tracked so narrowly on the conversations and actions of campaign elites—would have given a much different
answer to the questions: "Why did Clinton win in 1992?" and "Does American
democracy work?"

NOTES

1. See Campbell, et al., *The American Voter*. For a discussion of the "paradigm" formed
by TAV and its progeny, see Pomper, "The Impact of *The American Voter* on Political
Science."

2. Key's critics challenged his reliance on recall data, as respondents could suffer
selective memory in explaining why they voted as they did (Niemi and Weisberg 165–
66). Key also failed to discover whether citizens met the strict criteria for issue voting set
forth in *The American Voter* (Margolis 116–17). Key was not able to produce data, for
instance, that documented that voters cared deeply about the issues that Key claimed
influenced their votes.

3. See Nie, et al., *The Changing American Voter;* Pomper, "From Confusion to Clarity:

Issues and American Voters, 1952–1968," 425–28; and Pomper, *Voters' Choice.* For a review of the changing debate over issue voting, see Levine, *Presidential Campaigns and Elections: Issues and Images in the Media Age,* 77–108.

4. Studies of 1992 and 1996 continued to document the influence of issues on the voting decision. See, in particular, Abramson, et al., *Change and Continuity in the 1992 Elections* and Abramson, et al., *Change and Continuity in the 1996 and 1998 Elections.* Issues, however, were less of a clear influence in 2000 (Frankovic and McDermott, esp. 86–91).

5. In the film, the falsity of the TV image is conveyed as Susan immediately drops Jack Stanton's hand the instant the cameras are turned off.

6. Iowa's Tom Harkin promised a return to the old-fashioned, liberal traditions of the Democratic Party, including the virtues of big government as seen in Franklin Roosevelt's New Deal. Jerry Brown and his "Take Back America" rhetoric stressed a populist crusade against the hold of corporate elites on American politics. Clinton, in contrast, constantly emphasized policies, including tax relief, for the forgotten middle class. Clinton was not promising radical change but only those changes that would conserve the position of a besieged middle class. In the later primaries, Clinton strongly emphasized the policy differences between himself and Brown, who remained in the race and offered the only alternative for Democrats hoping to stop a Clinton nomination. Clinton ads attacked the unfairness and regressivity of Brown's proposed 13 percent flat tax and the havoc that such a tax change might wreak on the financing of Social Security. See Kolbert 68; Levine 252–53, 260.

7. Clinton's middle-class and moderate orientations were genuine. As governor of Arkansas, he headed the Democratic Leadership Council. The DLC was a group of more moderate or centrist Democrats, predominantly from the South, who attempted to steer the party away from what they saw to be the electorally disastrous consequences of the big-government liberal orthodoxy of the McGovern, Mondale, and Dukakis programs. See Hale, "A Different Kind of Democrat: Bill Clinton, the DLC, and the Construction of a New Party Identity."

8. For a profile of Tsongas and Clinton voters in various state races, see the exit-poll results that accompanied the following *New York Times* stories: Clymer, "Messages of Warning to Bush and of Hope for Democrats"; Rosenbaum, "Surveys Indicate Top Candidates Are Vulnerable" and "With Clinton Surging, Party Splits on Next Step."

9. Cutler would later direct *A Perfect Candidate,* a documentary on the brutal 1994 Chuck Robb–Oliver North Senate race in Virginia.

10. Later in the fall, Perot would decide to reenter the race.

11. According to Greenberg, the Democrats suffered their 1994 mid-term debacle in congressional elections as Clinton, in his first two years in office, drifted from his New Democratic roots and, as a result, was perceived by voters as a cultural liberal. See two works by Greenberg: *Middle Class Dreams: The Politics and Power of the New American Majority* and "Popularizing Progressive Politics," 288–89.

12. Borders.com's "The War Room" refers to "a shoestring budget" of $75,000. Ettinger's reference to $75,000 is cited by Karlin, who estimates the costs of the finished film at $350,000. Whatever its shortcomings, *The War Room* represents quite an achievement for low-budget filmmaking.

13. Wendy Ettinger to Phillip Weiss of the *New York Observer* as quoted by Borders.com's "The War Room."

14. Stephanopoulos, quoted by Karlin, "Filming Inside Clinton's Camp."

WORKS CITED

Abramson, Paul R., John H. Aldrich, and David W. Rohde. *Change and Continuity in the 1992 Elections.* Rev. ed. Washington, D.C.: CQ Press, 1995.

———. *Change and Continuity in the 1996 and 1998 Elections.* Washington, D.C.: CQ Press, 1999.

Bartels, Larry M. *Presidential Primaries and the Dynamics of Public Choice.* Princeton: Princeton University Press, 1988.

Borders.com. Description of *The War Room.* (6 August 2000).

Campbell, Angus, Philip E. Converse, Warren E. Miller, and Donald E. Stokes. *The American Voter.* New York: John Wiley, 1960.

Carroll, Jerry. "*The War Room*: A Peek Behind the Campaign Curtain." *San Francisco Chronicle,* 26 December 1993.

Clymer, Adam. "Messages of Warning to Bush and of Hope for Democrats." *New York Times,* 5 March 1992.

Elshtain, Jean Bethke. "Issues and Themes in the 1988 Campaign." In *The Elections of 1988,* edited by Michael Nelson, 111–26. Washington, D.C.: CQ Press, 1989.

Fiorina, Morris P. *Retrospective Voting in American National Elections.* New Haven: Yale University Press, 1981.

Frankovic, Kathleen A., and Monika L. McDermott. "Public Opinion in the 2000 Election: The Ambivalent Electorate." In *The Election of 2000,* edited by Gerald M. Pomper, 73–91. New York: Chatham House/Seven Bridges, 2001.

Gorov, Lynda. "Is 'Colors' About Clinton?" *Houston Chronicle,* 18 May 1998.

Greenberg, Stanley B. *Middle Class Dreams: The Politics and Power of the New American Majority.* New Haven: Yale University Press, 1996.

———. "Popularizing Progressive Politics." In *The New Majority: Toward a Popular Progressive Politics,* edited by Stanley B. Greenberg and Theda Skocpol, 288–89. New Haven: Yale University Press, 1997.

Hagstrom, Jerry. "So Now It Can Be Told." *National Journal,* 20 March 1993, 703.

Hale, John F. "A Different Kind of Democrat: Bill Clinton, the DLC, and the Construction of a New Party Identity." Paper presented at the annual meeting of the American Political Science Association, Washington, D.C., 2–5 September 1993.

———. "The Making of the New Democrats." *Political Science Quarterly* 110 (1995): 207–32.

Jacobson, Harlan. "*The War Room*: The 1992 Campaign Film Gives Credit Where Credit Is Due." *The New Democrat,* November 1993, 27.

Karlin, Susan. "Filming Inside Clinton's Camp." *New York Times,* 31 January 1993.

Kempley, Rita. "*The War Room*: A Peek at the Men Behind the Curtain." *Washington Post,* 12 November 1993.

Key, V.O., Jr. *The Responsible Electorate.* New York: Vintage, 1966.

Kolbert, Elizabeth. "Test-Marketing a President." *New York Times Magazine*, 30 August 1992.

LaSalle, Mick. "Shades of Clinton's Colors: Film Comes Across as Good-Natured." *San Francisco Chronicle*, 11 September 1998.

Levine, Myron A. *Presidential Campaigns and Elections: Issues and Images in the Media Age*. 2nd ed. Itasca, Illinois: Peacock, 1995.

Lipset, Seymour Martin. "The Significance of the 1992 Election." *PS: Political Science and Politics* (March 1993): 13–14.

Maisel, L. Sandy. "The Platform-Writing Process: Candidate-Centered Platforms in 1992." *Political Science Quarterly* 108 (1993–1994): 671–98.

Margolis, Michael. "From Confusion to Confusion: Issues and Voters, 1952–1972." In *Parties and Elections in an Anti-Party Age*, edited by Jeff Fishel. Bloomington: University of Indiana Press, 1978.

McCarthy, Todd. "The War Room." *Daily Variety*, 1 October 1993.

Miller, Arthur H., and Warren E. Miller. "Issues, Candidates, and Partisan Divisions in the 1972 American Presidential Election." *British Journal of Political Science* 5 (1975): 393–431.

Miller, Warren E., and Teresa E. Levitin. *Leadership and Change: The New Politics and the American Electorate*. Cambridge, Massachusetts: Winthrop, 1976.

Nie, Norman H., Sidney Verba, and John R. Petrocik. *The Changing American Voter*. Cambridge, Massachusetts: Harvard University Press, 1976.

Niemi, Richard G., and Herbert F. Weisberg, eds. *Controversies in American Voting Behavior*. San Francisco: W.H. Freeman, 1973.

Pollack, Joe. "Intriguing Style, Not Substance, of the Clinton Campaign." *St. Louis Post-Dispatch*, 14 January 1994.

Pomper, Gerald. "From Confusion to Clarity: Issues and American Voters, 1952–1968." *American Political Science Review* 66 (June 1972): 415–28.

———. "The Impact of *The American Voter* on Political Science." *Political Science Quarterly* 93 (1978).

———. *Voters' Choice*. New York: Dodd, Mead, 1975.

Popkin, Samuel L. *The Reasoning Voter*. Chicago: University of Chicago Press, 1991.

Rosenbaum, David E. "Surveys Indicate Top Candidates Are Vulnerable." *New York Times*, 12 March 1992.

Timmerman, David M., and Larry David Smith. "The 1992 Presidential Nominating Conventions: Cordial Concurrence Revisited." In *The Presidential Campaign: A Communication Perspective*, edited by Robert E. Denton Jr. Westport, Connecticut: Praeger, 1994.

Wattenberg, Martin P. "How Clinton Won and Dukakis Lost: Candidates As Dynamic Factors in U.S. Presidential Elections." Paper presented at the annual meeting of the American Political Science Association, Washington, D.C., 2–3 September 1993.

———. "Theories of Voting." In *Political, Parties, Campaigns, and Elections*, edited by Robert E. DiClerico. Upper Saddle River, New Jersey: Prentice-Hall, 2000.

"With Clinton Surging, Party Splits on Next Step," *New York Times*, 9 April 1992.

Luc Herman

Bestowing Knighthood

The Visual Aspects of
Bill Clinton's Camelot Legacy

John F. Kennedy and the first lady
preside over a Camelot White
House.

John F. Kennedy's presidential style continues to be epitomized by Camelot.
When it comes to appointing roles in the Camelot musical as it was performed
in the Kennedy White House, one might say that JFK was simultaneously King
Arthur *and* the Knights of the Round Table. He was the man of reason who
understood intricate situations and could make practical decisions, but he was
also young and forever growing, an idealist warrior—the so-called "knight in
shining armor"—whose every move was a stepping-stone in a policy that would
receive its fulfillment in his second term. Kennedy himself was allegedly pro-
jecting some major decisions, such as a potential withdrawal from Vietnam,[1]
onto his second term, but this scenario of growth was mainly concocted by the
early hagiographers, who interpret his murder in Dallas as a result of their
knight seeking out danger in order to contain it for the benefit of his country.
"Danger" in this application of the Camelot narrative referred both to the anti-

Kennedy feeling that was taking shape in certain sections of the Texas population and to a conflict within the Texas Democratic Party itself.

The American public was only too eager to accept this larger-than-life scenario, not least because the shock of the murder—combined with the grandness of the funeral rites—had, as Thomas Brown puts it, "humanized [JFK], yet elevated him above the ordinary mass of politicians and public figures" (Brown 3). The Camelot metaphor proved a perfect fit for the grandeur of the occasion. The growing suspicions surrounding the assassination as well as the possible involvement of federal and other officials reinforced the Camelot image even more, since Kennedy thus became a victim of the strife in his own castle. Instead of overcoming the danger he so bravely set out to eradicate, JFK fell at the hands of traitors who had conspired against him. With his blockbuster *JFK*, which came out late in the fall of 1991, filmmaker Oliver Stone tapped into this Arthurian vein and, in doing so, made it possible for Bill Clinton to ride a new wave of Kennedy popularity in his 1992 presidential campaign. In the following pages, Clinton's use of Stone's movie will be considered in conjunction with the historical documents the Clinton campaign used to develop the JFK angle for its candidate.

THE IMPORTANCE OF JFK

With his movie *JFK*, Oliver Stone turned the assassination game into a contest for cultural authority. The questions indeed were: who does the public think is speaking the truth? who appears as the most knowledgeable expert? and how does this person manage to acquire this kind of status? As Barbie Zelizer has argued, at least three sets of players have tried to enforce their version of the facts: the journalists (foremost among them Dan Rather of CBS); the independent critics (including Jim Marrs, Mark Lane, and especially Carl Oglesby, who is a prominent member of the Assassination Information Bureau); and the historians (Thomas Reeves, Richard Posner, and others), who have appropriated segments of the assassination tale in their wide-ranging representations of the historical record. Alongside these groups there have always been the writers and moviemakers, who have most often translated and probably also enhanced the popular Camelot narrative and its tragic conclusion on 22 November 1963, but who have made no claim to factual authenticity—Don DeLillo, for example, renders this attitude explicit in an author's note appended to his best-selling novel, *Libra* (1988).

Unlike the writers and moviemakers who had come before him, Oliver Stone entered the assassination game with "stature, prestige, media interest and access, finances, proven celebrity talent" (Zelizer 202), all assets in his bid for authority, a bid which rapidly came to the surface when he claimed he was acting as a historian, and not merely as an entertainer. As is well known, Stone maintains that the Kennedy assassination was the work of a group of high-ranking officials in the CIA and the FBI. Because they anticipated that Kennedy was going to pull out of Vietnam and also going to strike a deal with communism, they organized a so-called *coup d'état* for the benefit of their allies in the military-industrial complex—the latter term being posited through Eisenhower in the opening segment of the movie. As Christopher Sharrett put it early on, the Jim Garrison thesis taken up by Stone "undermines the very notion of constituency-based, representative democracy" (Sharrett 11), and as a result of this encompassing—and perhaps even outrageous—message, *JFK* did not fail to create a stir. In *Oliver Stone's USA,* edited by Robert Brent Toplin, a collection published nearly a decade after the Kennedy movie came out, Michael L. Kurtz still faults Stone for his "gross historical errors" (Kurtz 169), ranging from factual inaccuracies to the wide-ranging conspiracy thesis and including his "hagiographic depiction of John F. Kennedy as a champion of truth, justice, and peace" (Kurtz 172). However, Kurtz also credits the filmmaker for the decisive impact his movie had on the release of the official assassination records, which, for Kurtz, go a long way in showing that Stone was not totally off the mark with his explanation of the murder.

More important than the truth-value of this explanation was indeed the outcry the movie caused, especially in view of the presidential race that was going to take place in 1992. Stone succeeded in having his product of popular culture taken seriously as a vehicle of truth. The media followed his lead—one should perhaps say that Stone proved to be a perfect manipulator of the media—and together with him, Kennedy was all over the newspapers and television channels again at the end of 1991 and the beginning of 1992. Every talk-show host in the country requested Stone's appearance, and he honored quite a few of these invitations as part of what turned out to be a very successful promotional campaign for *JFK.* Stone's impact proved so big that other players in the contest for cultural authority with regard to the assassination felt they had to react in order to defend their position. In fact, as Kurtz has shown in great detail, some of them had already voiced their anger before the movie's official release date.

USING KENNEDY DESPITE STONE

Thanks to the conflict surrounding Stone that was fought out in the media, the key Kennedy TV clips from three decades earlier were shown over and over again. It almost seemed as if Kennedy was being marketed again, this time (given Stone's interpretation) as a commodity of subversion, as a product that gave every single American the possibility of doing something about the undemocratic control pervading society. In other words, early on in 1992, John F. Kennedy once more "held out a promise of change." This brief strand of Clinton campaign rhetoric suggests why his team strategically tapped into the suddenly revived vein of Kennedy popularity in order to multiply Clinton's own chances as the democratic contender for the White House. As Clinton's chief media consultant, Frank Greer, has indicated, JFK was indeed anything but the accidental hero of Clinton's race against George Bush.[2] Of course he might also have figured in the Clinton campaign if Stone had not made his movie—many politicians (Gary Hart perhaps most famously among them) have tried to invoke and even imitate JFK—but the controversy caused by Stone surely incited the Clinton people to increase their use of the former president. While there is no concrete evidence of the importance of Stone for the campaign, Clinton strategists Frank Greer and Mandy Grunwald must have had considered Stone's influence on the JFK image when they decided to look for visual materials that would concretize the link between their candidate and the former president.

Needless to say, they must first of all have weighed the exaggeration of Stone's conspiracy message against the extra points it might bring them in the polls, but probably the combination of the stir and the resulting popular perception of JFK as a democratic president slain by antidemocratic opponents must have been reason enough to use Kennedy once more in a Democratic campaign. The decision to ride the renewed Kennedy popularity must also have been taken in full awareness of the movie's many other controversial aspects. W.J.T. Mitchell, among others, has detailed the cinematic and ideological arguments that can be offered against Stone. His film can no doubt be regarded as an "unbearable tissue of clichés and stereotypes," not least because of Stone's portrayal of Jim Garrison "as a decent, normal family man whose domestic bliss is disturbed by a bunch of perverted, homosexual, rightwing plotters" (Mitchell 8). Exploiting the cliché is probably unavoidable if you want to drive home a point and your vehicle is a mainstream movie, but there are different ways of doing it. Thinking of Clinton's agenda concerning gay rights (resulting in an early proposal not to discriminate against gays and lesbians in the military), one wonders to what extent Stone's simultaneous evocation of American family values and homophobia affected (or should have affected) the campaign decision to play the Kennedy card. But, of course, the campaign team decided to go for it, and in retrospect one can safely say that the down-right coarseness of Stone's movie did not hurt Clinton one bit. In 1992, the gay community, in fact, became more and more hopeful about a Clinton presidency, so the Clinton-Stone link did not influence their judgment of the future president in any negative way. This attitude on the part of a special-interest group goes to show that Stone had succeeded in reducing his message to an easily digestible statement about federal involvement in the assassination.

One major reason for this success is Stone's unrestrained didacticism, which appears in a great many scenes, such as Jim Garrison's meeting with Mr. X at the National Mall in Washington; his long speech at the Clay Shaw trial in New Orleans; and also, in a less spectacular but even more pathetic way, in the scene where Garrison, seated on the front porch swing, explains to his children that he has to work late because he is trying to save America. Stone's manipulation of the spectator is not only a matter of the script; it is also very much an effect of montage—not just the speed with which Stone cuts from one image to the other but also the mixture of already existing footage with new scenes (which are sometimes hard to distinguish as such because they are in black and white and the image quality is not as good as it might be). All of these techniques overburden the spectators, undermine their critical powers, and make them susceptible to the thesis on offer.

Ironically, Stone's manipulation of the spectator works quite as oppressively as the control exerted by the state within the state that he is warning against, but apparently this paradox has not deterred the audience from buying the message. It takes a strong spectator to resist this director's stratagems and to create enough distance to call into doubt Stone's convictions. All in all, Stone's homophobia, his didacticism, and his glaring technical manipulation of the audience have easily been overridden by his vigorous reevocation of the Camelot legend, more particularly of the young hero slain by reactionary forces in his castle. Latching onto this narrative must therefore have seemed the logical thing to do for a Democratic candidate.

Finally, the lesson learned by Gary Hart must also have appealed to the Clinton team. JFK's heroic status was so strong as to negotiate all the negative revelations about his private life, which started to appear on a large scale in the media around the mid-1970s. Since the positive image was so deeply enshrined at the time the president's sexual infidelities came to light, it was not only able

Andy Sachs, Consolidated News Photos.

President John F. Kennedy passes the torch to a new generation.

to withstand this liability, but it even turned the flaw into a kind of virtue. Kennedy was such a stylish example of American political potency that it seemed almost logical that there might be other evidence of his virile style. The extramarital affairs might thus have functioned for the American public (male and female) as a concrete instance of the individual American's fantasy about his or her sexual resources. By virtue of JFK's status as a positive limit case in all other walks of life, this evaluation has in the long run transcended the negative moral judgments the affairs quite naturally evoked immediately after they were revealed. In Arthurian terms, one might even say that the tarnished blazon had become one more sign of true heroism. The downfall of Gary Hart has shown that this mechanism did not work for those who wished to walk in JFK's footsteps, and therefore Clinton strategists will have considered their politician's sex life before deciding on the Kennedy connection. It is difficult to say at this point exactly how much they knew, but it is abundantly clear that any doubts were overruled by the public perception of JFK in early 1992 and by the fact that they were able to concretize the JFK-Clinton connection with the help of historical materials.

FROM THE ARCHIVES: FILM FOOTAGE
AND A TELLING STILL PICTURE

The bridge for the Clinton-Kennedy connection is the footage of Clinton's visit as a teenager to the Kennedy White House on 26 July 1963. Just before his seventeenth birthday, Clinton was part of the Arkansas representation to Boys Nation, an annual visit to Washington by outstanding students sponsored by the American Legion. The group briefly met Kennedy in the Rose Garden of the White House. In 1992, during the preparation of the Democratic convention movie on Clinton, Chris Kepferle, a producer, and Frank Wear, a production assistant, were assigned by Greer and Grunwald to find a record of the meeting different from the picture they had received from Clinton early on in the campaign. After having learned the date of the meeting from the American Legion headquarters, they asked a Clinton supporter from Boston, Michael Casey, to go to the JFK Presidential Library to look at the film. Casey first saw the movie on 25 June 1992, and he was immediately aware of its campaign potential.

The American audience at large was first made aware of the footage during a biopic shown at the Democratic National Convention. In this brief campaign film, produced by Linda Bloodworth-Thomason and designed to avert the attention from anything that could be construed as an anti-American act on the part of its hero, Bill Clinton and his mother serve as frame narrators for the historical images in which JFK, after briefly taking the podium, is seen to go up to Clinton for a brief but steady handshake. The meeting took only four seconds on film, but in the biopic it is reproduced in slow-motion so that its effect could be stronger. Frank Greer (as quoted in Wilkie) commented that his candidate looked like "such a wholesome kid" (Wilkie 20).

Immediately after the footage of the meeting, Clinton's mother also mentions the snapshot taken of Bill and Jack at the time, which would become the central Kennedy reference in the rest of the 1992 campaign. The still picture, taken from an angle different from that of the motion picture footage, isolates the most important moment of the visit to the White House, and thus enhances the power of the clip. In the still picture, Kennedy and Clinton are seen to look each other in the eyes; Clinton, who slightly bows his head as a sign of respect, is clearly full of admiration for the president, while JFK looks upon the young man in front of him with a certain benevolence—no real interest, perhaps, but his facial expression is neutral enough to allow for positive interpretations. The president is standing tall, his handshake is strong, and in the back some bystanders are watching, which turns the scene into an even more enviable occasion.

In the context of a presidential race, Bill and Jack's eye contact does not fail to become effective. Seen against the background of the entire Kennedy campaign card, one may safely say that the picture even assumes the status of what (with a term borrowed from pragmatics) could be called a "performative": it performs an act through its mere existence. Irrespective of what actually went on so many years ago, irrespective of what was actually said, the presidential gaze becomes a sign of empowerment or—to catch the whole situation in Camelot terms—a sign of the knighthood Kennedy bestows on the young idealist in front of him. It is as if Kennedy were saying: "Bill, you must pull the country back together again when you grow up; you must lead when I'm gone." In the biopic, Clinton's mother reinforces the Camelot ritual by saying she knew upon his return from Washington that Bill was going to be in government. He had returned to Hope a different person, and so we are led to believe that what happened in Washington must have had a tremendous impact.

Two more points can be made about the footage. First of all, Clinton's own commentary on the clip underscores the mandate for future leadership. He says he happened to be in the front row and that JFK "just" came up to him because he was tall. The audience is obviously meant to realize that JFK came up to him because young Bill exuded the physical qualities of a leader—he was not just tall but also shining, having the charisma typical of a future leader. Secondly, Clinton's youth at the time of the visit handily confirmed the youthful energy he opposed to George Bush's alleged fatigue and occasional illness. Clinton's youth in the clip with Kennedy also indirectly, through association, signifies the youthful energy that was one of JFK's assets. As a result, and although they were separated by a good number of years, both Bill and Jack would be regarded as young and energetic warriors for the same good cause that is America.

All these strong effects of the clip and the picture cannot have been lost on the Clinton campaign team. Accordingly, they made the most of the two factual remainders of the Clinton visit to the White House. The picture especially was all over the Clinton commercials, and this doubtlessly contributed to his victory in 1992.

DEVELOPING THE KENNEDY REFERENCE?

Clinton's use of Kennedy was extended into the early days of his presidency. During the musical extravaganza on the eve of his inauguration, the organizers of the event screened two videoclips on a huge screen at the back of the stage; one of them was on Kennedy; the other one on Martin Luther King. During those first days in Washington, Clinton also paid a well-publicized visit to Kennedy's grave, just as Jim Garrison did in Stone's movie. There was no token African American present as in the movie, but coming at such a ritual moment, this visit certainly signified once more that JFK's political legacy was going to inspire Clinton's policies—or, to be slightly more pragmatic, the visit certainly made it seem as if this was going to happen, shrouding the upcoming presidency, as it were, in a cloak of political endeavor, creating expectations in order to gain momentum. Even more importantly, Clinton inserted a clear reference to Kennedy in his first State of the Union Address: "It has been too long—at least three decades—since a president has challenged the American people to join him in a great national march." "At least three decades" implies that Kennedy, according to Clinton, was the last American president to have challenged the American people and suggests that he, Clinton, wanted to model his plans on those of the man who knighted him in the Rose Garden of the White House.

All the examples of Clinton's use of Kennedy mentioned so far were successful. As has already been mentioned, there is a tradition of Democratic contenders trying to connect with JFK, and Clinton connected better than all of these, at least until the press started to turn the tables. This negative reaction started during his first year in office. In October 1993, Clinton understandably invited Richard Reeves for a two-and-a-half hour discussion of his *President Kennedy,* a dense account of the JFK White House. Jonathan Alter used the occasion in *Newsweek* to insist on the differences between the two presidents and closed his piece by submitting to Clinton Eleanor Roosevelt's advice to JFK: show a little less profile and a little more courage. And here is another early example from the mainstream press. Reflecting on the Paula Jones sexual harassment suit against the president, *Time's* Lance Morrow wrote in May 1994: "Bill Clinton possesses some of Kennedy's gifts—youth, energy, the most important job in the world. Clinton's problem may be that he learned a few wrong lessons from J.F.K. One better-left-unlearned text from the lout's side of Camelot might be the idea that a guy can get away with anything" (Morrow 60). Given the emphasis Clinton put on his Kennedy heritage in the 1992 campaign, this kind of sarcasm is probably inevitable.

On the basis of this early quotation, one can also easily see what was going to happen during the Monica Lewinsky crisis. As a result, Clinton's references to JFK became few and far between. He did not go as far as disavowing his king—there were occasions, such as an official event at the JFK library in Boston and the tragic death of John Kennedy Jr., that obliged him to confirm the link—but he and his advisers must have realized all too well that it had become difficult to score points with the public at large by evoking a sovereign whom he had come to resemble too much. Indeed, the libido parallel effectively put an end to the organized use of the Kennedy reference. As a result, the 1963 footage and picture assume their true proportions of marketing ploys. Kennedy only worked for Clinton as long as the latter was able to focus the media attention on a positive link between them.

Since this positive link was indebted to JFK's renewed popularity as a result of the Oliver Stone movie, Stone's fall from public grace during the second half of the first Clinton term further eroded the image. Allegedly after taking acid and watching Stone's 1994 film *Natural Born Killers*, two teenagers went on a rampage that led to two killings. When John Grisham, popular author of legal thrillers and a friend of one of the victims, decided to sue Stone, the latter lost much of his stature with the public at large—regardless of whether his film did indeed incite the teenagers to violence. If the JFK effect had not been worn off by then, it certainly took its definitive blow with this move by Grisham in early 1995. With the director of *JFK* in discredit and with Clinton's own philandering very much in the public eye, the president had no choice but to bury the connection with the king who knighted him as a teenager. But that connection did contribute to his win in the 1992 election, not least because the Clinton team decided to hit an American nerve—the JFK assassination—laid bare by the controversy surrounding a movie. As such, the 1992 presidential contest harbors a complex testimony to the manipulative power of the visual image. If Stone managed to manipulate his audience, then the JFK-Clinton materials redoubled that manipulation, not least because of the nostalgia evoked by the historical documents. Clinton paradoxically suggested innovation by a turn to the past, and it worked.[3]

NOTES

1. See Giglio 253–54 for a list of the statements that seemed to go in this direction.
2. See, for example, Wilkie.

3. Portions of this article were published earlier in *BELL* (Belgian Essays on Language and Literature). I am grateful to the editors for letting me use this material in a new and more visible context.

WORKS CITED

Alter, Jonathan. "Less Profile, More Courage." *Newsweek*, 1 November 1993, 4.

Brown, Thomas. *JFK: History of an Image*. Bloomington: Indiana University Press, 1988.

Giglio, James N. *The Presidency of John F. Kennedy*. Lawrence: University of Kansas Press, 1991.

Kurtz, Michael L. "Oliver Stone, *JFK*, and History." In *Oliver Stone's USA: Film, History, and Controversy*, edited by Robert Brent Toplin, 166–77. Lawrence: University of Kansas Press, 2000.

Mitchell, W.J.T. "Culture Wars." *London Review of Books*, 23 April 1992, 7–10.

Morrow, Lance. "Living in Virtual Reality." *Time*, 16 May 1994, 60.

Reeves, Thomas. *President Kennedy: Profile of Power*. New York: Simon and Schuster, 1993.

Sharrett, Christopher. "Debunking the Official History: The Conspiracy Theory in *JFK*." *Cineaste* 1 (1992): 11–14.

Wilkie, Curtis. "Retrieving a Political Past: Brief Film of 1963 Meeting With Kennedy Becomes Centerpiece of Clinton Pitch." *Boston Globe*, 13 August 1992, 20.

Zelizer, Barbie. *Covering the Body: The Kennedy Assassination, the Media and the Shaping of Collective Memory*. Chicago: University of Chicago Press, 1992.

David Haven Blake

HOLLYWOOD, IMPERSONATION, AND PRESIDENTIAL CELEBRITY IN THE 1990s

Sydney Ellen Wade (Annette Bening) is a lobbyist who becomes romantically involved with the world's most powerful and most famous widower in *The American President* (1995).

In Rob Reiner's film *The American President* (1995), the lobbyist Sydney Ellen Wade (Annette Bening) receives a phone call from the widower Andrew Shepherd (Michael Douglas), who also happens to be the president of the United States. Wade has been sitting in her sister's Washington apartment, bemoaning her embarrassing performance during a morning meeting at the White House. "I acted like a college freshman at a protest rally," she complains—and justly so, for not only had she accidentally insulted the president to his face, but later in a spirited display of resolve, she had briskly exited the Oval Office—only to discover that she was leaving by the wrong door. The president's evening phone call dramatically aggravates this embarrassment, for when she hears his voice, Wade assumes it is her friend Richard, to whom she had previously confessed her ordeals. "Oh, it's Andrew Shepherd," she sarcastically responds, "Yeah, you're hilarious Richard, you're just a regular riot." When the man on the other end insists that, no, he really is Andrew Shepherd, Wade mocks what she assumes is his juvenile impersonation game. "Well, I'm so glad you called," she informs the imposter, "because I forgot to tell you what a nice ass you have."

And then she hangs up. Whatever awkwardness Wade felt earlier in the day becomes minor when compared with her humiliation in learning that the impersonator she so confidently saw through was indeed the man he claimed to be.

The scene is important to the film on a number of levels: it establishes Shepherd's first nervous efforts to court a woman since the death of his wife, a courtship made particularly difficult by its coming from the isolated world of the Oval Office. More significantly, perhaps, Wade's repeated gaffes and indiscretions help characterize her as a female "Mr. Smith," Frank Capra's legendary senator (Jimmy Stewart) whose story Wade invokes throughout the film. Like Jefferson Smith, Wade is made to suffer a series of embarrassments before she evolves into a force passionate enough to reinvigorate the government—though compared to Smith's political naïveté, Wade comes off as hardened, cynical, and frankly unbelieving. Nonetheless, despite her background as a highly credentialed lobbyist, she is made to appear ridiculously combative and inexperienced when confronted with the masculine glamour of Shepherd's presidency. The phone call contributes to the film's larger pattern of humiliating this woman in front of her suitor before she can reclaim her dignity and, in the end, salvage the ideals of his presidency.

Even more, however, than issues of plot or characterization, the scene is valuable for its comic representation of presidential fame in the 1990s. In Wade's assumption that her friend was impersonating Shepherd, we have an important trope for the ways in which the president has become a celebrity, a man whose voice and image have such public currency that they are immediately recognizable in any context or setting. With its peculiar combination of social isolation and public ubiquity, the presidency generates legions of counterfeits that seem strangely more credible and realistic than the president himself. The film as a whole relentlessly affirms Shepherd's stable, physical identity, insisting along with its title character that the chief executive possesses a

Library of Congress.

Aaron Sorkin's model for Andrew Shepherd and Josiah Bartlet.

private, unmediated personality. The mistaken phone call suggests, however, that in a society saturated with the presidential image, the president himself can be simulated through imitation and masquerade. Having successfully asked the lobbyist to join him at a state dinner, Shepherd recommends that when his secretary calls with details for the evening, Wade should "give her the benefit of the doubt" and believe her when she states her name. The advice glosses over what this president wants to forget, that he is vulnerable to impersonation not because he is powerful but because he is famous.

The American President is not alone in its attraction to this motif, for through-out the White House comedies of the 1990s, we find an abundance of scenes involving the impersonation of the president. These range from momentary gags to larger, more extended considerations of the fragmented, variable nature of the president's public identity. Consider, for example, the film *My Fellow Americans* (1996), in which the two former presidents take refuge in the guise that they are simply entertainers hired to imitate their actual selves; or the opening of the film *Dave* (1993), which juxtaposes the president's arrival by helicopter on the White House lawn with the image of his counterfeit strad-dling a hog as part of a promotion for Durenberger Chevrolet; or Don Hedaya's performance throughout the movie *Dick* (1999), a performance so attuned to Richard Nixon's carriage and demeanor that one might say it actually rises to the level of caricature. All of these films join *The American President* in reflecting on the president as a cultural icon rather than as an expression of political agency. All represent the shrinking gap between the citizen and the spectator, the leader and the star, and politics and entertainment.

The prevalence of such scenes should not be surprising in the midst of a political culture that openly incorporates the acts of imitation and parody. Dana Carvey's impersonation of the elder George Bush—*for* the elder George Bush—suggests a world in which simulated presidents can have such popularity that they are virtually guaranteed the endorsement of authentic, political figures. This was not always the case. In 1962 White House aides did their best to dampen the public's enthusiasm for the record "First Family," which featured Vaughan Meader's uncanny impersonation of John F. Kennedy. Although Kennedy himself claimed to be amused by the recording, Arthur Schlesinger and Pierre Salinger worried about its high level of air play and worked hard convincing radio stations to strike the record from their play lists (Cull). Thirty years later, the Bush administration thought differently and invited Carvey to a public audience with the president. The event promised only political gains for the notoriously patrician Bush, who came off appearing slightly less defensive and slightly more populist than he had in his loss to Bill Clinton.

The acceptance of impersonation by the political establishment raises the larger question of who commands the public's interest in contemporary American society. Who lays claim to the people's affection in a heavily mediated age: the beleaguered politician or the transpartisan mimic? The culture has grown increasingly comfortable with this ontological puzzle over the last decades. In a move that would have shocked Franklin Roosevelt, whose White House had restricted all imitations of the president on the airwaves, contemporary politicians have begun to study their imitators. *Saturday Night Live's* impersonation of Al Gore's behavior during the 2000 presidential debates was so persuasive, for example, that the candidate's advisers made him watch it to learn from his mistakes. This willingness to engage the comedic sketch, to see it as revealing vital knowledge about a candidate, underscores the ways in which political handlers now perceive the impersonation as reliably representing widespread beliefs. The proliferation of such incidents invites scholars to consider the degree to which fame has emerged as a category for understanding the presidency. In an era of unprecedented media exposure, the president has clearly emerged as a singularly prominent personality, a man who, quite literally, plays the United States on the world stage. As the line between news and entertainment rapidly disintegrates, as voters at the polls reward the politician's high visibility, it seems logical for the public to expect its presidents to be both commanders *and* celebrities in chief.

Conceptions of fame have nearly always shaped American notions of political power, and it is important to remember that the desire for renown played a particularly important role in eighteenth-century political thought. Indeed to the Constitution's framers, it was vital to the cultivation of a bold but virtuous leadership. In *The Federalist*, for example, Alexander Hamilton described the "love of fame" as "the ruling passion of the noblest minds," arguing that it "would prompt a man to plan and undertake extensive and arduous enterprises for the public benefit" (Bailyn 363–64). James Wilson, Hamilton's fellow delegate to the Constitutional Convention, described fame's import in more explicitly psychological terms:

> The love of honest and well-earned fame is deeply rooted in honest and suscep-
> tible minds. Can there be a stronger incentive to the operations of this passion,
> than the hope of becoming the object of well founded and distinguishing ap-

plause? Can there be a more complete gratification of this passion, than the satisfaction of knowing that this applause is given—that it is given upon the most honourable principles, and acquired by the most honourable pursuits? (as cited in Wills 129)

What is interesting about both Hamilton and Wilson's comments is their focus on a leader's motivation and sense of purpose. "The pursuit of fame," as Douglass Adair explains, "was a way of transforming egotism and self-aggrandizing impulses into public service" (Adair 8). The founders "had been taught that public service nobly (and selfishly) performed was the surest way to build 'lasting monuments' and earn the perpetual remembrance of posterity" (Adair 8). Both a check against tyrannical impulses and an incentive to accomplish great things, the desire for renown suited a skeptical theory of political power that expected leaders to achieve greatness in the eyes of each other and history.

Contemporary assessments of presidential fame tend to focus less on the president's motivation than on his well-known image. The public does not determine the president's celebrity, awarding him its applause, as much as it contends with and appropriates his iconic presence. Hollywood impersonations of the president, in this respect, tend to reflect on a perceived gap between the president and the populace. They entertain the deeply democratic possibility that the executive office might ultimately be returned to the electorate. We are accustomed to the notion that the president acts as a spokesman for the citizenry, that as the only representative elected by the public at large, he serves as a ventriloquist of popular opinion. In his single, coherent voice, the president speaks for the many. Hollywood fantasies of impersonation approach the office differently, focusing less on its discursive qualities than on the trope of every American inhabiting the chief executive's body. Disseminated through the media, the president's physical characteristics—his dress, his speech, his face—all become signs of a peculiarly republican fusion of personality and publicity.

A highly literalized image of this process emerges from Ivan Reitman's film *Dave* (1993). By virtue of their uncanny resemblance, Dave Kovic, the director of a temporary employment agency, secretly fills in for the president who lies in a coma underneath the White House. Following Dave's exploits as he impersonates the president, the film considers whether, given the proper media attention, an average American could rejuvenate an office mired in political expediency. Combining common sense with an increasingly savvy handling of the media, Dave returns compassion to the Oval Office, saving, for instance, an educational program for homeless children that had been eliminated from the federal budget. He goes on, in the movie's conclusion, to rescue his honorable vice president from a plot to smear him with charges of dishonesty. The film fuses a Capraesque plot line with Andy Warhol's prediction that in the future every American will enjoy fifteen minutes of fame. Using the power of presidential celebrity, Kovic restores both virtue and integrity to a callous political establishment.

In contrast to *Dave*, however, in which an ordinary citizen is translated into the most powerful position in the world, the act of impersonation typically involves the public's diffusion of presidential authority. In what we might regard as a mediated exchange, the president speaks for the people, and in turn they possess his image and can make of it what they will. Anne Norton comments that the presidential sign is always vulnerable to subversion: an image on a campaign poster, she argues, can serve as a rallying point for supporters, but when the same image is made into a rubber mask, it signifies not acclamation but ridicule (Norton 92). Norton makes an important point, though it is important to qualify her association of subversion with scorn. As an exaggerated form of the mask, the act of impersonation reduces the president to a series of bodily and verbal quirks; it separates the president's media characteristics from his office, privilege, and legitimacy. While they certainly can be deployed for partisan purposes, acts of impersonation usually have less to do with politics than they do with popular culture. The joke—in order to work—must appeal to its audience not as fellow citizens but as a community of spectators mutually aware of an extended media performance.

The iconographic nature of the presidency emerges from Peter Segal's *My Fellow Americans* (1996). The film concerns two former presidents who are bitter political rivals, though each shares the humiliation of having been voted out of office. Played by James Garner and Jack Lemmon, former presidents Douglas and Kramer discover corruption in their successor's administration and must flee NSA operatives who have been ordered to kill them. The crisis forces the two rivals to embark on a picaresque journey that brings them into contact with the people who have rejected them.

The requisite education of these former presidents begins with a scene involving impersonation. Having been stranded in the country, Douglas and Kramer board a party train headed for a college basketball tournament in Ohio, and they are mistakenly assumed to be among a group of hired impersonators. "So what's the deal fellas? Bobby didn't say nothing about no presidents," an

Elvis look-alike confronts them. "Let's get one thing straight—no sharing tips." The setting importantly draws the former presidents into a carnivalesque atmosphere in which traditional hierarchies are inverted and mocked. A Marilyn Monroe confesses that she once had a fling with the real President Douglas and that he had been a disappointing lover. The carousers jeer the "imitation" presidents, mocking Kramer's media habits and catch phrases. Stripped of their political dignity, both men must contend with their images not as trusted statesmen but as figures ripe for parody. What the presidents come to realize is that while they have joined Elvis and Marilyn as icons of the country, they possess none of the stars' appeal. Adrift in the carnival of popular culture, disguised as imitations of themselves, they must perform their official identities, which prove to be their first steps in the rejuvenation of their political careers.

The prevalence of impersonation scenes in White House comedies is a useful index of the growing political import of publicity and fame. Beyond the rise of such entertainer politicians as Ronald Reagan and Jesse Ventura, a larger question has surfaced about the degree to which politics is represented through the prism of celebrity. Critics have remarked on the glamorization of the presidency since the Eisenhower administration hired the Young and Rubicam agency for its 1956 reelection campaign. Among the agency's many contributions was the development of a "star committee" of popular entertainers who agreed to make appearances on Eisenhower's behalf (Allen 131). One of the most insightful, though neglected, reflections on the changing nature of electoral politics was Budd Schulberg and Elia Kazan's *A Face in the Crowd* (1957). The film follows the career of Lonesome Rhodes, a drunken roustabout brilliantly played by a young Andy Griffith. Discovered in a small-town jail, Rhodes experiences overnight success as an Arkansas radio personality and then rapidly evolves into a television sensation and guitar-picking American icon. A wealthy general, who sponsors Rhodes's show, calls upon the entertainer to advise the conservative senator Worthington Fuller on how to run his upcoming presidential campaign. With devastating bluntness, Rhodes teaches the senator how to become more likeable to the sixty-five million people who watch his show each week. The rather priggish Fuller learns that he must express his conservatism in the folksy, down-home style preferred by Rhodes's audience, a style that Rhodes himself wields with demagogic power.

While Schulberg and Kazan overtly agonized over the subject, the staggering numbers of presidential movies released in the last decade were produced in a culture increasingly at ease with the role of entertainment in the political process. Although perhaps an extreme example, the 1995 premier of John F.

Kennedy Jr's *George* magazine perfectly embodied the logic shared by many of Hollywood's presidential comedies. Displaying a cynicism that remained strikingly devoid of self-irony, the magazine mounted a comprehensive effort to identify politics with celebrity. The first six issues, for example, displayed such stars as Cindy Crawford, Howard Stern, and Charles Barkley dressed in the costume of George Washington. A regular column titled "We the People" featured photographs of entertainers and politicians as they mixed at fundraisers and charity balls. Each issue ended with a column entitled "If I Were President" in which personalities from Rush Limbaugh to Claudia Schiffer were asked to describe their own political fantasy. As Kennedy wrote in an early editorial, the magazine was founded on the idea that "Much of politics, like the movies, is about starpower" (Kennedy 7).

As Kennedy's magazine was struggling to stay in print, however, its underlying principles were reaching their logical conclusion in the 2000 presidential campaign. With neither candidate able to attract much public interest, the media quickly inserted its own celebrities into the spectacle of presidential politics. The AP wire, for example, began to report the latest campaign jokes from late-night television, and the *New York Times Magazine* wondered whether Letterman and Leno were among the most powerful political commentators in the country. In 1962, Daniel Boorstin used the term "pseudoevent" to describe the media's creation of significance through publicity and hype. One wonders what Boorstin would say about the resurfacing of White House films just days before the 2000 election. Among the programs Americans could view on television the weekend before the election were *Dick, Primary Colors, Murder at 1600, Election, The American President,* and *The Best Man.* At times the entertainment event seemed to rival the actual campaign for ontological supremacy. The appearance of Eddie Vedder and Susan Sarandon at a Madison Square Garden rally, for example, earned Ralph Nader an appearance in *US Weekly,* though Nader himself was featured in only a stamp-sized photo while a picture of the laughing stars occupied a page and a half. The abundance of such materials indicates a moment in which public attention was replacing public opinion as the cornerstone of cultural identity.

Although critics on both the right and the left have resisted their efforts, Hollywood historically has associated the making of stars with the principles of popular sovereignty. David Marshall illuminates this position in arguing that the figure of celebrity embodies "the empowerment of the people to shape the public sphere symbolically," to select among a vast array of individuals a handful to be vested with significance and popularity (Marshall 7). Because in the end the famous rely upon the culture to give them specific meaning, they draw upon the same source of power as leaders and politicians (Marshall 47, 19). Celebrities have traditionally encouraged their fans to recognize the representative aspects of their renown. Consider Myrna Loy's explanation of stardom to a teenage admirer: "I am not my own boss. . . . I serve not one boss but several million. For my boss is—the Public. My boss is that very girl who writes me herself and thousands like her" (as quoted in Gamson 34). Several generations later, Marilyn Monroe would employ the same reasoning, declaring, "If I am a star, the people made me a star, no studio, no person, but the people did" (as quoted in Coombes 62). Obscuring their origins in advertising, celebrities have learned to suggest that their personal prestige is merely a reflection of the popular will. Ranting about himself in the third-person, the television demagogue in *A Face in the Crowd* boasts that he has the power to break presidents. Why? "Because the people listen to Lonesome Rhodes. Because the people love Lonesome Rhodes. Lonesome Rhodes is the people. The people is Lonesome Rhodes."

While clearly interested in the subject of presidential celebrity, recent White House comedies insist that there are differences between being the chief executive and being simply famous. *Dave* and *The American President* (along with the television program *The West Wing*) resist the postmodern tenor of a film such as *Wag The Dog* in which the president is an absent figure, a disembodied voice created wholly by packaging. In what proves to be the climax of his first term in office, Andrew Shepherd addresses the conservative Senator Bob Rumson (Richard Dreyfuss), whose personal attacks on his relationship with Sydney Wade have gone unanswered for weeks. Speaking through the White House press corps, he comments, "This is a time for serious people, Bob, and your fifteen minutes are up." Rumson, it is clear, has confused two identities; he has been impersonating a presidential contender by wearing his media trappings. Shepherd implies that the president is more than a celebrity: we should measure his seriousness by the endurance of his reputation. As Shepherd envisions him, the president is less a Warholian figure than a man motivated by what John Adams and Benjamin Rush understood as "the spur of fame," by which they meant character as it would be measured by the righteous judgment of history (Adams and Rush).

While Shepherd's remarks provide a fitting conclusion to his personal and political stories, he should not be granted the last word on presidential fame. Part of the appeal of these White House comedies is that they safely offer what

Dustin Hoffman, Anne Heche, and Robert DeNiro in *Wag The Dog* (1997).

historian Neil Harris has described as an "operational aesthetic." Harris coined the term in explaining P.T. Barnum's ability not only to fool the public but to have it delight in his revelation of the trick. Barnum's hoaxes fascinated his contemporaries because, for many of them, discovering how the deceptions "had been practiced, was even more exciting than the discovery of fraud itself" (Harris 77). In a decade distinguished by widespread distrust of government, White House comedies provided viewers with a privileged look into the artifice behind the presidency. Like Dave Kovic, like Sydney Wade, like Henry Burton in *Primary Colors* (1998), and even Stanley Motss in *Wag The Dog* (1997), viewers wander through these films amazed at the pollsters, spin doctors, dust busters, and pols all scheming to pull off another political hoax. Barnum's followers filled his museum—first, to see his exhibits and then to see how they had been duped. The White House comedies of the 1990s perform an analogous function: they promise working knowledge about how the government is supposed to operate and how it really does.

For stories concerned with politics, however, these films have little to say about political issues themselves. Harris's discussion of Barnum is particularly illuminating here. One consequence of the operational aesthetic, he explains, is that, while reveling in the hoax, the audience feels no need to reexamine broader questions about basic values. In the case of Barnum's museum, Americans became so intrigued with "observing process and examining for literal truth" that they did not push their inquiries beyond the gathering of information itself (Harris 79). Focused on the "aesthetic of the operational," on how Barnum's hoaxes worked, "Onlookers were relieved from the burden of coping with more abstract problems" (Harris 79). Appearing to expose the Oval Office to public view, Hollywood's version of the presidency fills a similar role. The films offer what might be called "realistic information" about how the White House works. They show Secret Service details, underground meeting rooms, lobbying sessions with Congress, and rivalry between cabinet members. At the same time these films confirm the strong cultural perception that, except for a few individuals, politics is ultimately corrupt. Instead of immersing audiences in contemporary political debates, they associate a successful presidency with a simple understanding of character. Andrew Shepherd is a "serious person"; his abusive critic is not. The difference assures that Shepherd will prevail.

In their effort to convey executive character, however, the films ultimately fall back upon their larger identification of the presidency with fame. *The American President*, for example, tries to counter Shepherd's celebrity with an affectionate, intimate portrait of his life both in and outside the Oval Office. All of that intimacy, however, comes at the cost of representing the president with the tools of the star. In the film *Being There* (1979), Chance Gardener (Peter Sellers) comments, "Mr. President, you are much smaller on television." In their own impersonations of the presidency, filmmakers greatly expand the presidential image, trading ubiquity for the solitary grandeur of the movie screen and the psychological weight of a complex citizen. In place of the morphed, fragmented figures of television, White House comedies offer something of a paradox—a private, coherent vision of a heroically scaled presidency. The entire subgenre is predicated on the illusion of intimacy that star-makers have recognized for decades; audiences become satisfied with seemingly private glimpses into the secrets of power and celebrity (see Schickel).

When applied to the presidency, this approach ironically suggests that film is ultimately a more reflective and a more authentic political medium than do newspapers or television. Compared to the image of a rapacious print and electronic press, filmmakers emerge as solid, rational citizens, persons capable of composing a judicious, coherent vision of the executive office. Television, in particular, appears in these films as an unreliable, partisan medium, an insidious disruptive force in American democracy that the linear narrative of the film must try to correct. Comedies such as *Dave* and *The American President* suggest that they faithfully depict republican character while the distortions of television do not. Emptied of political engagement, however, such portraits represent democracy as an uninterrupted spectacle in which the audience does not participate as much as it absorbs. Indeed, with the audience's silent consent, the Oval Office becomes a familiar, comfortable, and synthetically realistic place. As Hollywood's impersonation of American democracy at work, the president emerges from these comedies as just another "idol of consumption," to borrow Leo Lowenthal's famous phrase, a figure who expects nothing but to be observed and admired as part of the show (Lowenthal). What these White House films ultimately offer the public is not the opportunity to reenergize politics (as their narratives suggest) but to purchase their vaguely satisfying leaders for a series of one-hundred-minute terms.

WORKS CITED

Adair, Douglass. "Fame and the Founding Fathers." In *Fame and the Founding Fathers*, edited by Trevor Colbourn. New York: Institute of Early American History and Culture, 1974.

Adams, John, and Benjamin Rush. *The Spur of Fame: Dialogues of John Adams and Benjamin Rush, 1805–1813*. Edited by John A. Schutz and Douglass Adair. Indianapolis: Liberty Fund, 2001.

Allen, Craig. *Eisenhower and the Mass Media: Peace, Prosperity, & Prime-Time TV*. Chapel Hill: University of North Carolina Press, 1993.

Bailyn, Bernard, ed. *The Debate on the Constitution: Federalist and Antifederalist Speeches, Articles, and Letters During the Struggle over Ratification*. Part Two. New York: Library of America, 1993.

Boorstin, Daniel. *The Image or What Happened to the American Dream*. New York: Atheneum, 1962.

Coombes, Rosemary. "The Celebrity Image and Cultural Identity: Publicity Rights and the Subaltern Politics of Gender." *Discourse* 14 (1992): 59–88.

Cull, Nicholas J. "No Laughing Matter: Vaughn Meader, the Kennedy Administration, and Presidential Impersonations on Radio." *Historical Journal of Film, Radio & Television* 17 (1997): 383–400. *EbscoHost*. Roscoe L. West Library, The College of New Jersey. 5 December 2001 <http://ehostvgw5.epnet.com>.

Gamson, Joshua. *Claims to Fame: Celebrity in Contemporary America*. Berkeley: University of California Press, 1994.

Harris, Neil. *Humbug: The Art of P.T. Barnum*. Boston: Little, Brown, 1973.

Kennedy, John, Jr. "Editor's Letter." *George,* December 1995/ January 1996, 7.

Lowenthal, Leo. "The Triumph of Mass Idols." 1944. Reprint, *Literature, Popular Culture, and Society.* Englewood Cliffs, New Jersey: Prentice-Hall, 1961.

Marshall, P. David. *Celebrity and Power: Fame in Contemporary Culture.* Minneapolis: University of Minnesota Press, 1997.

Norton, Anne. *Republic of Signs: Liberal Theory and American Popular Culture.* Chicago: University of Chicago Press, 1993.

Schickel, Richard. *Intimate Strangers: The Culture of Celebrity.* Garden City, New York: Doubleday, 1985.

Sella, Marshall. "The Stiff Guy vs. The Dumb Guy." *New York Times Magazine,* 24 September 2000, 72–80, 102.

Wills, Garry. *Cincinnatus: George Washington and the Enlightenment.* New York: Doubleday, 1984.

John Matviko

TELEVISION SATIRE AND THE PRESIDENCY

The Case of *Saturday Night Live*

Dan Aykroyd as President William
Haney in *My Fellow Americans*
(1996).

The last quarter of the twentieth century saw significant changes in the relationship between American mass media, especially television, and the presidency. In the summer of 1974, Richard Nixon, after months of media revelations
about presidential wrongdoings, resigned as President of the United States.
The media, acting as the fourth branch of government, had pursued President
Nixon, and the judicial and legislative branches had followed. In a climate that
not only permitted but encouraged criticism of the presidency, television asserted its right to scrutinize and satirize the presidency—at first, in news programs, such as *60 Minutes,* and then later in entertainment programs, such as
Saturday Night Live. By the end of the century, however, as the distinction between news and entertainment blurred, presidential scandals dominated the
news, and titillation, rather than information, became the higher priority. Much
has been written about the blurring of news and entertainment; this essay will

instead explore what has happened to presidential satire by examining the history of *Saturday Night Live* (*SNL*).

In November 1975 the fourth episode of a new series called *NBC's Saturday Night* [1] began with a "cold" opening of Chevy Chase as President Gerald Ford. Chase's imitation of a bumbling Ford was more slapstick than satire; the audience's laughter and the later success of the show ensured, however, that making fun of presidents—whether by slapstick, parody, or satire—would be acceptable for late-night television. Skits about presidents, as well as comments about them on the show's mock newscast "Weekend Update," would soon become fixtures on the program as Richard Nixon (1969–1974), Jimmy Carter (1977–1981), Ronald Reagan (1981–1989), George Bush (1989–1993), and William Clinton (1993–2001) would all become targets.

BACKGROUND

Before *SNL*, satire, let alone presidential satire, was hard to find on prime-time television. The dominant comedy genres of the 1950s and 1960s were the sitcom and the comedy-variety show, and neither had a satiric edge. While *Father Knows Best* and *Leave It to Beaver* would eventually lead to *The Dick Van Dyke Show*, situation comedy would not deal sharply with issues until the arrival of *All in the Family* in 1971. The comedy-variety show, "TV vaudeville," consisted of slapstick, sketch comedy, and later, gentle spoofing of television itself on *The Carol Burnett Show*.[2] Notable in its attempt at topical satire was *That Was the Week That Was*, an NBC import of a successful British series—starring David Frost—that premiered in the fall of 1964. The show was satiric and often quite caustic; it even went so far as to aim some of its barbs at President Lyndon B. Johnson. The show's producers would fight numerous battles with the NBC censors, leading to the program's being temporarily taken off the air in the weeks preceding the Johnson-Goldwater election. NBC chose not to renew the series for a second season (Marc 123). Ahead of its time, *That Was the Week That Was* suggested that the medium was capable of political commentary through humor.

Two additional shows were important precedents for *Saturday Night Live*—*Rowan and Martin's Laugh-In* and *The Smothers Brothers Comedy Hour*. *Laugh-In's* quick visual style and one-liners sometimes were political, and some were even aimed at the president. More style than substance, *Laugh-In* was careful about whom it satirized; for example, because the show's head writer, Paul Keyes, was an occasional speechwriter for Richard Nixon, Nixon jokes disappeared entirely during the 1968 presidential campaign. Nixon, the candidate, would even appear on the number-one-ranked show uttering with unintended irony, "Sock it to ME?"(quoted in Hendra 216). Placing more emphasis on substance and clearly more satirical was *The Smothers Brothers Comedy Hour.* The show fought numerous battles with network censors, including one over a Pete Seeger song aimed at President Johnson ("We're waist deep in the Big Muddy/ And the big fool says to push on") (quoted in Spector 179). Presidential satire also came in the form of the "Pat Paulsen for President Campaign." Paulsen's popularity reached its peak on the eve of the 1968 election when a Pat Paulsen for President special drew far more viewers than a last-minute Hubert Humphrey speech (Hendra 218). Alas, battles with censors would eventually bring about the show's demise. As a memo from a CBS censor noted with unintended humor: "It's okay to satirize the President, as long as you do so with respect" (quoted in Hill and Weingrad 22).

The driving force behind the development of *Saturday Night Live* was Lorne Michaels. Raised in Canada, Michael's first American job was as a writer for *Laugh-In.* He then returned to Canada to coproduce and cohost comedy specials, only to return to America three years later to coproduce comedy specials for Lily Tomlin. NBC, which was last in the ratings, was looking for a program that would attract a younger audience (the eighteen-to-thirty-four demographic). Michaels assembled some of the best young comics from *National Lampoon, Second City,* and *The Committee* in a show that would feature live sketch comedy (Hill and Weingrad 37–47). On 11 October 1975, George Carlin guest-hosted the first show. Despite praise from many TV critics, the program struggled with low ratings for its first season. By the second season, however, *SNL* was a hit with the targeted demographic and had made stars out of a number of the Not-Ready-for-Prime-Time-Players, including Chevy Chase, Gilda Radner, and John Belushi (Hill and Weingrad 94–106).

GERALD FORD (1974–1977)

Chevy Chase's Gerald Ford imitation was a regular feature in the program's first two seasons, and it often opened the show. Typical was the 8 November 1975 program that opened with the Presidential Seal and a voiceover that announced, "Ladies and Gentlemen, the President of the United States." The camera slowly zoomed in on Chevy Chase as President Ford as a title self-reflexively told the viewers that, "This is not a good impression of President Gerald Ford." The next title continued "but Rich Little won't work for scale." Chase-Ford then sneezed into his tie and stumbled over the text. After the phone rings Chase-Ford tried to answer it by picking up a glass full of water and putting it to his ear. More phone problems were followed by more bumbling. The president then knocked over his visual aid and then fell over his desk. Picking himself up from the floor, Chase delivered the show's signature opening: "Live from New York, it's Saturday Night."

The Chase-Ford bits became a fixture on the program, and with the show's improved ratings, the recurring bit as well as jokes about Ford in the "Weekend Update" segment became a concern for the Ford reelection committee in 1976. In an effort to defuse the negative image, Gerald Ford's press secretary, Ron Nessen, suggested to Lorne Michaels that Nessen guest-host the program. Nessen's strategy was to play along with the gag, suggesting that President Ford could laugh at himself. Ford himself had earlier worked the strategy at the annual dinner of the Radio and Television Correspondents Association, where he appeared on the dais with Chevy Chase. Chase had done his Ford imitation along with a mock "Weekend Update" newscast consisting of Ford jokes. Ford followed with his own imitation of his media image: he got tangled in the tablecloth and then lost his speech as his notes scattered on the floor. To Chase he would say: "I'm Gerald Ford and you're not" and "Mr. Chevy Chase, you are a very, very funny suburb." Ford contributed to the Nessen appearance by taping three lines including the opening "live from New York, it's Saturday Night," and "I'm Gerald Ford and you're not" (quoted in Nessen 173–74).

With the exceptions of monologues by Johnny Carson and Bob Hope, jokes and other types of humor about the president were rarely found on television in the 1970s. While political jokes were a staple of Johnny Carson's opening monologue throughout his reign as the king of late-night television, Carson's humor was seldom malicious. And Bob Hope's monologues, while topical and often very pointed, were most certainly palliated by his known conservatism and his often public elbow-rubbing and golf-playing with the very objects of his humor. One had the feeling that both Carson and Hope, in the style of Will Rogers, liked the presidents they joked about. Lorne Michaels, as producer of *Saturday Night Live*, took a much different approach to the presidency. With Ford, and especially Nixon, the show went for the jugular. About the Nessen show, *SNL* writer Rosie Shuster stated: "The President's watching. Let's make him cringe and squirm" (quoted in Hill and Weingrad 184). Nessen appeared in a number of skits, most obviously one with Chevy Chase portraying the stumblebum president. By design, Nessen's appearances were surrounded by the raunchiest material the show had done to that point. Among the skits was a parody commercial for a douche called "Autumn Fizz" ("a douche with the effervescence of uncola"), characters humping in bed while the Supreme Court watched, and an Emily Litella (Gilda Radner) "Weekend Update" commentary on the upcoming "presidential erections." Some members of the press were quite critical of the program, and *Saturday Night Live* dominated Nessen's daily briefing the following Monday. Ford himself did not publicly comment, and his wife Betty said only that she found some of the White House skits "funny" and some of the other material "a little distasteful" (quoted in Nessen 175). Later, Nessen concluded that the show had been out to get him: "Looking back, it's obvious that my attempt to smother the ridicule of Ford by joining the laughter on *Saturday Night* was a failure" (Nessen 177).

Later in 1976 the show would satirize the first presidential debates held in sixteen years. Again, Chase played a befuddled President Ford. In answer to a lengthy question about the economy, a dazed Ford responded, "It was my understanding that there would be no math." One of the obvious questions that this raises is the possible effect it had on the election of 1976. Ford lost to Carter by slightly more that two percent or about 1.7 million votes (New York Times.com). Did *Saturday Night Live*'s presidential portrayal, combined with the media's seemingly endless attention to Ford's reported clumsiness, cost Ford the election? Ford himself dodged the question in 1999 when asked whether he thought Chase's impression had been harmful: "I never watched the show. . . . They're going to do what they want to, and if you criticize them, it gives them more space; so I just kept my mouth shut" (American Enterprise.com). On the other hand, Dick Cheney, Ford's chief of staff, saw it as important: "Chevy Chase on *Saturday Night Live* didn't help, either. Once you get to the point at which something becomes a stock gag on Johnny Carson's *Tonight Show* or one of those kinds of TV shows, that label sticks and you can't get rid of it" (quoted in Rozell 196). Nessen clearly believed that it contributed to Ford's defeat (Nessen 177). Hill and Weingrad, who wrote a history of the early years of the program, suggest that Chase and most of the cast believed that they contributed to Ford's defeat by "promulgating so effectively his image as a befuddled klutz" (Hill and Weingrad 188). *Saturday Night* even went beyond making the president "cringe and squirm" to trying ensure his defeat. On the Saturday before the 1976 election, in a segment called "Carter's unreleased commercials,"[3] the show replayed the Ford speech in which he pardoned Richard Nixon. Lorne Michaels's justification for the replaying was that the pardon had been forgotten. Michaels would later call the rebroadcast of the Ford speech one of his proudest moments (Hill and Weingrad 183).

RICHARD NIXON (1969–1974)

On the one hand, in the minds of many, Gerald Ford's sin was pardoning Richard Nixon. On the other hand, Richard Nixon's sin was being Richard Nixon. Although out of office, "Nixon" was found in at least seven skits in the show's first three years. Long after he was gone from the political stage, Nixon would remain on the *Saturday Night Live* stage in a *60 Minutes* sketch in 1983, a Nixon/Gingrich skit in 1994, and a Nixon/Clinton sketch in 1998. Dan Aykroyd, unlike Chase's Ford, looked and sounded like Nixon. The audience's reaction was also different: the hearty laughter at the slapstick found in most of the Ford sketches was gone—replaced by a we're-in-on-the-joke-and-we-love-what-you're-doing snickering.

The most famous of the Nixon sketches was the parody of Woodward and Bernstein's *The Final Days*. The long sketch included a drunken Pat Nixon, David and Julie Eisenhower, Sammy Davis Jr, and Henry Kissenger (John Belushi). The original opening written for the sketch had Lorne Michaels introducing it: "Hi, I'm Lorne Michaels. As producer of this show, I make weighty decisions every day. But this week, I had to make the toughest decision of my career: whether or not to ridicule Richard Nixon one more time." Michaels would go on to note that it would be "too easy" to "make light of a man who hadn't slept with his wife for fourteen years." Additionally, Michaels would note that "jokes about Alexander Haig's belief that Nixon and Bebe Rebozo were having a homosexual affair have no place on network television." The intro was discarded late in the week in favor of having Pat Nixon (Gilda Radner) writing in her diary (quoted in Hill and Weingrad 141). In the sketch, Nixon is seen talking to the portraits of former presidents Lincoln ("You were lucky. They shot you.") and Kennedy ("You! Kennedy. You looked so good all the time. They're gonna find out about you, too. The President having sex with women within these very walls. That never happened when Dick Nixon was in the White House. Never! Never! Never!"). The sketch was unmerciful; Nixon was portrayed as a half-crazy, anti–Semitic racist.

Of all the presidential skits aired on the show, "The Final Days" is probably the most vicious. The skit, and the program's attitude toward Ford and Nixon, did not go without criticism. Satirist Tony Hendra, in his book-length study of what he calls "boomer humor," criticized the show for not being satirical: "The reason Ford should not be President, *SNL* seemed to say, was that he didn't make it on television." Likewise, for Hendra, "The Final Days" sketch was "hardly state-of-the-art satire" (Hendra 438). *Doonesbury* creator, Gary Trudeau, also criticized the show in 1981: "For all its innovations this kind of satire tells society's nebishes that they are right about themselves, that they are nobodies, that to be so un-hip as to be disadvantaged, to be ignorant, to be physically infirm, or black, or even female is to invite contempt. . . . If this is to become a society intolerant of failure and uncompassionate in the face of suffering, then we are lost" (quoted in Hill and Weingrad 183).

JIMMY CARTER (1977–1981)

Compared to their treatment of Ford and Nixon, *SNL*'s handling of Jimmy Carter was relatively tame. Dan Aykroyd's Jimmy Carter first appeared on the show in 1976 when Aykroyd portrayed him talking about his life and presidential campaign. Aykroyd, throughout the Carter administration, beautifully mimicked the president's mannerisms and speech. Even critic Hendra was forced to admit that "(n)o one performer, caricaturist, or columnist caught the gluey sanctimoniousness of Jimmy Carter as perfectly as Aykroyd" (Hendra 443). Carter was a part of most of the programs during his presidency, and the skits look like a cartoonish historical record of his administration: "Carter says his sex life will carry on Democratic tradition," "Host (Julian Bond) and Andrew Young confront Carter about cabinet positions," "Carter generates electricity to broadcast energy saving message," "Carter urges Americans to burn 8% of their money to fight inflation," and "Reluctant Carter brings brother Billy along to Jerusalem." Most of these skits were topically satiric and most had some bite. The most famous skit of the Carter presidency, if presence on compilation tapes is an indicator, is "The Pepsi Syndrome," a takeoff on the then very popular movie *China Syndrome*. In the skit, Aykroyd as the president is exposed to radiation and becomes a mutant giant. While still funny today, the skit works better as a spoof of the movie rather than as a satire of the president. The Carter presidency paralleled what many consider to be the golden years of *SNL*—the late 1970s when the original cast of the show did most of its best work. Consequently, most are still funny today. And the Carter satires, perhaps because Carter was not connected to the hated Richard Nixon, were more Horatian than Juvenalian, certainly more good-natured than intolerant.

RONALD REAGAN (1981–1989)

Walter Truett Anderson, in his book on postmodernism, *Reality Isn't What It Used to Be*, argues that Ronald Reagan was our first postmodern politician: "Presented to the public as the antidote to a counterculture that was leading the march away from modern culture, he took the society even further from its connection to the certainties of the modern era. . . . (H)e understood the power of free-floating symbolism, rooted in nothing at all" (Anderson 165). This lack of a firm, definable target made it difficult for opponents and critics to attack. Even satiric texts, such as *SNL*, had difficulty with the "Teflon president."[4] Ford and Nixon were easy targets, but attacking the Reagan presidency proved difficult. In the show's history, six different actors portrayed Reagan, but none captured him like Chevy Chase as Ford, Dan Aykroyd as Nixon, or, later, Dana Carvey as George Bush. Having different actors portray Reagan may be a function of a changing cast, but the number of actors who portrayed Reagan may also signify the difficulty in finding someone who could mimic and satirize the popular, yet elusive, president. It could also be argued that the Reagan years coincided with what most critics consider a decline in the show's quality. Rather than coincidence, this may have been causation—the show declined because a weekly target of its satire, the presidency, was now held by a man whose immense popularity, even with *SNL*'s core audience, made satire difficult. Further proof can be found in the show's compilation program on presidential politics, *Saturday Night Live Presidential Bash*. First broadcast as a 1992 special in prime time and then later released on video, *Presidential Bash* is a two-hour collection of presidential skits from the first seventeen years of *SNL*. While Reagan was in office for almost half of that time, only three of the seventeen sketches deal with him, and in only one, "Mastermind," is he the featured player.

A sampling of the subjects of the Reagan skits demonstrates the show's inability to find effective satiric subjects. Before 1980, skits dealt with Reagan playing the blues organ and trying to suggest hipness, a campaign aide detailing Reagan's nap-filled schedule, and a spoof called "Invasion of the Brain Snatcher" where Reagan pods try to turn liberals into conservatives. Only the "Weekend Update" news portion contained any satire with bite. The trend would continue during his presidency. For example, Reagan's previous acting career was often parodied. In 1981, skits included Ed Meese getting to run the White House because he convinced Reagan that he was in a film and Reagan arguing that Frank Sinatra should be a presidential adviser because he, too, had a film career. (Joe Piscopo's Sinatra would end up in a number of Reagan skits through 1984, not so much because he was important to the Reagan administration but rather because he was easily one of the show's most popular recurring characters.[5]) Later in his first term, the show would satirize Reagan on racial issues ("Reagan uses ethnic clichés to communicate with Deng Xiaoping" and "Reagan asks Sammy Davis Jr. to hug Democratic frontrunners"), but for the most part the material was much like the recurring, but not very clever, 1982 monologue in which Howard Hesseman asked viewers to "moon Reagan."

SNL, during Reagan's second term of office, focused even less on politics in favor of more sketches ridiculing the Reagan family. From 1985 through 1988, the president appeared in fifteen episodes while Nancy Reagan appeared in eight. Increasingly, the program appeared to be moving away from the president to focus on easier targets. For instance, while the program did deal with Reagan's negotiations with Mikhail Gorbachev and the Russians, Nancy was frequently given equal time. A "Weekend Update" report in 1985, for example, showed Nancy and Raisa Gorbachev at Wardrobe Limitation Talks. Later, a 1987 *Phil Donahue Show* satire found Nancy being jealous of Raisa's growing popularity. A 1985 episode even had Reagan's son, Ron, as guest host. The show opened with a takeoff on *Risky Business* (1983) with Ron throwing a party while his parents were at Camp David. A later skit had Ron going "back to the future" on a *Hellcats of the Navy* (1957) set in order to reunite his parents. While fun to watch, these skits are more spoofs of the motion picture legacy than satires of a sitting president.

SNL's most interesting sketch of the Reagan years occurred in 1986. "Mastermind" opens with the president and a reporter discussing the arms to Iran/aid to the Contras problem. Phil Hartman as the president appears forgetful and unaware of what is going on around him. After dismissing the reporter, the president meets with his staff and suddenly takes charge of every detail of his efforts to continue his aid to the Contras. The meeting is interrupted as the president must meet his "11:30 photo opportunity with the Girl Scout who sold the most cookies." Back and forth, the skit alternates between the avuncular, kindly, and, perhaps, forgetful president we saw in countless media reports and the "take-no-prisoners" chief executive that *SNL* suggests is the real president. All of this is certainly satire, but of whom? And if the purpose of satire is to reform, who is to be reformed? In this case, it was certainly not Ronald Reagan. The satire might be of the American press corps who had accepted these "free-floating symbols" that are rooted in nothing. Or the satire could be aimed at television, which, according to Scheuer's *The Sound Bite Society*, "rewards simpler messages. It forces politicians and journalists alike to be more exposure- and image-conscious, focusing their attention (and that of viewing audiences) on the cosmetic and superficial values of individual presentation and away from issues and ideas" (Scheuer 34).

GEORGE BUSH (1989–1993)

Dana Carvey's George Bush first appeared in 1987 in the opening, announcing "I'm no wimp, I've staged a coup." The "I'm not a wimp" theme continued in the next *SNL* program as the show opened with "BushWhacked!" as Bush uses the Morton Downey approach to looking tough. *SNL* continued the Bush tough guy satire through most of his term in office, often teaming it with foreign-policy issues. From his first appearance, Carvey's George Bush was popular with the audience, and he often opened the show—indeed, from 1989 and into 1990, nine consecutive programs began with Carvey's George Bush. While a number of the skits through 1992 were topically satiric, Carvey's Bush is probably best remembered for how closely he mimicked the voice and style of the president. (Carvey claimed his George Bush was a melding of the voices of John Wayne and Mr. Rogers ["Relaxed Bush" B6].) The most interesting Bush opening was probably the appearance by Bush himself shortly after he was no longer president. After a "(L)adies and gentlemen, the former President of the United States," George Bush appeared live from Houston. The former president then imitated his imitator, even mimicking the exaggerated hand gestures that were part of Carvey's impersonation as well as using Carvey's "wouldn't be prudent." The former president showed up again in the Carvey-as-Bush opening monologue, telling him that he did not say or do a number of the things in the Carvey-as-Bush act.

Through the four years of the Bush administration, then, Dana Carvey demonstrated the uncanny ability to mimic. The humor, for the most part however, owed more to Carvey's ability to capture the voice and mannerisms of the original rather than to any satire of Bush's ideas, actions, or policies. It would be hard to picture Chevy Chase being invited to the Ford White House or Dan Ackroyd performing for Jimmy Carter. Yet a month after his 1992 defeat, Bush invited Carvey to the White House to perform for his family and staff, telling them "Dana's given me a lot of laughs" (quoted in "Relaxed Bush" B6).

WILLIAM JEFFERSON CLINTON (1993–2001)

Through the years of the Clinton presidency, *SNL*'s satire moved from satire about events and decisions to focus increasingly on the presidential scandals. Clinton's first appearance occurred during the 1992 Democratic primaries when he, Jerry Brown, and Paul Tsongas were shown pursuing the *Star Trek* vote. Phil Hartman's Bill Clinton, like Carvey's George Bush before him, closely matched the voice and mannerisms of the candidate.

Library of Congress.

The early Clinton satires focused on the debates and, after his election, some of his policies. For example, in early 1993, Clinton is shown eating at McDonald's while explaining Somalia, and later that year, he explains his health plan. By 1994, however, *SNL* has him blaming his wife for the Whitewater scandal and being investigated in a skit called "Real Stories of the Arkansas Highway Patrol." In 1996, Darrell Hammond replaced Michael McKean who had briefly replaced Phil Hartman. Hammond's tenure would

Bill Clinton draws bawdy attacks from *Saturday Night Live.*

begin in the fall of 1996 as the program featured the Clinton-Dole election campaign. As with the Ford-Carter election, the program took sides. For example, in the last program before the election, the show opened with Carvey's George Bush preparing Dole for his upcoming defeat. Chris Rock then did a stand-up monologue about Clinton and sexual harassment. Later in a mock Dole ad, a black man, a woman, and a gay say "don't vote." Still later, Bob Dole is seen rehearsing "his mean-spirited victory and concession speeches."

With the reelection of Clinton, the show turned again to Clinton's peccadillos as in early 1997 when Paula Jones attempted to identify the president's genitalia in a line-up. Current events, especially those with Janet Reno, would sometimes be satirized, but increasingly the humor dealt either with the sex scandals or with Clinton's marital problems. As the Lewinsky part of the scandal grew, Molly Shannon's Monica often appeared in multiple skits in a single episode. For example, a spring 1998 episode had her on the phone with Clinton and Saddam Hussein and later discussing oral sex with Oprah. And as media coverage of the scandal deepened, Will Ferrell's Kenneth Starr became a featured character. The satire in these sketches was not especially subtle; sometimes, it was not even original. Borrowing the premise of *Wag The Dog*, the beginning of the Saddam Hussein skit had Clinton asking Saddam "could you not let the inspectors in" and "couldn't you spray a few Kurds with anthrax?" In the introduction to the 1999 *SNL* prime-time special entitled *The Best of the Clinton Scandal*, Darrell Hammond summarized the difference between his Clinton and Dana Carvey's George Bush: "He got Iran-Contra, taking down the Berlin Wall, the Gulf War. I get Bill Clinton dancing around with busty ladies, dropping his pants; there's a fat lady with a tape recorder, a wife with a rolling pin. It's like *The Benny Hill Show*." Hammond's assessment was accurate: many of the Clinton sketches substituted burlesque for satire. The skits that did have subtlety and insight were often those that featured either the Republican opposition to Clinton or the media's handling of the scandal. For example, the opening sketch on the show that followed Clinton's impeachment trial had Newt Gingrich and Bob Livingston at a local bar drowning in their despair. "What the hell happened?" Livingston asks again and again. Finally, a confident President Clinton, with a woman at his side, appears out of a back room and triumphantly buys drinks for the clueless Gingrich and Livingston. As the president leaves, a bewildered Livingston can only ask, "What the hell happened?" Oprah, Barbara Walters, and cable talk shows were also satirized for their obsession with the White House dalliances.

Ironically, the target of most of the satire was not Bill Clinton but either the irate Republicans or the transfixed media. In contrast to *SNL*'s attitude toward Ford and Nixon, the show's approach toward Bill Clinton was downright affectionate. A number of factors might explain this phenomenon: first, the show was aimed at baby-boomers. *SNL* was among the first television shows to play with such taboo topics as sex, drugs, and the proper-thing-to-do. The goal was to attract and then keep many baby boomers in its core audience as well as adding new generations who would share these beliefs. Clinton was not only the first baby-boomer president, but his persona suggested that, even if he did not say it out loud, he shared at least some of the audience's liberated attitudes. In a skit immediately after the final Senate vote on impeachment, Clinton is shown with his staff trying to not gloat; yet the party becomes more and more about gloating. Rather than have a satiric goal, the function of the skit is to celebrate the Clinton victory with the *SNL* cast.

Actually, Clinton may be our first late-night president. Late-night television, as typified by *SNL*, the talk shows, and even *Politically Incorrect* rewards likeability and humor over other attributes. The master of this genre, of course, was Johnny Carson, who combined them both to such a degree that he might have been elected to almost any office he chose to pursue. The late-night persona is also irreverent ("politically incorrect"), occasionally sincere (although this is often undercut by an ironic stance), and frequently willing to test the boundaries of the acceptable. Clinton's election to the presidency in 1992 was greatly aided by his appearance on the late-night *Arsenio Hall Show*. On that show, Clinton played his saxophone and claimed (wink-wink) that he never inhaled. Through two terms of office, Clinton sort of "felt our pain" and tested the limits of what is considered acceptable presidential behavior. His popularity, through it all, remained high with the young. Even at the end of the House vote on impeachment, as members of his own party were expressing doubts about his character, his approval rating not only remained high, but it actually jumped from 61 percent to 71 percent (Pew Research Center, 1999). Clinton and *Saturday Night Live* were made for each other; it should not come as a surprise if, at some future point, the former president ends up a guest host or even a fixture on late-night television.

AL GORE AND GEORGE W. BUSH (2001–)

As in past election years, *SNL* followed the presidential contests from the primaries, through the debates, to the election. While the candidates were certainly criticized, some of the show's best satire was reserved for the media. At the end of the 2000 primaries, for example, the show opened with ABC's Ted Koppel and NBC's Tom Brokaw complaining on the telephone about how boring the upcoming Gore-Bush election was going to be. Ratings would plummet because neither of the candidates was very interesting. They are soon joined by CNN's Bernard Shaw who has *SNL*'s Molly Shannon in bed with him. The group is lamenting the lack of excitement in the upcoming general election when Brokaw makes a suggestion: "Hey guys, I've got an idea, why don't we all agree to take hold of the issues—go out and do some investigative reporting—old fashioned news. Screw the ratings." The group is silent for a moment, as though they are contemplating Brokaw's proposal, and then they all break out in laughter. Obviously the media would not seriously consider substantive issues!

Late-night television and especially *Saturday Night Live* were given credit for playing an important role in the 2000 election. After the third Gore-Bush debate, Peter Jennings asked Cokie Roberts to judge who won and who lost. Roberts answered that "(W)e have to see what the late-night comedians say"(Goodman A9). Roberts was probably only half joking. The Pew Research Center found in January 2000 that "(n)early half (47 percent of those under thirty) are informed at least occasionally by late night talk shows, with significant numbers saying the same of comedy shows (37 percent) and MTV (25 percent)." Not only does late-night television help determine the winner, it may also determine what the candidates say and do in the debates. In preparation for the second debate, Gore's advisors forced him to study Darrell Hammond's version of Al Gore in the *SNL* debates (Peyser 38). Gore's advisers saw the *SNL* mock debate as important to the campaign and possibly an effective teaching tool for Gore (Goodman A9). Additionally, both men, at their own request, taped segments for *Saturday Night Live's* "Presidential Bash 2000" aired two days before the election (Peyser 38). Regardless of how they were treated, neither candidate wanted to miss an opportunity to be on *Saturday Night Live* ("Cast and Crew").

CONCLUSION

For over twenty-five years, *Saturday Night Live* has attempted to satirize the president. In its early years *SNL's* humor reflected the counterculture's disdain for all things connected with the American Establishment—which included President Richard Nixon. In the 1980s, as Ronald Reagan's popularity grew and *Saturday Night Live's* hipness became mainstream, the program could not sustain the critical edge that was so much a part of its early years. By the administrations of the elder George Bush and William Clinton, the dominant style of its presidential humor became mimicry and burlesque as the media—rather than the presidency—became the target of its satire. While it may be still too early to tell, it would seem that this trend would likely continue with George W. Bush.

What do we make of this change in satiric targets from the presidency to the television medium itself? Television's increased role in our democracy certainly makes it a worthy subject for satire. But does satire, such as *SNL's*, explain or go far enough to suggest why or how citizens should reform the system?

Here, the Koppel-Brokaw-Shaw sketch described above may be illustrative. The skit suggests that television news has given up its provider-of-necessary-information-in-a-democracy function to concentrate on its more profitable entertainment function—in this case, focusing upon candidates who even the newscasters find "boring." The sketch, however, never addresses any of the causes—from increased media concentration to the "bottom-line" mentality that sees news as just another form of entertainment—for this shift. Indeed, an alternative reading of the newscaster sketch could view it as spoof rather than as satire—a humorous acknowledgement rather than an indictment of what television news has become. Finally, will presidential satire ever return to television? The answer would appear to be "no" for prime-time network television. Given the increasing dependence of the major networks on a "lowest common denominator" audience, the minimum required level of knowledge about its subject that satire requires would seemingly rule out such a likelihood. And while the occasional joke or satiric sketch might turn up on cable or late-night television, it is difficult to imagine a satiric show popular and thus profitable enough to justify its existence. The question needed to be asked at this juncture is critical—can American democracy function in a media age without a satirical bully pulpit?

NOTES

1. The original name of the program was *NBC'S Saturday Night* because ABC had just started a program called *Saturday Night Live with Howard Cosell*. With the demise of the Cosell program in 1977, NBC permanently shortened the name to *Saturday Night Live*.

2. The saddest case may have been *The Jackie Gleason Show: The American Scene Magazine*. In 1962, after having been away from television for a number of years, Gleason promised his new weekly program would feature "topical satire," but satire, topical or otherwise, never appeared. Instead, Gleason reworked the old *Honeymooners'* characters to save the show (Marc 121–22).

3. There is no official episode guide to *Saturday Night Live*. Serpas provides an excellent and up-to-date guide at <http://www.io.com/~serpas/snl.html.> All references to sketch titles that do not come from compilation tapes are taken from the Serpas database.

4. Lorne Michaels discussed the difficulty of getting an accurate "take" on the Larry King show that aired two days before *Presidential Bash 2000* and four days before the actual election: "until we found that take on Reagan ["Mastermind"], we really didn't have a take. We had sketches. We just didn't have a take" (*Larry King Live*).

5. A 1992 program would even open with Reagan giving a speech while Sinatra and Reagan's wife, Nancy, have sex.

WORKS CITED

American Enterprise. "Interview with Gerald Ford." 24 October 2000. <http://www.theamericanenterprise.org/taemj99j.html>.

Anderson, Walter Truett. *Reality Isn't What It Used To Be.* New York: Harper and Row, 1990.

Best of the Clinton Scandal. Videocassette. Trimark, 1999.

"Cast and Crew of *SNL* Preview Their 'Presidential Bash 2000,'" *Larry King Live.* CNN, Atlanta. 3 November 2000.

Goodman, Ellen. "Too Much Ham, Too Little Meat in Presidential Race." *The Columbus Dispatch,* 23 October 2000, A9.

Hendra, Tony. *Going Too Far.* New York: Doubleday, 1987.

Hill, Doug, and Jeff Weingrad. *Saturday Night: A Backstage History of Saturday Night Live.* New York: Beech Tree Books, 1986.

Marc, David. *Comic Visions: Television Comedy and American Culture.* Boston: Unwin Hyman, 1989.

Nessen, Ron. *It Sure Looks Different from the Inside.* Chicago: Playboy Press, 1978.

New York Times. "Election Results: 1976." 24 October 2000. <http://www.nytimes.com/learning/general/specials/elections/1976/results1976.html>.

Pew Reseach Center for the People & the Press. 5 February 2000. "The Tough Job of Communicating with Voters." 24 October 2000. <http://press.org/jan00mor2.html>.

22 December 1998. "Turned Off Public Tuned Out Impeachment." 24 October 2000. <http://www.people-press.org/impeach.html>.

Peyser, Marc. "Al and Dubya After Hours." *Newsweek,* 30 October 2000, 38.

"Relaxed Bush Stages White House Laugh-In." *Atlanta Journal and Constitution,* 8 December 1992, B6.

Rozell, Mark J. *The Press and the Ford Presidency.* Ann Arbor: University of Michigan Press, 1992.

Saturday Night Live Presidential Bash. Videocassette. HGV Video Productions Inc., 1996.

Scheuer, Jeffrey. *The Sound Bite Society.* New York: Four Walls Eight Windows, 1999.

Spector, Bert. "A Clash of Cultures: The Smothers Brothers vs. CBS Television." In *American History/American Television,* edited by John E. O'Connor. New York: Frederick Unger, 1983.

Part Four

Bibliographic Overview

Myron A. Levine

THE TRANSFORMED PRESIDENCY

The *Real* Presidency and Hollywood's *Reel* Presidency

The American presidency has undergone considerable transformation since World War II. As the presidency assumed new domestic and foreign-policy responsibilities, the number of staff members who work for the White House expanded; new advisory structures were also created to assist the president. The result has been the emergence of an enlarged, institutionalized White House that demands considerable managerial talent from a president. Another quite obvious area of change is in communications where advances in technology have provided skilled presidents with new tools of leadership—while at the same time also offering new forums for media critics and the president's opponents.

For a number of decades, Hollywood did not focus all that greatly on the presidency. After all, the decisions made by the nation's chief executive did not always make for compelling cinema. Stories outside of the White House—tales of war, protests, strikes, and social conflict—all provided more dramatic visuals and story lines. In recent decades, however, Hollywood has shown a renewed interest in a presidency that has assumed new, and sometimes even quite terrifying, policy responsibilities.

This essay reviews the vast literature, written by both presidential scholars and former White House insiders, that has traced the growth and transformation of the modern White House. Only by doing so can we gauge the degree of accuracy or inaccuracy of the portrait of the American presidency provided by Hollywood film.

THE WAY THINGS USED TO BE: THE WHITE HOUSE OF FDR

The growth of the presidential staff is often attributed to the forces set in motion by World War II and the postwar era. A brief look at the presidency of

Library of Congress.

Presidential power grew with the New Deal and World War II. Yet the White House staff under Franklin D. Roosevelt was considerably smaller and less institutionalized than the White House staff of today.

Franklin D. Roosevelt reveals a White House that was much smaller and, in important ways, quite different from the bureaucratized, institutionalized presidency of today.

In her Pulitzer Prize–winning *No Ordinary Time—Franklin and Eleanor Roosevelt: The Home Front in World War II*, Doris Kearns Goodwin describes a White House with the informality and intimacy of a "small, intimate hotel," where houseguests came and even stayed for years:

> The permanent guests occasionally had private visitors of their own for cocktails or for meals, but for the most part their lives revolved around the president and first lady, who occupied adjoining suites in the southwest quarter of the second floor. On the third floor, in a cheerful room with slanted ceilings, lived Missy LeHand, the president's personal secretary and longtime friend. The president's alter ego, Harry Hopkins, occupied the Lincoln suite, two doors away from the president's suite . . . Lorena Hickok, Eleanor's great friend, occupied a corner room across from Eleanor's bedroom. This group of houseguests was continually augmented by a stream of visitors—Winston Churchill, who often stayed for two or three weeks at a time; the president's mother, Sara Delano Roosevelt; Eleanor's young friend Joe Lash; and Crown Princess Martha of Norway. (Goodwin, *No Ordinary* 9–10)

Roosevelt valued Hopkins, the frail secretary of commerce and former head of the New Deal's Works Progress Administration, who wound up serving as the president's emissary to London, Moscow, Teheran, and Yalta:

> "Stay the night," the President insisted. So Hopkins borrowed a pair of pajamas and settled into a bedroom suite on the second floor. There he remained, not simply for one night but for the next three and a half years, as Roosevelt, exhibiting his genius for using people in new and unexpected ways, converted him from the number-one relief worker to the number-one adviser on the war. Later, Missy [LeHand] liked to tease: "It was Harry Hopkins who gave George S. Kaufman and Moss Hart the idea for that play of theirs, 'The Man Who Came to Dinner.'" (Goodwin, *No Ordinary* 37)

Hopkins, the president's sounding board, occupied the Lincoln Study, just doors away from the president's bedroom.

By today's standards, the Roosevelt White House was relatively small, personal, and homey. A ritual evening cocktail hour, where the president himself mixed the drinks, offered "intimate gatherings" (Goodwin, *No Ordinary* 34), a time for relaxation, gossip, and swapping jokes in an informal atmosphere. Cocktails, card-playing, movies, and gossip, all offered the president the opportunity to escape the burdens of the office and renew his energies (Goodwin, *No Ordinary* 419). The FDR White House was so "un-imperial" that FDR and his guests even had to put up with drab, simple, and overcooked meals—oatmeal for breakfast—as the president could not bring himself to replace his housekeeper (Goodwin, *No Ordinary* 198–99).

In the Roosevelt White House, interpersonal relationships were often quite close, as seen in the anecdote told about the time the president approached Churchill with the idea of calling the treaty among the twenty-six Allies the "United Nations":

> By far the best story was told by Harry Hopkins, who claimed the president was so excited by his inspiration that he had himself wheeled into Churchill's bedroom early one morning, just as the prime minister was emerging from his bath, stark naked and gleaming pink. . . . The president apologized and said he would come back at a better time. "No need to go," Churchill said: "The Prime Minister of Great Britain has nothing to conceal from the President of the United States!" (Goodwin, *No Ordinary* 312)

During Churchill's extended visits, the Rose Suite and nearby rooms served as the virtual headquarters for the British wartime government.

The FDR White House poses a stark contrast with the more layered, bureaucratized, and institutionalized presidency of today. Structured and hierarchical staff relationships, a businesslike atmosphere, and an earnestness of purpose all characterize the contemporary White House—as so well captured in NBC's award-winning *The West Wing* (Rollins and O'Connor). By comparison, the Roosevelt White House, with its fluidity, informality of structure, and absence of large numbers of staff, seems almost antediluvian.

Today in Washington, the professionalization of the White House press corps, the norms that govern press behavior, and the institutionalization of presidency-press relations are all markedly different from the Roosevelt years. Roosevelt's relationship with the press was characterized by a "mutual respect and professional intimacy" (Kernell 78) that would seem quite remarkable if it were to occur today. Faced with a growing press corps of two hundred reporters, FDR appointed the first presidential press secretary, Stephen Early (Kernell 79). Still, Roosevelt met the press "frequently and routinely" (Kernell 79) and maintained close, personal relationships with reporters:

> For seven years, twice a week, the president had sat down with these reporters, explaining legislation, announcing appointments, establishing friendly contact, calling them by their first names, teasing them about their hangovers, exuding warmth and accessibility. Once, when a correspondent narrowly missed getting on Roosevelt's train, the president covered for him by writing his copy until he could catch up. (Goodwin, *No Ordinary* 26)

By the second half of the century, advances in technology and a change in press corps norms (resulting from Watergate and Vietnam) would act to un-

Library of Congress.

John F. Kennedy was the first president to master the art of presidential television. He used televised press conferences as a means of communicating directly with the American people.

dermine the intimacy of presidency-press relations that had characterized the Roosevelt era.

John Kennedy was the first presidential master of the new medium of television. TV offered the president new opportunities to communicate directly with the public, bypassing reporters. Presidents no longer had to suffer the risks of being too available to the press. Presidential press conferences became less frequent; they also became less a means of providing hard answers to the questions of the press and more a stage from which the president could reach the American public directly. A press secretary and a communications director—and their burgeoning staffs—would also now stand as a buffer between an increasingly media-savvy president and a growing corps of increasingly investigative and adversarial reporters (Edwards 108–28; Grossman and Kumar 81–156; Kernell 65–94).

Presidents increasingly discovered the advantages of "going public" as part of their governing strategies (Kernell 11–48). No longer do presidents rely so exclusively on the insider-bargaining approach portrayed in the film *Advise and Consent* (1962, directed by Otto Preminger), where the president makes deals and twists political arms in an attempt to get things done and to gain Senate confirmation of a controversial cabinet nominee.

Advise and Consent portrays the old-style presidency of the 1950s and 1960s, a presidency that was soon to undergo great change. Today, in contrast, presidents supplement their insider-bargaining strategies with appeals to the public that rely on the assistance of staffs of pollsters, media-relations advisers, press spokespersons, speechwriters, and aides serving as liaisons to key political constituencies and interest groups (Edwards; Grossman and Kumar; Kernell; Tulis; Peterson 612–25; Patterson 129–84, 193–218; Spragens and Terwood).

There is perhaps no greater testament to the change in White House–press relations than *All the President's Men* (1976, directed by Alan J. Pakula), which not only recorded the new adversarialism of the Nixon era but which, in many ways, inspired a new generation of investigative reporting after Watergate. *All the President's Men* attributes the "cracking" of the Watergate story to the aggressive work of *Washington Post* reporters Bob Woodward and Carl Bernstein (played, respectively, by Robert Redford and Dustin Hoffman), who persisted despite the lies and the disinformation fed by the official White House press machine and even the occasional threat from high White House officials. One flaw of the film is that it underplays the role of governmental investigations in bringing down the White House. Woodward and Bernstein largely reported leaks from other government bodies; still, their stories (and those of other reporters) kept up the pressure for government action.

In one important way, press norms have evolved still further since Watergate. In the film, *Post* editor Ben Bradlee (Jason Robards) demands that every allegation be checked twice, that the *Post* as a responsible paper seeking to preserve its credibility will not print unsubstantiated allegations. In today's Washington, with the growth of cable television, the Internet, and other new media outlets, such a concern seems quaint. In reporting the news, a rush to publish has overwhelmed the older gatekeepers such as Bradlee and the *Post*. In the new Washington, much to the president's discomfort, rumors and unsubstantiated allegations are often circulated and amplified by the media.

Contemporary filmmakers have also shown a heightened concern with the problems posed by political manipulation. *All the President's Men* painted the portrait of a Nixon White House mired in lies and cover-ups. The comedy *Dave* (1993, directed by Ivan Reitman) and the darkly sardonic and paranoid *Wag The Dog* (1997, directed by Barry Levinson) suggest an even still greater power for "spin," image control, and deception in the hands of the presidential public-relations machine. In *Dave*, an ordinary citizen (Kevin Kline) is used

Dustin Hoffman stars as a famous Hollywood producer who is called upon by presidential aides to deceive the public in *Wag The Dog* (1997).

to double for the president who suffers a stroke while in bed with his mistress; in *Wag The Dog*, a White House media adviser (Robert DeNiro) works with the help of a Hollywood producer (Dustin Hoffman) to stage the illusion of a war in order to divert the public's attention from a presidential sex scandal (involving a Girl Scout!). Interestingly, in both films, it is a sexual dalliance that is at the root of the deception, a fact that says something about the nature of the public and media's fascination with the presidency. Such a preoccupation with sexual misdoings cannot simply be blamed on Bill Clinton. The president in *Dave* bears some resemblance to George Herbert Walker Bush; rumors of a sexual affair, never substantiated, had circulated about Bush. *Dave* is also so steeped in an anti-Washington populism that any average man is seen to be able to stand in and do a more capable job than Washington insiders.

"THE SWELLING OF THE PRESIDENCY"

For most of the nation's existence, presidential staffs were extremely small—for a while almost nonexistent. Jefferson had only one messenger and one secretary. Early presidents paid staff salaries out of their own pockets, oftentimes relying on the services of relatives. It was not until 1857 that Congress appropriated money for the first presidential staff member, a clerk. Even in the twentieth century, Woodrow Wilson had only seven full-time aides (Burke 417–19).

The growth of the White House is seen as the result of FDR's proactive efforts to meet the challenges posed by the Great Depression and fascism in Europe. The Executive Office of the Presidency (EOP) was created in 1939 to give the nation's chief executive new staff resources. Yet, by today's standards, the Roosevelt White House had very few staff members; in preparing his legislative initiatives during his first "hundred days," Roosevelt had to rely greatly on personnel loaned to him from other government agencies (Burke 419).

Roosevelt sought to avoid staff institutionalization. He wanted to maintain close control over staff members, to keep his aides "on a very short leash" (Pfiffner, *The Modern Presidency* 46).

FDR did not allow his White House staff to grow so large that he could not personally supervise each member's activities. As a result, even at the height of the war, his senior White House staff, not counting clerical aides, numbered no more than a dozen. And they had few assistants of their own; there was little of the staff layering so common today (Dickinson 20).

FDR sought the assistance of generalists whom he could flexibly assign to tasks as needed; he feared that staff members would regard fixed jurisdictional assignments as "hunting licenses" for unsupervised policy initiatives. FDR also employed a competitive model of staffing where he used the work produced by one aide to check on the work done by another. Roosevelt did not have a chief of staff, an institutional innovation that would later be introduced by Eisenhower; instead, the president handed out staff work assignments himself. Often attacked for being disorderly and confusing, the Roosevelt managerial approach had clear advantages: "staff parochialism, closed-mindedness, and complacency were less likely to take root" (Dickinson 19; also see Neustadt 220–21).

The numbers clearly document "The Swelling of the American Presidency" (Cronin and Genovese 302) over the course of the twentieth century. The White House had only 45 full-time employees in 1937; ten years later, under Truman, the number stood at 190. During the Nixon years, the number ballooned to 550 before peaking at 605 under George H.W. Bush and falling back to 543 during Clinton's first year. Even these numbers may understate the true size of the White House staff because there is no easy way to document the exact number of personnel from other executive branch agencies who are detailed on temporary assignment to various presidential offices.

The Executive Office of the Presidency has mushroomed to the point that it fills not just the White House but also the next-door Eisenhower Executive Office Building (formerly known as the Old Executive Office Building), the New Executive Office Building, and various townhouses and other offices in Washington. New responsibilities led to new presidential advisory structures: the National Security Council (begun under Truman); the Council of Economic Advisers; the Office of Policy Development (with both domestic policy and economic policy responsibilities); and the Office of Management and Budget (a very valuable tool for setting presidential priorities and establishing centralized control over executive-branch agencies). There are also lesser EOP offices: the Council on Environmental Quality; the Office of the U.S. Trade Representative; the Office for National Drug Control Policy; and the Office of Science, Technology, and Space Policy (Patterson 18, 49–95). Responsibilities for policy formulation and implementation, once lodged with cabinet members and their subordinates, are now increasingly lodged with the White House staff, aides whom the president more fully trusts.

There are important staff resources in helping a president to get his legislative program through Congress. Beginning with Eisenhower, an office of legislative liaison was set up in order to help maintain a two-way flow of communications with Senate and House members. The White House legislative-affairs office functions, as Bryce Harlow has observed, as "An Ambulatory Bridge Across a Constitutional Gulf" (Patterson 114).

MANAGING THE INSTITUTIONALIZED PRESIDENCY

The contemporary president must be an institutional manager capable of giving direction to and overseeing the actions of the presidential bureaucracy as well as executive-branch departments and agencies. Presidents have found personnel decisions critical to institutional management: "Second to none in importance and priority at the White House is the selection of the men and women whom the president wishes to have serve in policymaking positions in the administration—and serve at his pleasure, without tenure" (Patterson 219). The president fills approximately 635 White House positions and another 5,840 noncareer positions in the bureaucracy (Patterson 220–21). The Office of Presidential Personnel (OPP), working under the direction of the White House director of personnel, screens applicants and ensures that new recruits can be entrusted to deliver the president's policies (Weko). The importance of the White House personnel operation is seen in its staffing numbers. The early Reagan administration had 100 persons who worked for the OPP; in 1993, under Clinton, there were 130 (Pfiffner, *The Modern Presidency* 92–93). During its presidential transition, the Clinton personnel office optically scanned 160,000 resumes into its computer system (Patterson 226).

A president's chief of staff (COS) is a key figure in the managerial presidency, dispensing and coordinating the assignments handed down to other staff aides and monitoring their work; in effect, the COS exerts total control over the work of other staff. The chief of staff also controls the president's schedule and determines just who has the need to see the president; it is the COS who determines "where to draw the line," that is, when an issue is to be taken to the president (Patterson 351–52).

Jimmy Carter, in a reaction against ills revealed by Watergate, tried to govern without a chief of staff. Carter wanted to fashion a more open presidency and did not want a COS who would serve as a "stopper" at the Oval Office door, isolating him from other voices in his administration as had been the situation during the Nixon administration. The experiment, however, did not work. In the absence of a COS, Carter soon found that he, himself, was burdened with the detailed work of supervising staff. Without the guidance of a COS, there was also such great confusion in staff assignments and so much competition for the president's ear that, toward the end of his term, Carter finally relented and named trusted adviser Hamilton Jordan as COS.

The Office of Management and Budget (OMB) offers a critical resource for presidential management. The OMB does much more than simply help the president prepare his proposed budget. Working under the direction of the president's appointed budget director, the OMB ensures "legislative clearance," that each department's legislative requests are screened by the White House and reflect the president's program priorities. In essence, the OMB assists the president in setting his priorities and his preferred levels of spending for every discretionary agency program. Since Ronald Reagan, the OMB has also been an important tool to ensure centralized control over the rule-making process, restraining departments and agencies from issuing administrative regulations that conflict with the president's policy priorities. Critics complain that recent presidents have exerted such great control over the operations of the OMB that the "neutral competence" and professionalism of the office's dedicated careerists are being jeopardized (Burke 434–34; Campbell 266–68). A politicized OMB risks losing its credibility when it underestimates program costs or overestimates expected revenues in an effort to help "sell" the president's proposed budget.

In foreign policy, the National Security Council (NSC) plays a dominant role. The NSC was created under Truman in order to facilitate interagency coordination and to ensure that the expertise of all relevant agencies would be brought to bear on complex security decisions. The NSC seeks to assure the proper flow of paperwork, allowing the staff of each agency to comment on proposed courses of action. Under recent presidents, however, the NSC and the national security adviser (the president's appointed head of the NSC) have gained an importance beyond efforts at interdepartmental, collegial, decision-making. Under a number of presidents, the national security adviser has tended to serve more as a presidential adviser advocating his or her own policy preferences, enjoying the influence that can accompany a top White House staffer's close proximity to the president (Burke 426–28).

DISPLACING THE CABINET

Cabinet secretaries differ from presidential staff members in that the former do more than simply work directly for and advise the president; they also have line administrative responsibilities for the day-to-day operation of huge executive departments. These line responsibilities often draw departmental secretar-

ies away from the White House; these departmental chiefs may also develop
views on departmental matters that are somewhat different from those of the
president. As a result, over time, a cabinet secretary may lose some of a
president's confidence. White House staff members, in contrast, do not suffer
such split loyalties. To a great degree, members of the White House staff have
displaced the cabinet as the president's primary advisers (Warshaw).

Unlike classic cabinet government in Britain, the modern cabinet in the
United States does not serve as a collective decision-making body. Presidents
may choose to rely on the advice of individual cabinet members, but presidents have not found the cabinet as a whole to be a very useful collegial decision-making or consultative body. Lyndon Johnson's press secretary and special
adviser George Reedy observed:

> The cabinet is one of those institutions in which the whole is less than the sum of
> the parts. As individual officers, the members bear heavy responsibilities in ad-
> ministering the affairs of the government. As a collective body, they are about as
> useful as the vermiform appendix—though far more honored. (Reedy 73)

The tradition of ignoring the cabinet even goes back as far as Andrew Jackson,
who chose instead to meet with a "Kitchen Cabinet" of political cronies and
friends.

For the contemporary president, the cabinet is simply too large and di-
verse to allow the targeted discussion and informed give-and-take that complex issues require. A cabinet member responsible for veterans' affairs, housing,
or agriculture, for instance, may have little of substance to add in the midst of
a foreign-policy crisis. In responding to the Cuban missile crisis, John Kennedy
convened the Executive Committee (ExCom) of the National Security Council, not the cabinet, to review alternative courses of action. In the ExCom work
group, the president assembled a wide array of intelligence, diplomatic and
defense experts, cabinet officials, and White House staff aides—including
speechwriter Ted Sorenson and political associate Kenny O'Donnell—whose
judgment JFK valued (Allison and Zelikow 110–11; Preston 97–136).

In today's "cabinet of unequals" (Cronin and Genovese 291–92), secretaries in the "inner" cabinet enjoy greater influence than do secretaries in the
"outer" cabinet. The Departments of State, Defense, and Treasury constitute
the inner cabinet; the president turns to them for advice on crucial foreign
policy and economic policy matters that he must repeatedly face. The heads of
the other departments—Agriculture, Interior, Transportation, Health and
Human Services, Housing and Urban Development, Labor, Commerce, En-

ergy, Education, and Veterans' Affairs—work on matters that are less central to the president. These secretaries comprise an outer cabinet; their secretaries enjoy less frequent access to the president and are generally called upon for advice only on those occasions when their jurisdictional concerns gain primacy on the president's agenda (Cronin and Genovese 292–93).

The Justice Department is sometimes in the inner cabinet and sometimes in the outer cabinet. Attorney Generals Robert Kennedy and Edwin Meese were important consigliores, respectively, to JFK and Reagan. Janet Reno, in contrast, worked largely as an outsider, distrusted by Clinton and his top staff.

Presidents generally choose cabinet members on the basis of their abilities. Yet, political considerations—the racial, ethnic, gender, geographical, and political balance an appointee can bring to an administration—are often also important, especially in the selection of members of the outer cabinet.

Just how far "out" can an outer cabinet member be when chosen for political considerations? At a reception during the early days of his administration, Ronald Reagan did not even recognize "Silent" Sam Pierce, his secretary for Housing and Urban Development and the only African American in the cabinet; Reagan greeted his new department head with an it's-so-nice-to-meet-you, "Mr. Ambassador."

Even when individual cabinet members serve as presidential counselors, they compete with presidential staff for influence. Cabinet heads must spend the great bulk of their time outside the White House, running their departments and meeting with the representatives of various departmental constituencies (Hess 202); this means that cabinet secretaries are often absent from the White House when key matters are discussed. As a result, in the competition between White House staff and cabinet members, it is often the staff members who emerge victorious. National Security Adviser Henry Kissinger, not Secretary of State William Rogers, dominated foreign policy during Nixon's first term in office. Cyrus Vance, Jimmy Carter's secretary of state, eventually resigned, having lost his power struggle with more hawkish National Security Adviser Zbigniew Brzezinski.

What explains the drift of influence from cabinet members into the hands of White House staff? The president does not always fully trust the perspective of departmental secretaries who risk "going native" as they spend so much time with departmental bureaucrats and their constituencies. A departmental secretary is no longer simply the president's representative; he or she also, to some extent, becomes the advocate of the department's point of view. White

House staff, in contrast, work only for the president and pose no such problem of divided loyalties.

New presidents have regularly promised to lessen the dominance of White House staff and strengthen the role played by cabinet officials; but once in office, confronted with the difficulties of getting things done, presidents eventually come to see the advantages of drawing decision-making into the hands of trusted White House advisers. Of all the modern presidents, Dwight Eisenhower paid the greatest respect to the authority of individual cabinet officials and to the cabinet as an advisory body. "General Eisenhower" respected lines of organizational hierarchy and the authority of his appointees: "Under the Eisenhower system the cabinet officers were expected to run the daily operations of their departments without presidential interference" (Hess 59). Eisenhower attended frequent cabinet meetings—an average of thirty-four a year over his two terms (Greenstein 113), a marked contrast to the paucity of cabinet meetings convened by more recent chief executives.

Richard Nixon came to the presidency promising a return to a cabinet-centered government (Pfiffner, *The Strategic Presidency* 41); but within six months departmental secretaries were ignored, and cabinet meetings were virtually forgotten as White House staff aides drafted major domestic policy bills in relative secrecy (Nathan 42–43). Having failed to win legislative approval for much of his domestic agenda, Nixon adopted an "administrative presidency" strategy where White House officials were to exert strict control over the day-to-day actions of the executive departments (Nathan 45). As part of the plan to give Domestic Policy Adviser John Ehrlichman greater power over agency affairs, Nixon, on the heels of his landslide reelection in 1972, asked for the resignation of all cabinet and sub-cabinet appointees: "They could keep their jobs only if they agreed to live by the cardinal rule: the White House was to call all of the shots" (Dean 153; also see DiClerico 183–88 and Nathan). Only the intrusion of Watergate derailed the administrative presidency.

Jimmy Carter, reacting to the abuses of Watergate, promised to reverse the direction of White House power by revitalizing the cabinet. But, like his immediate predecessors, he, too, soon came to regard cabinet meetings as a waste of time; they were convened less frequently. Toward the end of his term, Carter sought greater White House review of agency actions and, like Nixon, even demanded the resignation of each cabinet member; he accepted five (Pfiffner, *The Strategic Presidency* 45–47; also see Campbell 59–61).

Ronald Reagan similarly sought to increase the involvement of cabinet members in policy by establishing a system of "cabinet councils" (Campbell 25–26, 150–52). These interdepartmental work groups met regularly with top OMB officials and other White House staff members who assured the fealty of the councils to the president's policy goals. While the system of councils did promote greater cabinet action in domestic policy, on the whole the cabinet councils dealt primarily with "secondary-level matters" (Newland 153–61); "many of the most important decisions were not made through the cabinet council apparatus" but by top-level White house officials "who often ignored cabinet council decisions" (Pfiffner, *The Strategic Presidency* 52).

Of all the contemporary Washington films, *Thirteen Days* (2000, directed by Roger Donaldson) perhaps does the best job of capturing the prominence of White House staff, the displacement of the cabinet in decision-making, and the different stature of inner and outer cabinet secretaries. The accuracy of the film is the result of the great deference that the filmmakers accorded historians who had examined the tapes of White House discussions during the Cuban missile crisis. Still, the movie is not without its flaws. The film heightens the drama (as if a film about the world on the brink of nuclear devastation needed an artifice to exaggerate drama) by unfairly painting the Joint Chiefs of Staff and other militarists as chomping at the bit to lead the nation to war. Also, as a matter of dramatic convenience, Kennedy confidante Kenny O'Donnell (Kevin Costner) is used as the inside-the-White-House "everyman" who allows the audience to see the unfolding of key inner-circle events through his eyes. While O'Donnell was a trusted JFK political lieutenant, tape recordings and other records of the ExCom meetings do not show that he played a great role at all in crisis decision-making—although, of course, we cannot know what influence, if any, he had on decisions that were made behind the scenes.

RISKS AND DANGERS: SYCOPHANCY, ISOLATION, AND COMPETITION

Departmental secretaries can be influential, but only if, like White House staff, they moderate their independent voice and submerge their policy views to those of the president. As George Reedy explains, "The secretaries do not have a political status and it is considered bad form for any one of them to deviate in the slightest from the line laid down by their chief—so bad that deviation usually spells an end to a public career" (Reedy 75–76). Modern cabinet members, like presidential staff, lack the political base necessary to express "the kind of dissent that a president should hear on a direct, personal basis if he is to remain in touch with reality" (Reedy 78). The tradition of cabinet loyalty is so strong as to mute internal criticism. Bill Clinton was able to appeal to this tradition in convincing Secretary of Health and Human Services Donna Shalala, a former university president with considerable professional stature, to mute her outrage upon having discovered that Clinton had deceived her and other cabinet members in his earlier denials of his sexual relationship with Monica Lewinsky.

Of course, presidents look for more than mere loyalty when choosing a departmental secretary; they also seek a person with the ability to manage his or her department. As a result, persons of stature with a reputation for independence—including James Schlesinger (under Gerald Ford), Jack Kemp and Alexander Haig (under Reagan), and Janet Reno (under Clinton)—can gain cabinet posts (Cronin and Genovese 279–81). Presidents are also often constrained when dismissing a maverick cabinet member. Clinton, facing continued criticisms over Whitewatergate, travelgate, the Lewinsky episode, and other matters allowed Janet Reno to remain in office despite the view of the White House that the attorney general was not a dependable team player.

White House staffers, lacking such stature, are even more prone than cabinet members to a sycophancy and a yes-man relationship that risks distancing the president from reality. In the "American monarchy" (Reedy 3), the presidency takes on certain aspects of royalty: "No one thrusts unpleasant thoughts upon a king unless he is ordered to do so, and even then he does so at his own peril" (Reedy 97). Staffers who gain their place in the administration as a result of their participation in the president's victorious election campaign are especially likely to see the president's priorities as their own.

The "one fixed goal in life" for a White House assistant "is somehow to gain and maintain access to the president" (Reedy 88). The result is a competition among White House staff members to curry the favor of the president and senior staff in order to gain increased responsibilities and status. The Nixon White House was so competitive that it was "in a state of perpetual internal flux" (Dean 20); offices were constantly being reassigned, altered, and redecorated, all serving as testimony to who was moving up and who was moving down the White House hierarchy. The most highly valued offices, of course, are those with proximity to the president and senior staff.

The great danger is that a staff member may sacrifice his or her independent judgment and concern for ethics in the race for advancement. John Dean, the presidential counsel whose tell-all Watergate testimony led to Nixon's demise, recalled his own early White House experiences of "climbing towards the moral abyss of the President's inner circle . . . thinking I had made it to the top just as I began to realize I had actually touched bottom" (Dean 21).

The White House is a place where "groupthink" regularly occurs and where courses of action desired by the president are rarely subjected to the most complete and exacting scrutiny. The culture of deference in the White House even helps to explain such major presidential disasters as Truman's overextension of the war in Korea, Kennedy's approval of the absurdly unrealistic Bay of Pigs invasion scenario, Johnson's continued escalation of the war in Vietnam, and Nixon's pattern of continued deceit in the Watergate cover-up (Janis 14-71, 97-130, 198-241). Indeed, writing after Watergate, Richard Neustadt admitted that his classic formulation of presidential power had underestimated the power of loyalty and the ability of misguided staff loyalty to lead a presidency to disaster (Neustadt 191).

The dangers posed by White House isolation and groupthink are especially severe when presidents, acting on the basis of incomplete advice, initiate unwise military interventions. As the Vietnam War dragged on, Congress in 1973 passed the War Powers Resolution (WPR), with its requirement that the president notify and consult with congressional leaders in advance of committing troops into situations of "imminent hostilities"; the consultation requirement was an attempt by Congress to break the isolation of White House inner advisory circles in a critical policy area. But the attempt has largely failed; in crisis after crisis since Vietnam, presidents have largely ignored the War Powers Resolution and have failed to consult with Congress in any meaningful way (Fisher 134–206).

On occasion, rivalries among staff factions can wind up breaking the circle of groupthink by bringing competing points of view to the president's attention. But such factionalism poses new problems for the president: the inability to get staff to act as a team; paralysis of action as decisions are delayed by continued internal debate; and the considerable damage to an administration caused by "leaks" as each White House faction uses the press to undermine the other (Morris 101–3).

The Reagan presidency suffered from the conflict among various staff factions. Clinton's first term was marred by the "chronic conflict" (Morris 97) between two White House factions, one committed to the more moderate New Democratic policy positions that the president had expressed during the campaign, and a second, more liberal faction that saw a Clinton presidency and a Democratic Congress as offering an opening to pass bold policy initiatives consistent with Democratic Party traditions. Plagued by the

internal conflict, Clinton soon came to express his regret that he did not de-
vote the same time and care in recruiting and screening his staff that he did in
selecting his cabinet (Morris 97).

Primary Colors (1998, directeed by Mike Nichols) observes how the sense of
shared mission, teamwork, and personal loyalty that develops during a presidential election campaign are carried over to a new president's staff. A less
salubrious picture of the presidency is presented by Stanley Kubrick's *Dr.
Strangelove* (1964), the ultimate satirical send-up of Cold War groupthink and
the unquestioned deference accorded military advisers. In *Dr. Strangelove*, President Merkin Muffley (Peter Sellers) and his advisers are both literally and figu-
ratively isolated from reality; confined in the War Room beneath the White
House, they set the world down the path toward nuclear doomsday.

THE IMPACT OF PRESIDENTIAL PERSONALITY AND STYLE

The exact relationship between a president and White House staff varies from
president to president. The tendencies toward isolation and staff factionalism
are inherent in the institutionalized presidency, but they are also dependent
on a president's personality and managing style. Not all presidents suffer equally

Infectious optimism, a good
sense of humor, and a
willingness to listen to
competing points of view were
all hallmarks of the Kennedy
leadership style.

from the risks of groupthink and isolation. As *Thirteen Days* recounts, John Kennedy encouraged the flow of a diversity of views. This is a perspective that is reinforced by Kennedy insiders. Speechwriter and Kennedy confidant Theodore Sorenson recalled that JFK wanted advisers to be "skeptical and critical, not sycophantic" (Preston 111). Secretary of State Dean Rusk similarly remembered that JFK "liked to have discussions that were more or less like seminars where various people around the table would be invited to speak up and present their views" (Preston 110–11). Kennedy did not want his advisers to serve as "filters to the president" but as a "debate team" that considered policy options from "multiple, conflicting perspectives" (George and George 211).

James David Barber's study of presidential character underscores the extent to which president-adviser relations are shaped by a president's personality. According to Barber (4–83), the dangers of isolation are most apparent in the case of ego-defensive, *active-negative* presidents who are compelled to action in order to compensate for their inner demons. These presidents see themselves as surrounded by enemies and attribute all criticisms of their policies to the ill motives of their attackers. Lyndon Johnson did not even allow his war councils to critically examine his policies.

Chester Cooper described how this process worked in a National Security Council meeting. "The President, in due course, would announce his decision and then poll everyone in the room—council members, their assistants, and members of the White House and NSC staffs. 'Mr. Secretary, do you agree with the decision?' 'Yes, Mr. President.' 'Mr. X, do you agree?' 'I agree, Mr. President,' would one-by-one give the assent that Johnson requested as he went around the table" (Goodwin, *Lyndon Johnson* 338).

LBJ had only a limited tolerance for dissenting points of view. He blamed scapegoats for the mounting protests against the Vietnam War and his declining approval ratings; he saw intellectuals, the press, knee-jerk liberals, Kennedyites, crackpots, and other conspirators as all being out to get him (Goodwin, *Lyndon Johnson* 329; Barber 44). Johnson saw Robert Kennedy, whom he always referred to as "Sonny Boy," to be the main villain (Barber 44). In the Nixon White House, the distrust and the sense of being besieged by "ruthless" enemies was so great that it led to a quite unhealthy do-it-to-them-before-they-do-it-to-you attitude (Barber 161–64).

The *passive-positive* presidents, by comparison, are compliant figures that play to the audience in a search for approval and affection. Ronald Reagan hated confrontation; he tried to "split the difference" to avoid offending competing advisers and was slow to fire top aides even when it was necessary to do so (Barber 224–31; George and George 225–26). Reagan possessed a strong foreign-policy vision, but its implementation suffered as the president was reluctant to establish discipline among competing staff factions (George and George 233). In the critical national-security policy arena, Reagan was a delegator, and his presidency suffered from a lack of firm control: "the president distanced himself to a surprising and dangerous degree from both the substance and the process of foreign-policymaking" (George and George 230). Barber's third type of president, the *passive-negative*, the increasingly rare type of executive who dislikes politics but who accepts the call to public service out of a sense of civic obligation, is similarly characterized by excessive reliance on staff and a tendency toward drift.

The *active-positive* president, according to Barber, has the healthiest personality. Brought up in an atmosphere of unconditional love and affection, the active-positive—FDR, Truman, Kennedy—is sure of who he is. He does not take criticism of his policies as criticism of himself as a person; he can learn from his mistakes, grow in office, and adapt flexibly to changing situations. Kennedy, for instance, learned from the Bay of Pigs fiasco. Amid the pressures of the Cuban missile crisis, Kennedy sought out a diversity of opinions and options; he also questioned the estimates of the agencies as to their capabilities (Barber 364–79; Janis 14–47, 132–58).

Barber's typology is provocative but not well grounded in personality theory (Hargrove 95). Presidents are complex figures whose behavior does not easily fall within one of Barber's four boxes (George; George and George 181; Nelson 210–11). Recent scholarship, for instance, has pointed to Eisenhower's successful leadership, including his more assertive command of the advisory process (Greenstein; Henderson), a portrayal that is quite at odds with Barber's characterization of Ike as "passive." Even the evidence on Kennedy is more mixed than Barber conveys. Kennedy revisionists charge that JFK often took conflict (especially with Castro) personally, that he exacerbated Cold War crises, and that he was not truly open to advice contrary to his tough, pragmatic foreign-policy interventionism (Fairlie; Miroff, *Icons of Democracy* 273–307; Miroff, *Pragmatic Illusions*; Wills).

Thomas Preston does not seek to classify a president's character; instead, Preston simply tries to assess the variety of ways that modern presidents have utilized their advisory systems in different policy areas (Preston 5–31). A president's relationship with his cabinet and staff will vary with his need to assert his power, his personal ability to see the complexities of issues, and his expertise or familiarity with a policy area. Eisenhower, Kennedy, and George

H. W. Bush, for instance, all came to the presidency with considerable foreign-policy experience and chose to rely on their own judgments in foreign affairs; in domestic policy, however, these executives were more reliant on the suggestions of advisers. Bill Clinton acted as his own "navigator" in domestic affairs, having had considerable experience as governor and having earned a considerable reputation for being a policy "wonk"; in foreign policy, however, he was less experienced, and his course of action was more dependent on the dominant views expressed in his advisory group (Preston 14–16). As Clinton grew in office and gained familiarity with the issues, he became more active in making foreign policy (Preston 31, 243–50).

The ability of a president to see the "complexity" of an issue has both benefits and drawbacks. Presidents who have a greater tolerance of complexity seek out more extensive contextual information and advice, including criticisms of potential courses of action. But such an extensive information search and deliberation can also slow down action. In contrast, low-complexity leaders, like Truman, who see the world in terms of "black-and-white" policy problems, are more likely to act decisively, relying on the recommendations of a few trusted experts without feeling the need to seek a wider discussion that explores every possible scenario (Preston 9–10, 32–63).

George W. Bush, in the early days of his presidency, exhibited the characteristics of a low-complexity leader, who had a low cognitive need for information and who saw issues in simple black-and-white terms. Bush had no intense need to personally dominate the decision-making process; he allowed a large policy role for advisers. The White House advisory system was hierarchically structured, in corporate-like fashion, with Chief of Staff Andrew Card jealously guarding the president's time. Policy memos written for the president were kept quite brief, and staff presentations were mandated to be short and to the point; there was little tolerance of extended and free-ranging discussions, which were seen as a waste of the president's time. Staff members were expected to assume the role of loyal team players.

Having served as governor of Texas, Bush possessed much greater familiarity with domestic issues, especially school reform, than with foreign policy. In the wake of the deadly attack on the World Trade Center, the president's tendency toward black-and-white thinking allowed him to deliver a relatively swift and decisive response against the Al Qaeda organization in Afghanistan. Sure of the correctness and the morality of the American cause, he did not unduly delay or limit the strike while advisers explored innumerable complexities and ramifications of American action: the possible destabilization of the

Library of Congress.

Bill Clinton was a self-professed policy "wonk" who enjoyed discussing the intricate complexities of issues.

region, the impact that the bombings could have on American relations with the Muslim world, and the impact that American action could have on both the Israel-Palestine conflict and India-Pakistan relations. Lacking intimate knowledge of the national security arena, the president turned to key inner-circle advisers—Secretary of State Colin Powell, Secretary of Defense Donald Rumsfeld, National Security Adviser Condoleezza Rice, and Vice President Richard Cheney—testifying to the importance of key foreign-policy advisers to inexperienced presidents. Bush's tendency to black-white thinking was also evident in his willingness to go to war against the "evil" of Iraq's Saddam Hussein and his continued development of weapons of mass destruction.

Hollywood has given fair attention to the discussion of presidential character (Rollins). Unfortunately, however, its movies have often been simplistic and melodramatic in their attempts to portray character. Biopics, such as Daryl Zanuck's *Wilson* (1944, directed by Henry King) and *Sunrise at Campobello* (1962, directed by Vincent Donahue and starring Ralph Bellamy as FDR), are little more than uncritical hagiographies. In *Wilson*, the president is portrayed as a man of uncompromising principle and virtue; Zanuck ignored the many flaws of Wilson's leadership that were apparent to Wilson's biographers of the day (Knock 100), flaws that would dominate the more serious interpretations of Wilson's character. As strange as it may seem, one of the best character portrayals of a president may well have been in the musical *Annie!* (1982, directed by John Huston), where viewers are given the sense of FDR's optimism and ebullience, the positive and uplifting spirit that allowed Roosevelt to inspire a nation during the dark days of the Great Depression and the setbacks early in World War II.

THE CHANGING ROLES OF THE VICE PRESIDENT AND THE FIRST LADY

The vice president and the first lady have assumed a new importance in the modern presidency that, not too long ago, was not at all typical. Such traditional wisdom as voiced by "Cactus" John Nance Garner, FDR's first vice president, that his office was not "worth a warm pitcher of spit" is simply dated. Still, even as late as the 1960s and 1970s, vice presidents like Hubert Humphrey and Spiro Agnew were often excluded from key decision-making councils.

It is the traditional vice presidency that has been presented in Hollywood film, to the extent that Hollywood has shown any interest in portraying the vice presidency at all. In *Thirteen Days,* Vice President Lyndon Johnson is shown as somewhat marginalized, with top Kennedy aides reluctant to bring him fully into the inner circle of decision. Even Oliver Stone's highly controversial *JFK,* which alleges the possible collusion of Lyndon Johnson in a cover-up of the Kennedy assassination, reinforces the perception of Johnson as a frustrated vice president who had been denied the power he coveted. Jim Garrison (Kevin Costner), the film's antagonist, asserts that Johnson was one of "the two men who profited the most from the assassination." When the film shifts forward to 1970, and Garrison, looking back on events, asks how it all started, his Washington informer "X" observes that "Money—arms, big oil, Pentagon people, contractors, bankers, politicians like LBJ were committed to a war in southeast Asia," and that Johnson and the others "knew Kennedy was going to change things." Stone's allegations are clear, albeit irresponsible.[1] Stone quite clearly believes in the heroic Kennedy; he gives great weight to the words of Kennedy's private confidants that he was planning soon to withdraw from Vietnam. Yet, Kennedy's promises must be weighed against his public statements and his record of escalation in Vietnam.

Today, however, the vice presidency has been transformed, and the vice president tends to act as a highly valued presidential advisor. Vice presidents enjoy considerable staff; they also have an office in the West Wing and access to key briefings and presidential meetings. To a great extent the reconstitution of the vice presidency began when Presidents Jimmy Carter and Ronald Reagan gave heightened prominence to their vice presidents, Walter "Fritz" Mondale and George Bush, respectively. Bill Clinton utilized Al Gore even more extensively. In each case, these vice presidents demonstrated their competence and earned the trust of the president, showing that they would subordinate their policy views and political ambitions to those of their chief and that they would never contradict or embarrass the president in public (Cronin and Genovese 328–38). In return for their fealty, they were rewarded with increasingly substantial policy responsibilities: Bush, for instance, served as Reagan's point man

Library of Congress.

Vice President Hubert H. Humphrey had gained considerable national respect as a result of his distinguished congressional career. Yet he was shut out of certain key decision-making processes by President Lyndon Johnson.

on regulatory reform and paperwork reduction; Gore was made responsible for the "reinvention" of government and also acted as a key presidential adviser on foreign policy. Bush vice president Dan Quayle, largely ridiculed by the press, did not fully pass the test of winning the president's trust; but he, too, grew in office and was given considerable responsibilities, attesting to the transformation of the vice presidency (Pika 547–52).

Vice presidents today are picked for their ability to govern and not just for the political assets they may bring to an electoral ticket. Compare the selection of Spiro Agnew and Richard Cheney. Nixon chose Maryland's Spiro Agnew as his running mate, having little knowledge of the man other than that the relatively unknown governor of Maryland would allow Nixon to bridge relationships with the more moderate Rockefeller wing of the Republican Party. George W. Bush's selection of Richard Cheney, in contrast, was obviously more the result of Cheney's extensive Washington experience and credentials in foreign policy, areas of Bush weakness, than of any concern for the three electoral votes from Cheney's home state of Wyoming.

Reflecting the changing role of women, and most conspicuous in the public stage occupied by Hillary Clinton, the first lady has gained a new primacy as a presidential adviser. An active spouse can be the "First Special Counselor" (Patterson 281), no longer just the wifely adjunct who devotes her time solely to hospitality duties and such tertiary policy matters as Lady Bird Johnson's efforts to beautify America by removing unsightly billboards and used-car dumps from along the nation's highways. The heightened role of the first lady is clearly evident in the transformation of the East Wing office. Hillary Clinton had a full-time speechwriter (later two); her personal staff numbered twenty and was supplemented by fifteen interns and another fifteen volunteers; additional staff worked for the White House Social Office (Patterson 292).

Still, as Hillary Clinton found out and as Eleanor Roosevelt had similarly discovered at an earlier time, the role of an activist first lady is fraught with danger. Little wonder, then, that Barbara Bush and Laura Bush, who devoted their time to such traditional "caring" policy areas as mental health and education, were less divisive figures who gained more unmixed public approval for their efforts.

Eleanor Roosevelt was a valuable complement to FDR, acting as the "eyes and ears" for the disabled president as she toured the nation. Eleanor's social policy convictions balanced Franklin's political pragmatism; she pushed him to act on behalf of the poor and excluded (Goodwin, *No Ordinary*). She also wrote a syndicated daily newspaper column. Eleanor Roosevelt, although widely popular, also often received public scorn for her failure to play a more traditional wifely role. She was eventually forced to give up the formal governmental position she had accepted as assistant director of the Office of Civilian Defense, as her actions in that office became the target of merciless criticism from Congress and journalists (Goodwin, *No Ordinary* 280–81, 323–26).

Like Eleanor Roosevelt, Hillary Clinton was an activist leader who gained newfound popularity but who also was a polarizing figure. She suffered for overtly violating traditional gender expectations, as when she announced that she would be known as Hillary Rodham Clinton, not just Hillary Clinton. During the election campaign, Bill had promised a new activist "partnership" fit for modern times—vote for one and get two dynamic leaders. Yet, in retrospect, it was clearly a political mistake for Bill to put Hillary in command of the cabinet-level task force charged with developing his national health-care initiative, his number one domestic priority. Hillary became a high-visibility lightning rod who attracted attacks that undermined the entire health-reform effort. The appointment was also unwise as it muted the normal give-and-take of policy development; ordinary aides would not willingly challenge the positions advocated by the president's wife (Patterson 284–85).

It is not only liberal, activist Democrats, like Eleanor Roosevelt and Hillary Clinton, who have seized greater influence beyond the confines of their East Wing offices. Nancy Reagan, too, played an important political role, but she did so largely behind the scenes. She suffered greatly as the press ridiculed her love of fashion, her concern for the furnishings of the White House, the inadequacy of her "Just say 'No!'" approach to drugs, and even her willingness to consult an astrologer. But, devoted to "Ronnie," she also served her husband well, seeking to protect his interests and even his place in history. In fact, Nancy may have been the only "disinterested adviser" (Neustadt 313) in a highly factionalized White House. Nancy policed White House personnel, urged the president to oust disloyal aides, kept White House chief of staff Donald Regan in check, and alerted the president to threats to his public standing (Patterson 312–14).

Overall, the president's spouse has gained a new primacy as a presidential adviser but still must be somewhat circumspect of traditional gender roles. Eleanor Roosevelt and Hillary Clinton at times were effectively punished for going too far and violating expectations. The lessons are simple: first ladies cannot hold formal positions of responsibility. First ladies can be active and will enjoy as much influence as the president allows, but the politically wise first lady will find it useful to shield the full degree of her influence from the American public and to pay at least some respect to traditional role expectations.

A TRANSFORMED PRESIDENCY

The White House has grown greatly and been transformed as the national government has assumed new domestic and foreign policy responsibilities. The growth of the EOP has provided presidents with important assets for leadership. But the growth of presidential staff also poses new problems of isolation and factionalism. Presidents must demonstrate considerable managerial abilities if they are to gain effective control of the institutionalized presidency and maximize their leadership potential.

But the contemporary Washington environment, with its extreme dispersion of power, does not lend itself easily to leadership. Curiously, it is an older film, *Advise and Consent*, that most clearly shows the limits of presidential power in the American political system.

Ironically, those presidents who are most recognized as "great" leaders are more often than not executives who sought to "preserve" order and minimize the potential of threatening change. The presidency has been transformed;

Vice President Kathryn Bennett takes charge of the situation room during the skyjacking crisis of Air Force One. *Air Force One* (1997).

but a transformed presidency is no guarantee of transformational leadership (Riley 435-40). It is perhaps here that Hollywood, in reifying a mythic "heroic" presidency, strays the furthest from reality.

NOTE

1. For a review of the great controversy surrounding Stone's *JFK*, see Stone and Sklar.

WORKS CITED

Allison, Graham, and Philip Zelikow. *The Essence of Decision: Explaining the Cuban Missile Crisis.* 2nd ed. New York: Addison-Wesley/Longman, 1999.

Barber, James David. *The Presidential Character: Predicting Performance in the White House.* 4th ed. Englewood Cliffs, New Jersey: Prentice-Hall, 1992.

Burke, John P. "The Institutionalized Presidency." In *The Presidency and the American Political System,* edited by Michael Nelson, 417–42. 6th ed. Washington D.C.: CQ Press, 2000.

Campbell, Colin S.J. *Managing the Presidency: Carter, Reagan, and the Search for Executive Harmony.* Pittsburgh: University of Pittsburgh Press, 1986.

Cronin, Thomas E., and Michael A. Genovese. *The Paradoxes of the American Presidency.* New York: Oxford, 1998.

Dean, John. *Blind Ambition.* New York: Simon and Schuster, 1976.

Dickinson, Matthew J. "Uprooting the Presidential Branch? The Lessons of FDR." In *FDR and the Modern Presidency: Leadership and Legacy,* edited by Mark J. Rozell and William D. Peterson, 13–35. Westport, Connecticut: Praeger, 1997.

DiClerico, Robert E. *The American President.* 4th ed. Englewood Cliffs, New Jersey: Prentice-Hall, 1995.

Edwards, George C., III. *The Public Presidency: The Pursuit of Public Support.* New York: St. Martin's, 1983.

Fairlie, Henry. *The Kennedy Promise: The Politics of Expectation.* New York: Doubleday, 1973.

Fisher, Louis. *Presidential War Power.* Lawrence: University Press of Kansas, 1995

George, Alexander L. "Assessing Presidential Character." *World Politics* 26 (1974): 234–82.

———, and Juliette L. George. *Presidential Personality and Performance.* Boulder, Colorado: Westview, 1998.

Goodwin, Doris Kearns. *Lyndon Johnson and the American Dream.* New York: St. Martin's, 1991.

———. *No Ordinary Time—Franklin and Eleanor Roosevelt: The Home Front in World War II.* New York: Touchstone/Simon & Schuster, 1995.

Greenstein, Fred I. *The Hidden-Hand Presidency: Eisenhower as Leader.* New York: Basic Books, 1982.

Grossman, Michael Baruch, and Martha Joynt Kumar. *Portraying the President: The White House and the News Media*. Baltimore: Johns Hopkins University Press, 1981.

Hargrove, Erwin C. "Presidential Personality and Leadership Style." In *Researching the Presidency: Vital Questions, New Approaches*, edited by George C. Edwards III, John H. Kessel, and Bert A. Rockman, 69–109. Pittsburgh: University of Pittsburgh Press, 1993.

Henderson, Phillip G. *Managing the Presidency: The Eisenhower Legacy—From Kennedy to Reagan*. Boulder, Colorado: Westview, 1988.

Hess, Stephen. *Organizing the Presidency*. Rev. ed. Washington, D.C.: Brookings Institution, 1988.

Janis, Irving L. *Groupthink*. 2nd ed. Boston: Houghton Mifflin, 1982.

Kernell, Samuel. *Going Public: New Strategies of Presidential Leadership*. 3rd ed. Washington, D.C.: CQ Press, 1977.

Knock, Thomas J. "History with Lightning: The Forgotten Film *Wilson*." In *Hollywood As Historian*, edited by Peter C. Rollins, 88-108. Lexington: University Press of Kentucky, 1983.

Miroff, Bruce. *Icons of Democracy: American Leaders as Heroes, Aristocrats, Dissenters, and Democrats*. Lawrence: University Press of Kansas, 2000.

———. *Pragmatic Illusions: The Presidential Politics of John F. Kennedy*. New York: Longman, 1976.

Morris, Dick. *Behind the Oval Office*. New York: Random House, 1997.

Nathan, Richard P. *The Plot that Failed: Nixon and the Administrative Presidency*. New York: John Wiley and Sons, 1975.

Nelson, Michael. "The Psychological Presidency." In *The Presidency and the Political System*, edited by Michael Nelson, 199–222. 6th ed. Washington, D.C.: CQ Press, 2000.

Neustadt, Richard E. *Presidential Power and the Modern Presidents*. New York: Free Press, 1990.

Newland, Chester A. "Executive Office Policy Apparatus: Enforcing the Reagan Agenda." In *The Reagan Presidency and the Governing of America*, edited by Lester M. Salamon and Michael S. Lund, 135-80. Washington, D.C., Urban Institute, 1985.

Patterson, Bradley H., Jr. *The White House Staff: Inside the West Wing and Beyond*. Washington, D.C.: Brookings Institution, 2000.

Peterson, Mark A. "The Presidency and Organized Interests: White House Patterns of Interest Group Liaison." *American Political Science Review* 86 (1992): 612–25.

Pika, Joseph A. "The Vice Presidency: New Opportunities, Old Constraints." In *The Presidency and the American Political System*, edited by Michael Nelson, 533-70. 6th ed. Washington D.C.: CQ Press, 2000.

———, John Anthony Maltese, and Norman C. Thomas. *The Politics of the Presidency*. 5th ed. Washington, D.C.: CQ Press, 2002.

Pfiffner, James P. *The Modern Presidency*. 2nd ed. New York: St. Martin's, 1998.

———. *The Strategic Presidency: Hitting the Ground Running*. 2nd ed. Lawrence: University Press of Kansas, 1996.

Preston, Thomas. *The President and His Inner Circle: Leadership Style and the Advisory Process in Foreign Affairs.* New York: Columbia University Press, 2001.

Reedy, George E. *The Twilight of the Presidency.* New York: World Publ./New American Library, 1970.

Reich, Robert B. *Locked in the Cabinet.* New York: Knopf, 1997.

Riley, Russell L. "The Limits of the Transformational Presidency." In *Presidential Power: Forging the Presidency for the Twenty-First Century*, edited by Robert Y. Shapiro, Martha Joynt Kumar, and Lawrence R. Jacobs, 435–55. New York: Columbia University Press, 2000.

Rollins, Peter C. "Hollywood's Presidents, 1944–1996: The Primacy of Character." *The World & I*, January 1997, 56–67.

———, and John E. O'Connor, eds. *The West Wing: The American Presidency as Television Drama.* Syracuse: Syracuse University Press, 2003.

Spragens, William C., and Carole Ann Terwood. *From Spokesman to Press Secretary: White House Media Operations.* Washington, D.C.: University Press of America, 1980.

Stone, Oliver, and Zachary Sklar, eds. *JFK: The Book of the Film.* New York: Applause Books, 1992.

Tulis, Jeffrey K. *The Rhetorical Presidency.* Princeton: Princeton University Press, 1987.

Warshaw, Shirley Anne. *Powersharing: White House–Cabinet Relations in the Modern Presidency.* Albany, New York: SUNY Press, 1996.

Weko, Thomas J. *The Politicizing Presidency.* Lawrence: University Press of Kansas, 1995.

Wills, Garry. *The Kennedy Imprisonment.* Boston: Little, Brown, 1994.

Appendix

John Shelton Lawrence

A FILMOGRAPHY FOR IMAGES OF AMERICAN PRESIDENTS IN FILM

CONVENTIONS AND METHODS

The 2000 Film & History conference offered a timely occasion for a presidential filmography posted at <http://www2.hnet.msu.edu/~filmhis/presidentialfilms/methods.html>. Additions and corrections to this filmography are welcome and should be sent to the author.

The titles and information are derived primarily from indexes or reviews for theater-released films from major studios, films reviewed in mainstream publications, or films with notable performers or directors. The most accurate and deeply indexed source for older films is the series of bound volumes published as the *American Film Institute Catalog of Feature Films*, which currently covers the period from 1893 to 1970, excepting only the period from 1951 to 1960, which is currently scheduled for release in 2003. In addition to providing careful plot summaries, AFI's index contains the "The President of the United States" and the names of individual presidents. This collection is available online to universities only from the Chadwyck Healy Company, and in this form is complete for the period from 1890 to 1970 (http://chadwyck.com).

In constructing the filmography, numerous films about the lives of Washington, Jefferson, Jackson, Lincoln, and Theodore Roosevelt have been excluded when the narrative content does not include their lives as presidents. And among films included, the presidential presence is frequently minimal. Fictional presidents are included and receive an (f) designation.

An apparent inconsistency in the *Variety* listings is the absence of page numbers. The older retrospective index volumes and review compilations provide review dates only. Where information is lacking, a ++++ symbol appears in the space.

A fascinating historical curiosity of the presidential film genre, *Variety*'s first review is listed immediately below, just as it appeared nearly a century ago.

Variety, 17 Oct 1908
"Life of Abraham Lincoln"
Chicago
This subject is said by the Essanay Company to be the first of the series called "Flashlights of American History." The pictures show the great American statesman as a boy, his father and mother, as well as those of other personages, according to history. Lincoln naturally appears also as a lawyer and a judge. The most interesting incidents are disclosed graphically. Nearly ever period of the life of Lincoln is produced. It pictures the assassination and the fight of the assassin. The series is one of the most interesting and instructive yet seen. It is an American historical lecture in motion. The actor who impersonated Lincoln has evidently studied the personality of the martyred President.

—Frank Wiesberg

A CHRONOLOGICAL FILMOGRAPHY: 1908–2000

The chronological filmography on the following pages is presented as tables in landscape format in order to make the films of each decade as accessible as possible. During the 1930s and during the latter half of the twentieth century, the number of films in each decade depicting American presidents grew too large for this type of grouping; therefore, for the 1930s, and for the 1960s through the 1990s, the decades are presented by halves or in smaller sections.

NOTE

A special thanks is due to Ken Dvorak, who Web-mastered the display of this list for the Film and History League.

1908–1919

Year	Title/Alternate	Genre	NYT	Variety	Actor/President	Plot	Director
1908	*Life of Abraham Lincoln*	Bio	+++++	17 Oct 1908: 11	Logan Paul/AL	Review of events in life	Phil Rosen
1909	*The Assassination of Abraham Lincoln*	Bio	+++++	+++++	+++++	+++++	+++++
1910	*Abraham Lincoln's Clemency*	History	+++++	12 Nov 1910	Leopold Wharton/AL	Story of clemency granted to solder who slept at his post	Theodore Wharton
1915	*The Birth of a Nation*	History	4 Mar 1915: 9	12 Mar 1915: 23	Joseph Henabery/AL	Southern rebellion against Reconstruction	D.W. Griffith
1919	*The Great Victory/Wilson or the Kaiser?*	War/ Propaganda	+++++	+++++	Fred C. Truesdell/WW	Atrocity film in which P. WW is persuaded to allow Alsatians to enlist	Charles Miller

Note: Frank Thompson's Abraham Lincoln: Twentieth Century Portrayals (Dallas: Taylor, 1999) contains a far more extensive listing for Lincoln films.

1920s

Year	Title/Alternate	Genre	NYT	Variety	Actor/President	Plot	Director
1924	*Iron Horse*	History	29 Aug 1924: 6	3 Sept 1924: 3	Charles Edw. Bull/AL	Railroad and national expansion	John Ford

Year	Title/Alternate	Genre	NYT	Variety	Actor/President	Plot	Director
1924	*The Life of Lincoln/The Dramatic Life of Lincoln*	History	+++++	+++++	George A. Billings/AL	Comprehensive life of AL from birth to assassination	Phil Rosen
1926	*Hands Up!*	History/ Comedy	18 Jan 1926: 26	20 Jan 1926: 40	George Billings/AL	Lincoln sends agents west for gold	Clarence Badger

1930–1935

Year	Title/Alternate	Genre	NYT	Variety	Actor/President	Plot	Director
1930	*Abraham Lincoln*	Bio	26 Aug 1930: 24	27 Aug 1930`	Walter Huston/AL	Episodes in AL's life	D.W. Griffith
1932	*Silver Dollar*	History/ Romance	23 Dec 1932: 20	27 Dec 1932: 14	Emmet Corrigan/ Chester A. Arthur	Life of silver baron Horace Tabor, whose fortunes are entwined with presidents and the gold standard.	Alfred E. Green
1933	*The Fighting President*	Docudrama	+++++	11 April 1933: 17	Franklin Delano Roosevelt (FDR)	Compilation of clips from FDR's public career	Allyn Butterfield
1933	*Gabriel Over the White House*	Political fantasy	1 April 1933: 18	4 April 1933: 15	Walter Huston/Judson Hammond (f)	President is touched by an angel in reckless accident, survives long enough to save nation	Gregory La Cava

Year	Title/Alternate	Genre	NYT	Variety	Actor/President	Plot	Director
1935	Grand Old Girl/Portrait of Laura Boyle/Woman Aroused	Drama	26 Feb 1935: 16	6 Mar 1935: 21	G. Gordon/The P (f)	Hometown school politics; principled principal rescued by president	John Robertson
1935	The Littlest Rebel	History/fantasy	20 Dec 1935: 30	25 Dec 1935: 15	Frank McGlynn/AL	Southern child (Shirley Temple) persuades Lincoln to release dad from POW camp	David Butler
1935	The President Vanishes	Political/Crime	1 Dec 1935: 18	11 Dec 1935: 19	Arthur Byron/P Stanley (f)	Businessman and "Gray Shirts" conspire for war	William A. Wellman
1935	Transatlantic Tunnel	SF	28 Oct 1935: 16	30 Oct 1935	Walter Huston/The P (f)	Futuristic, melodramatic story of tunnel building	Maurice Elvey

1936–1939

Year	Title/Alternate	Genre	NYT	Variety	Actor/President	Plot	Director
1936	Gorgeous Hussy	History/Romance	5 Sept 1936: 7	8 Sept 1936: 16	Lionel Barrymore/Andrew Jackson	Loose reconstruction of Jackson's relationship to tavern girl	Clarence Brown
1936	Hearts Divided	History/Romance	+++++	+++++	George Irving/Thomas Jefferson	Romance involving American and son of Napoleon	Franz Borzage
1936	Hearts in Bondage	History/Romance	+++++	21 Oct 1936: 18	Frank McGlynn/AL	Civil War tale of Merrimac and Monitor with romance subtext	Lew Ayres

Year	Title/Alternate	Genre	NYT	Variety	Actor/President	Plot	Director
1937	*Nation Aflame/Avenging Angels/My Life is Yours*	Political/ Crime	+++++	7 Apr 1937: 15	C. Montague Shaw/The P (f)	William A. Seiter	Victor Halperin
1937	*This is My Affair*	Crime	28 May 1937: 17	2 June 1937: 15	Frank Conroy/ Wm. McKinley	Secret agent of McKinley is betrayed	William A. Seiter
1938	*Of Human Hearts*	Historical	18 Feb 1938	9 Feb 1938	Frank McGlyn/AL	P plays role in reconciling alienated family members during the Civil War	Clarence Brown
1939	*Joe and Ethel Turp Call on the President*	Comedy	4 Jan 1940: 19	6 Dec 1939	Lewis Stone/The P (f)	Ordinary folks go visit the P and get their problems fixed	Robert B. Sinclair

1940s

Year	Title/Alternate	Genre	NYT	Variety	Actor/President	Plot	Director
1942	*The Remarkable Andrew*	Fantasy	6 Mar 1942: 17	21 Jan 1942	Brian Donleavy/A. Jackson; Gilbert Emery/TJ; Montago Love/GW	Jackson, TJ, & GW appear as ghosts to rescue AJ's falsely accused descendant	Stuart Heisler
1942	*Tennessee Johnson*	History/ Bio	13 Jan 1943: 18	16 Dec 1942	Van Heflin/ Andrew Johnson	Bio of Lincoln's successor	William Dieterle
1942	*Yankee Doodle Dandy*	Bio	30 May 1942: 9	3 June 1942: 8	Captain Jack Young/FDR	G.M. Cohan bio featuring meeting with FDR at White House	Michael Curtiz

Year	Title/Alternate	Genre	NYT	Variety	Actor/President	Plot	Director
1944	*Buffalo Bill*	Bio	20 Apr 1944: 22	15 Mar 1944	Sidney Blackmer/TR; John Dilson/ R.B. Hayes	Life of BB, leading him to celebrity among presidents	Henry King
1944	*Wilson*	Bio	2 Aug 1944: 18	2 Aug 1944: 10	Alexander Knox/WW	Dramatic reconstruction of WW's public life	Henry King
1946	*Centennial Summer*	Musical	18 July 1946: 20	29 May 1946: 10	Reginald Sheffield/ U.S. Grant	Centennial celebration set in 1876	Otto Preminger
1946	*Magnificent Doll*	History/ Romance	9 Dec 1946: 34	20 Nov 1946: 8	Burgess Meredith/ James Madison	Fantasy of romance between Dolly Madison and Aaron Burr	Franz Borzage
1947	*The Beginning or the End*	Docu	21 Feb 1947: 15	19 Feb 1947: 8	Godfrey Tearle/FDR; Art Baker/HST	Story of the development of the atomic bomb	Norman Taurog
1948	*My Girl Tisa/Tisa/ Ever the Beginning*	Drama	21 Feb 1948: 9	21 Feb 1948: 8	Sidney Blackmer/TR	Immigrant girl's family is cheated, TR intervenes to prevent deportation	Elliot Nugent
1948	*Silver River*	Western	22 May 1948: 8	5 May 1948: 8	Joe Crehan/U.S. Grant	USG & expanding U.S. silver product	Raoul Walsh

1950s

Year	Title/Alternate	Genre	NYT	Variety	Actor/President	Plot	Director
1951	*New Mexico*	History	14 July 1951: 7	2 May 1951	Hans Conried/AL	Violation of Indian treaty made with AL leads to uprising	Irving Reis

Year	Title/Alternate	Genre	NYT	Variety	Actor/President	Plot	Director
1951	The Tall Target	History	28 Sept 1951: 26	1 Aug 1951	Leslie Kimmel/AL	New York detective protects AL from assassination	Anthony Mann
1952	Red Planet Mars	SF	16 June 1952: 15	14 May 1952	Willis Bouchey/The P (f)	Scientists receive optimistic messages from Mars that threaten world	Harry Horner
1952	The Story of Will Rogers	History	18 July 1952: 10	16 July 1952	Earl Lee/WW	Will Rogers's career	Michael Curtiz
1953	The President's Lady	History/ Romance	22 May 1953: 31	11 Mar 1953	Charleton Heston/ A. Jackson	AJ's marriage to previously married/not legally divorced woman	Henry Levin
1954	Sitting Bull	History	26 Nov 1954: 24	15 Sept 1954	John Hamilton//U.S. Grant	Imaginary meeting of P and Sitting Bull results in peace	Sidney Salkow
1955	Court Martial of Billy Mitchell	History/ Docudrama	23 Dec 1955: 14	14 Dec 1955	Ian Wolfe/Calvin Coolidge	Heroic portrayal of Billy Mitchell trial	Otto Preminger
1955	Far Horizons	History	21 May 1955: 11	25 May 1955	Herbert Heyes/TJ	Lewis & Clark expedition w. romantic subtexts	Rudolph Mate
1955	Prince of Players	History	12 Jan 1955: 24	5 Jan 1955	Stanley Hall/AL	Story of Edwin Booth, actor and brother of AL's assassin	Philip Dunne

1960–1965

Year	Title/Alternate	Genre	NYT	Variety	Actor/President	Plot	Director
1962	*Advise and Consent*	Political	7 June 1962: 31	23 May 1962	Franchot Tome/ The P (f)	U.S. Senate in an acrimonious, McCarthyite phase	Otto Preminger
1963	*Cattle King/ Guns of Wyoming*	Western	+++++	19 June 1963	Larry Gates/ Chester A. Arthur	Rancher fights against cattle trail	Tay Garnett
1963	*How the West Was Won*	History/ Western	1 Apr 1963: 54	7 Nov 1962: 6	Raymond Massey/AL	Epic story of conquest in the West, with assassination attempt on AL	John Ford
1964	*Dr. Strangelove: Or How I Learned to Stop Worrying and Love the Bomb*	Political/ Comedy	31 Jan 1964: 16	22 Jan 1964: 6	Peter Sellers/ Merken Muffley (f)	Satiric treatment of nuclear weapons, which trigger mutual destruction of USSR and U.S.	Stanley Kubrick
1964	*Fail-Safe*	Political/ Drama	16 Sept 1964: 36	16 Sept 1964	Henry Fonda/The P (f)	Story of political crisis resulting from accidental command to bomb USSR w. nukes	Sidney Lumete
1964	*Kisses for My President*	Comedy	22 Aug 1964: 13	19 Aug 1964	Polly Bergen/ Leslie McCloud (f)	Prolonged "First Hubby" joke	Curtis Bernhard
1964	*Seven Days in May*	Political	20 Feb 1964: 22	5 Feb 1964: 6	Frederick March/ Jordan Lyman (f)	Right-wing plot to take over government because of nuclear treaty with USSR	John Frankenheimer

1966–1969

Year	Title/Alternate	Genre	NYT	Variety	Actor/President	Plot	Director
1967	*First to Fight*	WWII/ History	30 Mar 1967: 55	25 Jan 1967	Stepehen Roberts/FDR	Action in the South Pacific front	Christian Nyby
1967	*In Like Flint*	Spy Comedy	16 Mar 1967: 53	15 Mar 1967	Andrew Duggan/The P (f)	Woman seeks world power; switches her P for real one	Gordon Douglas
1968	*The Virgin President*	Comedy	+++++	+++++	Severn Darden/ Fillard Millmore (f)	Farcical episodes featuring a son who succeeds his dead father	Graeme Ferguson
1968	*Wild in the Streets*	Comedy/ Political	30 May 1968: 21	8 May 1968	Christopher Jones/ Max Frost (f)	Rock star elected as P, empowers youth	Barry Shear
1969	*The Monitors*	Comedy	+++++	+++++	Ed Begley/The P (f)	Irreverent skits including one with the P	Jack Shea
1969	*Putney Swope*	Comedy	11 July 1969: 19	9 July 1969: 6	Pepi Hermine/The P (f)	Satire of business, advertising, race; P is drug user	Robert Downey

1970–1975

Year	Title/Alternate	Genre	NYT	Variety	Actor/President	Plot	Director
1970	*Brand-X*	Comedy	+++++	+++++	Taylor Meade/The P (f)	Series of skits, including an interview w. P as his retarded wife sits nearby	Win Chambers

Year	Title/Alternate	Genre	NYT	Variety	Actor/President	Plot	Director
1970	Escape from the Planet of the Apes	SF	+++++	26 May 1951	William Windom/The P (≈)	Scientists time travel to escape from nuclear holocaust, find ape planet	Don Taylor
1970	The Forbin Project/ Colossus: The Forbin Project	SF	+++++	1 Apr 1970	Gordon Pinsent/The P (f)	U.S. and USSR create an out-of-control computer that insists on peace	Joseph Sargent
1972	Hail/Hail to the Chief/ Washington, D.C.	Comedy	+++++	24 May 1972: 26	Dan Resin/The P (f)	The P becomes dictator, creates prison camps for youth	Fred Levinson
1972	Richard	Comedy	1 Aug 1972: 30	26 July 1972	Richard M. Dixon & Dan Resin/RMN	Spoof of RMN's career	Lorees Yerby

1976–1979

Year	Title/Alternate	Genre	NYT	Variety	Actor/President	Plot	Director
1976	The Pink Panther Strikes Again	Comedy	22 May 1976: 32	15 Dec 1976	Dick Crockett/The P (f)	Joke-strewn rescue of world from death-ray device	Blake Edwards
1977	MacArthur	Bio	1 July 1977: 8	29 June 1977	Ed Flanders/HST; Dan Herlihy/FDR	MacArthur's military career and political conflicts	Joseph Sargent
1977	The Strange Case of the End of Civilization as We Know It	Comedy	+++++	+++++	Joss Ackland/The P (f)	+++++	Joe McGrath

Year	Title/Alternate	Genre	NYT	Variety	Actor/President	Plot	Director
1977	*Twilight's Last Gleaming/ Nuclear Countdown*	Drama	10 Feb 1977: 48	2 Feb 1977: 22	Charles Durning/The P (f)	Liberal, imprisoned general escapes, controls weapons, demands public truth about Vietnam policy	Robert Aldrich
1977	*Wizards*	Animated Cartoon	21 Apr 1977: III, 22	2 Feb 1977: 24	James Connel (voice)/ The P (f)	Dystopian future with battle between good and evil	Ralph Bakshi
1978	*Born Again*	Drama	+++++	6 Sept 1978: 22	Harry Spillman/RMN	Charles Colson's post-Watergate spiritual rebirth	Irving Rapper
1978	*Rabbit Test*	Comedy	9 Apr 1978: 53	22 Feb 1978	George Gobel/The P (f)	The first pregnant man: includes skit w. P	Joan Rivers
1979	*Attack of the Killer Tomatoes*	SF/ Comedy	+++++	31 Jan 1979: 22	Ernie Myers/The P (f)	Earth battles killer tomatoes	John DeBello
1979	*Being There*	Comedy	20 Dec 1979: III, 20	19 Dec 1979: 19	Jack Warden/ "Bobby" The P (f)	Parable of man who knows nothing becoming P's adviser	Hal Ashby

1980–1981

Year	Title/Alternate	Genre	NYT	Variety	Actor/President	Plot	Director
1980	*First Family*	Comedy	27 Dec 1980: 11	31 Dec 1980: 20	Bob Newhart/The P (f)	Addled P with alcoholic wife and sex-hungry daughter	Buck Herman

	Title	Genre			Actor/Character	Description	Director
1980	*Kidnapping of the President*	Drama	15 Aug 1980: III, 12	13 Aug 1980	Hal Holbrook/Adam Scott (f)	P is victim of a ransom kidnapping	George Mendeluk
1980	*The Nude Bomb*	Satire	9 May 1980: III, 12	7 May 1980	Thomas Hill/The P (f)	"Get Smart" episode saves world from clothes-destroying bomb	Clive Donner
1980	*Superman II*	Action	19 Jan 1981: C8	3 Dec 1980	E.G. Marshall/The P (f)	P's capture in the White House brings Superman to save the world	Richard Lester
1981	*Escape from New York*	Action	10 July 1981: C6	17 June 1981	Donald Pleasence/The P (f)	P held in futuristic New York—a prison	John Carpenter
1981	*The Final Conflict*	Horror	20 Mar 1981: C8	25 Mar 1981	Mason Adams/The P (f)	Third in *Omen* trilogy	Graham Baker
1981	*Kill and Kill Again*	Action	8 May 1981: C21	13 May 1981	Mervyn Johns/The P (f)	+++++	Ivan Hall
1981	*Legend of the Lone Ranger*	Action/Western	22 May 1981: C8	20 May 1981	Jason Robards/U.S. Grant	Grant kidnapped from presidential train, rescued by LR, Tonto	William Fraker
1981	*Ragtime*	Drama	20 Nov 1981: III, 10	13 Nov 1981: 3	Robert Boyd/TR	Interwoven lives of ragtime pianist and famous New Yorkers	Milos Forman

1982–1989

Year	Title/Alternate	Genre	NYT	Variety	Actor/President	Plot	Director
1982	The Soldier/ Codename—The Soldier	Action	3 Sept 1982: C11	26 May 1982	William Prince/The P (f)	Russians steal U.S. plutonium, threaten Middle East oil	James Glickenhaus
1982	Wrong is Right	Dark Comedy	16 Apr 1982: C8	7 Apr 1982	George Grizzard/ P Lockwood (f)	Absurdist, impotent P in world dominated by aggressive TV coverage	Richard Brooks
1983	The Right Stuff	History	5 Aug 1983: C13	27 July 1983: 21	Robert Beer/ Dwight Eisenhower	Dramatization of early days of space program	Philip Kaufman
1984	Dreamscape	SF	15 Aug 1984: C24	16b May 1984	Eddy Albert/The P (f)	Psychic genius thwarts plan to enter P's dream to kill him	Joseph Ruben
1984	Secret Honor	Drama	+++++	11 July 1984	Philip B. Hall/RMN	Monological ravings, meditations of drunken RMN	Robert Altman
1984	Slapstick of Another Kind	Comedy	+++++	28 Mar 1984	Jim Backus/The P (f)	Alien twins are messengers with world-saving messages	Steven Paul
1987	Amazing Grace and Chuck	Comedy	22 May 1987: C30	1 Apr 1987	Gregory Peck/The P (f)	Kid affronted by strategic weapons stops pitching, forces P to abandon nukes	Mike Newell

1990–1993

Year	Title/Alternate	Genre	NYT	Variety	Actor/President	Plot	Director
1991	JFK	Historical	20 Dec 1991: C1	16 Dec 1991	JFK incorporated through film clips	Conspiratorial exposition of Jim Garrison's theories	Oliver Stone
1991	The Last Boy Scout	Action	13 Dec 1991: B3	16 Dec 1991: 57	Ed Beheler/The P (f)	Violent investigation of pro football corruption	Tony Scott
1991	McBain	Action	23 Sept 1991: C15	30 Sept 1991: 70	Forrest Compton/P Flynn	Revenge film that takes Vietnam vet to Colombia	James Glickenhaus
1991	Naked Gun 2½—The Smell of Fear	Comedy	28 June 1991: B1	28 June 1991: 2	John Roarke/ George Bush Sr.	P's environmental advisor kidnapped by energy magnate	David Zucker
1992	Bebe's Kids	Comedy/ Animation	1 Aug 1992: 13	3 Aug 1992: 43	Rich Little (voice)/ RMN (robot)	African American journey through theme park	Bruce Smith
1992	Love Field	Drama	+++++	14 Dec 1992: 43	Bob Gill/JFK	Dallas women's experience of JFK assassination and aftermath	Jonathan Kaplan
1993	Dave	Drama	7 May 1993: B2	26 Apr 1993: 68	Kevin Kline/ Bill Mitchell (f)	Real P incapacitated by illicit sex; impersonator brought in	Ivan Reitman
1993	Hot Shots! Part Deux	Action/ Parody	21 May 1993: C5	24 May 1993: 44, 65	Lloyd Bridges/ Tug Benson (f)	P as bumbling sportsman	Jim Abrahams
1993	In the Line of Fire	Action	9 July 1993: H10	19 July 1993: 71, 94	Jim Curley/The P (f)	Long-term Secret Service agent lives through doubts about ability to protect the P	Wolfgang Peterson
1993	The Pelican Brief	Crime	10 June 1994: D16	20 Dec 1993: 30	Robert Culp/The P (f)	Murder of Spr. Ct. justices threatens to implicate White House	Alan J. Pakula

1994–1995

Year	Title/Alternate	Genre	NYT	Variety	Actor/President	Plot	Director
1994	*Clear and Present Danger*	Crime	27 Jan 1995: B8	1 Aug 1994: 44	Donald Moffat/ Edward Bennett (f)	P with drug links abuses intelligence/special ops agency powers	Philip Noyce
1994	*Forrest Gump*	Drama	6 July 1994: B1	+++++	Actual presidents incorporated by simulation	Dim-witted, genial fellow encounters famous people of his era	Robert Zemeckis
1994	*I.Q.*	Comedy/ Romance	23 Dec 1994: C8; 7 July 1995: B15	19 Dec 1994: 73	Curtis Keene/ Dwight Eisenhower	Einstein's romance scheme for niece brings Ike to Princeton	Fred Schepisi
1995	*The American President*	Political drama/ Romance	25 Apr 1995: D17	6 Nov 1995: 71	Michael Douglas/ Andrew Shepherd (f)	Widower P has affair and fights right-wing foes	Rob Reiner
1995	*Canadian Bacon*	Comedy	22 Sept 1995: C20	29 May 1995: 54	Alan Alda/The P (f)	Unpopular P drifts into war with Canada	Michael Moore
1995	*Nixon*	Bio	17 Dec 1995: H1	18 Dec 1995	Anthony Hopkins/RMN	Extended expo of Nixon's private and public life	Oliver Stone

1996

Year	Title/Alternate	Genre	NYT	Variety	Actor/President	Plot	Director
1996	*Courage Under Fire*	Drama	12 July 1996: C1	24 June 1996: 119	John Roarke/The P (f)	Exploration of friendly-fire deaths in Gulf War	Edward Zwick
1996	*Escape from L.A.*	SF	9 Aug 1996: C5; 18 Aug 1996: H27	12 Aug 1996: 32	Cliff Robertson/The P (f)	Future dystopian U.S. controlled by right-wing P	John Carpenter
1996	*First Kid*	Comedy	30 Aug 1996: C10	2 Sept 1996: 66	James Naughton/ P Davenport (f)	P at work on reelection has problem teenage kid	David M. Evans
1996	*Independence Day*	SF	2 July 1996: C2	1 July 1996	Bill Pullman/ P Whitemore (f)	Alien invasion prompts P to top-gun role in space	Roland Emmerich
1996	*Jingle All the Way*	Comedy	1 Dec 1996: H28	25 Nov 1996: 71, 73	Havery Korman/The P (f;	+++++	Brian Levant
1996	*Mars Attacks!*	Comedy	13 Dec 1996: C5	2 Dec 1996: 66	Jack Nicholson/ Art Land (f)	P sells out to Martians during campy SF invasion	Tim Burton
1996	*My Fellow Americans*	Comedy	20 Dec 1996: C20	+++++	Dan Aykroyd/ P William Hanna (f)	Bribery scheme penned on ex-Ps	Peter Segal
1996	*Spy Hard*	Spy/Parody	+++++	27 May 1996	Bruce Gray/The P (f)	Agent has task of averting world destruction	Rick Friedberg

1997

Year	Title/Alternate	Genre	NYT	Variety	Actor/President	Plot	Director
1997	*Absolute Power*	Crime	14 Feb 1997: C5	10 Feb 1997: 62	Gene Hackman/ Alan Richmond (f)	P involved in murder of sex partner, covers up	Clint Eastwood
1997	*Air Force One*	Action	25 July 1997: C1	21 July 1997: 37	Harrison Ford/ James Marshall (f)	P battles terrorists for control of AF1	Wolfgang Peterson
1997	*Amistad*	History	10 Dec 1997: E1; 13 Dec 1997: AR32	8 Dec 1997: 2	Nigel Hawthorne/ Martin Van Buren; Anthony Hopkins, ex-P John Adams	P manipulates court to mollify Spanish slave trade and the South; ex-P wins freedom of rebel slaves	Steven Spielberg
1997	*Contact*	SF	11 July 1997: C1	14 July 1997: 37	Bill Clinton clips	Science and romance-driven exploration of alien communication	Robert Zemeckis
1997	*Executive Power*	Crime	+++++	+++++	William Anderson/ P Fields (f)	P's sex partner at White House dies, P involved in cover-up	David L. Corey
1997	*Executive Target*	Action	+++++	+++++	Roy Scheider/The P (f)	The P is kidnap target	Joseph Merhi
1997	*Murder at 1600*	Crime	18 Apr 1997: C23	14 Apr 1997: 91	Ronny Cox/Jack Neil (f)	White House family sex crime combined with international crisis	George Cosmatos
1997	*The Peacekeeper*	Action	+++++	+++++	Roy Scheider/The P (f)	P kidnapped, requested to commit suicide on TV	Frederick Forestier

| 1997 | *Shadow Conspiracy* | Political thriller | 31 Jan 1997: C6; 9 Feb 1997: H33 | 3 Feb 1997: 43 | Sam Waterston/The P (f) | Conspiracy to assassinate the P | George Cosmatos |
| 1997 | *Wag The Dog* | Comedy | 26 Dec 1997: E7 | 15 Dec 1997: 58 | Michael Belson/The P (f) | P accused of molesting Girl Scout at White House contrives international crisis as distraction | Barry Levinson |

1998–1999

Year	Title/Alternate	Genre	NYT	Variety	Actor/President	Plot	Director
1998	*Armageddon*	SF/Action	1 July 1998: E1	29 Jan 1998: 37	Stanley Anderson/ The P (f)	Asteroid heads toward earth; P authorizes attempt to divert it	Michael Bay
1998	*Deep Impact*	SF	23 Oct 1998: E30	25 May 1998: 37	Morgan Freeman/ Tom Beck (f)	Asteroid threatens world; P commands effort to save it	Mimi Leder
1998	*Primary Colors*	Comedy	4 Sept 1998: E25	16 Mar 1998: 63	John Travolta/ Gov Jack Stanton	Satirical guide to Clinton's first campaign for White House	Mike Nichols
1999	*Dick*	Satire	10 Dec 1999: E40	2 Aug 1999: 32	Dan Hedaya/RMN	Teen visitors at White House battle RMN and cause Watergate crisis	Rod Lurie

2000

Year	Title/Alternate	Genre	NYT	Variety	Actor/President	Plot	Director
2000	*The Contender*	Drama	12 Oct 2000: E1; 6 Nov 2000: E1	11 Sept 2000: E1	Jeff Bridges/ Jackson Evans (f)	Republicans attempt smear of female Democrat VP candidate with sex scandal	Rod Lurie
2000	*Deterrence*	Drama	10 Mar 2000: E27	24 May 2000: 71	Kevin Pollak/ Walter Emerson (f)	P trapped in blizzard during crisis makes strategic decisions about Iraq	Rod Lurie
2000	*Thirteen Days*	History	25 Dec 2000: 1	4 Dec 2000: 1	Bruce Greenwood/JFK	White House decision-making in Cuban missle crisis	Roger Donaldson

CONTRIBUTORS

LINDA ALKANA is a faculty member with the history department and international studies department at California State University, Long Beach, and an editor for *The History Teacher*. She teaches critical thinking, protest movements, women's history, historical methodology, and world history. Her research interests lie in evaluating "how we know what we know," leading to her inquiries into the relationship between popular culture, film, and history. An avid book and film reviewer, she has also written articles on "Teaching Critical Thinking with Historical Methodology" and "Using a Film Clip Approach for Teaching World History." She can be contacted at lalk@csulb.edu.

DAVID HAVEN BLAKE teaches American literature and culture at the College of New Jersey. He is a graduate of Colgate University and Washington University in St. Louis. Blake's scholarly work has appeared in a wide range of journals, including *American Literary History*, *Michigan Quarterly Review*, and *Prospects: An Annual of American Cultural Studies*. Although his primary interest is nineteenth- and twentieth-century poetry, he has published essays on such political topics as Andrew Jackson, the Adams-Jefferson correspondence, and the House Un-American Activities Committee. Blake has recently completed a book-length manuscript on Walt Whitman and the culture of American celebrity. He can be contacted at blake@tcnj.edu.

DEBORAH CARMICHAEL, associate editor of *Film & History*, currently serves as an assistant director of the Oklahoma State University composition program for all first-year students. She was coeditor for the text entitled *The Great Plains: Writing Across the Disciplines* (Harcourt, 2001). Her most recent publication, "Main Street, Stillwater OK: Growing Up with Hollywood CA" appears in the *Chronicles of Oklahoma* 80 (2002). She has chaired conference areas of study for both film and literature topics at the regional, national, and international level. She can be contacted at debcar6569@aol.com.

CHARLENE ETKIND is an independent scholar whose Ph.D. from Bowling Green State University in American culture studies has involved her in a broad spectrum of popular-culture studies—including social effects of the Internet and has published a chapter entitled "Netsex: Empowerment Through Discourse," in *Cyberghettoes or Cybertopia: Race, Class and Gender Issues in Cyberspace* (1998). Other areas of study include gendered behaviors in motorcycle culture, and film-television studies. An article, "Violence on Television: Parbles for Modern Society," appears in the *Lamar Journal of the Humanities,* 1997. She has taught journalism and visual communications at the University of Toledo and the University of Missouri. She can be contacted at IRCresearch@go.com.

LUC HERMAN is associate professor of American literature and literary theory at the University of Antwerp (Belgium). He received his B.A. from the University of Antwerp, his M.A. from Harvard University, and his Ph.D. from Princeton University. He has published *Concepts of Realism* (Camden House, 1996) and edited a double issue of *Pynchon Notes* (1998) entitled *Approach and Avoid: Essays on* Gravity's Rainbow. He is currently writing a book on the contemporary encyclopedic novel and can be contacted at Luc.Herman@uia.ua.ac.be.

ROBERT E. HUNTER is a graduate student in the Ph.D. program in history at the University of Illinois at Chicago. He obtained his B.A. and M.A. from Ohio University. Specializing in twentieth-century American history, he is also interested in American popular culture and the history of technology. A former Guggenheim Fellow at the Smithsonian Institution's National Air and Space Museum, Hunter's dissertation examines the depiction of American atomic policy in film, radio, and television during the heyday of the Cold War. He can be contacted at zpn1@earthlink.net.

JAAP KOOIJMAN is assistant professor of film and television studies at the University of Amsterdam, the Netherlands. In 1999, he received his Ph.D. in American studies at the University of Amsterdam based on the book *And the*

Pursuit of National Health: The Incremental Strategy Toward National Health Insurance in the United States of America (Amsterdam/Atlanta: Rodopi, 1999). His writings on American politics and popular culture have appeared in *Presidential Studies Quarterly* and *The Velvet Light Trap*. He can be contacted through his website: www.jaapkooijman.nl.

MICHAEL G. KRUKONES is a professor of political science at Bellarmine University in Louisville, Kentucky, where he teaches courses in the areas of American government, political theory, comparative government, international relations, and politics and film. His areas of research specialization include presidential campaigns and politics and film. He has written a book entitled *Promises and Performance: Presidential Campaigns as Policy Predictors,* has contributed to works on *Ronald Reagan's America* and *Keeping Faith: The Presidency and Domestic Policies of Jimmy Carter,* and has had articles published in journals such as *Presidential Studies Quarterly, National Social Science Journal,* and *Innovative Higher Education.* He can be contacted at mkrukones@bellarmine.edu.

JOHN SHELTON LAWRENCE is emeritus professor of philosophy at Morningside College (Sioux City, Iowa) and currently an independent scholar and consultant residing in Berkeley, California. He received his B.A. from Stanford and his Ph.D. from the University of Texas–Austin. With Robert Jewett he has coauthored *The American Monomyth* (1977, 1988) and *The Myth of the American Superhero* (2002)—both studies of democratic and antidemocratic ideals in popular culture. With Jewett he has also written *Captain America and the Crusade Against Evil* (2003), a narrative history of holy-war ideology in biblical history and in American politics. He can be contacted at johnslaw@pacbell.net.

STUART LEIBIGER received his B.A. from the University of Virginia and his M.A. and Ph.D. from the University of North Carolina. He is currently an associate professor of history at La Salle University, specializing in early America. Before taking his current position, he worked as a historical interpreter at Thomas Jefferson's Monticello and as an editorial assistant at both the *Papers of George Washington* and the *Papers of Thomas Jefferson.* He has published numerous articles about the Founding Fathers in historical journals and has appeared on several television documentaries, including C-SPAN's Book TV. In 1999, the University Press of Virginia published his book, *Founding Friendship: George Washington, James Madison and the Creation of the American Republic.* He can be contacted at leibiger@lasalle.edu.

MYRON A. LEVINE is professor of political science at Albion College and the college's Justin L. and Marjorie Wardell Sleight and Norman R. and Alethea E. Sleight Endowed Professor of Leadership Studies. He received his Ph.D. from MIT and is the author of *Presidential Campaigns and Elections* and coauthor of *Urban Politics: Power in Metropolitan America*. His writings on the presidency have appeared in the *Presidential Studies Quarterly*; his analysis of the hit NBC series appears in The West Wing: *The American Presidency as Television Drama*, edited by Peter C. Rollins and John E. O'Connor (Syracuse University Press). He has served as a Fulbright lecturer at the University of Riga in Latvia and has received Fulbright and NEH awards for study in Germany, the Netherlands, and France. Having taught in the Czech Republic and briefly in Yugoslavia, he also maintains a special fondness for the films of Eastern and Central Europe. He can be contacted at mlevine@albion.edu.

JOHN MATVIKO is associate professor of communications at West Liberty State College. He received his master's degree from the University of Pittsburgh and has done additional graduate work at Catholic University of America and West Virginia University. He has been active in both regional and national popular-culture associations. He is a founding member of the Middle Atlantic Popular/American Culture Association and has served in many capacities for that organization including president and newsletter editor; he currently serves as associate editor for the organization's scholarly journal, *The Almanack*. For the past eight years he has edited *ACAN*, the newsletter of the American Culture Association, and he is also founding and current editor of *Rewind*, the newsletter of the Film and History League. He can be contacted at wayne121@attbi.com.

JOHN E. O'CONNOR is professor of history at New Jersey Institute of Technology (NJIT) and member of the federated department of history of NJIT and Rutgers University, Newark. He is cofounder of the Historians Film Committee and was editor/coeditor of its journal, *Film & History*, from 1979 until 1991. Also with Peter C. Rollins he coedited *Hollywood's World War I* (1997), *Hollywood's Indian* (1988), and *The West Wing: The American Presidency as Television Drama* (2003). He is author/editor of *Image as Artifact: The Historical Analysis of Film and Television*, compiler of the 120-minute *Image as Artifact* video compilation, and author of *Teaching History With Film and Television*, all published or copublished by the American Historical Association in 1990. In 1991 the American Historical Association honored him with the creation of its annual John E. O'Connor Award for the best historical film or video production.

ANDREW PIASECKI is a lecturer and course leader in the department of media and communication at Queen Margaret University College, Edinburgh. He has a B.A. in English with American studies from the University of Nottingham and an M.A. in drama and theatre studies from the University of Leeds. His teaching and research is in the areas of media and public relations, with a particular interest in developments in communication in the United States during the nineteenth and early twentieth century. Recent articles include, "Blowing the Railroad Trumpet: Public Relations on the American Frontier," *Public Relations Review* 26 (2000): 53–65 and "The Rock Island Line: A Mighty Fine Line," *Komunikacie* 1 (2000): 93–97. He is the Scottish representative for *Film & History* and can be contacted at apiasecki@qmuc.ac.uk.

LOREN P. QUIRING received his M.A. and Ph.D. from the University of Virginia. A former NEH Fellow at Harvard University, he now teaches film studies, literary theory, and world literature at the University of Wisconsin, Oshkosh. His scholarship includes articles on Frost, Stevens, Modernism, and Pragmatism, as well as papers on the historical construction of gender in American film and on the strategies for using film and television in the writing classroom. He can be contacted at quiring@uwosh.edu.

PETER C. ROLLINS is Regents Professor of English and American/Film Studies at Oklahoma State University. He is the editor-in-chief of *Film & History: An Interdisciplinary Journal of Film and Television Studies* and coeditor of such University Press of Kentucky books as *Hollywood as Historian* (2nd ed., 1998), *Hollywood's Indian* (1998), *Television Histories* (2001), and from the Syracuse University Press. *The West Wing: The American Presidency as Television Drama* (2003). His *Columbia UP Companion to American History on Film* (2004) is basic to the field. His films include *Will Rogers' 1920s: A Cowboy's Guide to the Times* (1976); *Television's Vietnam: The Real Story* (SONY, 1985); and *Television's Vietnam: The Impact of Media* (SONY, 1986) are on one cassette for home and classroom use after PBS and WTBS broadcasts. He was given a Lifetime Achievement Award by the national Popular Culture Association and the American Culture Association in 2002. For more information and contact, try www.filmandhistory.org and RollinsPC@aol.com.

BRYAN ROMMEL-RUIZ is assistant professor of history at the Colorado College, where he teaches early American and African American history. He received his A.B. from the University of California, Berkeley, and his Ph.D. from the University of Michigan. His writings explore a variety of topics, including film and history, history and computer technology, and early American history. His forthcoming book *Inventing a Black Atlantic: Afro-Americans in Rhode Island and Nova Scotia, 1750–1850* will be published by the University of Pennsylvania Press. Professor Rommel-Ruiz is also writing a book manuscript on film and history, entitled *American History, American Cinema: Historians, Hollywood, and Representing the American Past.* He can be contacted at bruiz@coloradocollege.edu.

IAN SCOTT is the programme director of American studies at the University of Manchester, England, where he teaches film and politics as well as history. He received his B.A. from Manchester Metropolitan University and his M.A. and Ph.D. from Keele University, both in England. He writes about the representation of politics, politicians, and political institutions in Hollywood film, including work on directors such as Frank Capra and Oliver Stone, and he also works on the history and cinematic portrayal of California. He recently published *American Politics in Hollywood Film,* and is currently writing about Frank Capra's longtime screenwriting collaborator, Robert Riskin, as well as the representation of California in films such as Roman Polanski's *Chinatown.* He can be contacted at Ian.Scott@man.ac.uk.

RICHARD SHENKMAN is an associate professor of history at George Mason University and the editor of George Mason University's HistoryNewsNetwork.org. He is the author of five books, including *Presidential Ambition: How the Presidents Gained Power, Kept Power and Got Things Done.*

DONALD E. STAPLES, professor of film and television at the University of North Texas, received his M.A. in cinema from the University of Southern California and his B.S. and Ph.D. in theatre, television, and film from Northwestern University. He founded the doctoral program in cinema studies at New York University and is the former president of the University Film and Video Association and the Society for Cinema Studies. Most of his film criticism may be found in *Films In Review,* and his best-known book is *American Cinema* (editor/contributor), the official film book of the United States government. He can be contacted at staples@cas.unt.edu.

SCOTT F. STODDART is the executive director of Special Programs and the director of Academic Advancement at Marymount Manhattan College, where he oversees the developmental and the honors programs. He also teaches cinema studies for the department of communications. After completing a dissertation on Sarah Orne Jewett at the University of Illinois, he taught as an associate professor of American literature and cinema at Nova Southeastern University for ten years. In addition to being the executive director of the Northeast Modern Language Association, he has published articles on the fiction of Henry James, E.M. Forster, Stephen Crane, F. Scott Fitzgerald, and on the plays of Stephen Sondheim. Also, he has published on the films of George Cukor, Martin Scorcese, Jane Campion, Jack Clayton, and Richard Kwietniowski. This spring, his first book will be published: *Prescriptive Lenses: Imaging the Gay Male in Hollywood Cinema, 1990–2000*. He can be contacted at sstoddart@mmm.edu.

J. TILLAPAUGH is assistant vice president for graduate studies and sponsored research at the University of Texas of the Permian Basin, where he is founding history faculty. He received his B.S. and M.A. from the University of Oregon and his Ph.D. from Northwestern University. His work in public history with historical preservation and popular culture include the founding of two museums. Recent articles include "Tom Lea: An Artist Correspondent in World War II," *Journal of America's Military Past* 26.2. He is finishing a book manuscript entitled *Fort D.A. Russell from the Mexican Revolution to the Border Patrol: A Twentieth Century Command in Texas*. Tillapaugh also uses Internet sources for portraying cultural history. A current project involves the development of the *Odessa Bush Home* on the campus of the University Texas of the Permian Basin. He can be reached at tillapaugh_j@utpb.edu.

JAMES M. WELSH, Ph.D., is professor of English at Salisbury University in Maryland, and the editor-in-chief of *Literature/Film Quarterly*, now in its thirtieth year of publication. He is author or coauthor of a dozen books, including *Tony Richardson: Essays and Interviews* (SUNY Press, 1999), *The Encyclopedia of Novels into Film* (1998), *The Encyclopedia of Stage Plays into Film* (2001), *The Encyclopedia of Filmmakers* (2002, 2 vols.), and *Shakespeare Into Film* (2002), all published by Facts On File, Inc. He can be contacted at jxwelsh@salisbury.edu.

DONALD WHALEY teaches American cultural history and coordinates the American studies program at Salisbury University on the Eastern Shore of

Maryland. He is a contributing editor of *Literature/Film Quarterly* and has guest-edited a special issue of that journal on Vietnam War movies. His essays on American culture have covered such topics as soul music and rockabilly, the history of anarchism, the writings of Gore Vidal, and the work of the southern documentary filmmaker Ross Spears. He can be contacted at dmwhaley@salisbury.edu.

INDEX

Note: In this index selected film and television characters have been indexed under the name of the character with the title of the film or television production in parentheses.